D1807352

The Birmingham Group

Robin Harriott

The Birmingham Group

Reading the Second City in the 1930s

Robin Harriott
Independent Scholar
Leintwardine, Hereford and Worcs., UK

ISBN 978-3-031-14382-3 ISBN 978-3-031-14383-0 (eBook)
https://doi.org/10.1007/978-3-031-14383-0

Cover illustration: travelib history / Alamy Stock Photo

This Palgrave Macmillan imprint is published by the registered company Springer Nature Switzerland AG.
The registered company address is: Gewerbestrasse 11, 6330 Cham, Switzerland

The enemy of study is distraction, and it is generally agreed that finding space, both temporal and physical, is something of a necessity. Time is indeed a precious commodity. I take this opportunity to thank my dear wife Elaine for keeping the hounds at bay and clearing a space for this undertaking. I have been particularly fortunate in this respect, and without her help and attention, this project would not have begun, let alone come to fruition.

Archives

Allen, Walter. Archive and Papers. Cadbury Research Centre. University of Birmingham.

A selection of Allen's novels, poems, criticism and correspondence.

Brierley, Walter. Papers. Derby Local Studies Library. Deposit DL282. A large selection of correspondence between Walter Brierley, Walter Allen and John Hampson. Copies of Brierley's Novels.

Halward, Leslie. Papers. Halward Collection, Birmingham Central Library. MS/1293/106/.

Collection of typescript talks, press cuttings and correspondence, including various playscripts.

Hampson, John. Papers. Special Collections Services. University of Reading. GB6 RUL 5091.

Copies of Hampson's published novels.

Acknowledgements

The seed of my intention to investigate the work of this unlikely, if not rather incongruous, literary coterie who met to discuss their writing in the urban-industrial manufacturing centre that was 1930s Birmingham germinated in 2016 when the University of Birmingham accepted my research proposal. Thanks are due in the first instance to Dr Rex Ferguson, who was encouraging of the project and who channelled it to Dr Daniel Moore, whose outstanding supervision, not to mention patient and diplomatic guidance, was invaluable in pointing me to aspects of the wider theoretical discussion I would not have considered and also for reining in some of my less-focused departures in order to bring the original project to a close. I would also wish to credit Dr Nathan Waddell for asking awkward questions and Tony Davies, now retired, for early encouragement on the English BA at Birmingham and who first piqued my interest in the Birmingham group writers. I also take this opportunity to register thanks to the many others past and present who made my intermittent periods of study at Birmingham so rewarding. Returning to academia following a somewhat extended interval is, to say the least, a challenge; however, the enthusiasm of both lecturers and fellow researchers was not only contagious but also supportive in providing the much-needed momentum to pursue my researches. Outside the academy, I would wish to record my gratitude to David Rees for a lifelong and enduring, at times stubbornly so, friendship and to Brian Whitehouse for early instilling a sense of self-belief. Also to Peter and Rhona Fear for good company, the latter of whom's comments regarding my psychological 'readings' were both insightful and thought provoking. I also take this opportunity to thank Molly Beck at Palgrave Macmillan for shepherding my book proposal and manuscript through the peer review and editorial process and for having invested her faith, time and enthusiasm in this project.

Abstract

The Birmingham Group: Reading the Second City in the 1930s

This project focusses upon the collective of working-class writers known variously as The Birmingham Group, The Birmingham School or The Birmingham Proletarian Writers, who, during the decade prior to the second world war were, for a brief period, active in the City of Birmingham and whose literary productions chronicled their fellow citizens' experience of life in the urban manufacturing centre that was the second city. Described as propagandistic: the imposition of political dogma on creativity; the literature of a party disguised as the literature of a class and often dismissed formally as conservative; lacking in invention, or simply the naïve emulation of bourgeois realism, working-class literature has often found itself on the receiving end of such negative critiques, given the absence of any close reading or more detailed engagement with their work, the writing of the Birmingham group has often been assumed to share in them. Though frequently referred to in footnotes, articles and discussions of working-class literature, a fuller consideration of the Birmingham group has not, to date, been forthcoming, as a consequence of which, whilst offering an emphatic repudiation of such dismissive assumptions, their work has remained overlooked, neglected and underwritten.

The book is distinctive in being the first dedicated solely to the works of the five writers: Walter Allen, John Hampson, Leslie Halward, Walter Brierley and Peter Chamberlain who comprise the Birmingham group's core members. Their writing contrasts the central 1930s socio-political issues of work and unemployment as experienced by the citizens of

Birmingham with those addressed in more familiar literary works deriving from locations centering upon single industry occupation alone e.g. Coal, Iron, Shipbuilding and Textile production. The narratives of the Birmingham group were not only alive to the 'technological turn' taking place in British manufacturing and its concomitant in a move away from traditional sectarian accounts of heavy industrial work, but also, in light of what came to be described as the 'ethnographic turn': the contemporary developments in Documentary Cinema, Mass-Observation, Reportage and Photo-journalism that were adopted and informed the Birmingham writers' active engagement in the reconfiguration of the traditional realist mode hitherto considered the only accessible representative medium for the working-class writer.

This examination of the Birmingham group's literary productions is therefore timely in as much that the works of this unlikely coterie are prescient *of* and responsive *to* changes in the traditional focus upon class as the primary and sole determinant in the discussions of working-class literature. It will contend that the Birmingham group productions of the 1930s both anticipate and respond to renewed critical considerations of working-class literature which seek 'to explor[e] the intersections of class with gender, ethnic and sexual identities, rather than reverting to earlier critical models from which these categories were largely absent'.* During the late 1930s W. H. Auden commented that the city of Birmingham was experiencing something of a 'boomlet', and whilst differing from more traditional accounts of working-class experience, the life of both City and Citizens, as chronicled in the narratives of this underwritten collective of writers, certainly deserves telling. It is hoped therefore that *The Birmingham Group: Reading the Second City in the 1930s* will contribute usefully to exploration of both place, epoch and the continuing production and discussion of working-class literature writing deriving from it.

* (Clarke & Hubble, Editors *Working-Class Writing; Theory and Practice*, 2018).

Contents

Abbreviations[1]

Allen, Walter—*Innocence Is Drowned*	***ID***
Allen, Walter—*Blind Man's Ditch*	***BM***
Brierley, Walter—*Means Test Man*	***MM***
Brierley, Walter—*Sandwichman*	***SM***
Brierley, Walter—'Transition'	***T***
Brierley, Walter—'Body'	***B***
Chamberlain, Peter—'Mr. Marris' Reputation'	***MR***
Chamberlain, Peter—'What the Hell?'	***WH***
Chamberlain, Peter—'Suburban Exercise'	***SE***
Chamberlain, Peter—'Belgravian Exercise'	***BE***
Green, Henry—*Living*	***L***
Halward, Leslie—'Belcher's Hod'	***BH***
Halward, Leslie—'Initiation'	***I***
Halward, Leslie—'A Broken Engagement'	***BE***
Hampson, John—'Man About The House'	***MA***
Hampson, John—*Saturday Night at the Greyhound*	***SN***
Hampson, John—*O Providence*	***OP***

Note

1. Throughout this book, I have used the abbreviations shown in bold italics to locate the Birmingham Group novels and short stories that constitute the primary texts herein and which refer to the editions shown in the 'List of Works Cited'.

CHAPTER 1

Introduction: 'They at Least Were Not Hybrids'

My interest in the affiliation of working-class writers known variously as the Birmingham Proletarian Writers, the Birmingham School or, more commonly, the Birmingham Group, was prompted by a brief reference to them during an undergraduate lecture at the University of Birmingham some thirty years ago. Armed with assumptions based upon recollections of the nineteenth-century 'Condition of England' novel or such later classics of the working-class canon as Robert Tressell's *The Ragged Trousered Philanthropists* and Walter Greenwood's *Love on the Dole* and with only vague notions as to what a working-class or proletarian literature ought to resemble, my initial encounter with the narratives of the Birmingham group was somewhat perplexing.[1]

Over time, critiques of working-class literature produced during the interwar period have come to regard it as irretrievably 'caught between the jaws of form and content', and, although praising its laudable imperative to promote social change, it was generally considered that such principled aims were purchased at the expense of literary expression.[2] *Seemingly* (I use the adverb provisionally) antithetical to modernist experimentation or social realism's commitment to political engagement, one's initial encounter with Birmingham Group narratives is unlikely to move far beyond this view, and in this respect it is not difficult to see how, as a consequence, their narratives have been consigned to critical oblivion. This book will offer a close reading and analysis of their novels and short stories to

R. Harriott, *The Birmingham Group*,
https://doi.org/10.1007/978-3-031-14383-0_1

demonstrate how, while diverging markedly from the work of their contemporaries, the Birmingham group writers' engagement with the familiar 1930s themes of work and unemployment actively challenges both prevailing and later evaluations of what a working-class text should be.

Neither aesthetically- nor philosophically naïve, as charged by some commentators, the narratives of the Birmingham group exercise restraint by voicing a soft-spoken radicalism and expressive ingenuity which paradoxically functions as a more powerful means by which to document working-class experience. The examples presented here will reveal how their collective achievement was realised through a combination of formal innovation and ideological addressedness not only unique in its time but prescient of more recent critical engagements with working-class literature that centre on a politics of form. Though dismissed as offering apolitical, at times quietist, representations of the working-class lives they document, or in failing to urge more traditional sectarian concerns, the narratives of the Birmingham group were nevertheless fully alive to aspects of working-class experience occluded by their more clamant, politically oriented literary counterparts. Their narratives respond to the plight of the working class by consistently giving voice to those considered peripheral or marginal, and, in so doing, present a holistic picture of working-class culture as it emerges from 'the routine activities of everyday life'.[3]

Beyond their dedicated promotion by Andy Croft some thirty years ago, this is the first extended critical study devoted solely to the narratives of the Birmingham group's constituent members Walter Allen, Leslie Halward, Peter Chamberlain, John Hampson and Walter Brierley.[4] 'Fenced-in' as they had been, between two major world conflicts and critical assumptions which viewed their work as merely illustrative of a localised outpouring of social-realism geared to issues of working-class life that were for a brief period fashionable, they have since suffered undue critical neglect. By employing methodologies and theoretical frameworks more sympathetic to the kinds of writing they actually produced, rather than reading their narratives against the prescriptive, frequently 'proscriptive', tenets of contemporary criticism, this study will argue that the Birmingham group writers are deserving of far wider critical acclaim than they have received hitherto. Functioning as a corrective to an overzealous approach, this study responds to Marina MacKay's and Lyndsey Stonebridge's caution that '[a]ny [work] which professes recuperative intentions risks making inflated claims about the reflected brilliance of the age—no doubt there were plenty of wretched novels produced in this period (as in any other) that have been deservedly forgotten'.[5]

In responding to Andy Croft's question: 'What are we to make today of these writings, this "Birmingham Group" of writers as different from one another as seems possible?' this book will maintain that the fictions of the Birmingham group retain enduring significance as both imaginative literary works and social documents.[6] Their narratives not only address the prevailing themes and issues of the interwar period but also anticipate, if not prefigure, more recent trends in the theorisation and re-evaluation of working-class writing. This prevenience is evidenced by the variety of formal innovations undertaken by the Birmingham writers in order to adapt and reconfigure traditional representational modes so as to accommodate subject material neglected and overlooked due to the prevailing emphasis of what was a politically charged and largely male-oriented discussion. As the Birmingham Centre for Cultural Studies (CCCS) English Studies Group paper 'Thinking the Thirties' makes plain, '[t]he Thirties, in literature and history, is a masculine decade. The politics, narrowly defined class politics from which issues of gender and sexual politics are excluded, are a male preserve, [manifest in and revealing of] a widespread crisis of masculine identity'.[7] In their introduction to *Working-Class Writing: Theory and Practice*, Nick Hubble and Ben Clarke stress that '[a]ny return to working-class writing must be informed by feminist, post-colonial and queer studies, exploring *the intersections of class with gender, ethnic and sexual identities*, rather than reverting to earlier critical methods from which these categories were largely absent' (my emphasis).[8]

In order to look more closely into the formative influences, affiliations and associations of the Birmingham group, this reading will have recourse to the autobiographies and correspondence of Walter Allen, Leslie Halward and John Hampson, which together form an invaluable resource in considering their accounts of working-class experience as they relate to each author's rootedness in the cultural life and community of the industrial metropolis they describe. It was this proximity to the working classes that enabled them to bridge the 'experiential gap' which, despite their undeniably ardent enthusiasm, frequently confronted and occasionally repelled those 'hybrid' proletarians of bourgeois origin who sought to document working-class experience.[9] In offering dispassionate, first-hand accounts of the lived-experience of their fellow citizens, the Birmingham group narratives may be considered a form of amanuensis. As Alan Sillitoe explains in his introduction to Walter Allen's *All in a Lifetime*:

> The common man, so called, is rarely able to tell his own story, each person has one, but any attempt to tell it, at least in writing, is likely to result in the distortion of the tale and the impatience of the reader [...] even though he may once have been a common man himself, he needs more than the emotional sympathy and dash of sociological reality which is often regarded as sufficient basis for such novels. Inspiration, imagination, and a certain distance are necessary to turn the material into a story which may be read with complete faith in its veracity. Many people may be writers, but few are artists.[10]

Christopher Hilliard develops this idea by appropriating Leslie Halward's formulation 'to write in my own language about my own people' as a chapter title in his *To Exercise Their Talents*, where he explains:

> One of the tasks of working-class writing was to correct the stereotypes and distortions produced by authors from other classes' [...] 'In their commitment to writing about "their" people, working-class writers implicitly accepted the idea that it was important to write about what one knew' [and that] for working-class writers, the importance of writing about the lives and places they knew lay in the value of honoring [*sic*] their communities with a truthful and artistically satisfying representation.[11]

Hilliard suggests this commitment took the form of a social obligation or duty, adding that '[t]o write a story of working-class life was an act of self-respect and community service. It was a point where the two meanings of the word "representation" coincide'.[12] His observation marks two aspects of the Birmingham group's narrative productions which this study will develop more fully. The first concerns the notion of the Birmingham writers' 'representative' role as spokespersons on behalf of their community; the second relates to their stylistic radicalism: the formal means by which they adapted language, the available representational modes, and developed literary strategies by which to communicate this material.

This introductory chapter had been divided into five sections. Section I, 'A Multiplicity in Unity: The Birmingham Writers and Their City', will provide an overview of the Birmingham group and their city including brief biographies of both writers and place to suggest how this urban manufacturing centre and its environs offered themselves as the locus for a new kind of socially engaged regional writing. Section II, 'Shaping Influences: Finding the Exotic in the Everyday', examines the work of authors who provided inspiration, encouragement and literary motivation in terms of their class origin, sense of place and formal innovation, these being, respectively, D. H. Lawrence, Arnold Bennett and Henry Green. Section III, '"Going Over": The Cultural Diaspora', will offer a survey of the prevailing literary discussion, particularly that relating to the phenomenon of left-leaning middle-class writers and intellectuals, the so-called fellow-travellers who, for a brief period during the 1930s, had sought political and social affiliation with the working classes. Section IV, '"At last the British are Coming": Prevailing and Contemporary Critiques of Working-class Literature', examines both prevailing and contemporary critiques of working-class literature by reference to some of the more stridently politicised discussion taking place in America during the 1930s. Section V, 'The Ethnographic Turn', will explore how the democratic impulse manifests in cinema, mass observation, photo journalism and reportage proved not only influential but was readily adopted by the Birmingham writers and underpins much of the critical framework employed both throughout and particularly in the final chapter of this book where montage and other technique deriving from these new media serve to illuminate wider aspects of the Birmingham group's formal strategies.

A Multiplicity in Unity: The Birmingham Writers and Their City

Functioning as something of an elder statesman/mentor figure to his Birmingham group companions, John Hampson (1901–1955) was the first of their number to experience a degree of literary renown. Published by the Woolf's Hogarth Press in 1931, *Saturday Night at the Greyhound* brought him overnight success. For a while, he was feted by the London literati in the shape of E. M. Forster, William Plomer, John Lehmann and others, his articles and short stories appearing in many of the acclaimed pre-war periodicals. Hampson Simpson's family wealth originally derived from a brewery business, though closer relatives, his great-grandfather and grandfather, had stepped briefly outside the world of commerce to manage the Theatre Royal in Birmingham. However, following the collapse of the brewery concern in 1907, the Hampsons moved to a terraced house in Leicester as described in Hampson's novel *O Providence*. His immediate family having fallen upon hard times, John consequently received little, if any, formal education owing to ill health as a child and commenced his working life in a munitions factory during the Great War. Periods of employment in hotels and public houses in London and the East Midlands followed, including a short spell in Wormwood Scrubs following his arrest for book theft. In 1925, he commenced work as a nurse to Ronald, the Downs Syndrome-afflicted son of a Birmingham couple, the Wilsons. Boarding and lodging were provided, thus affording a degree of security and enabling him the time and space to pursue his writing.

Despite harbouring adolescent dreams to 'retire from professional football [having played for Aston Villa] and to grow fat in [his] own pub', Walter Allen (1911–1995) would, in reality, pursue a somewhat different career trajectory. Born in Aston, Birmingham, he won a place at King Edward VI Grammar school, following which he gained an open scholarship to study English at the University of Birmingham. It was here that Allen made the acquaintance of Louis MacNeice, currently teaching classics under the distinguished tutelage of E. R. Dodds, and through whom he later became acquainted with W. H. Auden. Walter Allen is remembered more today as a critic rather than a novelist, yet, by the close of the pre-war decade, his first two novels: *Innocence Is Drowned* and *Blind Man's Ditch*—both set in Birmingham and drawing upon their author's experience of working-class life in the city—had been published. On the strength of the former's 'success' (though receiving positive reviews, it sold only a 'few copies'), and with Britain sliding into the closing stages of the 'phoney war' preceding the greater conflict to come, Allen moved to London, where he 'narrowly survived, writing book reviews and reports for publishers'.[13] Allen's critical works and his autobiography, *As I Walked Down New Grub Street* (1981), have been especially helpful in furnishing an overview of the contemporary literary climate and the figures with whom he associated.

Respectively, amateur boxer, dance band drummer, engineering apprentice, plasterer, short story writer, laureate of working-class romance and latterly radio playwright, Leslie Halward (1905–1976) was, for a brief period during the 1930s, 'greatly admired [...] his talent unrivalled'.[14] In *Let Me Tell You*, Halward records his birth 'over a pork butchers shop in what was then known as High Street, Selly Oak, Birmingham'.[15] He continues, 'There are three ways in which I might say that: (1) Apologetically, as if I were ashamed of it. (2) Arrogantly, as if I were rather more than proud of it. (3) Naturally, as if I were making a simple statement of fact. I would like you to credit me with method (3).'[16] Once familiarised with Halward's philosophy, more possibly his vocation 'to write in [his] own language about his own people', one is more inclined to 'credit' him with method (2), for Halward—even more so than his Birmingham group contemporaries, including ex-miner Walter Brierley—was chauvinistically working class. Though effusive in praise of his not inconsiderable achievement, Walter Allen confides, 'He had had very little education and had remained thoroughly working-class as if he gloried in being so, though I suspect, as much out of fear of the ways of life outside the working-class'.[17]

Having drawn John Hampson's attention following *The Listener's* publication of 'Frustration and Bitterness: A Colliery Banksman', Walter Brierley (1900–1972) became the beneficiary of both John Hampson's and Walter Allen's literary largesse. Prior to meeting the Birmingham writers, the Derbyshire writer had completed the manuscript of a second novel, *The Bare Heath*, a work in the style of Thomas Hardy. As he recalled, '[I] was not cut out for a miner. And because maybe [*sic*] of an imagination more alive than that of the average miner, I was more scared than the average.'[18] In 1917, Brierley attended Heanor Grammar school one evening each week to learn French. However, this introduction to the world of 'culture' only exacerbated his dissatisfaction with colliery work: 'this reading fed a sense in me that there was something better in life than the pit'.[19] Brierley's subsequent struggle with the dispiriting and psychologically debilitating strictures of the Means Test and his thwarted aspirations towards self-cultivation are vividly set out in the novels *Means Test Man* and *Sandwichman*. Despite his fearful reluctance to endure the collier's life as one of Orwell's 'grimy caryatids', Brierley's perspective as a miner-writer widens the scope of this study by showing how workers beyond the urban proletariat were experiencing the devastating effects of the inter-war slump.

In terms of detailed biographical information, Peter Chamberlain (1903–?) remains problematic. His whereabouts beyond 1955 when he was editor of a *Motor-Cycle* magazine, have proven difficult to ascertain. Unlike his fellow Birmingham group writers, Chamberlain's family owned a foundry manufacturing bedsteads and were relatively prosperous. Though unrelated to those more renowned Chamberlains, Joseph and Neville, his maternal grandfather had been Birmingham's first Lord Mayor, while his paternal grandfather, John H. Chamberlain, was curator of the Birmingham Art Gallery and, as an architect, painter, educationalist and poet, had become a prominent figure in Birmingham cultural life. In terms of social status, these factors distance Peter Chamberlain socially from his Birmingham group companions and in this respect moved him nearer 'fellow travellers' such as Henry Green, who, rather than being *of* the working classes, wrote *about* them. Chamberlain had attended Clifton College, and, according to Leslie Halward, he 'studied at the University of Birmingham for a short time', later becoming acquainted with John Hampson via Hampson's elder brother Jimmy, a famous racing motorcyclist at this time. [20] Although the irascible Halward seems to have been very taken with Chamberlain, Walter Allen recalls him as being 'very much the public school man, by which I mean that I found him arrogant'.[21] Allen recounts that '[Chamberlain] knew London at least as well as he did Birmingham and had his own circle there. He knew writers: he had met Anthony Powell', and 'numbered Hemingway, Fitzgerald and John O'Hara as his literary heroes.'[22] Allowing for a degree of envy amongst his possibly less-than-urbane Birmingham confrères, Chamberlain had nonetheless received enthusiastic approbation from beyond their ambit. V. S. Pritchett credited him as having 'revived the traditional humour of the English novel', and, in an encouraging review of Chamberlain's short story 'What The Hell?', I. A. Richards stated that it was 'the finest thing in English he had read for six years'.[23]

The authors mentioned above constitute the core members of the Birmingham group, as detailed by cross-references, autobiographical accounts and the recollections of its principal members. However, it is worth remarking here upon two significant omissions and additions. Firstly, Birmingham writer Kathleen Dayus was a contemporary of the Birmingham group, and whilst providing a vivid account of her poverty-stricken childhood and adolescence in Birmingham during the early decades of the twentieth century, the fact that her memoirs were completed in later life excludes them from the periodisation adopted here. Secondly, though his work does fall within this periodisation, I have also omitted the Halesowen-born writer Francis Brett Young. In many respects a regional writer, his novels exploited the urban industrial as their backdrop; where Birmingham becomes 'North Bromwich', and typical settings include the Black Country and Welsh Borders, Brett Young's stories reflect more closely the interests and intrigues of a bourgeois gentleman, rather than those of working-class experience. Conversely, I have included a writer frequently, though mistakenly, assumed to have been a member of the Birmingham group and to have hailed from working-class origins in the city: Henry Green. Chapter 1 will offer an extended account of his best-known novel *Living* (1929). Though published twelve months prior to the periodisation adopted here, Green's (neo-realist)/late modernist depiction of life in a Birmingham foundry is illustrative of the stylistic departures employed by a novelist who, while impatient with the bourgeois affectations of his own caste, proved an inspiration to Allen and Hampson: his work functioning very much as the template for their own formal departures.

It is something of a cliché to describe the setting of a novel as an additional character within it; however, if the Birmingham writers agreed on one thing, it was to document the life of their city's working classes, and, due to the fact that references to the city appear so frequently in their narratives, it is to Birmingham itself that this introduction now turns.

> They came from Birmingham, which is not a place to promise much you know Mr Weston. One has no great hopes for Birmingham. I always say there is something direful in the sound.[24]

In 1960, Birmingham became the adoptive home of literary critic, novelist and former professor of English at the University of Birmingham, David Lodge, and, as he remarks, these pronouncements uttered by the egregiously snobbish Mrs Elton, in Jane Austen's *Emma*, have been quoted against Birmingham ever since.[25] What follows therefore aims to re-adjust such unjust and dismissive misperceptions. Interestingly, David Lodge's move to Birmingham had been pre-figured thirty years earlier when Louis MacNeice first set foot in 'this hazy city' in order to take up a position as Lecturer in Classics at the University. Despite mentioning London, Spain and Ireland, MacNeice's *Autumn Journal* includes the following references to Birmingham where:

> Sun shines easy, sun shines gay, / On bug-house, warehouse, brewery, market / On the chocolate factory and the B.S.A., / On the Greek town hall and Josiah Mason; / On Mitchells and Butlers Tudor pubs, [26]

Despite his undoubted affection for the city and the people, it should be on record that the Parthenon-like 'Greek town hall' was actually modelled upon the Temple of Castor and Pollux in the Roman Forum and that the marble statue of Josiah Mason was, subsequent to MacNeice having penned these lines, unfortunately destroyed. It had originally stood outside the entrance to Mason College, once the recipient of donations from its eponymous founder, and was forerunner, owing largely to the efforts of Joseph Chamberlain, of the city's first university. Birmingham's regenerative impulse, its mania for demolition and reconstruction, as registered in the cyclical relocations of its central library, has become something of a civic pursuit. Phlegmatic as they are and well-schooled in the art of self-deprecation, Birmingham's citizens have long-since inured themselves to the more eclectic and somewhat irrational planning decisions of their city-fathers and likewise the critical estimations of outsiders. What might be urged, however, if one were attempting to define a particular Birmingham sensibility or outlook, would be the seemingly paradoxical values of individualism and co-operation, the combination of independence and self-reliance that have come to characterise both people and place, and which in turn derive from a combination of earlier Chartist and non-conformist involvement and the influx of peoples from many nationalities who have over time settled in the city and made it their home. Whilst a relative newcomer amongst Britain's provincial cities, Birmingham has claims to a history of progressive, reformist and non-conformist thinking. During the nineteenth century, a combination of the religious and political was manifest in the 'Civic Gospel' preached by the likes of George Dawson, Josiah Mason and John Bright, this being a fusion of the spiritual/material values that would later morph into Joseph Chamberlain's 'Municipality'. Indeed, Chamberlain's caucus-style electioneering and his promotion of the city during the latter years of the nineteenth century resembled forms of political activity and local government synonymous with American cities such as Detroit or Chicago, and found Birmingham operating as a virtual city-state independent of central government.

Unlike northern counterparts defined by the predominance of a single trade or industry, Birmingham's industrial expansion during the nineteenth century owed much to the high incidence of small-scale enterprises; its various trades undertaken in numerous small workshops, rather than the large workforces required of traditional: mining, steel, coal, 'heavy' industry. Historian Asa Briggs notes that in such small-scale working environments, 'relations between "masters" and "men" were close therefore, if not always good, and the economic and political philosophies that thrived locally were those which laid emphasis on 'mutual interests', interdependence' and 'common action'.[27] Briggs remarked that 'a large percentage of the workforce were skilled-tradesmen and relatively well-off economically'; what is perhaps more pertinent, in terms of Birmingham's further development in the engineering sector, was the fact that the city's Silver, Jewellery and Gunsmiths' 'quarters' were particularly well appointed with that aristocrat of the artisanal pyramid: the Toolmaker.[28]

As the 1930s began to pull away from the financial turmoil of the preceding decade, the economies of the Midlands, the South East and the Capital began to enjoy something of an upturn in their fortunes. As Chris Upton indicates, '[w]hen the "green shoots of recovery" began to appear in 1931, the city was at the forefront of growth, by 1937 unemployment was down to five per-cent'.[29] This recovery was accompanied by unprecedented economic and industrial expansion. Both the 'Chocolate factory' (Cadbury's at Bournville) and the Birmingham Small Arms ('B.S.A.') factory at Small Heath, each referenced by MacNeice, saw increased production and a concomitant reduction in the city's unemployment figure; this being further reduced owing to the expansion of the motor industry. Despite Asa Briggs' comment regarding Birmingham's proliferation of small-scale enterprises, or SMEs as they are now termed, Herbert Austin's car factory at Longbridge Birmingham became for a time the largest manufacturing plant in the world. Ancillary production spreads outwards as Joseph Lucas: electrics, Wilmot and Breedon: sheet-metal fabrications and car bodies, Dunlop: tyres, and a host of other producers each jostled to engage in supplying the automobile industry.

In order to accommodate the families of troops returning to a 'land fit for heroes' following the First World War and the thousands of extra workers pouring into the city during the peak of its expansion, numerous housing estates were under construction. During the period 1919–1939, some 105,000 homes, of which some 50 percent were council houses, were constructed. The largest estate, Kingstanding, which had provided the setting for several of Leslie Halward's short stories, saw the construction of 5000 municipal houses by 1939.[30] Here, under his father's tutelage is Jimmy, Halward's apprentice plasterer, taking his first awkward steps:

> "Now then," Joe said. "Shove the end of the lath well back against the wall. Keep 'em square now! They're a mile apart this end! That's better. Now tap the nail. Now hit it once. The nail, not your bloody finger! *Hit* it! *Once,* I said! Christ, how many more times? You'll break the bleedin' joist in half! He stood there laughing. "I thought you said you could do it! Come out of the road and let me show you again". (*I*, 59)

Later, not without a similar element of comic effect, readers are acquainted with the ritual of the morning tea break. Yet, beyond a keen documentary eye and such 'lived' comic interludes, Halward was also able to offer deep and sensitive psychological explorations of character.

With regular wage packets, shorter working hours and increasing amounts of leisure time, the city's myriad new homeowners eagerly sought entertainments to occupy themselves. Notwithstanding the misguided impression that her citizens were entrapped within a smog-benighted, stygian darkness, Birmingham's outer reaches enjoyed a green and leafy backcloth. As with the tree-lined arterial roads that serviced it, the city was the beneficiary of a profusion of parks, playing fields and areas of 'verdure' that even the disparaging Jane Austen would have been delighted 'to gaze upon'. Swimming pools and Turkish Baths proliferated, as did civic architecture, including the City Museum and Art Gallery, the latter containing a prized collection of Pre-Raphaelite paintings, along with a Science Museum, a central reference and many lending libraries. In 1900, the Town Hall featured the first public performance of Elgar's (Op.38) 'The Dream of Gerontius', though less sublimely some thirty years later it would host a gathering of Oswald Mosley's 'New Party', whose thuggish acolytes are described in Walter Allen's novel *Innocence Is Drowned*. Football was clearly a large draw, and references to Birmingham City FC and Aston Villa appear in several Birmingham group fictions. In 'A Christmas Story', Peter Chamberlain's protagonist rejoins drinking companions engaged in an earnest conversation about the 'Villa's' inside-right, while Henry Green's association with the workers at the family firm doubtless precipitated the following paean to Aston Villa: 'The Villa, The Villa, Come on the Villa. Mr. Connolly stood like transfixed with passion and 30,000 people waved and shrieked and swayed and clamoured at eleven men who play the best football in the world. These took no notice of the crowd, no notice' (*L*, 380). The County (Warwickshire) Cricket Club was founded in 1882, and, similarly confounding of common perception, Lawn Tennis was first played in Ampton Road Edgbaston in 1873, the Edgbaston Archery and Lawn Tennis Society being the oldest Lawn Tennis club in the world.

Beyond sport, cinema proved the most significant mass pursuit during the 1930s. Developments such as the arrival of 'talking pictures' and their exhibition in the numerous, and sumptuous, art deco 'picture palaces', bore witness to not only Cinema's 'Golden Age' but also the first nervous twitchings of the nation's cultural custodians as they contemplated its deleterious effects on the populace at large. During the middle years of the 1930s, cities such as Birmingham were beginning to see an improvement in living standards. Valentine Cunningham notes how citizens in wealthier areas of the country were only likely to realise and register the degree of poverty that still existed elsewhere when confronted with hunger marchers begging a few coppers in their cinema queues. It was here that large numbers of Birmingham's younger citizens were to be found, alongside their eighteen million counterparts nationwide who were visiting the 'pictures' each week and 'pushing 40 million pounds each year into cinema box-offices'.[31] Birmingham was particularly well served in this respect, her cinemas numbering some one hundred by the mid-1930s. That this owed not a little to the efforts of Balsall Heath born, Oscar Deutsch, is less well known. The entrepreneurial son of Hungarian immigrants, Deutsch opened his first cinema in Brierley Hill (near Dudley) in 1928 and his art deco picture palaces enjoyed an exponential increase reaching a total of 250 Odeon Cinemas nationwide by 1937.

By the late 1930s, Birmingham's philosophical and intellectual discussion had moved from the Lunar Society's venue at 'Soho House' Handsworth where, during the closing years of the eighteenth century, the '*lunaticks*', as they described themselves, had met each month at full moon to unwittingly precipitate in the industrial revolution.[32] Having relocated to 'Highfield House' in Selly Oak, the intellectual discussion during the 1930s was markedly less optimistic. The global capitalism inadvertently spawned by those frock-coated and bewigged proto-industrialists at Soho House had begun to unravel as the Western world moved inexorably from economic meltdown towards full-scale crisis. The mood at Highfield reflected this; in a single decade, the less-savoury aspects of political crisis, world recession and high unemployment, not to mention the rise of Fascism, civil war in Spain and augurs of an imminent global conflict, would each came calling; all subsequent discussion would shortly turn a decidedly sharp left. A kind of West Midlands Garsington, Philip and Lella Secour Florence's home functioned much as a literary salon where, according to Walter Allen, between 1930 and 1960, 'most English and American left-wing intellectuals visiting Britain must have passed'.[33] Amongst those named by Allen were the poets W. H. Auden, Stephen Spender, Henry Reed and Louis MacNeice, radio dramatist R. D. (Reggie) Smith, art historian Nikolaos Pevsner, architect Walter Gropius, biologist Julian Huxley, philosopher G. E. Moore and other notables such as William Empson, A. L. Rowse, John Strachey and Naomi Mitchison.

Besides the intellectual and literary firmament gathered at Highfield, another of the city's cultural networks had formed around its artists and painters. Conroy Maddox, John and Robert Melville, Emmy Bridgewater, Oscar Mellor and Desmond Morris comprised the core members of the Birmingham Surrealist Group. As regional exponents of what was an international movement, the Birmingham Surrealists are illustrative of regional movements in the creative arts. In *Surrealism in Birmingham (1935-1954)*, while keen to stress the Surrealist Movement's outward development geographically and psychologically, Michel Remy argues:

> A corollary was that the expansion of surrealism should not develop solely outwards, but also inwards, not only towards other countries but also within one and the same country. In other words, to the process of 'internationalization there must correspond a process of '*provincialization*.'[34]

Tessa Sidey also presses this view by suggesting that the Birmingham Surrealists presented a challenge to metropolitan assumptions. The importance of regional artistic production Sidey registers on behalf of the city's Surrealist painters is equally applicable to the literary endeavours of the Birmingham group writers, for as she maintains:

> The idea of a group of surrealist artists associated with Birmingham might register as highly improbable, even a surreal proposition. In fact no other British city can boast such a sustained association with this avant-garde movement. When art history in the West is largely written from the perspective of powerful centres, it seems valid to consider the cross-currents and initiatives that challenge established boundaries and, for a time, proved productive for a small group of committed artists associated with the city in the pre- and post-war period.[35]

However, as Walter Allen explains, 'it was in the Film Society more than anywhere else that young artists came together.' [36] And it was here under the aegis of E. R. Dodds that many of the city's creative spirits first encountered one another:

> Very soon after I graduated, [Dodds] invited me to a dinner he gave in a private room in the Burlington Restaurant to a group of young men whose mentor in some sense he was. Most of them were clerks in local government or industry. There were perhaps ten guests, among them the sculptor Gordon Herickx, who worked as a stonemason, Stanley Hawes, who became

> a documentary film director [...] the painter John Melville and his brother Robert.[37]

Allen continues, '[Although] I doubt whether Birmingham realised it, Dodds was a splendid man for such a city to have in its midst. How he came to be president of the Film Society I do not know but he was then at the centre of interest and activity in the arts and in the city.'[38] That the film society became the prime focus of the city's artistic and intellectual fraternity owed more to its showing of what we would now refer to as 'Art-House' productions, inclining more to the politicised documentary of Eisenstein than more commercial Hollywood fayre. Remembering the youthful enthusiasm of his first visit to see the Russian film '*We (are) From Kronstadt*', Allen records, '[he] was prepared in [his] excitement to believe it was the best film ever made anywhere'.[39] The Surrealist painter Conroy Maddox, in similarly effusive vein, likewise described how on Sundays 'we would go to the Film Society, and saw [*sic*] for the first time the works of Eisenstein, Cocteau, Pudovkin, Fritz Lang and others. Afterwards we would talk about the film or more imaginatively [*sic*]'.[40]

The film society had an indelible effect on Walter Allen; the techniques he learned from the cinematographers mentioned here surface in each of his first two novels. Often honing in on sibling rivalry and familial conflict, Allen adapts montage devices to present vivid, often cinematic imagery to contrast differing character perspectives. In the following, filmically lit interior monologue, Rose Gardiner resignedly contemplates the predicament of her husband's unemployment:

> Then she fell into an uneasy sleep with Dick lying beside her, eyes still wide open staring at the splash of light thrown on the wall by the street lamp. She did not need to be told that he spent the greater part of the night awake. Now she did not bother to wonder what he was thinking about. She knew: he thought himself unnecessary, unwanted, no longer a support to his wife and children, but a parasite. There were times when he sat in the house for days, without speaking a word, far away. It was enough to give you the creeps. (*ID*, 48)

Unlike their Surrealist counterparts, while meeting, discussing and encouraging of one another's literary endeavours, the Birmingham group writers neither committed to a group aesthetic nor issued a formal manifesto; their literary styles deriving instead from a variety of influences. MacNeice's assertion that they regarded the novel as 'social history' is helpful in providing a descriptive frame with which to consider their work, although his terminology might be tightened so as to emphasise and include the 'cultural and imaginative' aspects of their writing and thus distinguish their unique narrative style from varieties of proletarian fiction emanating from other conurbations or regions whose cultural traditions had been informed by single industry occupations alone. As we shall see, with the exception of Derbyshire ex-miner Walter Brierley, a close inspection of the Birmingham writers reveals a diversity of influence and social status, revealing less a commonality of purpose than a multiplicity in unity, a 'formation' in Raymond Williams' sense of the term, more divergent than has often been assumed.[41] Andy Croft sought to explain this diversity by indicating how the writing of Hampson, Chamberlain, Allen, Halward and Brierley

> [E]merged from a complex system of patronage and support, linking Codnor to Bloomsbury, Edgbaston to Iowa, critically encouraged and shaped by an intellectual, alliance of academic and freelance, professional and amateur, political and literary, anti-fascist and social democratic, homosexual and heterosexual, working-class and middle-class, town and gown, metropolitan and provincial.[42]

From this perspective, compared to other regional affiliations of working-class writers, where opportunities to associate with other creative artists or established literary figures did not exist, or where the 'negative' effects of higher education, as Orwell observed, may lead to estrangement from one's sociocultural origins, the Birmingham group writers were indeed unique.[43] The 'cultural capital' they acquired by means of 'educational opportunity' and 'professional association' was significant in shaping their 'literary world-view', and being 'provincial' in terms of their urban location proved no hindrance in this respect; indeed, for a brief period during the interwar years, certainly in terms of the cultural discourse in which they were immersed and the constellation of artists, writers, poets, painters and academics with whom they associated, 1930s Birmingham was experiencing something of a creative micro-climate.

Geographically plumb-centre, at the heart of the country's logistical canal, rail and road network, yet as far from the coast as it is possible to get, the 'romantic' associations of seaport, travel and overseas adventure clearly did not attach to this land-locked metropolis. I allude here to Walter Benjamin's essay 'The Storyteller: Reflections on the Works of Nikolai Leskov' in which Benjamin cites the German expression, 'when someone goes on a trip, he has something to tell about', and explains how people imagine the traveller as someone who has come from afar and thus impute romance and adventure to the act of storytelling.[44] However, as he indicates, '[people] enjoy no less listening to the man who has stayed at home, making an honest living and who knows the local tales and traditions'.[45] Rather than expressing a personal preference, Benjamin saw these antitheses as mutually advantageous or complimentary. His distinction between 'tiller of the soil' and 'trading seaman' marks the port of embarkation in Ken Worpole's exploration of working-class writing. He uses the 'trading seaman' archetype to recover the Liverpool-Irish writers Jim Phelan, James Hanley and George Garrett, who, as members of the merchant marine, had crafted modernist, proletarian fictions reflecting the 'dislocation', 'rootlessness' and 'often extreme psychological isolation' determined by their occupation.[46] The collective impulse to work in a tradition constructed upon class, place and local tradition: what is effectively the definition of a regional literature thus locates the Birmingham writers as 'tiller[s] of the soil'. In this respect, they were in good company for, as the following section will underline, their focus on aspects of urban industrial linked them to a burgeoning tradition of Regional writing.

Shaping Influences: Finding the Exotic in the Everyday

Of the many potential influences on the Birmingham group's outpouring of working-class narrative in the 1930s, perhaps the most significant in terms of having emerged from working-class stock himself, was none other than D. H. Lawrence. Having, 'pulled himself up by his bootstraps', and, notwithstanding Valentine Cunningham's characterisation of him as 'the lost leader of the proletarian novel', the Nottingham writer functioned very much as the Birmingham group's role model, owing to his all-pervasive influence references to him will be made throughout this discussion as appropriate.[47] Although a competent literary practitioner in his own right, the Birmingham group member most indebted to Lawrence, due largely to their regional (East Midlands Coalfield) mining connection was Walter Brierley. The extract from his short story 'Transition' below finds Brierley's narrator describing an anxious mother's thoughts following her son's first day at the pit and offers a flavour of this reluctant collier's writing.[48] Answering the door to a friend who had arranged to call on her son following his first day at the pit, the boy's mother explains:

> "'E's asleep Joe. Not washed or changed. I'll tell 'im you've been."
> She came back into the room with tense lips.
> "'E'll be t'same as t'rest. Lozzin about in 'is pit-muck till bedtime."
> She glanced at the boy, saw the pain of weariness in his features, and her mouth softened. "I wish wi'all my 'eart 'e'd been a gel."(*T*, 95)

The mother's sympathy is evident in her facial expression: the tensed lips registering concern at the boy's weariness and is enunciated in her wish that he'd been born a girl. Beyond romanticised notions of male camaraderie and manhood, pit work, as Lawrence had often shown, was physically hard, unremitting and, not to mention, dangerous. Brierley's intervention is to consider the occupation from the woman's perspective. Focalising her heart-felt anxiety in this way, the female voice and its concomitants, the nurturing roles of motherhood and domestic responsibility, those perspectives traditionally undervalued or overlooked by workerist accounts, are here restored and brought to the fore as Brierley actively interrogates the conventions of contemporary masculine 'positioning'.[49]

The remainder of this section will examine how two other writers: Arnold Bennett and Henry Green, proved influential in shaping the Birmingham writers' subordination of the 'political' in favour of the 'cultural' and reveal how their depictions of everyday urban experience might present as a powerful counterforce to the contemporary insistence that politics was all. The recognisable descriptions of life in the potteries provided by Arnold Bennett's *Clayhanger* doubtless contributed to his novel's success. As a study in social realism, Bennett's beliefs that literature should be accessible to ordinary people and that descriptive detail addressing their own lived-experience would be of interest were clearly factors in the appeal of his novels, not only to an increasingly educated working-class and middle-class readership but also to later writers such as Walter Allen who likewise sought to depict urban experience. As Raymond Williams indicates, 'the simplest descriptive novel about working-class life is already, by being written, a significant and positive cultural intervention. For it is not, even yet, what a novel is supposed to be, even as one kind among others.'[50] Such vociferous support for the value of unalloyed description is also evident in Salman Rushdie's observation that:

> *[D]escription is itself a political act.* The black American writer Richard Wright once wrote that black and white Americans were engaged in a war

> over the nature of reality. Their descriptions were incompatible. So it is clear that re-describing the world is a necessary first step to changing it…The novel is one way of denying the official, political version of events (my emphasis).[51]

Earlier in the century, purely 'descriptive' realist writing had enjoyed something of a bad press, especially in the wake of Virginia Woolf's chastisement of Bennett, Wells and Galsworthy in 'Mr. Bennett and Mrs. Brown' (1923). Their dogged recording of minutiae, the fictional creation of a 'dolls house' in which characters were merely 'placed', rather than (psychologically) 'explored', being the principal target of Woolf's censure. Walter Allen claimed the contrary however. A lifelong admirer of Bennett, the fact that Allen produced a critical volume dedicated to his work is testimony to the Staffordshire writer's influence upon his own narratives, not least his decision to choose Birmingham as the locus for his first two novels. Indeed, *contra* Woolf, Allen argues how, in Bennett's hands description functions almost as a creed or guiding principle, claiming: 'For Bennett that life is quotidian is exactly the point about it', adding:

> Bennett's aim was to unroll the panorama of life in time through all the tiny, detailed incidents of its thousand acts. It is the almost loving subjection to time as a succession of minutes, hours, months, years that makes *The Old Wives' Tale* the most impressive record we have in English of life in time, of birth, change and decay […] one is left with the feeling that never has the rhythm of ordinary life, life in time, been so faithfully, so surely transcribed.[52]

Clayhanger was marked out for Allen's especial praise, the character of Edwin being in his opinion 'one of the most attractive heroes in twentieth century fiction. Bennett, who believed inordinately in the 'interestingness' of ordinary things and ordinary people, was never more successful in revealing the 'interestingness' of an apparently ordinary man than in Edwin Clayhanger'.[53] One might also wish to add the 'interestingness' of an ordinary *place* which leads directly on to the consideration of the Birmingham group as potential inductees into the genre of regional writing. In the passage below, Walter Allen remarks on earlier 'condition of England' novelists for whom the industrial scene presented as a 'moral challenge':

> Disraeli, Mrs Gaskell, Dickens were Southerners for whom the industrial north was essentially alien; the industrial revolution that had made it was new and frightening, an affront to and a threat, and its towns were at once centres of a new kind of power and a new kind of man and the breeding places of a new kind of misery [...] For Bennett, the potteries were neither new nor frightening; they were the perfectly familiar home. Bennett's scene, as he realised himself, was fresh material for English fiction. It was in every way ugly, and yet however unpromising the surroundings there is a certain type of mind which craves for beauty, must find it, and where it is lacking, must create it for itself.[54]

Whist impressed by Bennett's subject material and choice of setting, rather than merely emulating the potteries writer by setting his own realist novel in Birmingham, Allen was also seeking a stylistic mentor. Born in 1905, five years before the publication of Bennett's *Clayhanger*, a writer more contemporaneous with Walter Allen, was Henry Green.[55] Published in 1929 when he was twenty-four years old, *Living* (page numbers referenced '*L*' below) describes the employers and employees at H. Pontifex and Sons, the family firm (an iron foundry) located in Bordesley, Birmingham. The novel established Green's reputation as a 'proletarian writer', an assessment which, given the prevailing requirement for a writer's 'working-class' credentials was, as will be shown, a little wide of the mark. Walter Allen initially judged Green's novel to be the prose-equivalent of W. H. Auden's poetry, adding, 'I knew nothing about Green at the time and assumed that, on the strength of the novel's setting and subject matter, he came from the working-class and had left-wing sympathies. *Living* seemed to me the conspicuous and most brilliantly successful English example of what we called the proletarian novel. I was, of course, dead wrong.'[56]

Discussing the formal element in what would today be described as a late Modernist work, Allen related how the style matched the novelty of the scene described: 'Bare repetitive, harsh, angular, sometimes deliberately clumsy, it is an admirable expression for the blackness and din of the foundry, at the same time as it is attuned to the vernacular of speech of the characters.'[57] However, it was Green's poetic rendering of familiar urban images that most impressed Allen: '[*Living*] showed me the Birmingham I knew caught from a totally unexpected angle.'[58] For Allen, it was Green's ability to defamiliarise archetypal cityscapes and pursuits: 'the football match, the day trip to the Lickey Hills, the infinities of red brick and the forever circling pigeons, [all] remain extremely fresh and vivid [...] as though set down for the first time. "New things," as Johnson said of Pope's poetry, are made familiar, and familiar things appear new.'[59] Chris Baldick agrees, saying Green's reimagining provides 'a realistic study of working lives and everyday rivalries, but in a modernist style whose syntactical oddities jolt us from habitual perceptions'.[60]

Just as Green's novel prompted Allen to ponder the imaginative potential of the urban industrial, so too his friendship with Louis MacNeice. Praising MacNeice's poem 'Birmingham', Allen recalls it 'showed me a city whose existence I had not suspected, a city enormously exotic and glamorous, though I could see that the exoticism and the glamour were truly properties of places I had known all my life'.[61] The writers discussed above would each prove influential upon Allen for, as he demonstrated in his own fictions, he had also learned that for the novel of urban life to be successful, its beauty, its poetry, would lie not so much in the matter presented but in the *way* it was presented.

As has been suggested, the work of the Birmingham group has generally been critically received as illustrative of a 'localised,' or 'provincial', writing. Unfortunately, the association of these adjectives with the parochial or small scale has, along with other misconceptions, militated against the wider critical reception of their work. The negative connotations of *provincial* are far-reaching, though fortunately the term is currently under a good deal of scrutiny—the modifier 'Regional' promising a more equitable assessment of such works. In *Regional Modernisms* (2013), Neal Alexander and James Moran choose the term over 'provincial', 'partly because it suffers less from pejorative connotations in ordinary usage, and partly because of its greater purchase as a geographical concept'.[62] K. D. M. Snell echoes these sentiments and has little hesitation in welcoming the urban novel into his discussion of the genre: 'The urban regional novel is such a crucial part of the genre that one cannot omit it. Nor does one want to regard cities as any less "regional" than other areas: without making any value judgements [...] the regional fiction of such areas should be treated accordingly.'[63] Snell attributes the disparagement of regional writing to 1940s and 1950s New Criticism, which, along with various other critical 'isms', encouraged the 'retreat from geography and history into a domain of pure "textuality" in which the principle of indeterminancy smother[ed] the possibility of social or political significance for literature'.[64] In Snell's opinion, the term 'regional'

> [I]s open to various understandings, but usually involves belittlement of any form of cultural life other than that supplied by the metropolis. It assumes metropolitan arbitration of taste, the superiority of metropolitan people and expression over those of locality—as though metropolis and locality were mutually exclusive terms.[65]

In his TV documentary considering the Birmingham group, David Lodge recounts how—along with many other writers and academics attracted to the provincial cities by the expansion of the university sector and the employment opportunities this provided during the 1960s—he was appointed as an assistant lecturer at the University of Birmingham. He remarks how his move

> [T]ransgressed a well-established rule of cultural life according to which, London, the capital, is the only place for an ambitious young writer of any kind to live and work in [and that] as soon as a young man or woman hears the call of the muse, they must pull up their roots and move into a bedsitter in Bloomsbury or Bayswater. That certainly has been the characteristic start to a literary career in this country from Shakespeare's time onwards.[66]

Reminiscent of MacNeice thirty years earlier, Lodge recalled how he first encountered the writing of the Birmingham group and discovered

> [T]hat here in [Birmingham], for a few years in the thirties, there flourished a literary life that was independent of the capital. There was even something called the Birmingham group of writers, now largely forgotten, but in their own way the object of considerable interest to metropolitan critics. The group was composed of short-story writers and novelists who had grown up in or near the city and wrote about it from a predominantly working-class perspective.[67]

In one of the first critical works to define the 'Regional Novel', Phyllis Bentley asserted that 'locality, reality and democracy are the watchwords of the English regional novelist' and that 'the regional novel expresses a belief that the ordinary man and woman are interesting and worth depicting'.[68] Little enamoured at the prospect of the urban-industrial novel contaminating her largely ruralist canon, Bentley's definition nonetheless chimes with Arnold Bennett's interest in ordinary things and ordinary people.[69] In this respect, discussions of the quotidian and regional may be seen to coalesce. As has been shown, owing to their rootedness in the city and their proximity to the locations, everyday lives and conditions of the citizens they describe, the Birmingham group writers were in a privileged position, one unavailable to 'outsiders' or their more middle-class literary colleagues, their dedication to describing the 'local and particular': the issues of cultural deportment arising from the urban-industrial municipality that was Britain's second city demand that her writers be included as exemplars of a regional writing. It is to situate their urban narratives in the broader, contemporary discussion of 1930s prose writing that the following section will primarily focus.

'Going Over': The Cultural Diaspora

Beyond the Birmingham group presenting as the city's' home-grown coterie of prose writers, metropolitan and intellectual 'outsiders' were at this time busily jostling to affiliate themselves with the working classes. This cultural tourism—subsequently attaining common parlance in Valentine Cunningham's coinage 'Going Over', borrowed in turn from Marx—has since encountered condemnation at the hands of both the writers themselves (the tourists) and social commentators alike, as evident in the following cynical, though perhaps justifiable, observation of Ronald Blythe:

> Working-class people took on a new fascination. For some of the upper-class Marxists, who had never seen the proletariat except as 'hands' or servants [...] the proles were beautiful [...] there was a *chic* in having one for a friend or lover, and it was noble to have working-class standards.[70]

In the TV documentary *As I Walked Down Bristol Street*, David Lodge remarks on this propensity, informing viewers:

> English literary culture developed a social conscience and a social curiosity in the thirties. This was of course a time of political and economic crisis: world recession, unemployment and the rise of fascism. There was, in short, a ready audience for young writers from provincial, preferably, working-class backgrounds who could put into words what they had observed or experienced.[71]

The reference used in the title of this introductory chapter is from Louis MacNeice's *The Strings are False: An Unfinished Autobiography*.[72] The 'hybrids' to whom he refers being those academics, writers, poets and proctor-intellectuals who, for a period during the 1930s, developed both an appetite for the writing of and a desire to affiliate with what were currently considered the superior workings of the proletarian soul. This section explores the wider discussion of working-class and proletarian writing during the 1930s, particularly the changing policies of Comintern during the interwar period and which proved so fundamental in shaping the contemporary theorisation and criticism of working-class literature and will consider the Birmingham group's response to this in terms of their political engagement and commitment. MacNeice's term thus functions as an entrée to the prevailing literary discussion during a decade in which airy ideals confronted harsh realities, where questions of engagement ran up against those of expression or, put more succinctly, where the *what* of content encountered the *how* of form. Reading the narratives of the Birmingham group writers against the grain of contemporary theorising this study argues that—amidst the clamour of metropolitan and Oxbridge proletarianising, sectarian tenets and sundry other contentions as to what a proletarian literature *ought* to be—taken collectively, their work presents as the practical resolution of several particularly heated debates.

English literary histories have frequently located the social conscience or democratic impulse of a period or an era in its poetry. In what may be considered something of a personal manifesto, Auden's 'Letter to Lord Byron' informs its eponymous addressee how the poet has discarded the idealised rural landscapes of the Georgians in order to savour instead 'the most lovely country that I know; / Clearer than Scafell Pike, My heart has stamped on / The view from Birmingham to Wolverhampton' [where] 'Tramlines and slagheaps, pieces of machinery, / That was, and still is, my ideal scenery'.[73] Written in 1936, Auden's poem registers much else besides worthy of note in respect of this project being his belief that 'novel writing [was] a higher art than poetry'.[74] However, the fact that some three years later the leading light of the poetic 'generation' named after him would turn his back on the collective idealism of what he now considered a 'low dishonest decade' has subsequently tainted the critical assessment of 1930s literature *tout court.* Elinor Taylor comments on 'the remarkable tenacity in [the] impression of thirties writing as the province of young, upper-middle-class, university educated, metropolitan (London-based) English leftists, the "little circle of English writers", as Spender called them, whose political phase ended with the departure of Auden and Isherwood for America and which was obituarised in Auden's "September

1, 1939"'.[75] Andy Croft expresses similar impatience, attributing the notion of 'failure' to 'critical re-readings of the so called "Red Decade" [which] have been content to merely explore "the early work of a small number of young, upper-middle class poets who once joined the communist party, but who quickly realised their mistake and the great risks to which they were putting their art, and who were all in long trousers by the time war came"'.[76] George Orwell likewise noted, 'the tendency to a sort of boy-scout atmosphere [whereby] the typical literary man ceases to be a cultural expatriate with a leaning towards the Church and becomes an eager-minded schoolboy with a leaning towards communism'.[77] Such belittling, though perhaps deserved, ought not condemn outright the ardour and enthusiasm of the Auden generation.[78] Possessing a level of self-knowledge that appears to have eluded other members of the Auden set with whom he is frequently associated, Louis MacNeice provides the following disarming, though nonetheless sincere, appraisal of his own class sympathies:

> My sympathies are Left. On paper and in the soul. But not in my heart or guts. On paper—yes. I would vote Left any day, sign manifestoes, answer questionnaires. Ditto my soul. My soul is all for moving towards the classless society. But unlike Plato, what my soul says does not seem to go. [...] With my heart and guts I lament the passing of class.[79]

In *British Writers of the Thirties*, Valentine Cunningham devotes a chapter to what might better be considered the Auden generation's 'well-intentioned', rather than 'insincere', aspiration to proletarian fraternisation, likewise Frank Kermode whose *History and Value* displays a similar reluctance to dismiss their attempt out of hand.[80] Nevertheless, a critical preoccupation with the indecision and perceived failure of commitment amongst certain 1930s poets does appear, owing to a measure of 'guilt by association', to have contaminated other aspects of the period's literary offering, notably its imaginative prose fiction, more specifically *working-class* prose fiction. As Benjamin Kohlmann and Matthew Taunton indicate, 'the popular narrative that has crystallized around writing and politics in the decade is fundamentally linked to the narrow and overwhelmingly male canon with which some previous critics worked'.[81] Elinor Taylor suggests: 'the a priori assumptions of 'failure' that dominate the literary memory of the thirties alienate us from experiments made in literary form, in cultural theory and in the political imagination no less than the entrenched terms of success do for modernist works.'[82] Her discussion clears a space for the 'recovery of resistance to the closure Auden announced on the outbreak of war: a consignment of the cultural radicalism of the thirties to a dead end, a "clever hope", and nothing more'.[83] Although Taylor's aims lie chiefly in establishing the decade's politicised literary engagement with the Popular Front, and seek to consider its respective 'successes and failures, through the lens of the British Communist novel', she acknowledges that 'other stories of the thirties are now being told' [for example] 'of women writers on the left, of working-class cultural producers'.[84] As detailed above, more recent critical rereadings have opened up the discussion of 1930s writing to more nuanced and less partisan considerations revealing how the production of imaginative writing during this period was not wholly predicated on ideas of masculine political engagement alone.[85]

That the economic and political turbulence of the 1930s met with a concomitant response in intellectual and literary circles is inescapable, and it was hardly surprising that the contemporary discussion of literature's 'social function' would percolate outwards from Oxbridge and the metropolis to the provinces. In *The Strings Are False*, Louis MacNeice describes how, following estrangement from his wife, '[He] began to go out a great deal and discovered Birmingham':

> Discovered that the students were human; discovered that Birmingham had its own writers and artists who were free of the London trade-mark. [That] the intellectual students were not so obsessed by politics as their contemporaries at Oxford or Cambridge, since, coming from the proletariat themselves, they were conscious of the weaknesses of the Prolet-Cult; some of them in fact were trying to achieve the old Oxford manner just at a time when the Oxford graduates were trying to declass themselves. [...] Reggie Smith, the son of a working man in Aston, and the one Birmingham student I met who had no complex about class, thought nothing was so funny as the Oxford and Cambridge proletarianisers. Not that he was one whose tastes are conditioned by reaction against their origins.[86]

Despite MacNeice's evident enthusiasm for their groundedness and, as he remarks, the honesty with which the Birmingham group writers rendered their environment, their work does present as something of an enigma. Written against a background of economic depression and high unemployment, they refrained from overt political didacticism, preferring instead to focus on how prevailing socio-economic circumstances were reflected culturally, and, in their view, more vividly by the presentation of domestic, community and workplace relationships. In some ways, this restrained approach may well account for their subsequent neglect, for based upon prevailing critical criteria, their narratives fell between two stools, their working-class subject material alienating them *canonically* from the curators of the Great Tradition on the one hand whilst their restraint and formal innovation distanced them *politically* from the purveyors of a prescriptivist Marxism on the other.[87]

It ought to be stated that, despite describing urban life from a working-class perspective, the Birmingham group's labelling as 'proletarian' writers is something of a misnomer; as the biographical thumbnail sketches above have shown, their working-class affiliation was more complex and wide ranging than hitherto assumed. The differences in their social status reflecting the fine shadings and gradations of a working-class community frequently, though mistakenly, considered monolithic. In *The Ideologies of Class*, Ross McKibbin comments on some common misconceptions:

> While characterised by extraordinary mutuality they were also marked by backbiting, gossip and a jockeying for social superiority. [...] All working-class communities were equally affected: single-status ones by the usual neighbourhood disputes (between those who kept the front step washed and blacked and those who did not, for example) while multiple-status communities displayed real social distances and much hostility between their members. The somewhat monolithic appearance the working-class presented to strangers concealed divisions which were at least as intense within communities as they were within the work-force.[88]

Again, as MacNeice discovered, the situation as reflected amongst Birmingham's 'working-class' *litterateurs* was far from straightforward:

> At this time, 1936, literary London was just beginning to recognise something called the Birmingham School of novelists. Literary London, hungry for proletarian literature, assumed that the Birmingham novelists were proletarian. Birmingham denied this; take John Hampson, Walter Allen, Leslie Halward—Hampson was a friend of E. M. Forster and was not employed as a labourer, Allen was a graduate of Birmingham University, Halward was a plasterer's labourer but even he could not be counted as of the sacred proletariat—his father had been a pork-butcher. It could be conceded however that they wrote about the People with a knowledge available to very few Londoners and that their view of the novel as social history had grown naturally out of their background instead of being, as in London, an apostasy from the view that the novel is primarily art. Though not accepting their

> theory of the novel, I found these Birmingham writers very refreshing; they at least were not hybrids; they were writing—and writing efficiently—on subjects they really knew.[89]

Valentine Cunningham remarks on the difficulty of defining proletarian writing and its practitioners, suggesting, 'It would be foolish, naturally to pretend that all "proletarian" fictions can be shunted together in one capacious category or that they were all written and read in the same way. There are big variations in kind and scope.'[90] Making reference to those who had gained George Orwell's seal of approval in the 1940 radio broadcast 'The Proletarian Writer', Cunningham suggests some additional candidates but remarks on the difficulty of adequately describing the qualities that constitute the 'working-class' writer and questions whether his *own* selections might really be described as proletarian:

> [Amongst] other possibles, some of them [are] a little hard, especially in the more-proletarian-than-thou 30s to place exactly in terms of class origin. Were V.S. Pritchett and Walter Allen proletarian? Was John Hampson? Was, for that matter Leslie Halward really? [...] Hampson was friendly with E. M. Forster, Walter Allen went to Birmingham University, prior to a career as a distinguished critic and later professor of English Literature. Halward's father sold pork chops. What class exactly—[Cunningham was citing MacNeice here—the question clearly niggled]—are pork butchers?[91]

Cunningham's inclusion of three Birmingham writers (he'd earlier mentioned Walter Brierley in a positive light, though by the same token he appears to have overlooked Peter Chamberlain) is nonetheless encouraging. It not only confers some recognition upon writers whose work this study will consider but also opens up the possibility of including works which, though not eschewing descriptions of proletarian life and experience, contain little in the way of overt political analysis.

'At last the British are Coming': Prevailing and Contemporary Critiques of Working-Class Literature

The fact remains that for a brief period during the 1930s, the appetite for working-class writing seemed insatiable with contemporary commentators increasingly urging the novel as a weapon in the class struggle. In order to ascertain the degree to which the 1930s novel had become politically 'weaponized', David Smith's *Socialist Propaganda in the Twentieth-Century British Novel* searched for examples of working-class writing that demonstrated a peaceful co-existence between art and propaganda.[92] Unfortunately, his survey provided little by way of affirmation, although Lewis Grassic-Gibbon's *A Scots Quair* and, that oft-cited 'classic' of working-class literature, Robert Tressell's *The Ragged Trousered Philanthropists* were, somewhat predictably, held as the paradigm texts.[93] In Chap. 5, titled 'At Last, the British are Coming', Smith focuses specifically upon the 1930s where, despite the prevailing clamour for more ideologically charged, working-class writing, only a dearth of 'revolutionary' novels were actually published.[94] It was only in 1936 with the commencement of the Spanish Civil War that Smith detected a trickle of revolutionary literature beginning to make its first 'cautious' appearance in Britain. For Smith, it seemed little had changed since the beginning of the decade, he cites the misgivings of the British delegates at the Second World Conference of Revolutionary Writers at Kharkov held in November 1930. According to Bob Ellis, 'There are many workers who write' [and] 'There are also people who write about the proletariat, but we have no proletarian writers', [a view] with which co-delegate Harold Heslop agreed, observing, 'It must be recognised that proletarian art in Great Britain is in a very bad condition—and is in fact hardly begun.'[95] According to Smith, the situation was highlighted in 1936 when the December edition of the American Marxist literary journal *New Masses* published Granville Hicks' 'The British are Coming', an article that in many ways reflected the triumph of hope over experience, his desires rather than their fulfilment, but which simultaneously registered America's exasperation at the reluctance of British writers to join the ideological fray.[96] The situation had not improved two years later when C. Day-Lewis likewise bemoaned the small amount of British revolutionary fiction, and—given the imminence of the Second World War—the fact that the number of committed British revolutionary novelists remained depressingly slight. Smith provides statistical evidence that underpins Day-Lewis' remarks:

> When one considers that in 1937—one of the peak years of extreme left wing activity—there were 1,817 new novels published, of which perhaps only six could have been said to be expressing unequivocal, revolutionary sympathies, the smallness of the movement is even more apparent.[97]

This doubtless proved discouraging for those expecting a degree of writerly solidarity in their pursuit of a progressive politics. The intervening eighty years have nevertheless enabled a degree of perspective on a decade which, whilst clearly awash with revolutionary intent, was self-evidently incapable of mobilising the promise of its rhetoric. Smith's statistics are inversely encouraging of this project as it relates to the Birmingham writers, for as he indicates:

> The point to be made is that alongside the fairly small body of unashamedly revolutionary fiction, and those few books which made clear their continued faith in parliamentary Socialism of the Labour Party variety, there was a much larger body of literature of social concern or social protest which either disdained politics altogether, or else treated the subject with varying degrees of objectivity, leaving the reader free to draw his own conclusions.[98]

It is not within the remit of this book to examine why the proletarian vanguard missed its 'historical moment', yet, having explored the many reasons as to why Marxism, or for that matter, a progressive politics of any colour had been doomed to failure in Britain, Ross McKibbin proposes the following as contributory factors:

> [A] working-class which was highly dispersed by occupation; having (appearances notwithstanding) a fairly low level of communitarian solidarity, following a number of competing associational activities and highly conditioned by inherited ideologies which emphasised a common citizenship, the fairness of the rules of the game and the class neutrality of the major institutions of the state [The Monarchy, The Parliament, The Nation itself].[99]

In terms of left-leaning doctrine, working-class autodidacts had not been slow in explaining Marxism's failure to ignite their political passions. Jonathan Rose argues, '[p]ut bluntly, the trouble with Marx was Marxists, whom British workers generally found to be too dogmatic, selfish and anti-literary.'[100] Referencing the personal testimony of workers, Rose suggests that the desire of middle-class intellectuals to politicise and fraternise with them was ultimately seen as condescending, he considers: 'early British Marxists dismissed as "bourgeois" the same canon of English classics that inspired generations of autodidacts, thus alienating the very proletarian intellectuals who might have proved the driving force behind a more creative Marxism.'[101] According to Rose, 'British working-people judged Marxism by the Marxists they knew, and concluded with good reason, that such people were not going to make a better world.'[102] By reading against the grain of David Smith's findings, one is able to appreciate how—despite the prevailing clamour of the Social Realists, Oxbridge and Metropolitan proctor-intellectuals, purveyors of prolet-cult and other left-leaning critical commentators urging the production of a more politically engaged literature—by far the greater quantity of British fiction produced during 1937 (and by extrapolation the decade) was motivated less by ideological engagement than a concern and interest in the everyday, lived-experience of its subjects. As Cunningham notes, 'In respect of their aims, ambitions, and the theory of a proletarian or socialist realist fiction, 'proletarian novelists' themselves could evidently differ as sharply as their fictional practices could vary.'[103]

In the US, the response towards an ideologically committed literature was more enthusiastic. Birmingham's Walter Allen, who visited Iowa University in 1935 to lecture on modern literature, was well placed to describe the situation there:

> [T]he social novelists of the thirties were mostly too young to have fought in the war… they had come to age in what later looked like an artificial paradise… Contemplating this world in ruins, attempting to render it in fiction, they took over the mood of the war books, a mood of anger and contempt for those who seemed responsible, the politicians and the industrialists, and of pity for their helpless victims. This was common to social novelists on both sides of the Atlantic; but when we place the American and English social novels of the thirties side by side we see the differences between them. The American novels, as a whole, are much more violent and radical. The twenties boom had soared to far greater heights in the United States than in England; the slump was therefore greater, and so was the sense of shock, outrage and betrayal.[104]

Much of the political discussion in the US was undertaken in the pages of the Marxist journal *New Masses*—the 'tag-line' of which asserted that it was '*prepared to act its role as a catalytic agent for the combination of literature and revolution*'—or alternatively, the John Reed clubs dedicated to: 'clarify[ing] the principles and purposes of revolutionary art and literature, to propagate them, to practise them'.[105] The implications for a literary convergence between Marxism and a patriotism built upon the somewhat paradoxical individualistic ideals of the American dream were clear to see. American Marxism sought a rapprochement by linking its doctrines with the revolutionary fervour upon which the modern country had been founded and where the ideas of freedom, instanced in its revolutionary disengagement with the 'Old Country', remained a guiding principle in the national psyche. Dedicated to the proliferation and dissemination of Marxist writing and ideology, *New Masses* numbered among its editorial staff: Michael Gold, Walt Carman, Whittaker Chambers, Joseph Freeman and Granville Hicks. In 1936, the writer, critic and committed Marxist James T. Farrell published *A Note on Literary Criticism* and, in what appeared to many a volte-face, displayed his impatience with the fervour of politically doctrinaire colleagues who demanded writers adopt the 'social-realist' party line. A staunch defender of the writer's freedom of expression, Farrell's assertion that 'he who would put literature in uniform is afraid of literature' neatly describes his position in respect of the contemporary dilemma. His preparedness to step back from the zeal of reformers, radicals and revolutionaries, in order to champion imaginative writing, presents as a refreshing intervention. Just as the Birmingham group writers sought to describe the lived-experience of their class counterparts, so too Farrell, who, as his biographer Alan Wald indicates, '[joined the] historic battle to create a place for working-class life experience in U.S. literature', his commitment to 'the interrogation of "experience" among the non-elite classes was key to his whole artistic project'.[106] Pointing to the bourgeois writer's difficulty in reconciling art with political engagement, Frank Kermode reflects, as had Walter Allen, that 'in such circumstances the Americans tended to be more explicit than the English about doctrine and its consequences'.[107]

Nevertheless, beyond the continuing discussion surrounding notions of political engagement, a further issue remained, and this is very much the sine qua non without which very little writerly or critical discussion might ensue: the question of publication.[108] The 'sociology of authorship' and the difficulties faced by the worker-writers aiming to see their work in print are covered comprehensively in Christopher Hilliard's *To Exercise Our Talents: The Democratization of Writing in Britain*, and, as this study will look at the Birmingham writers' encounters with their respective publishers during the course of this discussion, only brief reference will be made here.[109] Arguably less politically committed than American journals such as *New Masses*, the appetite for accounts of working-class experience nonetheless remained strong in British periodicals. Again, as with others who would later recant on such once-principled aims, John Lehmann provided a respected forum for worker writers during his editorship of the

Hogarth Press publication *New Writing*. And, launched in October 1934, Montague Slater similarly oversaw the publication of *Left Review*, which similarly aimed to encourage contributions from working-class writers and which provided a series of competitions adjudged by the sincere, though somewhat schoolmarmly, Amabel Williams-Ellis alongside such worker-writers as James Hanley, although, despite *Left Review's* noble sentiments, a whiff of condescension still managed to seep through.[110] H. Gustav Klaus registers his personal disquiet, commenting:

> Encouraging as the result[s] were, with up to fifty entries being received per competition, the whole enterprise (with Amabel Williams-Ellis telling the workers to avoid the use of jargon) had something patronising about it, and was, as Alick West later pointed out, based on a critical standard 'which was indistinguishable from the aesthetics current at the end of the nineteenth century'.[111]

In terms of packaging working-class experience as a product for literary consumption, Valentine Cunningham registers T. S. Eliot's 'cheap magisterial sneer' at the very possibility of a proletarian literature, and likewise George Orwell, whose review of Philip Henderson's *The Novel Today* remarks, '[Henderson] is careful to explain, proletarian literature does not mean literature written by proletarians,' prior to concluding in his characteristically irascible tone, '[it] is just as well, because there isn't any'.[112] Despite such seeming impatience, Orwell had himself had dealings with the worker-writer Jack Hilton, whose advice he eagerly sought and whose suggestion that he visit Wigan, 'for there are the colliers and they're good stuff', led to the former's *The Road to Wigan Pier*.[113] Not unduly enthusiastic regarding 'the wasted money, energy and piffle' that Orwell subsequently produced, Hilton's dealings with others of his stamp were even less amicable. Describing his irritation at 'silver-spoon, progressive editors' such as John Lehmann, with whom he dealt in the late 1930s, Hilton observed how 'these pups of University boys with a flairy flare [*sic*] for LIT, in the worst form are too *dictatorially* important (my emphasis)'.[114] D. J. Taylor's gloomy conviction registers little by way of encouragement: '[s]o much literary Marxism grew out of what was a largely social hierarchy [which] tended to keep working-class writers at bay. Such genuinely working-class writing that appeared in the mainstream periodicals of the 1930 was largely there on sufferance, and most of the attention it received was careful to stress its representative qualities rather than its individual distinction'.[115] Yet, unpromising as the prospects for worker-writers appeared, it should be remembered that not all 'patrons' of working-class literature 'patronised' their protégées in this manner; were it not for Edward Garnett, Ford Madox Ford and others (see Conclusion, pp. 206, 209), the voices of two distinguished Nottingham authors may have forever remained unheard.

Having offered this necessarily limited overview of the prevailing discussion, it would be useful to look at how more recent scholarship has approached the subject. As is doubtless becoming apparent, by seeking to situate the fiction of the Birmingham writers within the broader critical conversation, one is confronted with much disagreement and questioning as to what constitutes working-class writing, what representational forms it should adopt, who should be writing it and to what extent should it be politically engaged? That these questions are unresolved or, in the case of the Birmingham group 'un-posed', is due not only to the inadequate definition and theorisation of working-class writing as a whole but also to the prevailing emphasis on the type of overtly politicised engagement that remained a constant feature, in pre-popular-front critiques.

In *'What Life Means to those at the Bottom':* Love on the Dole *and its Reception since the 1930s*, Jack Windle surveys the critical reception of Walter Greenwood's novel from its publication in 1933 through to 2011 and draws two significant conclusions:

> Firstly, that criticism always reads into texts the pre-eminent concerns of its own time and setting, but with working-class texts which tend to be politically charged because of their contexts and contents, this is even more marked. [...] [Secondly] there is a gap of historical understanding between critics and working-class cultural production. Critics are overwhelmingly middle or upper-class, or else they are 'declassed' by their education and professional status. Furthermore they are at a geographical and cultural remove which renders impossible a full understanding of the local specificities that so crucially shape the style and tone of working-class writing.[116]

Taking the second point first, Windle, as had George Orwell, touches on the notion of 'embourgoisement' and considers that the deracination of working-class writers, owing to the 'benefits' of higher education, effectively alienated them from their class; the notion of such educational deracination is supportive of Frank Kermode's view that 'workers could not be writers without ceasing to be workers'.[117] The circularity of this proposition is dealt with more comprehensively in Chap. 4, although, as will be shown, the theme of 'self-cultivation' features as something of a trope in working-class writing and will be encountered in several of the texts under discussion here. Likewise its seeming inverse, the social realignment sought by educated, middle-class writers for whom 'engagement' and 'commitment' were watchwords. Windle's first point concerns the belief that the critical scrutiny of working-class texts from this period has continuing relevance for our own times.[118] The 'Lessons of History' trope or its inverse in 'Presentism' are still very much alive and kicking, though, as Windle records, critical commentators have on occasions been overly ambitious in their attempts 'to read into texts the pre-eminent concerns of our own time', thereby pushing working-class narratives far beyond their referential potential.[119] However, Alice Beja welcomes the fact that '[In America] the relationship between thought, literature and politics in the thirties [...] gave birth to radical studies, and proletarian novels and authors were revalued in the 1970s and 1980s in the wake of the development of cultural studies, gender studies [and] Afro-American studies'. Whilst raising the question of Legacy discussed more fully in this book's conclusion, Beja cautions that this tendency can also prove 'damageable [*sic*] to literary works' with texts being read as merely 'illustrative of one [social] trend or another'.[120] John Fordham also draws attention to this kind of 'misreading', attributing it to the fact that 'no overall theory of working-class writing has been developed to cope with the multiplicity of its forms'.[121] In seeking a critical framework with which to consider the writing of James Hanley, Fordham says he was attracted to the work of critical commentators who sought to investigate a work's inherent dialectic or ideological complexity, rather than proffering critical evaluations based solely by reference to a prevailing political orthodoxy or meta-narrative.[122]

As will become clear, the perspective adopted in this study aligns closely with the work of critics adopting a more dialectical and nuanced approach to working-class writing, one that places high value on implicit social comment achieved by means of the detailed description of *lived-experience*. The reference to 'descriptive content' is a nod to Karl Radek's injunction that 'proletarian art cannot content itself with the class struggle alone. It should describe processes that are going on in the classes themselves—their way of life, their psychology, their development, their strivings' and, rather than being overtly or directly propagandistic, should adopt formal procedures that enable the work's political content to emerge unobtrusively. Occupying a liminal space between high modernism's difficulty and interiority and social realism's commitment to political engagement, Birmingham Group narratives prove more responsive to a critical discussion directed at their intrinsic cultural value, rather than their summary dismissal at the courts of enquiry convened to dispose judgements founded upon politicised sectarian or workerist critiques concerned predominantly with what 'ought' rather than 'had' been written. This doctrinal aspect of what came to be termed 'socialist realism' was from the outset used as the stick with which to beat working-class writers whose texts were deemed insufficiently 'progressive' in this respect. In terms of the Birmingham writers' diminution of the political and augmentation of the cultural, the following observation from Simon Goulding's analysis of the novels of Patrick Hamilton is supportive. Discussing the influence of Russian Socialist Realism on British writers during the interwar period, he suggests:

> [D]espite the theoretical importance of *partiinost* (party-ness) it is *narodnost* (people-ness) that serves as the primary device of socialist realism within British Socialist Fiction of this period. It is the actual lives of the people, the quality, peril and joys of their existence that motivates writers such as Hanley, Garrett and Sommerfield.[123]

Owing primarily to the 'cultural', more specifically, 'domestic' issues and concerns they address, especially as registered in the autobiographical element that permeates their narratives and which is considered in the body of this study, the work of the Birmingham writers is equally ripe for inclusion here, for, as Goulding remarks of Hamilton, their narratives demonstrate 'a creative belief in writing about what one had seen and lived', and one where making plain the contrast between how things *were*, as opposed to *how they could or might have been*, was axiomatic.[124] The body of contemporary scholarship surrounding the 1930s and the working-class literature produced in this period continues to build. Recent studies by women writers such as Elinor Taylor's *The Popular Front Novel in Britain 1934—1940*, cited above, and important work by Nicola Wilson, whose *Home in British Working Class Fiction* 'puts family and marital relationships, gender, household finances, education and the kitchen table at the heart of what we understand about class', have both added to contemporary accounts of working-class literature cited elsewhere in this book and where it is hoped that in adopting a similar approach it too will resist the prevailing sectarian perspectives of this troubled decade and likewise the accounts of 'failure' that have permeated and distorted the literary discussion surrounding it.[125] The concluding section of this introduction will consider how the Birmingham writers' impulse to document the lived-experience of their urban counterparts would find accommodation within the collaboration of image and word that came to be termed the 'Ethnographic Turn'.

The Ethnographic Turn

During the interwar years, realist and modernist works had between them accounted for the majority of prose fictions produced, and although realism remained the principal means of literary representation, conflict between the proponents of each mode endured. As both a literary critic and practitioner of working-class writing, Walter Allen was conscious of the double-bind here, particularly that regarding the working-class writer's entrapment between the jaws of form and content. Allen observed that although many novels by working-class writers remain moving, their authors often lacked the necessary literary skill and education to make them more than 'pathetic documentaries', reliant on 'an over-emphatic naturalism'.[126] However, bourgeois writers, though doubtless conversant with a variety of modernistic literary techniques, frequently lacked lived-experience of working-class mores.

In terms of which representative mode might be most suitable for setting down accounts of working-class experience, Elizabeth Maslen indicates: '[Michael Levenson] rightly argues for a useful distinction between a narrow definition of the term "modernism" and the concept of "modernity" too often linked as inseparable.'[127] This is helpful for separating the representational form from a constraining and restrictive time frame, and ventures the possibility that 'realism' might similarly be de-coupled from its nineteenth-century 'Bourgeois' conception and re-configured as the medium with which to represent contemporary (1930s) reality. Nonetheless, it must be conceded that each mode was not without its critics. 'High-Modernism', Maslen continues:

> [Is] arguably restrictive in its approach to many of the concerns of twentieth-century life—that complex mixture of personal, social and political, a mix which often results in contradictions and confusions. [...] Meanwhile, the term 'realism', so often dismissed as in opposition to modernism [...] has provoked much impassioned rhetoric, not only among critics but among

> writers of fiction too. In the thirties, Samuel Beckett, for instance, refers to Marcel Proust's distaste for 'the realists and naturalists worshipping at the offal of experience'.[128]

A compromise needed to be reached and fortunately one would not be long in appearing, for with their temporal constraints now thrown off, the two prime representative modes might forge links with an emergent Documentarism.[129] As remarked above, during the pre-war decade, cinema had become the principal mode of entertainment, its tractor beams scanning the wider cultural universe and drawing all other artistic and literary forms into its orbit.[130] David Lodge clearly subscribes to this view identifying Christopher Isherwood, Graham Greene and Evelyn Waugh as 'representative fiction writers of [the interwar] decade [who] gradually shook off the influence of modernist fiction with its mythic and poetic bias and refurbished the traditional novel with techniques learned from the cinema.'[131] Based upon their adoption of similar practices, this study would naturally urge the inclusion of the Birmingham group writers alongside their better-known contemporaries here. However, it might be added that beyond cinema alone each of the elements constitutive of what became known as the 'Ethnographic Turn' would combine in providing more adaptable, up-to-date and sympathetically grounded methods by which to take the nation's cultural pulse.

In terms of more recent theorisations, though primarily concerned to challenge Modernism's highjacking of literary critical discourse during the interwar period, Kristen Bluemel's *Intermodernism: Literary Culture in Mid-Twentieth Century Britain* (2009) provides a timely intervention. Bluemel explains how the writers featured within *Intermodernism*'s pages—*contra* T. S. Eliot's claim that the 'duty of the poet, as poet, is only indirectly to his people: his direct duty is to his *language*'—saw their responsibility, as writers, primarily to 'the people' and that, by opening out areas of discussion hitherto occluded by the powerful counterforce of modernism, her collection of essays would focus on democratised forms of writing relating to 'people, work and community (original emphasis)'.[132] In his review of *Intermodernism*, Jesse Matz cites Laura Marcus, John Fordham and Nick Hubble's articles as justifications for the intermodernist project. Of the former he notes:

> Marcus proves that collaborations and conflicts between cinema and literature in these years were crucial to the formation of aesthetic, political

> and cultural categories critical to twentieth century culture. This discovery validates the claim for intermodernism as distinct from either modernism or postmodernism: here, the documentary impulse did not come after modernist aestheticism but instead shaped a modernism that persisted into activities joining aesthetic and realist imperatives.[133]

Matz argues that Fordham's article underpins Marcus' by providing 'proof that we need a new critical category truly to understand the social implications and aesthetic value of writing invisible to modernist, realist and postmodern critical perspectives'.[134] This is also a view to which Tyrus Miller aligns, for he likewise remarks upon the 'convergence and complementarity' in the documentary movement's deployment of both modernist *and* realist representative modes during the interwar period, seeing their marriage within the documentary form as the resolution of a hitherto conflicting and antagonistic relationship (my emphasis).[135]

As has been intimated, the past two decades have witnessed a renewed interest in the working-class writing of the 1930s. Scholars and critics of the genre such as Nicola Wilson, Elinor Taylor, Simon Goulding, Jack Windle, John Fordham and Nick Hubble represent a crop of writers and researchers whose critical approach aligns with the intermodernist intervention. The methodology deployed in this study follows the 'intermodernist' approach and will later, as indicated at the outset, adopt an 'intersectional' framework. Benjamin Kohlmann and Matthew Taunton suggest that 'the breakdown of ideological binaries of the Cold War has enabled literary scholars to produce more nuanced accounts of the political affiliations that characterised the inter-war years'.[136] They stress how their critical anthology adopts:

> [A] broad spectrum of political positions in which sexual, religious and racial identities combine with or rub up against class politics. In a related vein, feminist literary criticism played an particularly important role in laying the groundwork for a broadening and deepening of the thirties as a literary historical category. […] where popular narrative [had] crystallised around writing and politics […] linked to the narrow and overwhelmingly male canon with which some previous critics worked.[137]

The linkage between the strategies of more recent critical positions and the overview of the documentary and Mass Observation movements provided below will hopefully contribute to a fuller appreciation of the literary productions of the Birmingham group. The anthropological impulse, or 'ethnographic turn' predicated on revealing the political manoeuvres presented by a seemingly innocuous media, exploited the media's own devices by turning them in upon themselves to lay bare the ideological forces at work on the population at large.

The contemporary search for the 'factual imperatives' lying behind the 1930s constructions of Britain's popular press and media commenced with the work of the documentary filmmakers John Grierson and Paul Rotha, who had in turn been influenced by continental counterparts such as Walter Ruttmann, Sergei Eisenstein and Dziga Vertov, whose works they would later emulate. They were followed by the mass observers Tom Harrison, Charles Madge and Humphrey Jennings and later the era's two best-known writers of reportage, J. B. Priestley and George Orwell, each of whom had by 1937 completed their respective tours of England's industrial heartlands. Finally, in bringing a much-needed female perspective to bear, the novelist Margaret Storm Jameson's *Fact* article 'Documents' had proposed a theory of documentary writing that functioned very much as the interface between scientific 'fact gathering' and a creative 'prose' geared to the promotion and transformation of the national conscience.

Keith Williams' assertion that 'Documentary' might qualify as the 'Jakobsonian dominant' of the pre-war era is justifiable; however, this study will suggest that 'Image' might prove a better candidate and argues strongly for the latter's adoption as the hierarchical term.[138] In the BBC TV series 'The Age of the Image', presenter James Fox explains how visual media were used 'not only by the powerful but also the powerless in order to fight the great battle of ideas that defined the twentieth century'.[139] Fox illustrates his point by reference to the pioneering photoessays that featured in *Picture Post* magazine. Although the issue he considers had dealt with 1953s coronation of Queen Elizabeth II, the 'photo-essay' had been a regular feature of the magazine since its inception in 1938. Fox explains that 'photographs drove the story' but, more importantly, how, alongside resplendent images of Royalty, the magazine also made visible the ordinary people.[140] *Picture Post's* democratic impulse was remarked upon by Stuart Hall, who suggested:

> [T]he characteristic syntax, style and rhetoric of the 'Picture Post' photograph was a democratisation of the subject [where the] focus on participating actors and onlookers—representative and cross-sectional—raises the "unnoticed subjects" to a sort of equality of status, photographically, with the heroic subjects (here the Queen) and the activities they elsewhere depict.[141]

However, as Nick Hubble indicates, there is a strong case for reconsidering the centre of the democratising movement less as the 'Social Eye of Picture Post' than as 'The Social Eye of Mass-Observation', which had anticipated its techniques a year earlier.[142] Following its founders' credo that 'Collective habits and social behaviour are our field of inquiry, and individuals are only of interest insofar as they are typical of groups', the Mass Observation movement probed beneath the ideological veneer of contemporary reality in an attempt to determine the collective voice and attitudes of the population at large.[143] Hubble comments on the difficulty of satisfactorily pinning down Mass Observation's prospectus. He cites Jack Common, who dismissed Mass Observation as 'the attempts of nice young men to penetrate working-class pubs and to try to get to know the workers', and contrasts this position with that of Stuart Laing, who believed MO had a positive function 'in an anthropological context' because it 'fostered the idea of the Mass as an unknown which has to be explored [thus] anticipat[ing] a broadening of social consciousness within the rigid class society of England'.[144] Valentine Cunningham voices similar concerns describing the middle-class lineage of 'journalists, doctors, [...] the Left rent-a-crowd in the 30s and early 40s', not forgetting 'the usual heavily represented preponderance of public school accents' that did duty as mass observers, though, *contra* notions of middle-class lineage, it seemed B. L. Coombes and the young Walter Allen had each done a stint of mass observation.[145] And, Tom Jeffery argues that the mass observers 'were preponderantly from the lower middle class like the Mr Polly's and Hoopdrivers and Kippses: Few were in full-time education much past the age of sixteen, although many had won scholarships to secondary schools. Those who did go to university almost without exception returned to the lower middle class world as schoolteachers'.[146] Setting out (in the manner of a *vox populi*) to record everyday life in Britain, and using specific monthly directives in the form of questionnaires, participant observers interviewed members of the public to determine its attitude towards such current events as the abdication crisis or the Chamberlain government's policy of appeasement. Personal testimony was thus employed not only to register the life of the individuals interviewed but also in the attempt to calculate the shape and nature of a collective sensibility.

Nick Hubble indicates 'the concept of the 'image' [...] had a particular modernist resonance that entailed something more than the pictorial impression [alone]'.[147] By intimating *something* beyond 'pictorial impression[s] alone' Hubble invokes a discussion of the 'Dialectical

Image', the concept Walter Benjamin developed in his *Arcades Project*. Considered inscrutable, at best obscure, and meeting with no little apprehension on the part of Benjamin scholars, recent interpretations have proved more useful and are encouraging of the reading undertaken here with regard to the 'affective' potential of graphic imagery and montage effects as they might be deployed to explore the notions of commodification, reification, alienation and consumerism historically experienced by the individual subjects under capitalist relations of production. Benjamin claimed that images 'need to be rescued from aesthetic discourses and endowed with a *shocking*, that is to say, politically effective power' [...] for they '[contain] the potential to *interrupt* hence to counteract modes of perception and cognition that have become second nature (my emphasis)'.[148] The desire to shock people from their complacency was a, if not the, key aim of cinematographers, documentarists, mass observers and imaginative prose writers alike. Benjamin saw the process less as convulsion therapy than the need to reawaken individuals from the artificial dream state induced by their capitalist conditioning. Just as Storm Jameson saw the documentarist's task as gathering a repository of 'raw material' in the shape of 'facts', Benjamin sought to assemble a phantasmagoria: a reservoir of raw materials as preparation for the construction of images that could in turn be deployed to provide a reading of capitalist history based upon the juxtaposition of its archaic or redundant material objects. According to Max Pensky, as with surrealist artworks, 'the power to disorient or shock lay to a large degree in the defamiliarisation effect of seeing otherwise meaningless material objects suddenly removed from the context that determines their meaning'.[149] Benjamin's aim was to reveal how ideas asserting the 'comforting visions' of linear 'progression' or 'development' that underpinned traditional approaches to historiography were misguided and to show instead that 'history is precisely repetition, the absence of real change'.[150]

Despite differences in their prioritisation of objectives, Harrison, Madge and Jennings agreed that the Mass Observation movement should treat 'images' as social facts. In this they followed Ezra Pound, who had earlier defined the image as 'that which presents an intellectual and emotional complex in an instant of time'.[151] In his preface to *Some Imagist Poets 1916*, Pound explained, 'In the first place "Imagism" does not mean merely the presentation of pictures, it refers to the manner of presentation and not the subject' [...]. 'The "exact" word does not mean the word which exactly describes the object in itself, it means the "exact" word which brings the effect of that object before the reader as it presented itself to the poet's (observer's) mind at the time of writing the poem (making an observation)'.[152] Hubble suggests 'using the image, rather than the word [as] the unit of signification', enabled the Imagist poets to 'generate their own meanings separate from dominant narrative associations'.[153] '[T]he author', wrote Pound, 'must use his *image* because he sees it or, feels it, *not* because he thinks he can use it to back up some creed or some system of ethics or economics.'[154] Thus, in seeking a qualitative, rather than quantitative or *instrumental*, response to external stimuli, Pound ascribed subjective experience greater 'emotive' value than the purportedly objective. Surprisingly the notion of an 'emotional intelligence' has continued to gain critical currency amongst intellectuals. Theodor Adorno proposes, 'there's no reason to think a subjective, emotional "reaction" to an artwork could not also be a hermeneutically "precise" one.'[155] Virginia Woolf's article 'The Cinema' likewise touches on the nature of the image, although she found verbal imagery more effective than celluloid symbolism.[156] Saussaurian linguistics have been similarly invoked, and though *avant la lettre* in contemporary discussions of the 'image', Valentine Cunningham proposes Saussurian 'signifieds [as] mental versions of items in the world', though he is conspicuously silent as to whom these 'mental versions' may have belonged.[157]

In his introduction to the 1999 edition of *Mass-Observation: A Short-History*, Tom Jeffery draws attention to some omissions and 'absences' from his earlier (1979) account:

> One in particular would be inconceivable now for the short history shows little interest in how the concerns, appeal and organisational logistics of Mass-Observation were of particular relevance to women, especially but not only middle class women, creating private access to a collective forum and opening up consideration of the hitherto hidden in contemporary domesticity and femininities. Which in turn prompts the relationship to a wider tendency to the autobiographical and diary form in the late thirties, the presentation of individuality and personal record as the mass obliteration of war came to seem inevitable.[158]

Jeffery is hard on himself, for although published during feminism's second wave, the revised 1979 edition still managed to overlook issues of 1930s domesticity and femininities. The 'Lessons of History Trope' is currently very much alive and kicking, and it is to Tom Jeffery's credit that he indicates the potential of the Mass Observation archive as providing a valuable resource in the continuing feminist conversation. As Nick Hubble indicates: 'The value of exploring Mass-Observation is that the inclusive cultural consciousness [it registers] is not simply historical but valuable for confronting ongoing cultural and political concerns in Britain and similar problems created by the onset of modernity across the world.'[159]

The development of mass culture, which rose to prominence during the 1930s, while welcomed by consumers had become a matter of concern for the country's cultural arbiters, notably Q. D. Leavis, whose glum prognostications are well documented. Virginia Woolf held similar reservations, but nonetheless appreciated cinematography's expressive potential. Writing in 1926, she maintained that 'if cinema would only develop its own devices'; if the filmmaker were able to communicate thought and emotion through his medium, then he would have 'enormous riches to hand [...] 'his booty could be hauled in hand over hand'.[160] Less sanguine than Woolf, the 'easy pleasures' of popular culture, the cinema and popular music, met with the vehement opprobrium of Theodor Adorno and Max Horkheimer, whose *Dialectic of Enlightenment* excoriated the culture industry considering it an ideological tool for the domination of the masses rather than serving to reveal their plight under monopoly capitalism.[161] Yet, unlike his Frankfurt School colleagues, Walter Benjamin believed film might yet function politically by using its intrinsic techniques: dissonances, jump cuts, close-ups and deranging montages, in a manner not dissimilar to Brechtian theatre, in order to defamilarise everyday 'reality' and shake the audience from habitual perceptions.

Although such box office attractions as Alfred Hitchcock's *The Thirty-Nine Steps* (1935), John Ford's *Stagecoach* (1937) or George Cukor's *Gone With the Wind* (1939) held sway in the popular imagination of 1930s audiences, four weeks prior to the beginning of the new decade John Grierson's documentary film *Drifters* (1929) first appeared. In the Autumn 1933 edition of *Cinema Quarterly*, Grierson theorised the new form, then a relative novelty to British audiences, as follows:

> Documentary, or the creative treatment of actuality, is a new art with no background in the story and the stage as the studio product so glibly possesses. Theory is important, experiment is important; and every new development of technique or new mastery of theme has to be brought quickly into criticism.[162]

Grierson's documentary *way of seeing*, his 'creative treatment of actuality' was none other than technical manipulation; the mechanical splicing or editing of items 'out there' in the life world which, under his supervision, would become ideologically oriented and politically subversive. Keith Williams states:

> Grierson's own comments about *Drifters* (1929) reveal how he sought to demystify and render visible the economic and social structure behind a prosaic commodity. Dramatically telescoping spatial and social distances between labour and consumption, its imagery was intended to shuttle between life-and-death ocean drama and hustling fish-market to underline the process by which labour is converted into exchange value—'said agonies are sold at ten shillings a thousand ...for an unwitting world['].[163]

Although critical responses were varied and, at times, contradictory, Williams claims the bulk of 1930s fictional literature was magnetised by documentary:

> It eventually became an important position in the debate about the nature of the real, and the question of the most effective form for representing it, central to thirties culture in both Britain and America [...] The solution sought was paradoxical: an 'objective' art representing reality as soberly and authentically as possible, while at the same time 'baring its own devices' in an anti-illusionistic manner.[164]

The 'nature of the real and questions regarding the most effective medium for representing it' became the motive force propelling the documentary movement and is traceable in each of its manifestations. As will be seen, the Birmingham group writers adopted the devices and techniques of both commercial and documentary cinema, especially the juxtaposition of images described above, and these techniques figure powerfully in the presentation of class identity in each of Walter Allen's first two published novels. *Innocence Is Drowned* montages images of poverty against those of wealth, while *Blind Man's Ditch* pursues Walter Benjamin's aim to awaken slumbering individuals from the catatonic dream state induced by their capitalist conditioning. John Hampson deploys cross-class montage in *Saturday Night at the Greyhound* contrasting Ruth Dorme's metropolitan perceptions with the down-to-earth Ivy Flack and the calculating Clara Tapin. Early Soviet avant-garde filmmakers such as Eisenstein defined cinema as '"first and foremost, montage", [...] a tractor ploughing over the audience's psyche in a particular class context', while Dziga Vertov edited factual footage to make significant connections through 'non-discursive, montage "shocks" in order to reveal the socio-economic syntax behind the automatized surface of everyday reality'.[165] Lara Feigel explains how cinematic devices: cross-cutting, close-up, long shot and montage were adopted by the writers of imaginative prose during these years and describes the uses to which they were put, and this study builds upon her insights in the discussion of Walter Allen's and John Hampson's novels below.

The democratic impulses of documentary cinema and mass observation together excited a good deal of intellectual and creative interest. However, as with the charges levelled against its commercial Hollywood counterpart, documentary cinema was not wholly immune to criticism. Despite his early enthusiasm for the medium, W. H. Auden challenged documentary cinema's 'factual imperative', its desire to subordinate and represent individuals as types. Lamenting the documentarist's positivist disregard of the 'private life or emotions', he argued that these were 'facts like any others, and one cannot understand the public life of action without them'.[166] Invoking the issue of class, Auden contends, 'it is doubtful whether an artist can ever deal more than superficially (and cinema is not a superficial art) with characters outside his own class, and most British documentary makers are upper-middle'.[167]

In an article discussing the need and conditions for contemporary literary advance, Montague Slater suggested a prerequisite for any progress in this direction must derive from:

> [K]nowledge of the ordinary world of people and of things, the world of work, the world of everyday economic struggle [...] descriptive reporting is something which the tabloid press has almost replaced by wisecracks, which the revolutionary press has no room for, and which for one reason or another has a particularly revolutionary import (we have even invented a jargon name for it, *reportage*).[168]

Concluding that 'to describe things as they are is a revolutionary act in itself,' Slater's article resonates with the views of Raymond Williams and Salman Rushdie cited above.[169] Indeed, it was to 'describe things as they are' and discover 'the world of everyday economic struggle' that J. B. Priestley embarked upon his *English Journey* (1934) and George

Orwell took *The Road to Wigan Pier* (1937). As each work has been the subject of detailed critical scrutiny, I shall refrain from further discussion here beyond noting that in their respective use of the generic hybrid that was *reportage*, Orwell and Priestley aimed to locate 'the ordinary world of people and things' sought by Montague Slater.

Appearing in *Fact*, Margaret Storm Jameson's article 'Documents' might well be considered the manifesto of literary reportage. Two recent biographers of Storm Jameson, Jennifer Birkett and Elizabeth Maslen, each described their frustration in finding appropriate critical tools with which to evaluate her work. Birkett attributes this to the following fact: 'Only recently have the limitations of the categories and boundaries imposed by the methodologies of "scientific" criticism on twentieth-century artistic production […] begun to be recognised, and the return begun to kinds of criticism that can read the relations of cultural forms to cultural practices, and recognise the particular operations of particular texts.'[170] Maslen considers Jameson has '[fallen]-foul of the mania to define fictions with terminological labels: Modernist, Post-modernist, Realist (this last usually in a derogative sense and cited in opposition to modernism implying a medium that is incapable of manipulation being in essence conservative, reactionary and old-fashioned)'.[171]

In order to analyse the 'ground of reality' that constituted the country's sociopolitical DNA, Jameson believed her subject matter would be better observed holistically, by 'sounding' a 'cross-section' of social classes. Her concept of 'soundings' thus aligns with the aims of Mass Observation, whose '*May the Twelfth* (1937)—an account of the events surrounding the coronation of George VI compiled by more than two hundred observers—took a deep synchronic slice through British culture on a single day'.[172] However, Jameson stresses that this documentary evidence ('the facts'), once gathered, might provide the basis for a piece of imaginative writing, as Elizabeth Maslen explains:

> 'Soundings', as [Jameson] interprets the term, offer her readers a chance to measure the depths of a contemporary crisis through close inspection of a sample community containing all the critical elements. […] In her trilogy 'Mirror in Darkness', exploring the links between character and context, Jameson obeys her own rule of letting characters think and speak with as little interference from the author as possible, offering a range of men and women as 'soundings' from a cross-section of English society, revealing each as a product of their background, and how, as a result, each reacts to and is affected by the world they inherit.[173]

Jameson's fictional characters present a cross-section of British society precisely because she believed the 'ideological imaginary' she sought to expose had permeated *all* levels of society. Although Aldous Huxley's *Point Counter Point* and Virginia Woolf's *Mrs Dalloway* were bourgeois 'collective' novels, the practical working out of Jameson's theory in the working-class novel was first realised in John Summerfield's *May Day* (1936). However, the Birmingham writers John Hampson and Walter Allen were likewise keen to exploit the representational potential of the multi-protagonist novel, and this will be explored more fully in the analysis of their novels below. Storm Jameson theorised that what was required in contemporary fiction already existed in another form, documentary film, and she proceeded to enumerate the formal criteria by which this new literature might be accomplished:

> The narrative must be sharp, compressed, concrete. Dialogue must be short—a seizing of the significant, the revealing word. The emotion should spring directly from the fact. It must not be squeezed from it by the writer, running forward with a 'When I saw this, I felt, I suffered, I rejoiced…' His job is not to tell us what *he felt* but to be coldly and industriously, presenting, arranging, selecting, discarding from the mass of material to get to the significant detail, which leaves no more to be said, and implies everything (my emphasis).[174]

Again the process described here—the search for the significant detail (the appropriate image)—chimes with the Mass Observers' treatment of the 'image as social fact'. In her eschewal of emotion, her insistence on brevity and her deployment of key words, namely 'concrete', 'coldly', 'industriously', 'selecting' and discarding', one might be persuaded that in terms of this formalised protocol, Storm Jameson's 'Documents' ought function as the de facto manifesto of the Birmingham group writers. Yet, despite having corresponded with and praised the work of Liverpool writer James Hanley, Jameson was disparaging of the proletarian novel per se, considering it 'an abortion'; few, if any, examples of working-class writing appeared in her reviewing, and it is unknown whether she ever encountered the work of the Birmingham group.[175] Nevertheless, as the following reviews, critical notices and statements reveal, the stylistic parallels between her criteria and Birmingham group practice are striking, each of which might function as a paraphrase of Storm Jameson's aesthetic:

The writing is so transparent, the observation so unexaggerated, that we seem to see everything with our own eyes. And what we see in these few figures is the life of a whole class. Edwin Muir on Walter Allen's *Blind Man's Ditch*.[176]

The style at first appears harsh, even crude: it is in fact the verbal expression of an abhorrence of anything like fine writing or verbal decoration or the obviously charming. Its angularity reflects the angularity of a mind intransigently honest, not cynical but unillusioned and sardonic, stoic. Walter Allen on John Hampson's prose style.[177]

Once again, without emotion, without propaganda, with a calm that succeeds where sound and fury would have been futile, Mr. Brierley has given us a picture of contemporary life almost unbearable in its truth. Anonymous review of Walter Brierley's *Means Test Man*.[178]

Halward made himself the most objective of writers and the most economical; his stories are stripped; his prose is admirably direct and terse; no opinions are expressed. Walter Allen on Leslie Halward.[179]

If you want to touch your reader's heart you must be cold. I don't want to know how *you* feel about the matter, I want to know how *your* characters feel. Why belabour your reader with a long-winded, detailed description of a scene by moonlight when a sharper impression is given by the statement that the light of the moon was reflected by a bottle lying on the roadside. Leslie Halward discussing how Chekhov had influenced his own style.[180]

The filmmakers, mass observers and writers mentioned in the foregoing each believed their work should prove socially transformative, as H. Gustav Klaus indicates:

> In this sense, documentarists understand themselves as propagandists, who, admittedly, generally confine themselves to tracing and spotlighting social evils. The *causes* of these problems are seldom documented, *solutions* rarely proposed. The leading mass-observers, for example, did hope to collect the material necessary to bring about a change in society; yet they practised political restraint in other areas. One thing alone was clear: 'Whatever the political methods called upon to effect a transformation, *the knowledge of what has to be transformed [was] indispensable* (my emphasis)'.[181]

The influence of the documentary movement pervades the Birmingham group narratives. Though Leslie Halward and Walter Brierley had less access to the wider social cross-section that informed Storm Jameson's fictions, the narratives of Walter Allen, John Hampson and Peter Chamberlain each deploy varieties of 'cross-class montage'. Another feature common to their reconfiguration of the realist form was to be found in the eschewal of a single central protagonist, usually the single, revolutionary or heroic figure. Birmingham group narratives, particularly those of Walter Allen and John Hampson, being recounted in social or collective novels constructed from a variety of viewpoint characters and perspectives. Barbara Foley applies generic labels to working-class novels which fall outside the categories of bildungsroman or traditional realist mode, though this study considers the term 'multi-protagonist novel' provisionally captures the generic distinction.[182] Walter Allen's *Blind Man's Ditch* offers a cross-section of social classes, whereas John Hampson's *Saturday Night at the Greyhound*, while certainly a 'social' or 'group' novel is, as with Allen's *Innocence Is Drowned*, restricted to a smaller cast of working-class characters often the family gathering in conflict with itself. Suggesting 'social' or 'collective' novels as the appropriate form with which to address working-class experience, Foley cites the American left-wing novelist Meyer Levin:

> [T]he group method which eliminates the central character, and uses the interwoven experiences of many characters of equal value for the building of a story, is particularly *á propos* for the social novel. By its very lack of a central character emphasis, it declares democracy. Moreover, its multi-viewpoint character makes possible a more complete analysis of social forces than can usually be shown in central character stories.[183]

The literary function was thus both perspectival and democratic; it was believed that eliminating the central protagonist, subordinating the narrative voice and deploying a range of narrative viewpoints would heighten of the reality effect. Whilst an undergraduate at the University of Birmingham, Allen had been impressed by Aldous Huxley's *Point Counter Point*, which, rather than employing a single linear plot, was related through a number of parallel and interlinking storylines related from differing character perspectives. Following the publication of his second novel, a *New Statesman* reviewer remarked how the collectively structured Birmingham of Walter Allen's *Blind Man's Ditch*, aspired to being a 'provincial *Point Counter Point*'.[184] Allen was certainly attracted to the idea of building 'closed little communities', as he recounted to Andy Croft:

> You know it was a great period, a great time for the novel of specific place [...] it was a time when a lot of people were experimenting with novels written from several points of view [...] the influence of cinema was tremendous, I think, on the 'montage; novel [...] what I usually used to do was to try and get on the page the image as a film-director might present it. That was what I was after, and I think everybody was after ['].[185]

Allen adopted this approach enthusiastically, and one can imagine episodes prefixed by the snap of the clapperboard or movie slate in each of his first two novels: *Innocence Is Drowned* and *Blind Man's Ditch*, likewise in John Hampson's *Saturday Night at the Greyhound*. Again, as with montage, interest in a 'collective' cinematic vision of society became common cause with documentarist, mass observer and imaginative prose writer alike.

While producing working-class slices of life such as 'A Christmas Story', which recalls the exploits of a young unemployed youth and a pensioner as they attempt to earn a little seasonal income by clearing snow, or the events that transpired in the smoke room of the Railway Hotel where 'Mr. Marris' earned his 'Reputation', Peter Chamberlain also produced experimental pieces in the form of 'Snapshot Documentary'.[186] Here in parodying and subverting a documentary realism traditionally focused upon working-class mores, Chamberlain turns the camera back upon his own social caste to present short 'found vignettes' of his middle-class peers. His 'What The Hell?' provides a critique of rabid consumerism which, by interrogating the forces that drive it, is illustrative of the false hope and redundancy provided in the varieties of 'wish image' that permeate Walter Benjamin's *Arcades Project*.

Work, unemployment, housing and education are recurrent themes in much working-class writing of this period, and the work of Birmingham group is no exception. Their chief concern was to illuminate the quietly lived stoicism of working-class, urban existence and to delineate the unheroic lives of ordinary individuals. Their subject matter, unlike the wider social remit of Margaret Storm Jameson, was often restricted to 'sunken' or 'submerged population groups', E. M. Forster's 'unthinkables' and those 'lesser mortals' discovered in the first-hand narrative accounts that historians E. P. Thompson and Lawrence Stone so valued.[187] In this respect, the Birmingham writers clearly—whilst functioning as the representative spokesmen or amanuenses identified by Christopher Hilliard—wrote on behalf of class counterparts who, as Alan Sillitoe indicates, were frequently unable to articulate the shortcomings of the system that ensured their exploitation, social deprivation and hardships.

In terms of a content predicated upon the exploration of the decade's principal themes, the fictions of the Birmingham group anticipate Karl Radek's assertion that proletarian art should not be confined to detailing the class struggle alone, instead '[i]t should describe the processes that are going on in the classes themselves—their way of life, their psychology, their development, their strivings'.[188] On a formal level, their narratives frequently had recourse to autobiographical forms, and in this respect it might be argued they had little need to *gather* the kinds of documentary 'evidence' Storm Jameson proposed; indeed, John Hampson's *Saturday Night at the Greyhound* (1931) may well provide the paradigm here for Hampson, as Helen Southworth points out, 'knew of what he wrote', the novel describing his own first-hand experiences when, at the request of his sister Mona, he visited the Derbyshire village of Ashover to assist her in running a public house.[189] Renamed as the eponymous 'Greyhound Inn' of the novel, he appears pseudonymously as the archetypal Hampson figure Tom Oakley, who, seeing more than the other characters, attempts to hold domestic body and soul together. Hampson's novel is analysed in Chap. 3, by reference to Max Saunders' account of 'autobiografiction'—a genre with which, one would hazard, the Birmingham writers were unfamiliar, but one that brings together more recent developments in the field of life-writing and one to which their narratives retroactively respond. Though newly recovered, this critical frame offers a theoretical context in which to consider the novel's innovative elements and demonstrates its marked departure from the traditional realist mould to which it has frequently, though erroneously, been likened.

This book will therefore break with traditional accounts of 1930s working-class writing by bringing the social eye of the documentary movement; the literary reconfigurations manifest in the multi-protagonist novel and the formal experimentation and technical departures discovered in contemporary cinema into constellation so as to read the Birmingham group narratives *against* the tide of prevailing theoretical and critical interventions. The following chapters will reveal how the imaginative fictions of the Birmingham group, while eschewing direct political didacticism, share common purpose with the de-mystificatory aims of Documentarist, Mass Observer, and the Writer of Reportage alike. Their choice of subject material and its depiction in a body of socially oriented, imaginative prose fiction was a conscious act that repeatedly laid bare the social actuality:

'the reification and privatization of contemporary life [...]—the tendential law of social life under capitalism—', to which Fredric Jameson alludes in *The Political Unconscious*.[190] By pursuing this approach, it will be argued that the Birmingham group writers respond with self-assurance, originality and invention to conceptions of what working-class literature *ought* to resemble by broadening its remit to include the discussion of women, the family and notions of identity occluded by the narrower and traditional focus derived from male-orientated, sectarian criteria. Chapters 2 and 3 have been arranged thematically to examine how Birmingham group narratives engage with the themes of work and unemployment. Described as the most universal of human activities, work has been the subject of much social, political and critical scrutiny. Contending that 'work' is not merely a 'backcloth' or 'setting' for narratives of working-class life but constitutes the 'decisive experience', Raymond Williams considers the 'distinctive physical character' of a working-class industrial area as 'formative': productive of a 'primary kind of consciousness' rooted less in the purposive than in satisfaction of the basic essentials.[191] The Birmingham-based narratives of Allen, Halward, Hampson and Chamberlain are illustrative, if not pre-figurative, of this process; their depictions of intergenerational conflict in the working-class family unit clearly point up the Williamsite perception that 'the particular "structure of feeling" of an epoch is to be located in the prevailing "material life, social organisation and dominant ideas"'.[192]

Following the economic aftershocks of the Wall Street crash that brought the previous decade to a close, Chap. 3 will explore the Birmingham writers' response to work's antithesis: unemployment. While the adaptability of Birmingham's smaller scale manufacturing units enabled the city to enjoy a faster recovery than other regions dependent on a single, heavy industry, for many during the 1930s the possibility of any return to full employment remained a dream rather than a reality. Having personally experienced how insecure work and unemployment impinged upon the family unit, the Birmingham writers were able to document its tribulations both veraciously and sympathetically. Taken together, Chaps. 2 and 3 offer qualitative accounts of the prevailing crisis and focus upon the Birmingham writers' sensitive treatment of these universal issues.

Chapter 4 will refocus a little in order to consider what Matthew Taunton and Benjamin Kohlmann describe as 'the decade's radical investment in neglected and non-normative (queer, female, proletarian) identities', in order to open up this discussion and reveal how Birmingham group narratives actively respond to more recent critical interventions.[193] It is hoped this approach will recover the identities and experiences of those whose lives had been either occluded or overlooked due to the dominance of the largely 'all male cast' hitherto predominant in both the working-class canon and the criticism of its texts. Pamela Fox's *Class Fictions* problematises the notion of working-class identity by adjusting further the critical focus from characterisation towards authorial subjectivity. Constructed, as the characterisations or protagonists in working-class fiction frequently were, from their authors' own lived experience, the notion of authorial subjectivity has proven a fruitful line of enquiry in this exploration of identity in working-class literature.

In order to address the innovative formal approaches adopted by the Birmingham writers, the last of this study's three 'analytical' chapters will therefore adopt two distinct theoretical frameworks. To explore how authorial subjectivity shapes their writing, this chapter will have recourse to the recently unearthed hybrid form: 'Autobiografiction'. As Max Saunders' recovery of this early twentieth-century model of life-writing reveals, 'autobiografiction' offers itself as an appropriate hierarchical term and also a capacious formal mode against which to read the Birmingham group narratives and continue the exploration of authorial subjectivity and identity begun by Pamela Fox. The chapter will also adopt an intersectional framework as the optic through which to consider what Kohlmann and Taunton describe as the decade's 'radical investment' in notions of identity.[194] Alongside the swing towards a more holistic consideration of working-class literature, recent discussions have considered twenty-first-century emphases on identity thinking to be detrimental: serving to fragment, undermine and dissipate the class-oriented objectives of traditional political struggle. The rationale adopted throughout this study, whilst engaging enthusiastically with notions of identity and intersubjectivity, urges the retention of a 'Class Vivid' approach, where, to extend the painterly metaphor, class issues should still remain the primary concern. Describing feminism as the template for the other intersectional categories, namely race, gender, ethnicity and sexuality, Nancy Fraser argues: 'For me, [it] is not simply a matter of getting a smattering of individual women into positions of power and privilege within existing social hierarchies. It is rather about *overcoming those hierarchies*' (my emphasis).[195] Whilst clearly contentious, Fraser follows Victor Wallis (see p. 142), and others, viewing liberal feminism as the 'handmaid of capitalism' which, by failing to confront the hierarchical assumptions of neoliberal society *collectively*, serves only to narrow the focus on the ever-widening gap between the rich and poor, and which, until such time as the injustices of capitalist maldistribution are fully countenanced, will remain solidly in place. It seems appropriate therefore to explore the Birmingham writers in the light of these more recent critical interventions, not only in terms of this study's chronological arrangement but also in terms of suggesting how the Birmingham narratives may provide a legacy which, despite the absence of certain more recently framed intersectional categories in their narratives, do nevertheless raise questions of identity *and* a class-based critique. In this way, the Birmingham writers not only pre-figure the criteria of more recent critical interventions but also offer themselves as a heritage for the kinds of working-class literature being undertaken by the more recent writers following in the tradition.

Notes

1. Beyond the readings of the Birmingham group's works provided here, a further impetus to this project stemmed in part from the tacit encouragement provided by the reprinting and reissue of the Birmingham group novels inaugurated by Andy Croft and Philip Gorski. Their respective recoveries of Walter Brierley's novels *Means Test Man* and *Sandwichman* stimulated my aim to recover the work of the remaining and, in my opinion, equally overlooked, members of the Birmingham group. Although the Hogarth Press reprints of Walter Allen's *All in a Lifetime* and John Hampson's *Saturday Night at the Greyhound* remain available, It is hoped that some of the value of this study lies in its having provided the footings for further exploration and will thus follow Croft et al. by precipitating the reprinting of other of the Birmingham group's novels, especially the collected short stories of Leslie Halward and Peter Chamberlain that are either currently out of print or remain prohibitively expensive or difficult to access.
2. Roy Johnson, 'The Proletarian Novel', *Literature and History,* 2. (1975), p. 93.
3. Joanna Bourke, *Working-Class Cultures in Britain 1890—1960: Gender, Class and Ethnicity* (London and New York: Routledge, 1994), p.4. Cited in Nicola Wilson, *Home in British Working-Class Fiction* (Farnham, Surrey: Ashgate, 2015), p. 15.
4. Andy Croft, 'The Birmingham Group: Literary Life Between Two Wars', London Magazine, 23. (1983); *Red Letter Days* (London: Lawrence & Wishart, 1990).

5. MacKay, Marina and Lyndsey Stonebridge, eds, *British Fiction After Modernism: The Novel at Mid-Century* (New York: Palgrave Macmillan, 2007), p. 5.
6. Andy Croft, 'The Birmingham Group: Literary Life between Two Wars', *London Magazine,* 23 (1983), p. 21.
7. CCCS paper 'Thinking the Thirties', (1979) cited in Nick Hubble, *The Proletarian Answer to the Modernist Question* (Edinburgh: Edinburgh University Press, 2019), p. 26.
8. Clarke, Ben and Nick Hubble, Eds, *Working-Class Writing: Theory and Practice* (Switzerland: Palgrave Macmillan, 2018), p. 5.
9. 'Hybrids': the somewhat pejorative term used by Louis MacNeice to describe the contemporary, middle-class phenomenon of working-class fraternisation. Louis MacNeice, *The Strings Are False: An Unfinished Autobiography* (London: Faber and Faber, 1965), p. 155.
10. Alan Sillitoe, Introduction, p. i. Walter Allen, *All in a Lifetime* (London: The Hogarth Press, 1986).
11. Hilliard refers to the combination of 'representativeness' and 'strangeness' felt by working-class writers: the 'individualized sense of being different—sometimes, a sense of being in the grip of an almost otherworldly desire to write.' Christopher Hilliard, *To Exercise Their Talents: The Democratization of Writing in Britain* (Cambridge Massachusetts: Harvard University Press, 2006), p. 128.
12. Ibid, p. 118.
13. Walter Ernest Allen (1911–1995). 'Bernard Bergonzi (Oxford Dictionary of National Biography', 2004).
14. Walter Allen, *The Short Story in English* (Oxford: Clarendon Press, 1981), p. 280.
15. Leslie Halward, *Let Me Tell You* (London: Michael Joseph Ltd, 1938), p. 23.
16. Ibid.
17. Walter Allen, *As I Walked Down New Grub Street* (London: Heinemann, 1981), p. 69.
18. Walter Brierley, Andy Croft introduction, p. viii. Walter Brierley, *Means-Test Man*, 2011 edn (Nottingham: Spokesman, 1935.
19. Ibid.
20. Leslie Halward, *Let Me Tell You,* p. 250.
21. Walter Allen, *As I Walked Down*, p. 68.
22. Ibid.
23. Ibid.
24. Jane Austen, *Emma* (London: Penguin Books, 1996), p. 255.
25. David Lodge, 'Birmingham Dire? Blame Jane Austen', *Daily Telegraph.* 4 April 2008.

26. Louis MacNeice, 'Autumn Journal' Part VIII, *Collected Poems* (London: Faber and Faber, 1979), p. 114.
27. Asa Briggs, *Victorian Cities*, 1990 edn (London: Penguin Books Limited, 1963), pp. 186–187.
28. Ibid.
29. Chris Upton, *A History of Birmingham* (Stroud: Phillimore & Co Ltd, 1993), p. 197.
30. Ibid, p. 196.
31. Valentine Cunningham, *British Writers of the Thirties* (Oxford: Clarendon Press, 1988), p. 280.
32. The members described themselves as 'Lunaticks', a pun on lunatics. Jennie Uglow, *The Lunar Men: The Friends Who Made the Future 1730-1810* (London: Faber and Faber, 2002).
33. Walter Allen, *As I Walked Down*, p. 37.
34. Michel Remy and others, *Surrealism in Birmingham 1935—1954* (Banbury: Birmingham Museum and Art Gallery, 2000), p. 7.
35. Tessa Sidey, Ibid, p. 15.
36. Walter Allen, *As I Walked Down*, p. 42.
37. Ibid.
38. Ibid.
39. Ibid, p. 39.
40. Silvano Levy, *Surrealism in Birmingham*, p. 25.
41. The formation of the form. This whole range of conscious, half-conscious and often apparently instinctive shaping, 'The historical process of the objective establishment of certain critical conventions to represent a specific social experience'. The concept of Williams' 'structure of feeling' developed from 'the accessible evidence of actual articulations [representations of contemporary sociocultural reality] in texts and works I could read. It developed as an analytical procedure for actual written works'. Williams believed that such works provided a record of something which was a much more general possession, 'the area of interaction between the official consciousness of an epoch—codified in doctrines and legislation—and the whole process of actually living its consequences'. Raymond Williams, introduction Geoff Dyer, *Politics and Letters: Interviews with New Left Review* (London and New York: Verso, 2015), pp. 158, 159; Raymond Williams, *The Long Revolution* (London: The Hogarth Press, 1992), p. 48, 40.
42. Andy Croft, *Red Letter Days*, p. 181.
43. George Orwell. 'The Writer in the Witness Box', Discussion between George Orwell and Desmond Hawkins. BBC Home Service, 6 December 1940. *The Listener*, 19 December 1940.

44. Walter Benjamin, 'The Storyteller: Reflections on the Works of Nikolai Leskov', https://arl.human.cornell.edu [accessed 26/02/2020]. p. 1
45. Ibid.
46. Ken Worpole, *Dockers and Detectives: Popular Reading Popular Writing* (London: Verso editions, 1983), p. 79.
47. Valentine Cunningham, *British Writers*, p. 321.
48. Walter Brierley, 'Transition' in Michael Harrison, *Under Thirty: An Anthology* (London: Rich & Cowan, 1939), pp. 82–95.
49. Lisbeth Goodman, Editor, *Literature and Gender* (London: Routledge/ The Open University, 1996). p. viii.
50. Raymond Williams, Chapter 6 'Working-Class, Proletarian, Socialist: Problems in some Welsh Novels', pp.110–121. In H. Gustav Klaus, *The Socialist Novel in Britain* (Brighton: Harvester Press, 1982). p. 111.
51. Elizabeth Maslen, 'The Case for Storm Jameson', In Mackay, Stonebridge Eds, *British Fiction After Modernism*, 33–41, p. 35.
52. Walter Allen, *The English Novel: A Short Critical Introduction* (London: J.M. Dent & Sons Ltd, 1954), pp. 309–310.
53. Ibid.
54. Ibid, p. 305.
55. From the perspective of 2019, Green is considered to be a late modernist writer. Whilst his choice of subject material and setting clearly encouraged Allen to write about his own city, Green's employment of montage technique was also highly influential.
56. Walter Allen, *As I Walked Down*, p. 133.
57. Walter Allen, *Tradition and Dream: The English and American Novel from the Twenties to Our Time* (London: J.M. Dent & Sons Ltd, 1964), p. 216.
58. Walter Allen, *As I Walked Down*, p. 134.
59. Ibid.
60. Chris Baldick, *The Oxford English Literary History, Volume 10, The Modern Movement* (Oxford: OUP, 2004), p. 186.
61. Walter Allen, *As I Walked*, p. 92.
62. Alexander, Neal and James Moran, eds, *Regional Modernisms* (Edinburgh: Edinburgh University Press, 2013), p. 9.
63. K.D.M. Snell, Ed, *The Regional Novel in Britain and Ireland 1800—1990* (Cambridge: Cambridge University Press, 1998), p. 3.
64. Ibid, p. 16.
65. Ibid, p. 48.
66. David Lodge, *As I Was Walking Down Bristol Street*. (Independent [Central] Television Production. (1983).
67. Ibid.

68. Phyllis Bentley, *The Regional Novel*, p. 6. Cited in K. D. M. Snell, Rd, *The Regional Novel in Britain and Ireland*, p. 2.
69. Andy Croft indicates, '[Bentley's] regional novel was written in places like "Wessex" and Barsetshire [...] a sort of literary orthodoxy based on class and geography, into which the "Group" would not fit'. Andy Croft. 'The Birmingham Group: Literary Life between Two Wars', p. 16.
70. Ronald Blythe, *The Age of Illusion: Glimpses of Britain between the Wars 1919—1940* (Oxford: Oxford University Press, 1963), p. 109.
71. David Lodge, *As I Was Walking Down Bristol Street*. TV Documentary.
72. Louis MacNeice, *The Strings Are False*, p. 155.
73. W. H. Auden and Mendelson, Edward, Ed, *The English Auden: Poems, Essays and Dramatic Writings 1927—1939*, (London: Faber and Faber, 1989), 'Letter to Lord Byron', Part II, p. 175.
74. Ibid, Part I, Stanza 14, p. 171.
75. Elinor Taylor, *The Popular Front Novel in Britain 1934—1940*, Chicago: Haymarket Books, 2018), p. 2.
76. Andy Croft, *Red Letter Days*, p. 21.
77. George Orwell, *Inside the Whale and Other Essays* (Harmondsworth: Penguin Books, 1940), p. 30.
78. Virginia Woolf's essay 'The Leaning Tower' drew attention to the privileged and expensive educations enjoyed by these public schoolboys and remarked upon the seeming ingratitude she perceived as reflected in their poems plays and novels: 'full of discord and bitterness, full of confusion and compromise'.
79. Louis MacNeice, *I Crossed the Minch*, (London: Longmans, Green, 1938), pp. 125, 127.
80. Valentine Cunningham, *British Writers*, pp. 211–240. Frank Kermode is less sceptical of the 'Auden Generation's aims, cf. Chapter Three, 'Mixed Feelings' in, Frank Kermode, *History and Value* (Oxford: Clarendon Press, 1988), pp. 42–62.
81. Benjamin Kohlmann and Matthew Taunton, *A History of 1930s British Literature*, (Cambridge: Cambridge University Press, 2019), pp. 4, 5.
82. Elinor Taylor, *The Popular Front Novel*, p. 22.
83. Ibid, p. 4.
84. Ibid.
85. Ibid, pp. 4, 2.
86. Louis MacNeice,*The Strings are False*, p. 154.
87. Philip Gorski. Introduction p. xv. *Sandwichman* (London: Merlin Press, 1990). In their introduction to the fifth Edition of Raman Selden's guide to literary theory, Peter Widdowson and Peter Brooker discuss the long-term legacy of Literary Theory suggesting: '[O]f all the theoretical discussion of literature over past decades, perhaps the most notable has been

the deconstruction of the canon—of an agreed selection of "great works" which are the benchmark for the discrimination of "literary value", and without which no literary education can be complete. The theoretical challenge to the criteria on which the canon is established, together with the arrival on the agenda of more marginal kinds of literary and other cultural production hitherto excluded from it has at once caused a withering of the old verities and an explosion of new materials for serious study.' Widdowson and Brooker legitimise the Intermodernist intervention, in respect of its contestation of the established (bourgeois) literary canon, and support the retrieval of texts once viewed as peripheral or marginal to earlier, more 'discriminating' notions of literature, and simultaneously question traditional critiques and prescriptions of what a working-class literature might or ought resemble. Raman Selden, *A Reader's Guide to Contemporary Literary Theory* (Harlow: Pearson Education Limited, 2005).

88. Ross McKibbin, *Ideologies of Class: Social Relations in Britain 1880-1950* (Oxford: Oxford University Press, 1990), pp. 24, 25.
89. Louise MacNeice, *The Strings are False,* pp. 154, 155.
90. Valentine Cunningham, *British Writers,* p. 309.
91. Ibid.
92. Had Smith placed his thumb on the scales? According to Nick Hubble, rather than a serious attempt to find texts illustrating the peaceful co-existence of art and propaganda, his project aligned more with the reactionary politics of the Thatcher era. Nick Hubble, *The Proletarian Answer,* p. 27.
93. David Smith, *Socialist Propaganda in the Twentieth-Century British Novel* (London: The Macmillan Press Ltd, 1978), p. 51.
94. David Smith, Ibid. Smith's chapter title 'At Last, The British Are Coming' was taken from Granville Hicks' *New Masses* article (xxi, 15 December 1936, pp. 23–4). Both register a sense of irony.
95. Ibid.
96. Ibid, p. 52.
97. Ibid.
98. Ibid.
99. Ross McKibbin, *Ideologies of Class,* p. 24.
100. Jonathan Rose,*The Intellectual Life of the British Working Classes,* Second edn (New Haven/London: Yale University Press, 2001), p. 298.
101. Ibid, p. 299.
102. Ibid.
103. Valentine Cunningham, *British Writers,* p. 309.
104. Walter Allen, *Tradition and Dream,* p. 141.
105. Walter Rideout, *The Radical Novel in the United States* (1956), pp. 144, 145, in, David Smith, *Socialist Propaganda,* p. 54.

106. Alan M. Wald, 'Introduction to the Morningside Edition', p. xxiv, In James T. Farrell *A Note on Literary Criticism* (New York: Columbia University Press, 1992).
107. Frank Kermode, *History and Value,* p. 93.
108. Alice Beja. 'Proletarian Literature, An Unidentified Literary Object', *L'Atelier* 7, 1 (2015), p. 1.
109. Christopher Hilliard, *To Exercise Their Talents.*
110. Alick West expressed some scepticism regarding the journal's use as a forum for creative writing, and indeed this had begun to abate in proportion to the emergence of political tensions in the outside world. I provide a fuller account of the patronisation and *patronising* of working-class writers during the 1930s in 'Submerged Voices: A Brief History of Condescension,' Volume X, 'Unheard', *Ad Alta: The Birmingham Journal of Literature* (Birmingham: Birmingham University, 2018), pp. 19-31.
111. H. Gustav Klaus 'Socialist Fiction in the 1930s: Some Preliminary Observations', *Renaissance and Modern Studies,* Vol. XX, (1976), p. 21. Cited in: Ronald Paul, "A Culture of the People': Politics and Working-Class Literature in *Left Review,* 1934-38'. *Left History,* 8, 1. p. 66.
112. Cunningham, *British Writers,* p. 306
113. Jack Hilton, *Caliban Boswelling.* University of Nottingham Library. JH/1/1/24/.
114. Hilliard, 'Modernism and the Common Writer', *The Historical Journal,* Vol. 48, No. 3 (September, 2005). pp. 769–787. p. 776.
115. D. J. Taylor, *The Prose Factory: Literary Life in England Since 1918,* (London: Vintage, 2016), pp. 105–106.
116. Jack Windle, *'What life means to those at the bottom':* Love on the Dole *and its reception since the 1930s, Literature and History,* 2 (2011), 35-47. p. 47
117. Frank Kermode, *History and Value,* p. 34.
118. 'Presentism'. Cf. Jonathan Freedland article, 'The 1930s were humanity's darkest, bloodiest hour. Are you paying attention?'. The 1930s, a byword for mass poverty, violent extremism and the gathering storm of world war. The 1930s is not so much a label for a period of time than rhetorical shorthand—a two-word warning from history.' *The Guardian* Long Read. Saturday, 11 March 2017.
119. Jack Windle, 'Love on the Dole: What Life Means', p. 47.
120. Alice Beja, 'Proletarian Literature, an Unidentified Literary Object', *L'Atelier,* 7. 1. (2015), 68-78. p. 76.
121. John Fordham, *James Hanley Modernism and the Working Class* (Cardiff: University of Wales, 2002), p. 2.
122. Ibid.

123. Simon Goulding, *'From Where I Stand,' Orientation and Location in the Textual Landscape: An Analysis of the Novels of Patrick Hamilton and George Orwell* ' (Unpublished PhD Thesis University of Birmingham, 2006).
124. Ibid.
125. Nicola Wilson, *Home in British Working-Class Fiction* (Farnham: Ashgate, 2015), p. 1.
126. Walter Allen, *Tradition and Dream,* p. 215.
127. Elizabeth Maslen, 'The Case for Storm Jameson', in Mackay and Stonebridge Eds, *British Fiction After Modernism,* 33-41, p. 35.
128. Ibid.
129. Rather than using it in the pejorative sense, I employ the term *documentary* here in the sense of the movement synonymous with documentary film/cinema as defined by John Grierson and Paul Rotha and following the political imperatives of Sergei Eisenstein. Tony Davies uses the term 'contested space' in order to describe the unexplored potentialities within realism itself, whereas I use it here, in the sense of the 'demilitarised-zone' or the 'no-man's-land' existing between the antagonistic assumptions of literary modernism on the one hand and realism on the other. Tony Davies. 'Unfinished Business: Realism and Working-Class Writing', in Jeremy Hawthorn, Editor, *The British Working-Class Novel in the Twentieth Century* (London: Edward Arnold, 1984), 125-136. p. 135.
130. Williams, Keith and Steven Matthews, *Rewriting the Thirties: Modernism and After,* 1997 edn (Harlow. Essex: Longman Limited, 1997), p. 164.
131. David Lodge, *Working with Structuralism: Essays and Reviews on Nineteenth and Twentieth-Century Literature* (London: Routledge and Kegan Paul, 1981), p. 8.
132. T. S. Eliot cited in, Kristin Bluemel '*Intermodernism: Literary Culture in Mid-Twentieth-Century Britain* (Edinburgh: Edinburgh University Press, 2009), p. 6.
133. Jesse Matz, Review of 'Kristin Bluemel '*Intermodernism: Literary Culture in Mid-Twentieth-Century Britain* (Edinburgh: Edinburgh University Press, 2009), in *Modernism/modernity,* 18.3. September (2011). 665-667. p. 666.
134. Ibid.
135. Tyrus Miller, 'Documentary/Modernism: Convergence and Complementarity in the 1930s', *Modernism/modernity,* Volume 9. (2002) 225-241. <https://muse.jhu.edu/article/23489> [accessed 14/09/2016]
136. Kohlmann, Benjamin and Matthew Taunton, *A History of 1930s British Literature* (Cambridge: Cambridge University Press, 2019), p. 4.
137. Ibid.

138. Matejka, Ladislav and Krystina Pomorska Eds: *Readings in Russian Poetics: Formalist and Structuralist Views* (Michigan: Ann Arbor, 1978). pp. 82–7. 'We may seek a *dominant* not only in the work of an individual artist and not only in the poetic canon, the set of norms of a given poetic school, *but also in the art of a given epoch viewed as a particular whole*' (my italics). From Keith Williams chapter 'Post/Modern Documentary: Orwell, Agee and the New Reportage' discussion of the Jakobsonian 'dominant' cited in Williams and Matthews, Eds, *Rewriting the Thirties*, p. 164.
139. James Fox, BBC Television Programme *The Age of the Image*, Episode 2, 'Power Games'. Broadcast Tuesday 10 March 2020.
140. Ibid.
141. Stuart Hall cited in Nick Hubble, *Mass Observation and Everday Life* (Hampshire: Palgrave Macmillan, 2006), p. 162.
142. Ibid.
143. Stuart Laing chapter 'Presenting Things as They Are': John Sommerfield's May Day and Mass Observation', in Frank Gloversmith, *Class Culture and Social Change: A New View of the Thirties* (Sussex: The Harvester Press, 1980), p. 153.
144. Nick Hubble, *Mass Observation*, pp. 2, 3.
145. Valentine Cunningham, *British Writers of the Thirties*, p. 338.
146. Nick Hubble, *Mass-Observation*, p. 81.
147. Ibid, p. 6.
148. Max Pensky, 'Method and Time: Benjamin's Dialectical Images' *The Cambridge Companion to Walter Benjamin* (Cambridge: Cambridge University Press, 2004), 177–198. p. 179.
149. Ibid, p. 186.
150. Ibid, p. 190.
151. Ezra Pound, 'Some Don'ts by an Imagiste' in *Imagist Poetry* ed, Peter Jones (Harmondsworth: Penguin Books, 1972), p. 130.
152. Ezra Pound, Preface to 'Some Imagist Poets 1916'. In Peter Jones, *Imagist Poetry*, pp. 136, 137.
153. Nick Hubble, *Mass-Observation*, p. 6.
154. Ezra Pound, article 'Vorticism', 'Fortnightly Review', London, September 1914, p. 468. In Peter Jones *Imagist Poetry*, p. 21.
155. Theodor Adorno, '*Minima Moralia: reflections from damaged Life*', translated by E. F. N. Jephcott (London: Verso, 2005) pp. 69, 70. Cf. David James', 'Zadie Smith's Style of Thinking', Post45, 5, 22/09/2020. pp. 1–11. Providing a useful entrée into 'affect studies', this article would form the basis of an illuminating, alternative analysis of the 'sentimental' aspect in Birmingham group narratives.

156. Virginia Woolf, 'The Cinema', *The Nation and Athenaeum,* xxxix. No.13. 3 July (1926).
157. Valentine Cunningham, *British Writers of The Thirties,* p. 6
158. Tom Jeffery, 'Mass Observation Archive Occasional Paper 10' (Sussex: University of Sussex, 1999), Introduction 1999 edition of *Mass Observation: A short history.*
159. Nick Hubble, *Mass-Observation,* p. 6.
160. Virginia Woolf, 'The Cinema' *The Nation and Athenaeum.* xxxix (1926).
161. Stuart Jefferies, *Grand Hotel Abyss* (London: Verso, 2016), p. 186.
162. John Grierson, *Cinema Quarterly*, Autumn 1933, p. 8.
163. Williams and Matthews Eds, *Rewriting the Thirties,* p. 166.
164. Ibid.
165. Richard Taylor, *The Eisenstein Reader*, pp.82, 56. Cited in Lara Feigel 'Buggery and Montage: Birmingham and Bloomsbury in the 1930s' in Anna Burrells and others Eds, *Woolfian Boundaries* (South Carolina: Clemson University Press, 2007), 51-57. p. 54.
166. W.H. Auden. Review of *Documentary Film.* By Paul Rotha. *The English Auden,* Ed, Edward Mendelson, p. 354 et seq. ; Valentine Cunningham, *British Writers,* p. 338.
167. Auden, Ibid.
168. Montague Slater, *Left Review,* May 1935, pp. 364–5, in Stuart Laing chapter 'Presenting Things as They Are' in Frank Gloversmith, *Class Culture and Social Change,* p. 142.
169. Ibid.
170. Jennifer Birkett, *Margaret Storm Jameson: A Life* (Oxford: Oxford University Press, 2009), p. 5.
171. Elizabeth Maslen, 'The Case for Margaret Storm Jameson', in Mackay, Stonebridge Eds, *British Fiction After Modernism,* 33-41. p. 33.
172. Kohlmann and Taunton, *A History of 1930s British Literature,* p. 3.
173. Elizabeth Maslen, 'A Cassandra with Clout: Storm Jameson, Little Englander and Good European', in Kristen Bluemel, *Intermodernism,* 21-37. p. 27.
174. Ibid.
175. Margaret Storm Jameson, *Journey from the North,* Part 1, cited in Jennifer Birkett, *Magaret Storm Jameson,* p. 149.
176. Edwin Muir, advertising copy/review from '*The Listener*' (1939) cited in Walter Allen's *Blind Man's Ditch.*
177. Walter Allen, *Tradition and Dream,* p. 226.
178. The *TLS,* 11 April 1935. The *TLS* reviewer praised Brierley's 'detachment', as did the *Economist* reviewer who praised its '*unemphatic* manner'. Cited in Croft, introduction to *Means Test Man,* pp *xii, xiii.*
179. Walter Allen, *The Short Story in English,* p. 275.

180. Leslie Halward, *Let Me Tell You*, pp. 227–228.
181. H. Gustav Klaus, *The Literature of Labour* (Brighton: The Harvester Press, 1985), p. 131.
182. Stuart Laing cites John Summerfield's *May Day* as the epitome of the reportage novel. Whilst not accentuating the political element as much as Sommerfield, Henry Green had employed cinematic techniques in *Living* some seven years previously. Barbara Foley offers a comprehensive discussion of the 'collective' and 'social' novel in *Radical Representations: Politics and Form in U.S. Proletarian Fiction, 1921-1941* (Durham and London: Duke University Press, 1993) pp. 362–441.
183. Meyer Levin, 'Novels of Another War', *The Clipper*, 1: 5 (August 1940), in Barbara Foley. *Radical Representations*, p. 363.
184. Andy Croft, *Red Letter Days*, p. 256.
185. Walter Allen letter to Andy Croft cited in Croft, *Red Letter Days*, p. 256.
186. Bashir Abu-Manneh, *Fiction of the New Statesman 1913-1939* (Delaware: University of Delaware Press, 2011), pp. 193–197.
187. Frank O'Connor, 'The Lonely Voice' from Charles E. May. Editor: *Short Story Theories* (Athens, Ohio: Ohio University Press, 1976), p. 88. Various terms for the working classes have included Frank O'Connor's: 'submerged population groups', Matthew Arnold's 'Sunken' and E. M. Forster's 'unthinkables'. The term 'The Precariat' is a compound deriving from proletariat/precarious.
188. Karl Radek, Speech delivered to the Soviet Writers Congress (1934). 'Contemporary World Literature and the tasks of Proletarian Art', Marxist Internet Archive, <https://www.marxists.org/archive/Radek> [accessed 26 October 2020]
189. Helen Southworth. Introduction, John Hampson, *Saturday Night at the Greyhound* (Valancourt Books: Richmond, Virginia, 2014). The Greyhound, Grovelace was a fictionalised version of The Nettle Inn, in Ashover Derbyshire.
190. Fredric Jameson, *The Political Unconscious: Narrative as a Socially Symbolic Act* (London and New York: Routledge, 1983), p. 4.
191. Raymond Williams, Phil O'Brien, 'The De-Industrial Novel' in Clarke and Hubble, *Working-Class Writing*, 229–246. pp. 229, 230.
192. Raymond Williams, 'The Welsh Industrial Novel', *Culture and Materialism: Selected Essays* (London: Verso, 2005), pp. 213–229.
193. Kohlmann and Taunton. *A History of 1930s British Literature*, pp. 8, 9.
194. Ibid.
195. Nancy Fraser, 'How feminism became capitalism's handmaiden'—and how to reclaim it'. *The Guardian*, 14 October 2013.

CHAPTER 2

This Working Life: Work and the Workplace

Comrades who when the sirens roar
From office shop and factory pour
'Neath evening sky;
By cops directed to the fug
Of talkie houses for a drug
Or down canals to find a hug
Until you die
– W. H. Auden ('A Communist to Others', Stanza 1 (1932)[1])

Though a later version of Auden's poem would substitute the opening line's 'Comrades' for 'Brothers' indicating a realignment—a slackening of the party line perhaps—in Auden's political positioning, and whilst, as Adrian Ceasar suggests, 'ostensibly addressing the working-class,' the opening stanza's tone of predestinate, inevitability, certainly in the light of later developments, may also be read as a somewhat condescending summation of proletarian existence.[2] The semantic tension arising from this uncertainty reflects simultaneously the conflicting attitudes of attraction and repugnance held by contemporary leftist intellectuals towards their recently rediscovered working-class brothers and sisters whose rescue from penury and exploitation it had been, at least for a few years during the 1930s, their aim to assist. Though later revising or recanting such altruistic interventions outright, the opening lines of Auden's poem provide the urban industrial mise en scène for the Birmingham group writers'

R. Harriott, *The Birmingham Group*,
https://doi.org/10.1007/978-3-031-14383-0_2

longer-term, authentic and more sincere investment in their accounts of working-class experience.

The theme of work as the universal human activity permeated the realist tradition informing the nineteenth-century condition of England novels that developed in parallel with the industrial revolution. The Romantic tradition's emphasis on nature asked pointed questions regarding the benefits of the industrial revolution and these would be reiterated by Victorian reformers such as Thomas Carlyle, John Ruskin and William Morris, who each spoke with lofty erudition on work's importance and degradations. Carlyle's 'Gospel of Work' declaimed on the sacredness of man's labour, although, as with Ruskin and Morris, his views were more applicable to those engaged in artisanal or artistically creative labour; the kinds of alienating, repetitive industrial work available to their working-class contemporaries affording little opportunity for spiritual salvation.[3] Contrary to such noble sentiments, 'Work', as experienced in the division of labour intrinsic to modern industrial production, was characterised less as one's sacred duty than as arduous repetitive servitude and long hours: an existential necessity, undertaken at best dutifully, more often, reluctantly.

Recent studies have adopted less negative positions however. In their research into the ideals of intellectual development and self-cultivation addressed in Chap.4 of this study, Kate Soper and Martin Ryle suggest: 'work considered in an abstract philosophical-anthropological sense, is not dispensable to self-realisation. To argue that people would be better fulfilled if they did less work is not to argue that they would be more fulfilled if they did none.'[4] They are aware that:

> Human beings derive satisfactions from the forms of objectification of themselves provided by work, the social orientation of their labours, the deployment of skills and expenditure of effort involved. This is a satisfaction associated with subordination of the self (to the needs of the community at large, to the demands of a collective practice or operation, to the sheer rhythm of physical exertion, and so on); it is distinct from the expressive and self-reflective forms of self-realisation that derive from culture.[5]

H. Gustav Klaus is supportive of this position, explaining:

> It is in the thematisation of work, in all its particulars and consequences that the central tradition of proletarian story-telling finds its most frequent and

common expression. Work as necessity, as ethos, as toil, but also in numerous concrete concerns such as the physical side of the labour process.[6]

Contrary to traditional realist accounts of workers as *sub species aeternitatis* and in opposition to 'classic nineteenth-century middle-class perspectives' that saw industry as 'merely a factory building that issues smoke,' H. Gustav Klaus and Stephen Knight trace:

> [A] shift from the Captain of Industry novels of the early Victorian period, through the capital and labour genre of the following decades, to an emphatic concentration on the working-class environment. In its growing confidence, even militancy, this type of working-class novel becomes the dominant form in the first half of the twentieth century [...] The representation of the work of ordinary men and women and the analysis of its economic, social and political implications are the unique contributions of industrial fiction to the literature of the nineteenth and twentieth centuries.[7]

The representation of work and 'the analysis of its economic, social and political implications' is central to situating the narratives of the Birmingham group in a world increasingly structured around the commodification and exchange values of industrial capitalism, especially during an era in which the existential threats of economic depression, inordinately high unemployment figures and imminent world-scale conflict were present. However, as Chris Baldick has observed:

> A curious feature of most English Industrial novels of the thirties, as in the 1840s and 1850s, is that they devote little, if any, space to the description of work itself. [...] novels about factory or colliery life tend to steer clear of the shop floor and coal face in favour of the strike meeting, the pub, or the family kitchen. Given that several prominent novels of working-class life in the Thirties were concerned principally with the unemployed, the omission of the labour process has an evident justification.[8]

In providing accounts of work and the workplace in a variety of occupations, the novels and short stories of the Birmingham writers prove the exception to this rule. Indeed, thematically speaking, the discussion of work can be seen, albeit indirectly, to run through the opening two chapters of this book, for as Chap. 3 will reveal, in a world where individuals are defined in terms of their occupation and the kinds of work they undertake, to be out of work, is tantamount to non-existence. Rather than being a neutral position defined by its antithesis, the psychological damage and darker implications wrought upon individuals owing to their unemployment or forced estrangement from it, inversely affirms work's more positive value as an activity pursued for reasons beyond the purely remunerative.

The momentous changes taking place in the industrial restructuring of 1930s Britain would have significant social and historical implications for the working classes. This chapter will not only address the contextual element, that is, the representations of work and workplace in the formative experiences of the men and women who feature so prominently in Birmingham group fictions, but also attend to the formal means, that is, the innovations by which its authors sought to extend and re-configure traditional narrative modes in order to depict the contemporary experience of work. Again, as Gustav Klaus explains: 'In sum, what was at stake was not whether to retain or write-off the (traditional realist) novel form, but how the genre could be "*umfunktioniert*" [re-configured] so as best to serve its overriding purpose, an imaginative grasp of reality, but now [in] the historical interests of the working class."[9]

In *Dividing Lines: Poetry, Class and Ideology in the Thirties*, Adrian Caesar undertakes a re-evaluation of the decade's poetic legacy. As the title of his opening chapter, 'The Myth of the Hungry Decade', implies, Caesar aims to problematise received accounts of pre-war socio-economic history—in particular those portraying an England tottering on the brink of revolution or about to sink under economic depression—in which he finds '[*a*] *rhetoric of dramatic exaggeration* prompted other generalisations without adequate supporting evidence' (my emphasis).[10] Caesar's purpose is to challenge the dominance of the so-called Auden Generation poets whose work he suggests aligned with the ideological position inherent in a rhetoric from which his account steps back in order to present a more considered overview. Such self-distancing from received accounts is not to understate the gravity of contemporary social and political issues, for he decries the intolerably high levels of unemployment that dogged these years and which, by the winter of 1932–1933, had touched three million and failed to drop significantly below this for the remainder of the decade. Nevertheless, in the interests of a less-emotive response, he counsels 'it is salutary to remember that there was never less than seventy-five per cent of the population *in* work (my emphasis)'.[11] Caesar's use of the percentage 'employed', as opposed to the more usual 'unemployed' statistic, does provoke reconsideration for as he suggests, '[a]gainst the regional unemployment affecting Northern Ireland, industrial Scotland, the North East, South Wales and Lancashire, one has to balance the new industrial structure which was being established in the South of England'.[12] This position is echoed by historian Chris Cook, who suggests, '[t]he crisis in the traditional industries that had once helped make Britain the workshop of the world had been exacerbated by the heavy *concentration* of these industries in certain areas' (original emphasis).[13]

The following discussion appropriates aspects of Caesar's re-envisioning, for the social and economic developments he describes have significant implications for the discussion of work and its centrality in the writing of Birmingham group. While the traditional, large scale and labour-intensive industries of shipbuilding, coal, steel and cotton were suffering inordinately due to changes in demand and the increasing instability of world markets, a boom was taking place in the manufacture of domestic consumer durables; light electrical goods were in increasingly high demand following the integration of the country's electricity supply in the National Grid (1933). As with the South and the South East, the towns and cities of the Midlands, notably Birmingham, where, as Auden noted, 'there [was] a boomlet on', and neighbouring Coventry both experienced high levels of industrial expansion during this period, significant testimony to this effect was evident in the fact that as major manufacturing centres they were both heavily bombed during the Second World War.[14] In addition to the work ethos deriving from the combination of non-conformism and the Civic Gospel preached by Birmingham's Victorian elders, the city was home to a proliferation of small to medium-scale engineering firms able to 're-jig', both literally and metaphorically, depending upon the invisible hand of market requirements. Examples here naturally included the manufacture of armaments and munitions manufacture during the Great, and similarly in the run up to the Second World War, each of which found the 'city of a thousand trades' well placed to respond to fulfil the relevant upsurge in demand. As related in the introduction, in addition to its plethora of small to medium-scale artisanal concerns in the Jewellery and Gunsmiths quarters; having a major motor manufacturer in the shape of Herbert Austin's motor company at Longbridge and, owing to the multitude of components required in automobile manufacture, the city's car parts and ancilliary producers held virtual monopolies on the supply of their products to the country's other motor manufacturers. Again, as Chris Cook explains:

> The paradox of Britain in the thirties was that the country was effectively becoming divided into two nations: a prosperous South, of new industries, low unemployment and a rising standard of living, and a distressed North. Thus, whilst the unemployment rate in Jarrow was 67 per cent, in St. Albans it was 3.9 per cent, in Coventry 5 per cent and in Luton 7 per cent.[15]

Caesar claims those of the working population fortunate enough to remain in employment consequently saw an increase in living standards calculated at between about 15 and 18 percent.[16] Providing quantitative data to support this North/South differential, he suggests, 'these figures help towards an understanding [that] the most pertinent political question of the decade as far as Britain is concerned was 'not why the swing to political extremism was so great, but why it was, in fact so small'.[17] Again, this inverted perspective supports Ross McKibbin's assertion regarding the British working-class' lack of enthusiasm for any form of rejectionist politics and bolsters Caesar's argument that, despite their well-intentioned impulse, the politicisation and social passing of the 'Auden Generation' and other Leftist intellectuals stemmed from what was essentially a misreading of the contemporary situation, as P. D. Anthony suggests:

> There is little evidence [...] of industrial employees [...] rejecting the demands of the industrial environment. This may be because the demands are essentially acceptable, or because the workers see their work as instrumental to other satisfactions [...] Although there is no opposition from the worker there seems to be a great deal of sympathy for his lot. It seems that the failure of the unions and workers to follow the 'proctor-intellectuals' and students to the barricades may be the result of fundamental differences of perception in which the intellectuals' sympathy for the workers is not reflected by the workers' view of themselves.[18]

Statistical evidence aside, if one requires a qualitative view of the experience of work, working conditions, the specific nature of those extrinsic satisfactions or, most important of all, the 'workers' view of themselves' during this period, it is necessary to look elsewhere, for, as E. P. Thompson explains:

> [At] this point a further series of difficulties begins, since the term 'standard' leads us from data amenable to statistical measurement (wages or articles of consumption) to those satisfactions that are sometimes described by statisticians as 'imponderables'. From food we are led to homes, from homes to health, from health to family life, and thence to leisure, work discipline,

> education and play, intensity of labour and so on. From the standard-of-life we pass to way-of-life. But the two are not the same. The first is a measurement of quantities: the second a description (and sometimes an evaluation) of qualities. Where statistical evidence is appropriate to the first, we must rely largely upon 'literary evidence' as to the second.[19]

The industrial restructuring of the Midlands and South East described by Chris Cook certainly locates Birmingham at the temporal and geographical epicentre of such developments. Nevertheless, without wishing to question the Gradgrindian efficacy of statistical data, if we require an insight into the effect of such transformations on the lives of working people, it is to the 'literary evidence' one must turn. Thompson accords imaginative narrative high status as the discourse best equipped to evaluate the 'imponderables' statisticians found so troubling, and his observations thus prompt a move from quantitative socio-economics to an examination of the decade's literary offering. Citing Raymond Williams, Phil O'Brien asserts that 'work and the industrial landscape have not simply provided backdrops or settings to stories about working-class life; work is the "decisive experience", giving rise to a "structure of feeling" predicated on and emerging from the "distinctive physical character" of a specific working-class industrial area.'[20] As had Thompson, Raymond Williams saw that it was in the literary representations of a period that one might experience 'the area of interaction between the official consciousness of an epoch and the whole process of actually living its consequences'.[21]

Discussing some of the better-known working-class novels published during the 1930s, Chris Baldick references Walter Greenwood's *Love on the Dole*, Walter Brierley's *Means Test Man* and John Hampson's *Saturday Night at the Greyhound*.[22] His selection of Greenwood and the two 'Birmingham Group' writers is encouraging for, as has been intimated, it locates the urban industrial within wider discussions of the regional novel, hitherto the preserve of distinctly rural fayre.[23] Baldick's reiteration of the naturalistic and autobiographical elements he finds in these works is consistent with his observation that whilst 'modernist experimentation [has] commanded more critical attention, realist fictions still comprise the mainstream of the English novel during this period'. However, Baldick omits to mention that some working-class novelists and members of the Birmingham group in particular were similarly likewise engaged in a process of formal experimentation. H. Gustav Klaus considered the reconfiguration of the traditional *realist* novel a necessary step in communicating the 'ideological correlate' he believed the term 'socialism' '[sought] to comprehend', which, in his view, determined the value of a literary work: the fact that it was written 'in the historical interests of the working class.'[24] Klaus touches upon the theme of political commitment that permeated the discussion of working-class literature during the pre-war decade and which is addressed in the discussion of Henry Green's *Living* below and also by reference to Theodor Adorno's discussion of the 'non-propositional content' of the artwork in the following chapter.

As suggested in the introductory chapter, rather than being regarded as a 'school' or movement dedicated to an agreed project or manifesto, Birmingham group writers may better be considered as sharing a 'multiplicity in unity'. Their *unity* is evident in a similarity of content; a shared project to chronicle the lives of their working-class contemporaries, their *multiplicity* consisting in the differing formal styles with which they represented this content, the adoption of which derived in turn from their differing gradations: social status and aesthetic education, within the working class. In this respect, their literary productions challenge the monolithic conception of the working-class writer offered by commentators such as Roy Johnson and Carole Snee. Johnson claims the '[working-class writer's] probable lack of an aesthetic education—the sheer lack of time and leisure in which to read—[might] militate against his [*sic*] developing the skills necessary to transcend bourgeois aesthetic values'.[25] However, Snee suggests 'the written word [was] not a means of communication specifically valued by the working-class'. As there was no available working-class fictional practice upon which to draw, working-class writers simply aped the available (naturalist or realist) modes, these being 'the most readily available [means] of expression for writers not schooled within a literary tradition'.[26] This chapter repudiates these characterisations by referencing aspects of the Birmingham writers' formal innovations that clearly demonstrate a willingness to experiment within, often beyond, the parameters of the narrowly realist tradition beneath which their narratives have generally been subsumed.

A Fellow Traveller? Henry Green: Birmingham's Adoptive Proletarian

As a member of the working class and, in terms of his literary success, Nottingham's D. H. Lawrence functioned very much as the 'class-exemplary'/ 'local-boy-made-good' role model for each member of the Birmingham group and, owing to a shared regional association, Walter

Brierley in particular. However, somewhat nearer in spirit, subject matter and stylistic ambition, at least to Walter Allen and John Hampson, was Henry Green. Deriving from Green's experience of work in a Birmingham foundry, his *Living* (1929) remains—in the estimation of several writers and critics—'the best proletarian novel ever written'.[27] As mentioned in the introduction, Green's novel may appear as a somewhat incongruous addition, not only falling outside this book's remit in terms of periodisation but also, despite its setting and subject matter, owing to the fact it was written by a member of the middle classes who was neither a Birmingham citizen, nor member of the Birmingham group. However, Green's inclusion owes more to the critical attention his novel received following publication and which it continues to excite. Widely read and praised, Green's late-modernist rendering of working-class life problematises the definition of what a working-class text ought to be. It is included here as a 'case in point', rather than functioning as a paradigm text or Arnoldian 'touchstone' against which to test the merits or otherwise of Birmingham group writing. *Living* functions not only as a referential narrative framework against which to determine the boundaries in the prevailing art/politics debate but also as a barometer of critical tastes during the interwar period.

Contemporary novels of the industrial workplace were, as Chris Baldick indicates, relatively few and far between; works written in the historical interests of the working class are even less so, and more recent critics clearly mourn a missed opportunity here. H. Gustav Klaus regrets the 'empty space' existing due to 'the remarkable absence of novels of factory life, which could have claimed to deal with a situation familiar to and typical of millions of people'. However, he grudgingly concedes that Walter Allen's assessment of *Living* as 'the best English novel of factory life' may have some justification.[28] An equally perplexed Chris Baldick advises readers, 'if we look for a convincing fictional treatment of life inside a factory, we have to turn the clock back to the late Twenties and read Henry Green's *Living* (1929)'.[29] As does Allen, Baldick praises Green's novel for 'a striking originality that manages to extract from the world of a Birmingham engineering works a melancholy beauty while remaining true to the unglamorous facts of industrial routine'.[30]

That *Living* continues to receive plaudits whilst simultaneously provoking controversy is clear and Walter Allen's periodic re-evaluations of the novel and its author chart his own misconceptions. In his appreciation of Green in 'An Artist of the Thirties', *Folios of New Writing* (Spring 1941), he claims:

> [*Living*] remains, after twelve years, the best novel of factory life written by an Englishman. It is a remarkable tour-de-force: as a Birmingham man, who spoke with the local accent for the first fifteen years of his life, I can vouch for the accuracy of the dialogue and scene, and as an employee at a foundry I know that the description of the life there and of foundry technique is as correct.[31]

By the time he had come to write this, Allen's assumption, 'on the strength of the novel's setting and subject matter,' his former belief that '[Green] came from the working-class and had left wing sympathies,' had been duly revised.[32] Noting how the novel's 'subject matter and style gave its author honorary membership, as it were, of a literary movement to which he never really belonged,' Allen hastens to add, 'in the thirties it was the subject matter, life among the factory workers in Birmingham, that gave it its immediate attraction'.[33] That the political zeitgeist would exert a powerful influence upon a working-class novel's critical reception is apparent in the following passage where, recounting his youthful enthusiasms, Allen remarks (perhaps a little guiltily) how one's literary tastes undergo continual reassessment: 'We believed we were interested in politics and in saving the world, fighting for the working class against unemployment, fascism, and the threat of war. And we were quite serious and sincere. But in fact, though we didn't know it, we were as much swayed by aesthetic considerations.'[34] As the opening sentence of Allen's article makes clear:

> "The pink decade" the nineteen thirties have recently been christened, but in spite of the sneer, for any writer of the 'thirties to have been non-political, to have aimed at pure art, is in a way itself suspect; and Henry Green is very possibly the only pure artist among the novelists of the thirties'.[35]

Escaping the conventions of the 'over-emphatic naturalism', he considered a flaw in working-class writing, Allen was impressed by Green's ability to capture 'the poetry of working-class life'.[36] This he believed was realised in 'a poetry of observation' where incidents such as the Welshman Arthur Jones' impromptu song recital—given to celebrate the birth of his son—or the recurring image of the homing pigeons were 'symbolic at once of escape, of the life beyond the labyrinth of brick, and of the attachment to home and the familiar scene'.[37] The following passages are illustrative in that they underscore Raymond Williams' view that work and the industrial landscape provide a 'sense of the quality of life at a particular place and time: a sense of the ways in which particular activities combined into a way of thinking and living'.[38] The following passages find Green's narrator depicting his characters' thoughts by using imagery appropriate to their experience within the industrial setting. During Bert Jones and Lily Gates' journey to Liverpool, each articulates secret misgivings; here the novel's homing pigeon leitmotif serves as an extended metaphor for Lily's mixed emotions:

> For as racing pigeon fly in the sky, always they go round above house which provides for them or, if loosed at a distance from the house then they fly straight there, so her thoughts would not point away long from the house which had provided for her.' [...] so Miss Gates, in her thoughts and when these ever threatened to climb up in the air, was always coming bump back again to Mr. Craigan. And again, as when we set off impetuously sometimes then all at once we have to stop as suddenly just how little we are rushing off for becomes apparent to us, so, now first excitement was over, for first time it was plain to her just what she was after. She wanted to better herself and she wanted a kid. (*L*, 348)

Similarly, as evident in the following passage, unable to establish his parents' whereabouts in the increasingly deprived Liverpool neighbourhoods in which they searched and of which he was becoming increasingly ashamed, it is appropriate that Bert's insecurity and self-doubt concerning his future with Lily is expressed, not in abstract terms, but through reference to workplace processes with which he was more familiar:

> [H]e had seen it like setting job up on a lathe, the foreman looking on and others in the shop watching him. Job was difficult, he'd been in two minds to begin or not. Now he was alone, lathe had stopped and he was alone. Job was going wrong [...] Anything a bit out of the way and he couldn't do it, He blamed himself. What was the good in trying to better yourself when you couldn't hold a better job. Now if he went on with this bit in the lathe he would hopelessly spoil it. [...] he couldn't ask her to take on any wife's life in this town, the ordinary kind of life anywhere, when she'd come out to get on in this world. (*L*, 360)

Walter Allen remarked upon the novel's linguistic experimentation, considering it 'accurately match[ed] the scene as Green saw it. Bare, repetitive, harsh, angular, sometimes deliberately clumsy, it is an admirable expression for the blackness and din of a foundry, at the same time as it is attuned to the vernacular speech of the characters'.[39] Described by Valentine Cunningham as a the nearest anyone got to a 'Worker's Pidgin', a fuller account of the novel's linguistic innovations is provided by Ramon Lopez Ortega, who suggests that these 'were devised to commit Green's experience of factory life to paper' and therefore represent his '[compulsion] to find the language which would express that first hand [*sic*] insight into working-class living'.[40] Less an attempt to convey the Birmingham accent phonetically, Green's omission of articles and conjunctions (asyndeton) was made to communicate the sparseness of the proletarian environment and to reflect 'the restricted code usually employed in working-class communication'.[41]

Compared with Allen's and Baldick's effusive evaluations, H. Gustav Klaus offers a more tempered assessment, for whilst praising *Living* for 'a number of qualities not always to be found in socialist novels', he is unable to discern any sense of social responsibility or collective action in the novel and, although conceding that 'in some of its more [lyrical] moments the novel springs to life,' he considers:

> [T]he overall impression one gets of the life of the workers is still one of hopelessness, monotony and lethargy, and it is telling that the more vivid scenes are those that deal with eternal 'timeless' events in the life of this class like conception, pregnancy and birth, whereas there is nothing to suggest that the workers ever take matters into their own hands to improve the harsh conditions under which they live and work. They endure but they never act.[42]

Aware that Green was no socialist, H. Gustav Klaus was nonetheless disappointed to find so little evidence of class-consciousness or collectivity in Green's representation of the workers or the action they take. He suggests their inertia exposes *Living* to the 'kind of reproach Engels made with regard to Margaret Harkness' *City Girl* by '[showing] the working-class figures as a passive mass, unable to help itself and not even [making] any attempt to help itself'.[43] In 'Fictions of Class and Community in Henry Green's "Living," Marius Hentea mitigates the seeming inertia of Green's foundry workers by suggesting the unconventional, less-confrontational industrial relations existing in some of Birmingham's smaller scale manufacturing units was not a figment of "Green's bourgeois prejudice" but represented instead his acquaintance with the "Birmingham way," the means by which the city avoided traditional large scale corporatism and where industrial mobilization proved difficult due to the large number of migrant workers the city attracted'.[44] Nevertheless, it should perhaps be remembered that only three years prior to *Living*'s publication in 1929, Jesse Eden had led a walkout at Birmingham's Joseph Lucas auto-electrical company and organised a further industrial action in 1931 which involved some 10,000 female (press shop) workers in a protest against 'Fordism', the imposition of so-called speed-up, latterly 'time and motion', techniques aiming to improve productivity.

As has been indicated, Klaus' theory of the novel requires that—irrespective of its author's class and beyond a work's thematic and sociological criteria—a further 'ideological correlate' is necessary to determine the value of a literary work, this being precisely what the term 'socialist' seeks to comprehend. In what is a distinctly Marxist formulation, Klaus explains: 'A novel written in the historical interests of the working-class, should reveal a standpoint consistent with the class-conscious sections of that class.'[45] Clearly stipulating political commitment as the gauge by which one should measure the value of a working-class text, Gustav Klaus follows closely the argument outlined in Walter Benjamin's essay 'The Author as Producer', in which Benjamin asserts that 'commitment is *simultaneously* political *and* esthetic (my emphasis)', and he enjoins compromise by arguing that, in addition to the correct political tendency, a work must also demonstrate the correct *literary* tendency.[46] Benjamin's assertion aligns closely with the readings adopted throughout this study. However, the early (pre-popular-front) years of the decade saw critical assessments clearly biased towards the political or propagandistic and generally in accord with the opinions of those who found modernism's affectations and experimentation inimical to the kinds of progressive content urged by the Left. Yet, to consider that 'realism and experiment as implacably opposed to one another', or that modernist or late-modernist writers had merely contracted out of society, were inward-looking and socially irresponsible is, as Andrzej Gasiorek suggests, to adopt the 'simplistic' account of modernism adopted in the post-war period by writers such as C. P. Snow, Kingsley Amis and others who, in advocating a return to realism, were censorious of what they saw as modernism's solipsistic and aesthetic affectations.[47] Lyndsey Stonebridge and Marina MacKay likewise comment on this tendency, although they attribute the 'polemical separation of the 'referential' and 'aesthetic' largely to the 'legacy of modernist manifesto making itself' [which they consider] 'is not only of doubtful relevance to earlier novelists, but also potentially damaging for those who followed'.[48] Fortunately, as remarked in the introduction, a dialectical approach more accommodating of both positions was slowly beginning to emerge.[49] That such 'simplistic accounts' of modernism have proven stubbornly resistant is evident in Carol A. Wipf-Miller's 'Fictions of "Going over": Henry Green and the New Realism', in which she claims:

> [T]he political shift that earned the thirties the epithet "The Red decade" had its concomitant aesthetic shift as the younger generation of writers "went over," so to speak, from modernism to a new realism, from an aesthetic ideal of formal autonomy to one that pursued an active and politicized engagement between life and art.[50]

Wipf-Miller sees this 'new realism' as a ditching of the aesthetic in favour of a more muscular, politicised discourse. Rather than seeking to overturn traditional 1930s orthodoxy however, she aims 'not only [to relocate] Green in the context of thirties leftism, but also [to place] these movements in a dialectical relation to modernist aesthetics and values defined as their antithesis'.[51]

During an interview in which he cited Isherwood's claim that *Living* was the 'best proletarian novel ever written', Terry Southern asked its author whether he considered the artist or writer should be socially aware. Green answered, saying, 'the writer must be disengaged or else he is writing politics. Look at the Soviet writers.'[52] Green's response engages directly with the notions of commitment taken up by H. Gustav Klaus, Walter Benjamin and Theodor Adorno that are discussed elsewhere in this study; however, owing to his general distrust of ideologies and lacking the conviction of Left facing contemporaries, Green was not persuaded to urge the progressive, political content required of a socially oriented criticism. Yet, despite such strident a-politicism, it would be mistaken to assume that Green was unconcerned with the experience of his co-workers. As J. McAleer indicates, '*Living* is a book about how people really live: their hopes, but also their compromises and defeats, and the way those defeats may not be so bad after all. Green neither romanticizes his proletarian characters nor pretends to hold out radical solutions for them.'[53] As Andrzej Gasiorek maintains, it is important not '[to confuse] authorial detachment with authorial disinterestedness',[54] In a BBC broadcast Green asserted, 'we are all individuals and each writer has something to communicate.'[55] That the 'something' Green wished to communicate was of vital, human interest is evident in the following passage, where, following a bad dream, Lily Gates prays for a child:

> Lord give me a child that I might wash him, feed him, give him life. Yes, let him be a boy. Give him blue eyes, let him cling to me with his hands and never be loosed from me. Give him me to love that I'm always kissing him and working for him. I've had nothing of my own. Give him me and let him be mine, oh, oh give me a life to work for, and give me the love of him, and his father's.[56]

From H. Gustav Klaus' perspective, Green was unable to adopt a 'standpoint consistent with the class-conscious sections of the working-class' his 'going over' may have implied, and he insists that Green's focus on such 'universal' scenes only serves to 'reinforce the hopelessness of workers' lives'.[57] However, Green sincerely believed that for the working class 'Children [...] as of course really for every class, are the only creative thing they can do'.[58] Based less upon sentiment or condescension, Green's assertion was congruent with his fundamental belief in the importance of babies and childrearing as human activities transcendent of contemporary economic or political concerns. In thus gesturing to the homely and familial, Green approaches the fascination for 'the continuous flow and recoil of sympathy' and the 'essential process of living' Raymond Williams had perceived in the writing of D. H. Lawrence.[59]

Perhaps the most significant elements of Green's writing for our purposes and those proving most influential in the work of Birmingham writers Walter Allen and John Hampson were his formal innovations. These are to be found chiefly in his deployment of cinematic techniques, cross-cutting, cross-class montage and suppression of the narrative voice or a concomitant of this being achieved by the use of free-indirect speech. Writing to Nevill Coghill, Green explained that *Living* '[is] written in a very condensed kind of way in short paragraphs, hardly ever much longer than 1½ to 2 printed pages & often very much shorter. A kind of very disconnected cinema film'.[60] As has been suggested, documentarism, not in the realist sense of close attention to detail, but in the Eisensteinian or Griersonian sense of de-mystification was, in its many shapes and forms, certainly in the ascendant during the pre-war decade. Valentine Cunningham references Green's 'deft cinematic cutting between different people and families, between home and work, between the classes (sweating foundry workers followed for example by Mrs Dupret and her son talking about dances and how tiring they are)'.[61] In this respect, Lara Feigel considers Green's *Living* 'as startling in its overt cinematic montage as in its sympathy for its working-class protagonists'.[62] However, while 'an enthusiastic cinema fan [...] like several 'highbrow' writers, [Green] tended to be more captivated by popular than avant-garde cinema, seeking pleasure rather than left-wing enlightenment'.[63]

Unburdened by the sense of guilt and inner conflict assailing those 'attempting', as Stephen Spender expressed it, '[to] cut themselves off from the roots of their own sensibility in order to align themselves with the more democratic tastes of mass culture', Green's 'going over' might thus be seen less as a desire to align himself with the 'working' class than a bid to escape the arrogance and mundane pre-occupations of his own milieu.[64] In this respect, *Living* communicated the sheer joy of Green's escape to new surroundings, and his experience at the Farringdon works of Pontifex, the family firm in Tyseley, Birmingham, which, contrasted with mid-1920s Oxford, he found positively congenial. In a letter informing his mother of his intention to 'come down' prior to completing his final year, Green described the futility of university life in an environment where 'everyone is rich and vapid or poor and vapid & one & all talk about Oxford day and night'.[65] As Wipf-Miller suggests, though retaining the 'return ticket' to his social origins, 'in his work, "Going over" is not an artificial identification with the other; rather, it recovers the *real* self he felt he had lost to the conformity and mass-produced tastes of his own class'.[66] On the publication of *Loving*, which featured a cast of characters redolent of the undergraduates described in his letter, it would seem that Green had finally redeemed his 'return ticket'. Nevertheless, besides its lyrical passages, *Living* presented its author's Auden-like appreciation of the urban industrial landscape by rendering authentically, and as never before, the lives and aspirations of the workers who inhabited it.

If emulation was to be considered a form of flattery, then Walter Allen's and John Hampson's adoption of the cinematic techniques they discovered in *Living* are fitting testimony to the work of Birmingham's adoptive proletarian. Although Robert Tressell's *The Ragged Trousered Philanthropists* is frequently hailed as the most successful, progressive novel in the working-class canon, Green's *Living* possibly represented its polar opposite: being the most overtly 'aesthetic'. In demarcating the boundaries of working-class narrative by reference to this more widely known work, this chapter sets up a critical paradigm with which to consider the narratives of the Birmingham group writers. It is this book's contention that, in bridging the rhetorical space between story and discourse without compromising imaginative (aesthetic) potency or political efficacy, the narratives of the Birmingham group will be shown to align with more recent theoretical and critical expectations of working-class literature.

Following her analysis of *Living*, Lara Feigel's discussion of Green's adaption of filmic technique embarked upon a different course in order to focus on the 'darker side of thirties cinematic writing'.[67] Here, in a world increasingly filmed and photographed and one in which reality itself appears as a simulacrum, Feigel claims that, having accepted the cinematic quality of their surroundings, certain 1930s writers—notably Christopher Isherwood, Stephen Spender and Edward Upward—began 'to [figure] consciousness itself as a camera or projector,' its 'subjects merely absent actors.'[68] In short, Feigel sees the 1930s as pre-figurative of the 'hyperreality' that Jean Baudrillard saw as permeating the post-modern condition, whereby, in adopting personae or passively existing as though in a performance, individuals, rather than operating under their own volition, become detached from reality. Feigel believes the subjective apprehensions expressed in Isherwood's Berlin novels 'work against the hopes for clear-sighted witnessing and political change' wrought by more politically engaged literary works which adopt the techniques of avant-garde/documentary cinema, to counsel against a surrender to inanition. Citing Walter Allen's *Blind Man's Ditch*, she suggests that such novels pointedly caution against 'camera consciousness' by underlining the dangers of passively registering or internalising the idealised lives or existence of characters featured in commercial/Hollywood movies.

John Hampson had noted that Walter Allen's novels were 'concerned with existence in the thirties', and, with fascism nearing its apogee as Allen was writing *Blind Man's Ditch*, the very performative abandon his novel cautions against could be found stirring restlessly in the darker imaginings of some European nations. More recently, J. M. Coetzee reminds us how the 'fascism as theatre' which surfaced in the films of Leni Riefenstahl revealed that, 'for ordinary Germans, the only identity on show was a fascist identity in fascist costume and fascist postures of domination and obedience'.[69] Walter Benjamin censured the aestheticisation of politics by arguing instead for a politicisation of aesthetics; aesthetics here understood as linking back to its Greek origin as perception: 'a theory of experiencing the world'.[70] In this aspect, Allen's novel certainly underpins Raymond Williams' formulation that artworks offer insights into the contemporary 'structure of feeling', and the following reading of Allen's novel will therefore extend Lara Feigel's discussion by examining a range of characters living in a performative world shortly to encounter the dark shadow of fascism and one in which the dangers of internalising cinematic hyperreality would be made glaringly apparent.[71]

Walter Allen: 'As a Film Director might present it': *Blind Man's Ditch*

Unlike the conventional investigation/denouement crime fictions of Agatha Christie or Dorothy Sayers, Allen's novel is more a 'why-' than 'who-dunnit', the reader's interest generated by speculating on the motives, rather than the identity, of the perpetrator. Enthusiastically adopting Henry Green's way of telling the story, 'mainly in very short episodes rather in the manner of a film, the author cutting from character to character, from scene to contrasted scene', Walter Allen explained his aim was to get the image on the page 'as a film-director might present it'.[72] Cinematic techniques such as cross-cutting, close-up/long-shot and montage effects each proved invaluable in the crafting of Allen's 'closed little communities', enabling him to present a cinematic and social cross-section of character viewpoints and perspectives.[73] Following Green's *Living*, and in retaining a loose plot structure, Allen's *Blind Man's Ditch* was largely episodic. The novel traces a sequence of events leading to an opportunistically planned payroll snatch that culminates in a murder. By making recourse to its compositional and stylistic devices, this reading of Allen's novel illustrates how techniques derived from the cinema came to play an important role in the Birmingham writers' reconfiguration of the realist novel during this period.

As intimated above, the less beneficent influence of popular cinema, the commercial Hollywood movie in particular, began to attract critical opprobrium, and this had gathered apace during the decade with cultural commentators of the Left claiming that commercial cinema was an ideological tool deployed in the interests of a bourgeois society to lull the masses into a state of comatose inactivity—the lexicon of narcotics being frequently deployed—and impassive credulity. Lara Feigel points out that several of Allen's characters seem 'gripped in a paralysing detachment from external events and from each other'.[74] Below is the epigraph from *Blind Man's Ditch* in which Allen describes the criminal assault towards which his novel inexorably works. Described cinematically in the form of a trailer, the images appear as a projection or shadow play of the events detailed later in the novel:

> The old man's shadow, spindled and contorted in grotesque parody, moved jerkily along the sun-bloomed surface of the wall. A Green van rattled to a stop and obliterated it. When it emerged again the shadow bobbed up and down as though twitched violently by a string. A second shadow cut across it in mimic assault. It hinged to the ground as though the string had been cut, and decomposed into a pool of blood. (*BM*, 8)

Lara Feigel cites this extract, suggesting, 'The epigraph gives the murder a cinematographic inevitability. It takes place textually before the characters have decided to enact it, which undermines their volition, suggesting that they are merely fulfilling their automaton-like roles in a pre-determined scene'.[75] Again, images of a barbiturate-infused drowsiness pervade, Ralph Bond was in no doubt that 'the social purpose of the cinema was to act as a drug, for it is just as much propaganda to prevent people thinking as to make them think in certain directions'.[76] Feigel references George Orwell's apostrophisation of the working-class cinemagoer 'standing on the street corner, indulging in a private daydream of yourself as Clark Gable or Greta Garbo, which compensates you for a great deal', though elsewhere it seemed Orwell's ire was aimed more purposively at the producers of entertainments that held their audiences in such intellectual contempt.[77] Such negative remarks did not remain wholly unchallenged however: recording his visits to the Trocadero at the Elephant and Castle and clearly unperturbed by the prospect of his ideological interpellation, Denis Norden countered: '[m]y generation learned how to be human beings from films. You learned how to smoke from films [...] you learned how to hold a cigarette [...] in a sense everything you learned about being a unit in modern society came from films.'[78] Nevertheless, the notion that audiences or writers might passively internalise the fantasy offerings of a cinematically mediated world, or worse, may have preferred to exist in one, was abhorrent to the likes of cultural commentators such as Theodor Adorno, who considered this 'the worst kind of bourgeois sadism' [...] 'if only for the simple reason that in a communist society work will be organised in such a way that people will no longer be so tired and so stultified that they need distractions'.[79]

As with medicine, it is first necessary to determine the cause before considering the cure. That people wished to escape the drudgery of work or quotidian anxieties was surely not unreasonable. However, an existential disquiet of a darker tenor had begun to gnaw away at the collective conscience. In *British Writers and the Approach of World War II*, Steve Ellis explains that, sandwiched between economic depression and imminent world war, expressions of a deeper concern had become manifest in a 'literature of anxiety'. Referencing the almost-forgotten genre of the 'Munich crisis novel', Ellis describes how the Edwardian writers Shaw, Wells and Woolf each registered and responded to the sense of catastrophe pervading E. M. Forster's essay 'The 1939 state', which, as its punning title implies, aimed to describe the neurosis currently assailing both national and individual psyches.[80] Published in November 1939, five months after Forster's essay, Allen's novel provides a gallery of individuals living under the shadow of potentially apocalyptic events and urges the necessity of collective political engagement by challenging the disabling detachment engendered by the palliative effects of commercial cinema.

The novel's title may derive from the biblical reference (Matthew 15:14), 'Let them alone: they be blind leaders of the blind. And if the blind lead the blind, both shall fall into the ditch', a biblical idiom which accurately conceptualises Allen's pairing of the spiritually blind, con man character James Bartholomew and his enticement of the depressed and rudderless Eugene Lorimer into performing a criminal act. Conversely, it may relate to the fates of Eugene Lorimer and Workers Educational Association instructor Ronald Anderson, in their attempts to woo the proud and independent Rosamund Miller—an activity at best misguided as the following extract from W. B. Yeats 'A Dialogue of Self and Soul' makes clear:

> I am content to live it all again
> And yet again, if it be life to pitch
> Into the frog-spawn of a Blind Man's Ditch,
> A blind man battering blind men;
> Or into that most fecund ditch of all,
> The folly that man does
> Or must suffer, if he woos
> A proud woman not kindred of his soul.
> (W. B. Yeats, *A Dialogue of Self and Soul*, Part II, Stanza 3)[81]

We first encounter English literature tutor Ronald Anderson at the Workers' Educational Association class he teaches one evening each week. By day, Anderson is a schoolmaster at King James Grammar School, a position secured following the breakdown of a previous relationship which had ended in his partner's suicide.[82] Having once entertained literary ambitions, a moment of maudlin reflection induces Ronald Anderson to ask himself: 'why had not his teachers when lecturing on great literature not warned him: "My dear boy this is beautiful and profound; but do not think it is life"' (*BM*, 151). Diffident regarding his school-mastering abilities, he considers himself better suited to tutoring the night school class attended by the idealistic Eugene Lorimer, who initially appears as a protégé: an echo of his former self.

Eugene Lorimer works as a maintenance electrician but is studying literature in order to 'improve' and ultimately to divest himself of an occupation he loathes. In this he follows the well-trodden path of those other working-class auto-didacts before him and which leads, in the context of the present discussion, from Hardy's Jude Fawley to Jack London's Martin Eden along to E. M. Forster's Leonard Bast and on to Arthur Gardner, the protagonist of Walter Brierley's *Sandwichman*. The following discussion of Eugene's educational aspiration pre-empts the exploration of self-cultivation I develop more fully by reference to the Brierley's novel in Chap. 4. Allen's characterisation of Eugene diverges from standard treatments of the working-class auto-didact for, as intimated by Ronald Anderson's misgivings above, Allen was himself not wholly without reservations regarding the benefits of cultural improvement or the vicarious experience to be gleaned from literature or film.

Beyond their acquaintance at night school, the lives of Ronald Anderson and Eugene Lorimer converge in their relationship with Rosamund Miller, the career-minded journalist employed by a local paper, who owns her own apartment, and who, for the 1930s, supplies a convincing portrait of the independent, self-possessed, career woman. Unfortunately, as in Yeats' poem, each character's relationship with her founders in 'most fecund ditch of all': the blind man's ditch of their 'folly'. Ronald Anderson, being older and more emotionally resilient, finds another partner and eventually adjusts to a less-elevated version of his youthful imaginings by settling to a career as schoolmaster. Whereas, mourning the termination of his brief relationship with Rosamund, Eugene Lorimer suffers a breakdown. Emotional despair and distraction render him susceptible to the criminal machinations of the morally vacuous, con man James Bartholomew, who manipulates him into committing the violent assault on Mr Overs, the elderly war veteran who later dies of his injuries. Allen's 'closed little community' is also populated by other characters whose lives intersect with and are montaged against the performative, constructed personae of his protagonists. However, it is in probing beneath what John Hampson referred to as the 'trim undistinguished façade which a provincial town presents to a stranger' and exploring the socially submerged sections of the community that Allen's novel moves both toward and beyond conventional conceptions of the crime novel genre.[83]

The following passage finds Eugene Lorimer performing his duties on the Saturday morning nearing the end of the working week. Having been called to the workbench of 'Snowball', a co-worker who, reluctant to overexert himself so near finishing time, claims his machine is malfunctioning, Eugene quickly traces the 'fault':

> "How long's this saw been in?" he asked.
>
> Snowball sprang to his feet, took his hands out of his pockets. "Christ Almighty!" he said, "I put it in new last week. There ain't nothing wrong with the saw."
>
> "No, and there, ain't nothing wrong with the motor or the starter either," retorted Eugene. "You mustn't half have been, busy, mate, if you only put that saw in last week." He put his pliers and screwdriver back in his pocket.
>
> "Trying to be funny, ain't you?" Snowball said. The threat was automatic and meaningless. Bloody hell! He'd have to put a new one in himself after all, and he'd been hoping to get enough power out of the motor to carry him over until Monday. But he was a philosophic young man. Might as well get it done. He stood with head on one side for a moment, looking at the saw. Then he began to sing softly to himself and set to work. (*BM*, 48)

Despite his scepticism concerning Snowball's claims, Eugene's attitude to work is no less cynical. Before reporting back to the electrician's shop, and with just fifty minutes before 'knocking-off time', he decides to have 'two drags and a spit' and cautiously makes his way to the lavatories. 'You had to be careful,' Allen's narrator informs us. 'The doors to the WC were half doors only, reaching from knee to shoulder; and they had no bolts. It was dangerous because the foremen used the same conveniences' (*BM*, 48). On entering the cubicle, Eugene sits down with half a Woodbine cupped in the palm of his hand, 'A surreptitious cigarette was one of the good things, and a few puffs in the lavatory tasted better than any number any other time' (*BM*, 49).

This extract again finds Allen following Henry Green in using cross-cutting techniques to present what Chris Baldick describes as 'the unglamorous facts of industrial routine', by revealing the quotidian nature of factory work and workers' attitudes to it. By juxtaposing or cinematically montaging the figures of Eugene and Snowball, Allen begins to shape their individual identities. Despite their differing status within the factory hierarchy, each views his work as merely instrumental: solely a means to extrinsic satisfactions, their mutual indifference and alienation registered in the petty acts of micro-resistance described here. Outside the workplace, Eugene aspires to intellectual advancement via his pursuit of literature and the arts, whereas Snowball spends his earnings on football and Max Miller. Recounting Snowball's suggestion that Eugene accompany him to see Max Miller at the Hippodrome, Eugene apostrophises 'Max Miller indeed!' following which Allen's narrator provides a left-handed compliment, 'He pitied Snowball, was priggishly sorry for him' (*BM*, 49). Eugene's condescension derives from his academic pretensions, though again, as the narrator cautions, 'If he did not realise them the future would be unbearable, life not worth living. [...] But the knowledge of his ambition isolated him. To achieve it, it was necessary to cut himself away from everything he had been associated with' (*BM*, 33). Eugene's intellectual aspirations thus illustrate the 'shame dynamic' Pamela Fox perceives in working-class culture, in which narrative description functions as a form of 'resistance' expressing individual needs and desires, *distinct* from trade unionism, labourism or *master narratives* exhorting a more organised or collective agenda (my emphasis).[84] Fox conceptualises working-class fiction as a 'playing-out' of the shame dynamic operating in working-class experience, and her views are therefore intrinsic to notions of educational aspiration and attainment amongst both the working-class characters and their authors as discussed in this book. Eugene's desire for knowledge and his idealisation of learning are each outputs of the shame dynamic Fox describes, and although seeing desire as a pattern of resistance based upon a perceived 'lack' or sense of disadvantage, Fox is also aware of its negative aspects; she cites T. A. (Tommy) Jackson's warning against the ideological dangers of reading the canonical texts of English literature: the 'Best Books' as recommended by his Working Men's College instructor, believing they accomplish assimilation rather than class awareness:

> Insensibly, preoccupation with these 'classics' treated as a single category—the Best—caused a student to slip into regarding Culture as a fixed Mind-world in which one either ascended with the geniuses to supreme heights or sank with the dullards and the dunces to the uncultured slime … one acquired a complete detachment from—if not downright contempt for—the 'uncultured' vulgarity and sordidiness of everyday life.[85]

Such embourgeoisification writ large may have troubled Walter Allen. Born into the working class and, as his sympathetic characterisations testify, sharing a thoroughgoing allegiance to and understanding of it, his early novels occasionally betray a regret that his education and literary aspirations set him on a Lawrentian trajectory away from his cultural origins. Allen was fortunately grounded enough to 'self-correct'; however, it is precisely against entering a world of literary or cinematic abstraction and severing one's links with reality that his novel cautions.

Cutting from Eugene's clandestine cigarette musings to the office of 'Woman's Editor' at the 'Daily Herald and Evening Star', we first encounter Rosamund Miller adding the finishing touches to the 'Women's Interests' column. It is appropriate that Rosamund occupies the position of Women's Editor; she is proficient in her work and clearly derives intrinsic satisfaction from it, being, one may presume, well remunerated, she is able to enjoy such material comforts as the 1930s might offer in the form of a luxury apartment, a telephone and independence. However, Rosamund appears to have internalised her job title to the extent that in the public sphere she presents as an edited version of herself. Following the breakdown of her relationship with the married features editor of a northern daily, she has moved to the Midlands in order to pick up the emotional pieces and begin life afresh. A competent professional whose self-worth is defined by her position, Rosamund nevertheless finds life on a provincial paper boring, tired of filling copy space with syndicated agency features, she dreams of a scoop. As with Eugene, she seems detached from the quotidian existing in an emotionally disconnected world of her own imaginings. Gazing down at the teeming life in the street below her office, she speculates detachedly on the meanings of people's expressions and movements. Lara Feigel observes how in viewing reality as though watching a film, '[Rosamund] bemoans her own, apparently inevitable disengagement from the scene'.[86] Despite her Garbo-like persona, she resembles more closely Henry Green's Lily Gates. As Allen's narrator confides to the reader:

> [F]or a moment she wished passionately that she could experience everything, thinking: I have sacrificed too much. She wanted for a moment to have her job, her independence, a man and a child and all at one time. But it was impossible; to have independence you must sacrifice all the other things. You could have men, but not one man; lovers, but not a lover. She did not dare ask herself whether the sacrifice was too great. (*BM*, 246)

It is prior to a performance of Shaw's *Arms and the Man* at the 'Little Theatre' that Rosamund first observes the self-conscious Eugene Lorimer desperately, not to say pretentiously, clutching his copy of Coleridge's *Biographia Literaria*, and determines to enliven the tedium of her existence by adopting him as temporary amusement and distraction. It is apposite that Rosamund should pick one so involved in his own self-creation. Allen montages her inner thoughts with those of Eugene who is at this point reflecting, somewhat phenomenologically, upon how his own 'performance' might be critically received:

> In the balcony of the Little he felt very much alone, but besides being envious and fearful he was proud. Sitting there, waiting to see a performance of *Arms and the Man*, reading the *Biographia Literaria* half-comprehendingly as in a foreign language during the overture, was a symbol of himself and of the ambition that he thought of as himself; what made him proud was not so much reading Coleridge, watching Shaw, as the *sensation* of reading Coleridge and watching Shaw (my emphasis). (*BM*, 63)

On first setting eyes upon Rosamund, Eugene feels he dislikes her intensely:

> She was remote from anything in his experience. Out of memories of Hollywood films he built up a background for her, of chromium furniture, green glass-topped tables [...] against which she stood, posed elegantly with a frost-green glass in her hand, a figure seen in a slick film or advertisement in the expensive weeklies you glanced at from time to time in the reading-room of the public library. (*BM*, 64–65)

It was 'as though he had walked into a cinema and seen himself upon the screen with Rosamund'. (*BM*, 112). Lara Feigel observes how Eugene 'figures her [...] as a Hollywood character, 'a figure seen in a slick film or in an advertisement in the expensive shiny weeklies that you glanced at from time to time in the reading room at the public library' (*BM*, 65). As Allen's, knowing and world-weary narrator explains: '[Eugene's] relationship with Rosamund, [...] was like something in a book. And this thrilled him, because life in books seemed finer to him and more real than actuality. He was in love with art and abstractions' (*BM*, 138). That people consciously engage in their identity construction was discomfiting to Allen who like T. A. Jackson, was himself a lover of cinema and the arts, but nonetheless saw that filmic emulation or living one's 'life in books' might prove destructive. Eugene's love of art and abstractions parallels that of the younger Ronald Anderson, although the latter had at least retained a residue of self-knowledge. Again montage enables Allen narrator to juxtapose Eugene's fantasy projection of Rosamund with the groundedness and down-to-earth perspectives embodied in his mother:

> She frowned, threading a needle. The Sunday paper lay beside her in her chair, but she had not read it. Later she would look at the back page of pictures and tut-tut the bathing girls. [...] but work was her drug; she felt guilty if her hands were not busy [...] she had come to accept life as that; work always, standing over a hot stove, blackleading a grate, washing clothes, ironing, back-aching work; [...] work that made the eyes ache. She complained of the work continually but in it she found her chief pleasure. (*BM*, 113, 4)

Contrasted with the independent Rosamund Miller, Eugene's mother seems enslaved to prevailing domestic convention in the shape of 'the woman's lot', and, though continually complaining of her workload, she appears to derive from it the kinds of satisfaction indicated by Soper and Ryle (see p. 56). Montaged against photos of bathing girls in the Sunday paper, Allen's narrator tells us that '[s]he had let her hair grow and kept it in place with myriad hairpins though she refused to have it cut, "Me go to a hairdresser at my age!" She found the notion utterly incredible. "Besides, your dad wouldn't like it"' (*BM*, 26).

Following his affair with Rosamund, who had become bored and not a little alarmed at his gaucherie and emotional indigence, the vulnerable Eugene falls under the spell of petty crook James Bartholomew. A spiv, and prey, as with other characters in the novel, to their filmic imaginings, he craves money and the cinematically ordained Hollywood fantasy of the 'good life' he imagines it will facilitate. More disconcertingly, he is prepared to engage in criminal activity in order to achieve it. Having returned home following an unexplained absence of three years, Bartholomew is feverishly planning a further crime. Like other characters in the novel, he finds it difficult to distinguish between the real and the imagined. We first encounter him preparing to visit his old school where a long-serving master is due to receive a retirement presentation. In a sequence mirroring Eugene Lorimer's self-conscious imaginings, Bartholomew 'rehearses' his 'role' for the event. In this 'performance', he has cast himself as a British volunteer invalided out of active service in the Spanish Civil War and, to add a little dramatic gravitas to his deception, has cultivated a limp. 'Limping expertly into the school, James Bartholomew watched himself limp expertly into school.' Allen makes Bartholomew's calculated dissimulation authentic by relating it in the third person, as though he were regarding his performance from the perspective of an observer: 'an impressive figure, the more distinguished because of the limp and the stick he leaned on; an ambassador perhaps, with a medal on a gold chain at his chest like the man in the De Reske advertisement' (*BM*, 66). Bartholomew's preposterous self-construction clearly draws upon cinematic projections of the heroic figure: 'But Bartholomew was enjoying himself. He was doing an act' (*BM*, 68). Allen's character juxtaposition continues when Bartholomew, the deceitful, work-shy con man is contrasted with his moral nemesis: Mr Overs the be-medalled First World War veteran, whose assault Bartholomew would later contrive and whose 'old soldier's incorruptibility was an affront to him'. 'Bartholomew did not know when he had hated a man so passionately' (*BM*, 148).

Eugene's Lorimer's unassuming brother Harry proves the exception to 'the paralysing detachment' in which so many of the novel's characters seem gripped. Wearing his blue, sand-stained labourer's overalls and attempting to catch a few moments sleep following a wearying shift at the foundry where he is employed, Harry belies his labourer's status in being sensitive, intelligent and politically radical. When the family retire to bed, he remains downstairs listening to a gramophone recording of Mozart's *The Magic Flute*. During a domestic altercation in which Eugene asserts he no longer intends to attend Sunday school, Harry interjects on his behalf proposing a visit the town hall instead, 'You come and hear Clem Atlee, our kid!' Just as such existential renderings of family life: 'the continuous flow and recoil of sympathy' had found expression in D. H. Lawrence's works, so too in Allen's multi-protagonist novels where families are periodically locked in noisy disagreement and intra-class conflicts are shaped from differing perspectives. Following a political meeting and evening session spent addressing publicity envelopes on behalf of the Labour candidate, Harry has returned home and settled to his supper. His sister Alice and her fiancée Phil wait politely at the table while Harry finishes his meal. Phil, a small-time entrepreneur who fancies himself a wit, winks conspiratorially at Harry's sister and proceeds to ask Harry about the meeting. 'Barely able to conceal his enthusiasm,' the ingenuous Harry recounted 'what Mr. Attlee and Miss Wilkinson had said, how they had defied Hitler, Mussolini, General Franco, and the National Government [...] "It was great", he said at the end' (*BM*, 114). Following Harry's enthusiastic account, Allen focalises Harry's disingenuous interlocutor Phil who

> [S]lick with Clark Gable moustache, sporting in plus fours, stifled a yawn. He was bored. Spain meant nothing to him: he had Alice and his sports car. He regarded Harry with good-humoured contempt: he was only a labourer after all, and Phil had small sympathy with labourers. He was in authority, boss over a score of girls. It had pleased him to condescend to Alice. He saw himself as an employer of labour. (*BM*, 115)

Winking at Alice, Phil goads Harry scoffing, 'What we want in this country is a Hitler!' Harry is dumbstruck, shaking with anger he rises violently from the table shouting, 'I ain't eating my supper with any bleeding fascist!' and hurriedly leaves the house slamming the front door behind him. Later we find him alone in a crowded pub disconsolately remonstrating with himself and brooding over Phil's deliberate provocation. Unlike Eugene, Harry is disinclined towards academic attainment and content to work as a labourer. Nevertheless, as he takes an active interest in politics and possesses an innate sense of social justice. Yet, as his outburst at the insensitive and politically vacuous Phil demonstrated, Harry regrets his inarticulacy, 'The trouble is, I got no education, he thought. He was suddenly sad. I got a vote, that's all' (*BM*, 120). He recalls with bitter satisfaction how in a previous employment the owner of the firm chaired a meeting at which the local Conservative candidate was to speak. His boss explained how this would provide the candidate with an opportunity to address the workers man-to-man, following which they would be 'permitted' to ask questions. At the appointed moment, though lacking confidence and unsure quite how to frame his words, Harry is repeatedly prompted by his increasingly impatient boss. Finally, in a spirit of sincere and innocent inquiry, Harry speaks up: 'I'd like to ask why you pay your workers less than Union rates?' (*BM*, 123).

Allen leaves the predictable consequences of Harry's impassioned inquiry to the reader's imagination, though we learn that following his masterly rhetoric and having taken up the foreman's instruction to collect his cards the following day, Harry would remain unemployed for six months. Yet, as Allen's narrator explains: '[For Harry] the memory was a touchstone and a talisman. It comforted him. For a minute at that meeting it had been as though a bomb had exploded; and he had thrown it. For a minute reality had broken through' (*BM*, 123). Despite his inarticulacy and political naïvety, Allen's Harry Lorimer expresses the sense of social responsibility and collective will that H. Gustav Klaus had sought but was unable to discover in Henry Green's *Living*. In a novel peopled by characters locked in the realm of their filmic imaginings and their 'paralysing detachment from external events', Allen's Harry Lorimer offered a groundedness that functioned as the still centre in a cinematically mediated world.

Blind Man's Ditch was completed in midsummer 1939, by which time its author, encouraged by the publication though meagre proceeds from the sale of *Innocence Is Drowned* the previous year, was now living frugally in London. In his autobiographical memoir, Allen describes receiving a telephone call from Louis MacNeice in which the poet, clearly presenting with symptoms of the '1939 state', informed Allen that war was imminent and, having sold his car for £14, suggested they spend the proceeds on lunch at the Café Royal. Having recently completed a novel cautioning against the internalisation of cinematically mediated reality, it was ironic, though, given the circumstances, not unreasonable perhaps, that 'floating on Brandy and cigar fumes' Allen and MacNeice should seek some temporary respite by taking a taxi to the Tottenham Court Road, where a cinema was showing one of their favourite Westerns.[87]

'As Unpolitical a Man as I Have Ever Met': Leslie Halward

Walter Allen, whose description of Leslie Halward supplies this subheading, and John Hampson had each set out to reconfigure the traditional realist novel by recourse to the repertoire of technical devices they had discovered in documentary film. Their receptivity to its inventory of formal innovation registered obliquely a dissatisfaction with the traditional realist apparatus and thus set their work apart from that of fellow Birmingham group writer Leslie Halward, who, rather than reconfiguring the traditional mode, found its more extreme variant in a naturalism that was entirely adequate for his purposes. Walter Allen distinguishes between the English and French forms of naturalism explaining that 'the French were interested in character as an instance of general laws that can be deduced from it, [whereas] for the English character tends to be an end in itself, which is to say that whereas the French write as moralists the English write as humorists'.[88] Halward's 'English' naturalism certainly accords with Allen's distinction, although his detailed character studies challenge Allen's assertion that naturalism 'turned away from psychological analysis'. On the contrary, Halward's naturalism explored the deeper psychological motivation of his characters whilst retaining a searching objectivity uncontaminated by authorial hand-wringing or what Margaret Storm Jameson terms the 'distorting gloss of the *writer's* emotions and self-questionings'.[89] In a talk given to the Birmingham Booklovers' Society, Halward explained his position by reference to the correspondence of his mentor Chekhov:

> YOU, may weep and moan over your stories,' he said in one letter, 'You may shed as many tears as you like, but your pen must shed nothing but ink.' And again, 'If you drop a tear you will strip the subject of it's [*sic*] severity and of everything worthy of attention in it. [...] When the good writer wants to make you sad, he does so by being as matter of fact as if he were telling you that the hero was lighting a cigarette'.[90]

He continued, '[t]hat seems to me to be the secret—to write *as if* you'd been a witness and were quite unaffected by the affair, and *not as if* you were heartbroken because of what happened' (my emphasis).[91]

The modern short story tradition in which plotless stories and the adoption of 'less mechanical versions of the surprise ending or twist-in-the-tail effect' that occupied the minds of popular 'magazine freelances' exerted a powerful influence on working-class writing during this period; for, as Christopher Hilliard observes, 'it is a tradition that has largely been ignored in critical discussions of thirties writing, in part because of the attention paid to the influence of the documentary forms.'[92] The fact that the short story merited consideration beyond its function as a *divertissement* is evident from the prevailing critical discussion. In *The Modern Short Story: From 1809—1953*, H. E. Bates champions the genre in its own right, rather than as a diminutive 'doll's-house' version, sketch or trial run for its more expansive cousin the novel. In the chapter 'Lawrence and the Writers of To-day', Bates praises Halward along with other exponents of the modern [Chekhovian] form such as V. S. Pritchett, Elizabeth Bowen and Arthur Calder-Marshall, who, in his opinion, formed 'the backbone of the English short-story today'.[93] Identifying his milieu as 'bricklayers, plasterers, love in the front room, and the Saturday football match in Birmingham', Bates believed Halward had broken with the stereotyped tradition of the artificially plotted short story and imbued the modern form not only with his own individual qualities but also with 'the realism and poetry it had sadly lacked.'[94]

Bates' views were echoed by Edward J. O'Brien in his introduction to Halward's collection of short stories *Gus and Ida* (1936). Though registering the achievement of his Birmingham group companions, it was upon Halward that O'Brien lavished his most effusive praise. Commending the technical mastery, objectivity, lack of sentimentalisation and 'the most self-sacrificing elimination of incidental beauties and irrelevant perceptions', he placed the Birmingham writer on a par with Katherine Mansfield, 'the only other English author of our time who was capable of this continuous self-denial'.[95] The comic element in Halward's stories would doubtless have appealed to Margaret Storm Jameson, who believed it was essential to 'get some fun out of [writing]. Nothing is less to our taste than the inspissated gloom of naturalism. A novel by Ignazio Silone, *Fontamara,* offers itself as a model—this tragic bitter story of a village is extremely funny, and sticks faster in the memory by it'.[96] Turning to the working-class characters who populate Halward's anthology *To Tea on Sunday*, O'Brien explained that its author was uninhibited by the trepidation which, unlike their American counterparts, makes contemporary English writers reluctant to engage in any 'spontaneous social contact outside their own class'.[97]

While eschewing a directly propagandist stance or ideological critique, Henry Green and Walter Allen had presented an implicit though powerful indictment of the dominant ideology by means of their formal experimentation and innovation. Neither 'genre resistant' nor, despite a somewhat chauvinistic protectiveness regarding 'his people', overtly political, Halward's short narratives are far from ideologically benign. By virtue of their subject matter alone, they lend support to Raymond Williams' view that 'working-class texts operate as a significant and positive cultural intervention'.[98] As touched upon in the discussion of Storm Jameson's 'soundings', by providing a glimpse of the lives of individuals existing beneath the veneer of contemporary bourgeois society, and describing aspects of what was still a relatively unexplored social grouping, Halward's project supplies the needs of Lawrence Stone, who advocated a historiography constructed from narrative accounts. Indicating that imaginative writing 'is organised chronologically; is focused on a single coherent story; is *descriptive* rather than *analytical*; is concerned with people not abstract circumstances; and deals with the particular and the specific rather than the collective and statistical' (my emphasis), Stone defines the particular branch of historical analysis he terms 'prosopography' as a rationale that 'seeks to create lists of biographical notes, covering both the political elite and [importantly] "*lesser mortals*"' (my emphasis).[99] Stone's belief in the qualitative potential of imaginative writing thus parallels that of E. P. Thompson mentioned above, and, as we shall see in the following chapter, the work of historian H. L. Beales and broadcaster R. S. Lambert, who, rather depending on statistical data alone, placed a higher premium on qualitative information.

The feelings of respect, anxiety, self-defeat and disappointment that surface in Halward's stories are illustrative of the strikingly powerful counterforce of 'Class Shame' that Pamela Fox finds in both working-class writers and their narrative depictions. Conventionally received as either 'straightforward political tracts' or, more recently, as 'examples of a marginalised, radical discourse suppressed by dominant culture', Fox addresses 'another, equally important, dynamic at work: the encoding of dominant desires and gestures in narratives governed by a restrictive model of class-conscious politics and writing'.[100] Though not included in her survey, Halward's short narratives provide an opportunity to examine the 'reproduction-resistance circuit' which Fox considers 'suggest[s] ways in which shame (beyond being a liability) might function as a resource in working-class culture and literary practice' and through which she attempts to relocate working-class writers and their narratives in a cultural middle ground between individual agency and bourgeois emulation.[101] Her intervention is especially relevant to the arguments presented here, for 'working-class texts' often frustrate the 'usually well-intentioned' expectations of Marxist theorising and critical perspectives seeking 'oppositional strategies', or likewise workerist or sectarian critiques which 'categorically condemn the reproduction of dominant values and celebrate "counter hegemonic" acts'.[102] Fox argues that class shame presents as 'a particular stance of "resistance theory" operating "as a class tool and survival strategy [that] competes with more militant discourse to shape the presentation of working-class experience"'.[103] Repudiating conceptions of social and cultural production developed by intellectuals such as Althusser, Bourdieu and others, she urges readers and critics of working-class literature to follow Willis, who, while respecting their aims, questions 'the astonishingly pervasive power' these theorists attribute to the 'dominant culture' which, whether in the ideological apparatus of education or family 'fails to allow for the possibility of momentary awareness and opposition among students, children, and workers'.[104] According to Fox, such failure 'posits a hopelessly abstract, static model of social relations' that, as Willis claims, 'cannot account for specific, lived "struggle and contestation", [...] 'the field of a creative, collective self-making in the subordinate class'.[105]

Leslie Halward's various employments as toolmaker, die-sinker, bricklayer and plasterer and leisure pursuits including cinemagoing, a spell as a dance-band drummer and bouts as an amateur boxer each attests to his working-class lineage. Despite Valentine Cunningham's difficulty in assessing whether, as the son of a pork butcher, Halward might 'really' be considered working class, Walter Allen had no such qualms considering Halward:

[P]ure Brummie, speaking no other tongue than the Birmingham accent, the product of working-class Birmingham [...] At first glance he struck you as sullen, from the combination, I think, of his accent, the seemingly unhealthy urban pallor of his skin, and a broken nose he had acquired as an amateur boxer.[106]

As Edward J. O'Brien records, for a brief period during the 1930s Halward's star was in the ascendant. That this was possibly an output of the intellectual fetishisation of working-class writing which, for a short time, captured the imagination of middle-class readers and publishers eager to satisfy their appetites and is touched on below by Walter Allen, who, commenting upon Halward's two published collections of short stories, claims:

> [T]he stories of working-class life collected in *To Tea on Sunday* and *The Money's All Right* seem to me without rival in British English. For a few years in the Thirties, [Halward] was naturally and properly much admired. He was thought of, of course, as a proletarian writer, but I am sure that meant nothing to him. He was as unpolitical a man as I have ever met, as much likely, I think, to vote Conservative as Labour.[107]

Allen's comments light upon issues raised in the introduction regarding those best qualified to write about working-class experience and whether accounts of working-class life should be ideologically prescriptive. As we have seen, whilst eschewing any progressive content, Henry Green's modernist, 'outsider' depiction of the urban-industrial had excited a mixed though largely affirmative critical response. Yet, although Halward undoubtedly possessed the appropriate working-class credentials, he was in many ways just as apolitical as Green. However, the disadvantages hinted at by Walter Allen do resonate with Roy Johnson's, not wholly unjustified, observation that '[their] probable lack of aesthetic education [...] militate[ed] against [working-class writers] developing the skills necessary to transcend bourgeois aesthetic values'.[108] Undeterred, however, Halward's chauvinistic 'class-pride', as distinct from 'class-consciousness', combined with a love of Chekhov—whose works he sought, read and emulated—to motivate his implacable desire to pursue self-expression in literature. He describes his 'calling' in *Let Me Tell You*: 'The stories I liked best and tried to improve were those about my own people, the working-class. Now I was getting somewhere. I knew what I wanted to write.'[109] As Christopher Hilliard observes, Halward's aim 'to write in [his] own language about [his] own people' was little short of a vocation. Hilliard addresses the idea that working-class writers viewed themselves as 'spokesmen' or 'representatives' of their class by suggesting, in somewhat biblical terms, that 'the transforming power of a revealed truth shaped a variety of events and movements during the interwar period'. Just as those volunteering as mass observers, or participating in hunger marches brought 'incontrovertible, breathing evidence of deprivation into the heart of prosperous towns and cities, *committing the experience of the poor and unemployed to print was a gesture toward the same end* (my emphasis)'.[110] Citing Walter Allen's assertion that Halward was 'the most unpolitical man he [had] ever met', Hilliard explains:

> The spokesman role that working-class writers adopted was not shaped exclusively by the politics of poverty and unemployment, but also by an impulse to present rounded, humane pictures of "their people." To write a story that accurately portrayed working-class life was an act of self-respect and community service. It was a point where the two meanings of "representation" coincide.[111]

Prompted by his abhorrence of class 'outsiders', Halward exercised a protective, at times almost obsessive, desire to conceal 'his people' from the gaze of predatory anthropologists, mass observers, politicians and others whose accounts of working-class experience merely derived from 'casual contact and occasional eavesdropping'. In a talk given at Fircroft College, he stressed that 'the most important of the qualifications required by those who write about the working-class, [...] is that they be *members* of that class' (my emphasis).[112] He cautioned those intending to write about 'his people' against adopting a superior or condescending tone, whereupon he launched into the following broadside on the debilitating effects of education:

> Another cause of this superiority complex is education. Here of course I'm bearding a number of Lions in their den. But I'm convinced of the truth of this statement. I'm quite sure that the worst thing that could happen to a young working-class man who, possessing natural talent and a desire to write about his people but not as yet the ability to express himself—the worst thing that could happen to such a young man is that he be sent to College or to a University. Once such a person gets "education" into his system, becomes a student and has a taste of culture all is lost.[113]

Despite his robust condemnation of tertiary education, Halward was nevertheless eager to reference the encouragement he received from none other than Ivor Evans, professor of English literature at Queen Mary College, University of London.[114]

Leslie Halward: 'Belcher's Hod'

Leslie Halward's workplace narratives not only move us 'from dry statistic to way of life', but also affectively for, if we seek an immersive account of what it was actually like to experience manual work from the perspective of an individual engaged in it, then it is to Halward we must turn.[115] The remainder of this chapter is devoted to the short story 'Belcher's Hod' Leslie Halward's character study of an ageing bricklayer's labourer on one of Birmingham's myriad pre-war housing developments. Derived from its author's own experience of work on the city's construction sites during the 1930s, the story is described as 'a minor masterpiece' by Paul Lester and as 'a subtle story enshrined in the form of an anecdote' by Walter Allen, and although each considers some deeper significance maybe attached, both read the story as a 'bigger they come, harder they fall' parable. E. M. Forster praised this story's economy of means and objectivity but, more importantly, Halward's 'ability to write from within' and 'make his class come alive', yet, whilst supportive of his achievement, such considerations overlook aspects of Halward's story that relates to the more complex questions relating to working-class subjectivity encoded in Pamela Fox's *reproduction-resistance circuit* mentioned above.[116] Walter Allen's suspicion that, his brusqueness aside, Halward was possibly fearful of life outside the working class ties in with Fox's claim that a 'shame dynamic' operates as 'cultural 'static' in working-class experience. Manifest in a sense of lack or disadvantage, this dynamic affects not only the life experience of working people but also working-class authors in whose narratives it surfaces. Such 'cultural static' is manifest in the notions of reputation and shame that abound in 'Belcher's Hod', which, despite its brevity, proves particularly responsive to the implications of Fox's theory.

> Everybody in the building trade knew or had heard of Jim Belcher. Belcher was a plasterer's labourer, a great barge of a man who gloried in his own strength and boasted of the beer he could drink. He was about fifty and had been in the building trade all his life. He knew his job. He had worked with master craftsmen, gauging the stuff for them to use, cleaning each tool for them as they put it down, in the days when work was done leisurely and well. For six months now he had been working on an estate where the houses, every one alike, were thrown up overnight and the plaster slapped on the walls, he said he believed, with a shovel. (*BH*, 1)

Here, presented with a minimum of fuss, is Jim Belcher. We're told Jim constructed his own 'hod'—a 'V'-shaped, boxlike container mounted on a long wooden pole designed for the building labourer to carry bricks, mortar or plaster mix to the 'trades', the skilled workers: bricklayers, joiners and plasterers employed on the building site. As befitting his own 'barge-like' proportions, Jim's giant hod was something of talking point:

> It was an immense size. He had made it himself and had painted the outside a brilliant green. He was very proud of his hod. 'It takes a man,' he would say, 'to carry that.' He carried it, full of wet floating, with superb ease. He would let nobody else use his hod or even touch it. Every night before he knocked off he washed it and dried it with rags as carefully as if it were made of gold. (*BH*, 2)

Having sketched in Jim's credentials and those of the hod by which he is symbolised, Halward's exposition effectively ends Jim's self-assurance, powerful physique and magnificent hod having coalesced in the intense sense of pride and self-regard that constitute his workplace reputation. Coming so early in the story, this catalogue of attributes effectively sets him up for his inevitable fall. However, the following reading will argue Jim's fate is more 'problematic' than 'proverbial'.

Following an evening of excessive drinking at a local public house, Jim is carried home by a group of his workplace companions, whereupon his wife leaves him downstairs to sleep on the sofa. During the night, Jim is nauseous and vomits in the sink, though despite which, waking at five the following morning and still feeling the worse for wear, he sets off to work as usual. On arriving at the building site, he asks the foreman if he can be 'signed-off' for half-an-hour at lunchtime to 'wet his whistle'—in drinkers' parlance: 'a hair of the dog'. Following a 'medicinal' pint, he encounters Charlie Tull, an old drinking companion, and inevitably further drinks ensue. Several pints later, apropos of nothing, Jim turns to Charlie. 'My daughter', he informs his semi-inebriated interlocutor, 'is a whore'. Seemingly nonplussed, possibly on account of the quantity of alcohol consumed, Tull merely nods and sways in acknowledgement. Jim continues: 'She went to Liverpool with a bloke', Tull nods again, 'He was married', says Jim (*BH*, 4). Voicing his dissatisfactions as they step outside the pub and, presumably still aiming to elicit some response, Jim watches helplessly as his companion—his drunken condition exacerbated by the fresh air—collapses to his knees on the pavement. Swaying uncontrollably and helpless to assist, Jim looks on as two bystanders lift his drunken companion to his feet and take him home.

On reporting for work the next day, Jim is immediately ordered home by the foreman. An argument ensues, and the situation quickly escalates to a confrontation with Jim raging at the foreman and a group of attendant workers, 'Is there a man amongst you as could make me go home?' [...] 'There ain't a man amongst you as could do it, I ain't going home, I'm stopping here' (*BH*, 5). In a final act of drunken belligerence, Jim attempts to intimidate Curly, another labourer currently loading his hod: 'Why don't you get a bloody hod?' he shouts. Further antagonisms follow when, having fetched and, with some difficulty set his giant hod up in preparation, Jim proceeds to show Curly the 'right' way to do it. Reaching for a spade, Jim loses balance and glimpses his hod as it falls to the ground, its shaft breaking off beneath the box. 'It was broken! *His hod was broken!* It could easily be repaired, but he could not think of that' (*BH*, 8). Jim is momentarily transfixed. 'What the hell's the matter with you man?' asks Curly, 'I broke me hod', said Jim. Curly sympathises, but Jim demands Curly helps retrieve his hod. 'What for' asks Curly? 'Give it to me!' demanded Jim. In what seemed a parody of funereal solemnity, Curly proceeded to place the damaged hod in Jim's outstretched arms tucking the shaft under his right arm. On returning home defeated, Jim enters the parlour with tears running down his cheeks, 'Look Mother, I broke me hod' (*BH*, 9). At which point, the story ends.

Having valorised work to the extent that he has come to define himself through it, Halward's Jim Belcher might initially seem to have enlisted in the ranks of Roy Johnson's 'dependable proletarian[s]'.[117] The term appears amongst Johnson's list of subsidiary values attaching to such fictional embodiments of the 'puritan work-ethic' as Jim Belcher: an honest day's work; the employee who 'refuses to cheat his employer by having time off'; 'support of monogamy and the nuclear family'; 'respect for private property and middle-class legality', all of which reflect a working-class subjectivity that depicts workers as 'perfect pawns of [the] employing class'.[118] In adopting this stance, Johnson follows the 'reproduction' critique, which according to Pamela Fox was that adopted by those who perceive working-class literary endeavour as the naive emulation of traditional bourgeois forms and, by so doing, obliquely giving support to bourgeois morality. While this reading takes the view that Halward's short stories present as anything but an endorsement of the dominant ideology, there are elements of Johnson's critique that need to be addressed. As Ross McKibbin suggests:

> [M]any working men were individualist by occupation or temperament, and such individualism was not, except in one or two cases, overridden by an active sense of community. This cultural and vocational diversity was typified and advanced by the unions. Craft-pride, real and legitimate if exaggerated, was deeply divisive and more than one local Labour Party foundered on disputes between 'skilled' and 'unskilled' unions.' The status consciousness which accompanied class-pride undermined working-class *esprit de corps* as much as it did that of any other class.[119]

From a Marxist perspective, in serving as an embodiment of the puritan work ethic replete with the associated moralities of decency and pride, the behaviour of Halward's protagonist will doubtless be construed as 'assimilationist'. However, for Pamela Fox these factors demonstrate conversely a form of 'resistance' by showing the need felt by members of the working class to 'win back [the] momentary sense of autonomy and self-respect' she believed was constitutive of the essential 'difference' in the narratives of working-class writers.[120] Given his experience on the building sites of interwar Birmingham, it is highly probable that Halward had encountered a real-life Jim Belcher, whose 'hardman' persona interested him and inspired this characterisation. In *Masculinities*, Raewyn. W. Connell cites the work of Mike Donaldson, whose researches into manual work identify strength, insensitivity and toughness as more 'reflect[ive] of economic realit[ies]' than machismo pure and simple.[121] Donaldson claims:

> [W]orking-men's bodily capacities *are* their economic asset, are what they put on the labour market. But this asset changes. Industrial labour under the regime of profit uses up the workers' bodies, through fatigue, injury and mechanical wear and tear. The decline of strength, threatening loss of income or the job itself, can be offset by the growth of skill—up to a point. It is at that point, unless he is very lucky, that his labouring days are over.[122]

The masculine ethos of the building site was not, and perhaps still isn't, an environment known for delicacy of expression, or one kindly disposed to emotional candour.[123] Reputations have to be earned and maintained, toughness, brawn and hard-graft being the requisite attributes. Opportunities for the discussion of one's domestic disappointments or the finer shadings of everyday anxiety are few, if non-existent, the nearest thing to counselling or psychotherapy, a 'man-to-man' in the local pub which—in offering a neutral space between private and public spheres—provides a suitable setting in which to unburden one's anxieties. In line with Chekhov's' dictum, 'I want to know how your characters feel not how you feel', Halward's narrator effectively withdraws from the narrative leaving the incensed and disillusioned Jim Belcher to vent his dissatisfactions.[124] Given the vitriol of his outburst, one is left in no doubt that his daughter's elopement with a married man drew heavily on Jim's emotional economy. Yet to describe her as a whore is to exaggerate grossly her misdemeanour. Rather than choosing a more delicate form of expression, Jim's bluff and bluster ought instead be construed as a deliberate subterfuge, a means of concealing his shame while simultaneously forestalling the censure and opprobrium he anticipated from the wider working-class community.

Communicated in plain, workmanlike prose, eschewing figurative language while shaped in a syntax rarely stepping beyond the simple sentence, and, rather than 'abandoning' the 'crude vigour' of working-class speech fearing it might not be artistically 'correct,' Halward unashamedly reinstates it.[125] His stories display a remarkable ear for the cadence of his fellow Birmingham citizens and facilitate the reader's visualisation of them as they engage in the quotidian struggle. Citing Basil Bernstein's work on the production of socio-linguistic codes, Pamela Fox explains that the '*public* language' used by working-class speakers is 'primarily a means of making *social* not *individual* qualifications'.[126] Contrasting this restricted code with the access of middle-class speakers to 'a formal language rich in personal, individual qualifications and characterized by complex, causal connections', Fox considers working-class language is 'tough' language, incapable of expressing intimate feelings. Its very structure prohibits the articulation of 'experiences of difference'.[127] Less a display of outrage, Jim's outburst might therefore be better read as a cry for help, signifying simultaneously a sense of deep-felt shame and personal crisis. In his clumsy attempt to provoke a discussion with his drinking companion, Jim had risked 'self-exposure'. Citing the work of cultural studies pioneer Helen Merrell Lynd, Fox explains how, in this respect, shame may serve an emancipatory function:

> The dual experiences of exposure and vulnerability, which are part and parcel of the shame dynamic, not only wound; they aid in the production of self-knowledge, community and social critique. After suffering involuntary exposure, one can *choose* to expose that exposure, as it were to another: "If … one can sufficiently risk uncovering oneself and sufficiently trust another person, to seek means of communicating shame, the risking of exposure can be in itself an experience of release, expansion, self-revelation, a coming forward of belief in oneself". Self-awareness and confidence become possible because in the process of revealing the shame of being shamed, often one is exposing oppressive societal norms and values as well.[128]

Whether Jim Belcher was able to access the emancipatory consolation of his self-exposure is unknown; nonetheless, coming to terms with his daughter's elopement was clearly difficult, her disappearance with a married man further evidence of a world out of step with his own moral precepts. For contemporary readers of Halward's story, Jim Belcher's shame is both illustrative and revealing of the 'oppressive societal norms and values' prevalent during the pre-war decade. The application of Pamela Fox's 'shame dynamic' to Halward's story prompts a consideration of how bourgeois notions of morality were emulated by the working-class community where, according to Fox, '[t]he need to represent one's self and family as decent, self-sufficient members of the community derived as much from other working-class spectators as from condescending middle-class investigators'.[129] The tension between contemporary moral values and Jim's protective instinct towards his daughter present as the ideological subtext to Halward's story, which, rather than offering the 'readerly' assurance of the traditional realist text, renders it closer to the kind of 'open' text described by Fredric Jameson whose hermeneutic necessitates:

> [T]he rewriting of the literary text in such a way that the latter may itself be seen as the rewriting or restructuration of a prior historical or ideological *subtext*, it being always understood that that "subtext" is not immediately present as such, not some common-sense external reality, nor even the conventional narratives of history manuals, but rather must itself always be (re) constructed after the fact.[130]

In this respect, Halward's story departs from traditional realist or naturalist narratives which offer a hierarchical discourse culminating in affirmative closure by moving closer to Catherine Belsey's 'interrogative text' where 'points of view' are brought 'into unresolved collision or contradiction' and where the reader is called upon to supply or venture meaning.[131]

In terms of presentation, the episode in which Jim inveighs against his daughter's 'shameful' behaviour complies with Edgar Allan Poe's requirement that the short story should contain 'no word written of which the tendency, direct or indirect, is not to the one of pre-established design'. Occurring both typographically and emotionally at the heart of Halward's story, Jim's somewhat elliptical reference to his daughter's behaviour suggests an inner conflict oscillating between profound shame and protective anxiety. It was perhaps inevitable that Jim's excessive self-regard would encounter its nemesis in the form of his public humiliation and exposure on the building site. True to Poe's dicta, Halward had sown the seeds of Jim's discontent in the opening paragraph of his story. Jim's lifetime in the building trade and his vicarious pride at having worked with master-craftsmen 'in the days when work was done leisurely and well' are contrasted with the shoddy workmanship on the site at which he is currently employed, where 'the houses, every one alike, were thrown up overnight and the plaster slapped on the walls with a shovel' (*BH*, 1). While the broken hod symbolises Jim's physical fatigue, it also stands in for the more profound spiritual crisis set in motion by the elopement of his daughter, the last straw in the sequence of assaults on his self-esteem. Less epiphany than weary resignation, Jim's workplace 'breakdown' represents his realisation that the puritan work ethic embodied in his notion of the 'grafter' is no longer a valued attribute. Pamela Fox explains how an individual's confrontation with contemporary behaviours:

> [F]inally hinges upon the clashing of different social and moral "values" in specific locations at specific moments, highlighting the trauma experienced by members of communities marginal to dominant culture: those most likely to feel shame are those made to feel "inappropriate" by dominant cultural norms.[132]

However, Jim's workplace perturbations are nothing compared to his private misgivings. The close-knit domestic unit he and his wife struggled to maintain is now the subject of public opprobrium. The working-class community was ill-disposed towards the female party in extramarital affairs, especially involvements where the absconding, and generally breadwinning, male spouse might lead to the family's impoverishment. Gossip and 'local talk', as Pamela Fox indicates, 'took on a policing function' for 'reputation was a prime concern in working-class culture, across regions and borders, and proved burdensome, as well as empowering'.[133] Jim's moral code is unheeded by a daughter whose behaviour represents the rejection of both her father's and her community's value system underlining Raymond Williams' observation that the social character of an epoch may be revealed in the conflict between 'generations who never quite talk the same language'.[134] In this respect, Jim's daughter joins other heroines of working-class fiction such as Henry Green's Lily Gates, Walter Greenwood's Helen Hawkins, Brierley's Jane Cook and Leslie Halward's own, chocolate-factory, production-line worker Ida, all of whom, as Pamela Fox points out, attempt to 'mark out an individual identity' [...] '[in order to] escape] the bleakness of working-class experience [and] class subjectivity associated largely with oppression and hemmed in by numbing factory work and/or overcrowded, often violent households'.[135] Rather than seeking assimilation, Jim's daughter's quest for distinctness is motivated less from a desire to emulate bourgeois or dominant culture than the search for a personal identity. According to Fox, this search 'both competes with and complements their mission of class solidarity [and] creates a model of subjectivity that ultimately falls into neither bourgeois nor Marxist categories.'[136] Likewise her father Jim, who, in seeking individual agency—rather than merely functioning as the unquestioning 'good subject' of bourgeois interpellation—moves beyond the figure of 'pliant and dependable proletarian', to align with such literary counterparts as Tressell's Frank Owen or Brierley's Jack Cook, who each offers:

> [P]articularly striking examples of a hybrid consciousness. Through their negotiations of public and private arenas, they on one level certainly reveal their affiliations with the introspective sealed off psyches of avant garde literature. Yet their privileged difference from other working-class figures never goes all the way; it is mediated or balanced by their shared material class position and, finally, their class allegiance. Shame dictates their desire to escape the working-class 'mass,' but they know they cannot. And, more importantly, should not. [...] At times the narratives may fall short in making this prized, quasi-individualist identity work toward radical ends [...] But that's ultimately not the point. In the end, the result of such ideological and formal tensions is an amalgam representing nothing less than a new class subject and cultural form.[137]

This reading has shown the 'resistance dynamic' operating not only across but also within class boundaries. Seeking to understand resistance as 'a refusal of dominated, along with dominant culture', Fox stresses the importance of attending to 'the variety of ways in which members of marginal or subordinate groups redefine for themselves what is at stake as they mediate cultural and economic forces'.[138] Halward's characterisations not only resist the deterministic conception of naturalism, whereby members of the lower-orders simply flounder as passive subjects, but also master narratives which consider working-class texts as naïve reproductions of the dominant ideology; they gesture instead towards agency by suggesting how working-class individuals are consciously active in their own self-fashioning. J. McAleer's assertion that Henry Green's *Living* 'is a book about how people really live: their hopes, but also their compromises and defeats', is also applicable to Halward's narratives, where representations of class struggle are seemingly apolitical, taking place entirely within the working-class community.[139] As Walter Allen commented:

> For two or three years he was greatly admired. Then there was the war, and the magazines that had published him disappeared. After the war, his kind of writing was no longer fashionable. He seems to have been powerless to change it. His was a trapped talent. For all that, his achievement within that talent was unrivalled in England at that time.[140]

The works discussed in this chapter have sought to situate contemporary working-class writing in the liminal space between propagandist rhetoric on the one hand and formal experimentation on the other. As I have shown, Walter Allen and Leslie Halward each reconfigured traditional narrative forms to serve their own ends. Following the example of Henry Green's *Living*, Allen appropriated the techniques of cross-cutting and montage specific to a documentary film 'not only to interpret creatively and in social terms the life of the people as it exists in reality' but also to caution his readers against the superficiality of contemporary experience as depicted in the politically emasculating, soporific confections of the Hollywood movie industry and, by extension, the machinations of the bourgeois order it aimed to mystify and obscure.[141] Leslie Halward's accounts of workplace experience, rather than urging political consciousness, developed the scientific objectivity of naturalism to explore his protagonist's inner thoughts and emotions. Despite Croft's claim that he 'rarely describe[ed] psychology', Halward's portrait of Jim Belcher provides a perceptive and sympathetic account of the anguished fragile soul that lay beneath the tough exterior of his ageing workman.

The discussion of work, its centrality and fundamental importance in people's lives continues in the following chapter where I examine its inverse, namely unemployment, the spectre of which haunted 1930s Britain. In the wake of the global depression that gripped the West following the Wall St Crash of 1929, the critical perspectives applied to working-class writing intensified. As Ramon Lopez Ortega remarks, unemployment lurked behind all the recurrent images—poverty, the fruitless search for work, life on the dole, the Means Test, the hunger marches, the strikes.[142] Questions as to whether working-class texts ought to function as a weapon in the class struggle or whether they were to be considered on their literary merits alone were frequently iterated during this period. The critical criteria used to frame these questions had been shaped by Comintern policy, the most significant moment of which being the change from the third 'class against class' period begun in 1928, to the softening of approach registered by the adoption of Popular Front policies in 1934. As Kenneth Ledbetter indicates, this change had considerable implications during the early years of the decade where '*only* novels concerned with the proletariat in social relationships (*i.e.*, class conflict) in which the revolutionary movement was portrayed as larger than life and where the quickening class-consciousness of the worker was [often] *anticipated* rather than honestly described could expect sympathetic treatment in leftist journals (my emphasis)'.[143] The following chapter will trace the reception and fortunes of the Birmingham group's narratives as they sought to negotiate the turbulence of this critical climate.

Notes

1. W. H. Auden, 'A Communist to Others' August 1932. *The English Auden,* Edward Mendelson ed, *The English Auden,* p. 120.
2. Adrian Caesar, *Dividing Lines: Poetry, Class and Ideology in the 1930s* (Manchester: Manchester University Press, 1991), p. 50. Bernard Bergonzi remarks that 'For a long time the Auden of the thirties has been conventionally regarded as a political, committed poet writing with an end in view'. However, perhaps indicative of a further change in Auden's adherence to the party line, 'A Communist to Others' was later dropped from *Collected Shorter Poems.* Bernard Bergonzi, *Reading the Thirties: Texts and Contexts* (London: The Macmillan Press, 1978), pp. 137–8.
3. Thomas Carlyle, *Past and Present,* Chapter XI, Labour.
4. Ryle, Martin, and Kate Soper, *To Relish the Sublime: Culture and Self-realisation in Postmodern Times* (London: Verso, 2002), p. 186.
5. Ibid.
6. H. Gustav Klaus, *Tramps Workmates and Revolutionaries: Working-Class Stories of the 1920's* (London: Journeyman Press, 1993), p. 5.
7. Gustav Klaus, H. and Stephen Knight, *British Industrial Fictions* (Cardiff: University of Wales Press, 2000), p. 3.
8. Chris Baldick, *The Modern Movement,* p. 185.
9. H. Gustav Klaus, *The Socialist Novel in Britain,* p. 3.
10. Adrian Caesar, *Dividing Lines,* pp. 10, 11.
11. Ibid, p. 12.
12. Ibid.
13. Chris Cook, 'The Work Ethic in the 1930s,' *History Today,* 33. 7. (1983) <https://www.historytoday.com> [accessed 14 July 2018], Unpaginated (pull out article).
14. Auden, 'Letter to Lord Byron' Stanza II, Part 5, p. 197.
15. Ibid.
16. Adrian Caesar, *Dividing Lines,* p. 12.
17. Ibid. Caesar cites John Stevenson's essay 'Myth and Reality: Britain in the Nineteen-Thirties' *Crisis and Controversy,* ed. A Sked and C. Cook (London, 1976), pp. 90–110. Stevenson's figures are challenged by Alan Howkins and John Saville in *The Nineteen Thirties: A Revisionist History,* although acknowledging the difficulty of establishing an accurate figure, they remark upon the fluctuations and influence of seasonal work in the building trade or the effect of temporary lay-offs in the motor trade owing to seasonal variations in demand. *The Socialist Register* 1979, pp. 89–100. Downloaded from the *Socialist Register Website.* Transcribed and marked up by Eidie O'Callaghan for the Marxist Internet Archive.

18. P. D. Anthony, *The Ideology of Work* (London: Tavistock Publications Limited, 1977), p. 288.
19. E. P. Thompson, *The Making of the English Working Class* (London: Pelican, 1963), p. 230.
20. Raymond Williams 'The Welsh Industrial Novel' in Williams (ed.), *Culture and Materialism: Selected Essays*, (London: Verso), pp. 213–229, cited in Phil O'Brien, chapter 'The Deindustrial Novel: Twenty–First–Century British Fiction and the Working-Class' in, Clarke, Ben and Nick Hubble *Working-Class Writing: Theory and Practice* (Switzerland: Palgrave Macmillan, 2018), pp. 229, 230.
21. Raymond Williams, *Politics and Letters*, p. 159.
22. Chris Baldick, *The Modern Movement*, p. 184.
23. Ibid. Chris Baldick mentions the 'Civic' novels of Winifred Holtby and Lettuce Cooper as presenting 'a panoramic view of contemporary society as attempted in certain regional novels of the thirties', describing theirs as 'civic fictions' and suggesting that they extend the kind of civic realism originally found in George Eliot's *Middlemarch*. Here Walter Allen's *Blind Man's Ditch* and Hampson's *Saturday Night at the Greyhound* might usefully be considered in similar terms.
24. H. Gustav Klaus, *The Socialist Novel in Britain*, p. 3.
25. Roy Johnson, 'The Proletarian Novel', *Literature and History*, 84-95. p. 93.
26. Carole Snee, 'Walter Brierley: A Test Case', in *Red Letters: Communist Party Literature Journal*, 3. (Autumn 1976), 11-13. p. 11.
27. Notably Christopher Isherwood, Walter Allen and Harold Heslop, who (mistakenly) believed Green to be of 'proletarian stock' and that, along with James Hanley, Green was among a 'new school of writers' who offered some potential to reinvigorate the working-class novel. Similar claims have been voiced by David Lodge and Jeremy Treglown.
28. H. Gustav Klaus, 'Socialist Fiction of the 1930s' in John Lucas, *The 1930s: A Challenge to Orthodoxy* (London: Harvester Press Ltd, 1978), p. 30.
29. Chris Baldick, *The Modern Movement*, p. 185.
30. Ibid.
31. Walter Allen, 'An Artist of the Thirties' in John Lehmann ed, *Folios of New Writing*, Spring (London: Hogarth Press, 1941), p. 153.
32. Harold Heslop had also been of a similar view, believing the author belonged to 'a new school of writers including James Hanley'. Valentine Cunningham, *British Writers*, p. 322.
33. Ibid.
34. Allen's re-evaluation parallels Terry Eagleton's assertion that literary priorities are often in a state of flux 'a work may be realist in June and anti-

realist in December'. Walter Allen, 'Thirties Fiction: A View from the Seventies', *Twentieth Century Literature,* 20 (1974), p. 246.

35. Walter Allen, in John Lehmann, Ed, *Folios of New Writing*, Spring 1941, p. 153.
36. Walter Allen, *Tradition and Dream,* p. 215.
37. Ibid, p .216.
38. Raymond Williams 'The Welsh Industrial Novel' in Williams (ed.). *Culture and Materialism: Selected Essays*, (London, Verso). pp. 213-229. Cited in Phil O'Brien, 'The Deindustrial Novel: Twenty-First-Century British Fiction and The Working-Class', in Clarke, Ben and Nick Hubble, eds, *Working-Class Writing*, p. 229.
39. Walter Allen, *Tradition and Dream,* p. 216.
40. Valentine Cunningham. *British Writers*, p. 320. Ramon Lopez Ortega, 'The Language of the Working-class Novel in the 1930s'. In H. Gustav Klaus, *The Socialist Novel,* 122-144. p. 124.
41. Ibid.
42. H. Gustav Klaus, 'Socialist Fiction of the 1930s', in John Lucas, *The 1930s: A Challenge to Orthodoxy,* pp.13-41.p. 31.
43. Ibid.
44. Marius Hentea, 'Fictions of Class and Community in Henry Green's "Living"', *Studies in the Novel,* 42 (2010), p. 326. In smaller industrial units such as the Green's foundry, more familial/co-operative industrial relationships may have obtained. However, industrial unrest was not uncommon in Birmingham. Jessie Eden led women press workers to down tools at Birmingham's automobile electronics manufacturer Joseph Lucas in 1926 and in 1931 where protests against 'Speed Up' led 10,000 employees to walk out in a single week.
45. H. Gustav Klaus, *The Socialist Novel In Britain,* p. 1. Klaus's position follows Walter Benjamin's theory here, although Benjamin also insisted upon the necessity of a work's Literary Correctness.
46. Walter Benjamin, The Author as Producer', *Selected Writings, Volume 2.* Editors: Jennings, Michael W., Howard Eiland, Gary Smith (Cambridge, Massachusetts: The Belknap Press HUP, 2005 p. 777.
47. Andrzej Gasiorek, *Post-War British Fiction: Realism and After* (London: Edward Arnold, 1995), pp. 3, 5.
48. MacKay and Stonebridge, *British Fiction after Modernism,* p. 3.
49. The Intermodernist approach, as exemplified in the writing of John Fordham et al. encourages the recovery of working-class texts and a more dialectical, as opposed to sectarian, critique.
50. Carol A. Wipf-Miller, 'Fictions of "Going Over": Henry Green and the New Realism', *Twentieth Century Literature,* 44.2. 135-154. p. 136.
51. Ibid, p. 137.

52. Terry Southern, Interview with Henry Green published in 'The Paris Review', 1958. In, *Surviving: The Uncollected Writings of Henry Green* (New York: Penguin Books, 1992), p. 247.
53. J. McAleer, *Popular Reading and Publishing in Britain, 1914—1950* (Oxford: Clarendon Press, 1992). Cited in Jeremy Treglown, *Romancing: The Life and Work of Henry Green* (London: Faber and Faber, 2000), p. 92.
54. Andrzej Gasiorek, *Post-War British Fiction,* p. 35.
55. BBC Broadcast published in 'The Listener', November 1950. In Henry Green, *Surviving,* p. 142.
56. Henry Green, *Loving, Living and Party Going* (London: Viking, 2005), p. 278. A similar celebration of universal verities is evident when the Welshman Arthur Jones provides an impromptu song recital following the birth of his son. p. 265.
57. H. Gustav Klaus, *The Socialist Novel in Britain,* p. 1.
58. Jeremy Treglown, *Romancing,* p. 92.
59. Raymond Williams, *Culture and Society 1780-1950* (Harmondsworth: Penguin Books, 1982), p. 205.
60. Ibid, p. 72.
61. Valentine Cunningham, *British Writers,* p. 332.
62. Lara Feigel, *Literature, Cinema and Politics 1930-1945* (Edinburgh: Edinburgh University Press, 2010), p. 5.
63. Ibid.
64. Stephen Spender, The Left-Wing Orthodoxy', *New Verse,* 31-32 (Autumn 1938) cited in Williams and Matthews, Eds, *Rewriting the Thirties,* p. 79.
65. Jeremy Treglown, *Romancing,* p. 68.
66. Carol A. Wipf-Miller, 'Fictions of "Going over"', p. 145.
67. Ibid, p. 122.
68. Ibid.
69. J. M. Coetzee, 'The Man Who Went Shopping For Truth' *The Guardian* 20 January 2001. Review of Walter Benjamin, *The Arcades Project,* translated from the German and French by Howard Eiland and Kevin Mclaughlin. (Belknap Press/Harvard University Press, 2002).
70. Matthew McManus, *What is Post-Modern Conservatism? Essays On Our Hugely Tremendous Times,* Chapter 'Benjamin, Aesthetics and the Political Practices of the Alt Right', Matt McManus and Erik Tate', (Hampshire: Zero Books, 2020), p. 72.
71. Raymond Williams, *The Long Revolution* (London: The Hogarth Press, 1992), p. 48.
72. Walter Allen Interview with Andy Croft 5 April 1982. Cited in Andy Croft, *Red Letter Days,* p. 256.
73. Ibid.
74. Lara Feigel, *Literature, Cinema and Politics,* p. 136.

75. Ibid.
76. Ralph Bond 'Cinema in the Thirties' in Jon Clark and others *Culture and Crisis in Britain in the 30s* (London: Lawrence and Wishart Ltd, 1979), p. 245.
77. George Orwell, *The Road To Wigan Pier*, p. 79; Review of the *Lady in Question*. (1940) In *The Collected Works of George Orwell*. Vol. 12. p. 291. Cited in Lara Feigel, *Literature, Cinema and Politics*, p. 117.
78. Juliet Gardiner, *The Thirties: An Intimate History* (London: Harper Press, 2011), p. 652.
79. Adorno to Benjamin in Fredric Jameson Ed, *Aesthetics and Politics* (London: Verso, 1977), p. 123.
80. Steve Ellis, *British Writers and the Approach of World War II* (Cambridge: Cambridge University Press, 2015), p. 1.
81. W. B. Yeats, 'A Dialogue of Self and Soul', *W. B. Yeats: The Poems*, Ed, Daniel Albright (London: J. M. Dent & Sons Ltd, 1992), p. 284.
82. Allen's 'St. James' is based upon King Edward's Grammar School for Boys in Aston, Birmingham, where Allen was a pupil, and which, as he told David Lodge, 'by virtue of its stained-glass windows and a curriculum including Latin, aspired to public school status'. Independent Television documentary 'As I was walking Down Bristol Street'. Central Television. Production number 1250/82, (1983).
83. John Hampson, 'Movements in the Underground', John Lehmann Editor: *The Penguin New Writing*, No 28, July 1946, (Harmondsworth: Penguin Books Limited, 1946), p. 138.
84. Pamela Fox, *Class Fictions: Shame and Resistance in the British Working-Class Novel 1890-1945* (Durham: North Carolina: Duke University Press, 1994).
85. T. A. Jackson autobiography *Solo Trumpet: Some Memories of Socialist Agitation and Propaganda*. (1953) pp. 21, 22. In Pamela Fox, *Class Fictions*, p. 35.
86. Lara Feigel. *Literature, Cinema and Politics, 1930—1945*, p. 136.
87. Walter Allen, *As I Walked Down*, pp. 113, 114.
88. Walter Allen, *The English Novel: A Short Critical History* (London: J. M. Dent & Sons Ltd), 1969.
89. Postgate, Raymond and Margaret Storm Jameson, eds, Storm Jameson 'Writing in Revolt; Theory and Examples', *Fact*, Number 4 London, (1937), 9-18. p. 13.
90. The Papers of Leslie Halward. 'A Talk to Birmingham Booklovers' Society', 24 September 1937. Birmingham Reference Library. MS 1293/106.
91. Ibid.
92. Christopher Hilliard, *To Exercise Our Talents*, p. 154.

93. H.E. Bates, *The Modern Short Story: From 1809-1953* (London: Robert Hale, 1941), p. 203.
94. Ibid, p. 206.
95. Ibid.
96. Ibid, p. 16.
97. Edward O'Brien, Introduction, pp. ix, x. Leslie Halward, *To Tea on Sunday.*
98. Raymond Williams, 'Working-class, Proletarian, Socialist: Problems in Some Welsh Novels'. In H. Gustav Klaus, *The Socialist Novel in Britain,* 110-121. p. 111.
99. Dion Smythe, *The Oxford Handbook of Byzantine Studies* (Oxford: Clarendon Press, 2008), p. 176.
100. Pamela Fox, *Class Fictions,* p. 2.
101. Ibid, p. 3.
102. Ibid.
103. Ibid, p. 2.
104. Ibid, p. 4. Paul Willis was a member of the Centre for Contemporary Cultural Studies Birmingham University between 1972 and 1981.
105. Ibid.
106. Walter Allen, *As I Walked Down*, p. 69. ; Valentine Cunningham asked whether, as the son of a Pork Butcher, Leslie Halward was 'really' working Class. Cunningham, *British Writers of the Thirties,* p. 306.
107. Walter Allen, *As I Walked*, p. 69.
108. Roy Johnson, 'The Proletarian Novel', *Literature and History,* 2. (Oct 1975), 84-95. p. 93.
109. Leslie Halward, *Let Me Tell You,* p. 164.
110. Christopher Hilliard, *To Exercise Our Talents*, p. 118.
111. Ibid.
112. Leslie Halward. 'Writing About the Working-Class.' Halward Papers. Birmingham Reference Library MS 1293/106/28, pp. 6, 8.
113. Ibid.
114. Ibid.
115. E. P. Thompson, *The Making of the English Working Class*, p. 20.
116. Paul Lester, *The Road to Excelsior Lodge: The Writings of Leslie Halward* (Birmingham: Protean Publications, 1988), p. 9; Walter Allen, *The Short-Story in English,* p. 276.
117. Roy Johnson, 'The Proletarian Novel', p. 88.
118. Ibid.
119. Ross McKibbin, *The Ideologies of Class*, p. 37.
120. Pamela Fox, *Class Fictions,* p. 203.
121. Mike Donaldson, cited in R. Connell, *Masculinities*, 2nd edn, (Berkeley: University of California Press, 2005), pp. 55, 83.

122. Ibid.
123. A recent *Guardian* article (17 March 2017) revealed construction workers amongst those at greatest risk of committing suicide in the National workforce. 'Forward For Life', an organisation which provides suicide prevention training, attributed much of the problem to the simple fact that 'Blokes don't talk'.
124. Leslie Halward, 'Introduction to Literature.' *The London Mercury,* 1938, p. 518.
125. Roy Johnson, 'The Proletarian Novel', p. 92.
126. Basil Bernstein, 'Class, Codes and Control'. Vol 1, *Theoretical Studies Towards a Sociology of Language*. (London: Routledge, 1971). Cited in Pamela Fox, *Class Fictions,* p. 105.
127. Ibid.
128. Ibid. p. 16.
129. Pamela Fox, *Class Fictions,* p. 98.
130. Fredric Jameson, *The Political Unconscious: Narrative as a Socially Symbolic Act* (Routledge: London, 1981), p. 28.
131. Catherine Belsey, *Critical Practice* (London: Routledge, 1980), p. 92.
132. Pamela Fox, *Class Fictions,* p. 13.
133. Ibid, pp. 98, 97.
134. Raymond Williams, *The Long Revolution,* p. 48.
135. Pamela Fox, *Class Fictions,* p.185.
136. Ibid, p. 203.
137. Ibid, p. 204.
138. Ibid, p. 3.
139. J. McAleer, *Popular Reading and Publishing in Britain,* in Jeremy Treglown, *Romancing,* p. 92.
140. Walter Allen, *The Short Story in English,* p. 280.
141. Laura Marcus, Paul Rotha's gloss on Grierson's definition that documentary was the 'Creative Treatment of Actuality'. In Laura Marcus '"The Creative Treatment of Actuality": John Grierson, Documentary Cinema and "Fact" in the 1930s', in Kristen Bluemel, *Intermodernism,* 189-207. p. 190.
142. Ramon Lopez Ortega, 'The Language of the Working-Class Novel of the 1930s'. In H. Gustav Klaus, *The Socialist Novel,* p. 122.
143. Kenneth Ledbetter, 'Henry Roth's Call It Sleep: The Revival of the Proletarian Novel', *Twentieth Century Literature; A Scholarly and Critical Journal,* 12 (1966). 123-130. p. 123.

CHAPTER 3

Feeling the Pinch: Unemployment

This chapter addresses the Birmingham group's response to the sociopolitical issue which came to define the 1930s: unemployment. As remarked in the introductory chapter, the Birmingham group writers have incurred a measure of guilt by association due largely to contemporary and later critical evaluations which perceived working-class writing as either enslaved to the conventions of naturalism or of credulously emulating a realist mode whose formal conventions it was unable to transcend. The consequences of this were manifest in an overdetermined documentary content or an aesthetically impoverished style where artistic skill was considered subordinate to political expression. This chapter repudiates such somewhat timeworn assessments by showing that, in their adoption of a variety of formal devices, Birmingham group writing presents less as constrained *by* or merely reproducing the traditional realist mode, but rather the reconfiguration *of* it. The narratives of the Birmingham writers therefore challenge the assertion that the formal element in working-class writing is overwhelmed by the stridency of its political message. This chapter will demonstrate how, rather than forcibly expressing an authorial viewpoint, the politically progressive element in their work arises unobtrusively from the dramatisation and description of incidents and situations within them, these in turn being presented in a manner more nuanced than clamant and often as a direct result of the formal devices employed.

R. Harriott, *The Birmingham Group*,
https://doi.org/10.1007/978-3-031-14383-0_3

Emerging as a result of the failure and dissolution of Ramsay McDonald's Labour administration, the UK's National Government of 1931 was a hung parliament. Embattled by the pressures of global depression, and lacking an alternative source of revenue, McDonald sought to reduce the treasury's outgoings by a reduction in the benefit payable to unemployed workers. The introduction of what later became known as 'The Means Test', appeared, especially to supporters of the party of labour, as the 'last straw' in a gathering and collective sense of dissatisfaction; viewed as intrusive, intimidating and unwelcome, it rapidly became the most hated government institution between the wars.[1] Though the situation in Britain was dire, Walter Allen considered 'the twenties boom had soared to far greater heights in the United States [...] the slump was therefore the greater, and so was the sense of shock, outrage and betrayal'.[2] That contemporary literature should engage directly with the events now confronting so many Americans was stated in Joseph Freeman's introduction to *Proletarian Literature in the United States*:

> Social themes today correspond to the general experience of men, acutely conscious of the violent and basic transformations through which they are living, which they are helping to bring about. It does not require much imagination to see why workers and intellectuals sympathetic to the working class—and themselves victims of the socio-economic crisis—should be more interested in unemployment, strikes, the fight against war and fascism, revolution and counter-revolution than in nightingales, the stream of middle-class consciousness, or love in Greenwich Village.[3]

As its dust jacket announces, the stories within the covers of *Proletarian Literature in The United States* were concerned 'to recognize the intimate ties between art and the social milieu from which it springs'. While giving the solipsistic focus of literary modernism short shrift, Freeman cautioned that, although the promotion of a proletarian ideology was important, this was not to be approached by heeding the strictures of a prescriptive 'party line' or by taking the form of a 'thesis' as propounded under the strictures of social-realism. He believed that 'the true artist *should focus instead upon communicating the experience from which that thesis had arisen*' (my emphasis).[4] Thus, despite the more radical tone of America's literary response, Freeman, as did James T. Farrell, championed the primacy of imaginative prose writing in conveying to a wider readership the lived-experience of those affected by the crisis.

An example of litotes, the expression 'feeling the pinch', used in this chapter's subheading, offers itself as a textbook example of understatement, its usage deriving from the 1880s; it aimed to ironise and distance members of the working class from the stigma attaching to their poverty. Again, as mentioned in the introduction, images from this period still haunt the collective memory whether in Dorothea Lange's photographs of depression-hit America or of British newsreel footage showing cloth-capped Jarrow Crusaders marching south to publicise their immiseration.[5] In 1931, BBC provided a series of broadcast talks on the subject of unemployment with speakers including Seebohm Rowntree, Herbert Morrison and John Maynard Keynes, with the Conservative prime minister Stanley Baldwin summing up. This congregation of notables registered the gravity of the situation and marked the beginning of a reversal in laissez-faire attitudes constructed on the 'assumption' that the collapse of prosperity might prove only a 'temporary continuance': might simply 'go away'.[6] As Juliet Gardiner indicates, further talks followed, as William Beveridge—whose interest in a system of national insurance would later provide the blueprint for the Welfare State—set out to 'diagnose the disease of unemployment', discovering that 'contrary to the myths of social-malingering, or the inactivity of that residual section of the population who would always be unemployable for reasons of physical or moral deficiency, as perpetuated in the popular press', its causes were structural in origin.[7] Gardiner indicates that Beveridge regretted he had not made his talks more 'human'; rather than assailing his radio listeners with abstract notions and yards of statistics, he reflected he should have talked more about the social consequences, how *actual people* were affected, for he had begun to appreciate (my emphasis):

> There is not a special class or kind of people who constitute the unemployed. They come from almost every calling and have as great a variety of interests and capacities as any other member of the community. They are ordinary decent people like ourselves to whom an extraordinary misfortune has happened.[8]

A Qualitative Deficit: Filling the Statistical Gap

Central to Beveridge's discussion was the distinction he made between 'abstract notions and yards of statistics' and 'the social consequences of how actual people were affected' in short, the difference between quantitative and qualitative accounts of unemployment. Despite the profusion of statistical (quantitative) evidence provided in contemporary reports and surveys, the broadcaster and editor of the *Listener* R. S. Lambert and the historian H. L. Beales each considered qualitative evidence of far greater value in fostering public awareness of the human cost and tragedy of unemployment and had become increasingly impatient with what they considered the sociologists' delay in enquiring into the 'psychological and social', as distinct from 'economic and political effects'.[9] Believing they had opened up a new area of study into the 'psycho-pathology of human communities affected by profound disturbances in the basis of economic life', Beales and Lambert sought qualitative evidence in the shape of personal accounts and testimonies that would 'fill the statistical gaps where quantitative material [was] not available'.[10] As has been shown, there was a consensus that, compared with statistical, scientific, philosophical or political forms of discourse, imaginative literature—more specifically, imaginative, working-class literature—was more attuned to describing the psychological damage visited upon working people by unemployment and more effective in communicating its hardships to readers (as yet) untouched by its consequences. Discussing the novel's discursive 'function', Terry Eagleton indicates: 'The difference between science and art is, not that they deal with different objects, but that they deal with the same objects in different ways. Science gives us a conceptual knowledge of a situation; art gives us the experience of that situation.'[11]

Whilst the depredations of long-term unemployment remained the focus of much 'quantitative' investigation during the 1930s, it was in accounts such as those published by Beales and Lambert that middle-class readers began to appreciate:

> How little, indeed do we yet know of what unemployment means, not in terms of economic loss, but in terms of human experience. If we are asked such questions as: "When a man loses his job, how long does he continue looking hopefully for a new one, or: when does he resign himself to life without economic incentive?" or: "Is the general effect of long-continued unemployment stimulating or deadening to the individual's interest in politics and public affairs?" our answers at present must be based on surmise and casual scraps of evidence. We have hardly yet discovered where the shoe pinches physically, and how much more ignorant are we of the intellectual and moral changes involved.[12]

Walter Brierley: Frustration and Bitterness: A Colliery Banksman

First appearing in *The Listener* and later collected and published in more permanent form by Gollancz in 1934, Beales' and Lambert's *Memoirs of the Unemployed* followed in the footsteps of *Die Arbeitslosen von Marienthal*, the first systematic analysis into the sociological effects of unemployment conducted by a team of social psychologists from the University of Vienna.[13] The 'Stage Theory' of unemployment they propounded was based upon an analysis of accounts provided by the redundant textile workers in Marienthal, an Austrian village in which the entire workforce had been terminated owing to the economic depression.[14] Walter Brierley's contribution to Beales' and Lambert's memoirs came about via an acquaintance of his wife, who had suggested he provide an article detailing the effects of unemployment upon himself and his family. Entitled 'Frustration and Bitterness—A Colliery Banksman', Brierley's piece was based upon personal experience, although—despite *The Listener's* requirement that the memoirs should provide factual detail as set out in a short memorandum stating they should be autobiographical, in the sense of being 'non-fiction'—it did register stylistically as a departure from the offerings of his fellow contributors. In a subsection entitled 'Selfishness Bred of Unemployment', Brierley describes, in a language reminiscent of Puritan writer John Bunyan, the spiritual and psychological damage wrought by unemployment: the inner questioning, the creeping within oneself, the sense of inferiority, despair, shame and social isolation, the nagging doubts and negative feelings that conspire to undermine the self-esteem of the workless individual. He records, 'it has made me, who once prided myself on a generous and self-sacrificing nature—a real follower of Christ—a selfish person.'[15] Brierley articulates the psychological debilitations of having to depend upon the state for money without having honestly earned it and how his loss of faith in everything except his own capabilities leads to constant rumination and self-loathing. Unemployment's corrosive effects construct a cynicism in which even the friendliest of gestures: the offer of a cigarette, or the buying of a drink, is seen as condescension and contaminates intersubjective experience to the extent that the 'striving of others for position in politics, trade union or cooperative societies' is considered disingenuous, rather than socially oriented or altruistic, though a residue of redeeming decency and self-knowledge was evident in his admission that, given the opportunity, he would probably have behaved in similar fashion.

Brierley's *Listener* memoir moves beyond a purely autobiographical account towards a mode more usually encountered in novelistic discourse. This is illustrated below where snatches of entreaty alternate with snatches of narrative to foreground the speaker's thought processes:

> It follows of course that family life is made more difficult, testiness creeps in and often condemnation of a system is transferred illogically to the irksome limitations of the married state.
>
> "If one were only single, without restraint, limitations."
>
> "If it were not for the child."
>
> These thoughts, sometimes expressed, give, when they do find an outlet in speech, occasion for a warm altercation, the resulting bitterness of which is only erased by periods of unintelligent silence.[16]

Here, Brierley combines self-awareness with an appropriate grammatical form (the conditional/subjunctive) in order to render his inner feelings, and, though clearly unaware of contemporary psychological terminology, in remarking upon the 'periods of unintelligent silence' he displays not only emotional intelligence but also prescience in his identification of the behaviour pattern which contemporary psychology terms 'passive aggressive'. Brierley's 'stylised' account thus presents as a bridge between quantitative, report-based, discourse and imaginative prose fiction. That such accounts might engage the sympathies of the wider public is mentioned by Brierley during a talk he gave in 1965 for a BBC Midlands Radio programme, *Turning Point*, in which he described how, following publication of his *Listener* contribution, the Bishop of Worcester's wife invited 'my wife, my son and me to spend a fortnight at Hartlebury Castle'.[17] Brierley's 'memoir' had also caught the attention of the Birmingham writer John Hampson. As Christopher Hilliard remarks, 'Working-class writers with contacts in publishing and literary circles [...] could be instrumental in helping newer writers into print', and he illustrated this point by reference to the Birmingham writers, noting how 'the ripples spreading out from [them] reached out to other working-class writers'.[18] Hampson's interest would prove fortuitous, and it was following Brierley's barely disguised plea for assistance in the extract below that Hampson, and later Walter Allen, would collaborate with him on the novel *Means Test Man*, which would open the doors to the Derbyshire writer's first literary success.

> Long ago I bought a typewriter and have had some minor successes. I study the styles of the great novelists and write and write and write. Only a few days ago I finished a novel I had been working on for over a year. If it is ever accepted (and if it is not, my optimism will lose none of its quality) I hope the reviewers will take it into consideration that the author is an unemployed miner, subjected monthly to the Means Test inquisition, knowing neither security nor normal comfort—matters creating a state of mind decidedly incompatible with that necessary for sustained effort.' This then, my success in the literary field—I never dream of a bestseller—seems the only light in our domestic darkness.[19]

Again, Christopher Hilliard describes how, following an introduction to Walter Allen, the two Birmingham writers each read drafts of the novel Brierley alluded to above—it appeared that Brierley had been smitten with a desire to write not dissimilar to that described by Leslie Halward—and, via friends and contacts, Allen and Hampson made strenuous efforts to get his writing published.[20] Hampson saw the potential in Brierley's work early and appreciated the ex-miner's innate literary style, developed emotional intelligence, psychological insight and 'gift of irony', which—combined with subject material derived from his life experience—would prove invaluable in a novel focusing upon the debilitating effects of unemployment, as these affect not only the workless individual but also his family and, more broadly speaking, his class. In April 1934, Hampson wrote a detailed letter to Brierley advising him as to the form his novel might take. He suggested structuring it around the days of the week and progressively heightening the dramatic tension in the days leading to the visit of the *Means Test Man*. Structured on this premise, the novel was episodic rather than plot based and closely resembled the device Hampson had employed in his own novel *Saturday Night at the Greyhound*, and which had originally been conceived as a three-act play. Walter Allen would likewise adopt an episodic, 'day to day' format in *Innocence Is Drowned*. That Allen was an enthusiastic collaborator in the Brierley project is evident from a further letter in which Hampson comments, 'I'm glad that Allen supported my demand for a "day to day" novel. I am quite sure that such a book will do a great deal to establish you as a considerable writer. The novel "*a la* Woolf" can come later.'[21] More detailed advice would follow with Hampson proposing the novel ought to include 'reminiscences of bygone days when Jack [Brierley's principal character] was free from the spectre of unemployment, [...] make capital of each and every difference between the man in employment and the man workless.

The idea of contrast, is, I feel, important'.[22] Reflecting on 'happier times' becomes a minor trope in the unemployment novel and, as will be shown, it recurs in several of the works analysed below. Assenting to a suggestion of Brierley's, Hampson agreed:

> You could still use the idea of the family who are determined to keep their self-respect and the family who let things go.' [...] Your main figure, must be a man of common sense, with great personal honesty, so that he is conscious of his own feelings and weaknesses. Do keep the people near earth, let them have a few high asperations [*sic*] but make those fleeting. The more detachment you get the better, and do give your gift of irony full play. I am certain that you can produce a very powerful novel. You do know that I am willing to help in any way that I can. [23]

The correspondence with Brierley was not all one-way-traffic. The fact that the Derbyshire writer acted so readily on Hampson's and Allen's suggestions is not to characterise him as a novice or time-serving literary apprentice. The two Birmingham writers were confident in their assessment of his potential, and their interest in his work exceeded mere curiosity.[24] As commentators such as Christopher Hilliard and Andy Croft have pointed out, the notion of patronage was always a determining factor in the development of the contemporary working-class writer, as would be revealed in the commercial success of Brierley's novel; it was owing to the dissemination of his work 'through friends of friends of Hampson's that the book found its way to Methuen [who] published it'.[25]

This chapter will explore how the issue of unemployment was addressed in both the novels and short stories of the Birmingham group. Beginning with Walter Brierley's novel *Means Test Man*, it will move on to an analysis of John Hampson's modernist short story 'Man About the House' before concluding with a reading of Walter Allen's *Innocence Is Drowned*.

Walter Brierley: *Means Test Man*

First published in 1935, it is owing to its re-evaluation and rescue by Andy Croft that *Means Test Man* was reissued by Spokesman Books in 1983 and remains currently available. Unlike the works of his lesser-known counterparts, Brierley's first published novel has begun to accrete a good deal of critical discussion. Rather than revisiting well-trodden critical ground therefore, this reading will focus on aspects of the novel which, though having received less critical attention, remain central to the consideration of a work described by some as the Birmingham group's 'most celebrated production'.[26] I shall initially examine how Brierley drew upon working-class speech patterns, tone of voice, satire and irony to determine the extent to which these essentially linguistic devices are constitutive of the novel's political orientation. Following which I consider how the influence of D. H. Lawrence prompted Brierley to experiment with elements of an expressionist technique that found him reaching beyond the formal parameters of the traditional realist/naturalist novel.

> Old Humphrey never attempted to soften the broad Derbyshire dialect he used when speaking to anyone. The children were always expectantly amused when they saw him take his stand behind the big bible…
>
> … "Ar'm gooin' ta ex ya a kind a riddle. Yo'll a'e ta listen."
>
> "Ner…
>
> "As greyn as grass an' isna grass? / An' bears a yeller flower; / As many spikes as yo can cernt / In twenty-fower hower."
>
> -no pause. "Wot is it?"
>
> "Gorse," called out a few voices at once.p
>
> Old Humphrey showed the pleasure he felt. " Ar m'lad. Ar m'gel. Goss. That's it Goss. Yo mun ex ya mothers an' faythers that w'en ya get omm". (*MM*, 71–2)

It is not uncommon to find renderings of regional accent or dialect forms permeating working-class narratives, and, as the above passage illustrates, *Means Test Man* was no exception. However, other speech-based elements, for example 'tone of voice' and the 'ironic stance', indicative of a particular 'attitude' to the external world deriving from working-class speech communities, more possibly a working-class 'consciousness', appear to have been overlooked. These factors combine with others—for example, the use of figurative forms, arising from what John Fordham, following Lukacs, describes as the worker's 'reified consciousness'—which, when taken together, leave their characteristic imprint on Brierley's style.[27] Richard Hoggart remarks on the importance of finding the appropriate register in his discussion of 'Tone' in autobiographical writing:

> [I]t is more difficult to find your style if you are from the working classes. Almost any ex-working-class writer can produce reasonably lifelike dialogue by sprinkling 'daft' and 'mucky' in odd places… it is easier for certain socially-conditioned manners and tones to express themselves, because so much of our writing has traditionally been expressed in those tones of voice.[28]

Hoggart describes how, on a rereading Lawrence's *Sons and Lovers*, he noticed for the first time that 'its movement, its "kick", its voice, were those of a working man who had become articulate and—instead of acquiring idioms foreign to his deep-rooted ways of feeling—had kept the rhetoric of his kind and so (this is the point) could better say what *he* had to say'.[29] Henry Green's *Living* to some extent illustrates the inverse of this process. Ramon Lopez Ortega discusses Green's search for a suitable language by which to render his working-class subject material; material that represented for him a completely different way of life, and one for which most available means seemed inadequate.[30] Though undocumented, it is clear that Brierley likewise sought an appropriate linguistic form or register by which to communicate his experience. Like Green, we may surmise that his innovations were motivated by a desire to break, at least temporarily, with literary conventions he found unequal to his task and develop an authorial voice 'to say better what he had to say'. It becomes evident that, at times, Brierley adopts the representational strategies of modernism, more specifically expressionism, rather than resorting to such stalwarts as the documentary realism or 'over emphatic' naturalism with which working-class writers had generally been associated.

Chronicling a week in the life of the Cook family—Jack, an unemployed miner, Jane, his wife, and their young son, John—*Means Test Man* is fuelled by insights gained from Brierley's experience of unemployment in the East Midland (Derbyshire) coalfield, and, while clearly indebted to its author's repository of lived-experience, the novel moves from 'formal' autobiography to develop those levels of psychological awareness and emotional intelligence that had first surfaced in his *Listener* contribution. Whilst nurturing and maintaining a sense of solidarity and encouragement with colliers' and their families facing similar circumstances, for those unfamiliar with its debilitating effects, the novel would offer an authentic portrayal of the psychological damage and inner turmoil to which the victims of unemployment were subjected and stoically endured. Brierley's account of the Cooks' emotional trauma during the week leading to the visit of the Means Test inspector is cyclical in that, rather than a periodic or random check, it was an experience to be endured each and every week during the period of unemployment. As with Walter Greenwood's *Love on the Dole*, this structural circularity immediately subverts the bourgeois realist novel's linear trajectory towards resolution and affirmation. Effectively placing his protagonists under a form of 'house arrest' and locked into a cycle of dreary, seemingly interminable repetition, the movement of Brierley's novel is generated largely by the alternation of viewpoint characters and accounts of their respective state of mind. Brierley's description of what effectively amounts to incarceration is not to cast the novel as the unremitting exercise in 'over-emphatic naturalism' that Walter Allen attributed to many working-class novels, for paradoxically Brierley's alternation of viewpoint character and his psychological explorations work alongside his documentation of quotidian detail to imbue his characterisations with depth and veracity.[31]

At the novel's outset, the Means Test inspector's visit is described as 'that agony-day once a month, he dreaded it, more for [his wife's] sake than his own; it almost killed her every time' (*MM*, 3). Brierley employs figurative language, namely agony, dread and killed, to communicate the emotional violence, economic frustration and the enforced conviviality unemployment brings upon the erstwhile sacred confines of the mining family's domestic space. Providing the setting for Brierley's exploration of 'the psychological states of a very small number of characters locked in a closed world of material circumstances', the euphemism 'Hearth and home' metonymically captures the womblike, inviolate sanctuary of the miner's home, registering simultaneously its restricted dimensions and the suffering family ensconced therein.[32]

In the closing pages of the novel, Brierley's narrator describes the Means Test inspector's visit as a spiritually demeaning and harrowing experience:

> The master and mistress of the household—the two heads of a home—husband and wife in their castle—English. And this man sat here at the table where grace used to be said, where friends used to come and laugh over tea, always on the first Sunday in the year, that nearest to John's Birthday. And this man sat where those friends had sat, he was like a lord and they stood trembling before him. No, that wasn't the relation at all, there was something soulless in this, callous. Means Test. It was something else besides a means test, it tested one's soul, one's being and the soul and the being were poorer every time. It could not but leave them worse, disturbing as it did the calm and quietness of the inner life. However far back into one's self one retreated, still the test followed, measuring, measuring. (*MM*, 263)

Employing anaphora ('And this man'), Brierley deconstructs the bourgeois maxim that 'An Englishman's home is his castle' and, in deploying what John Hampson referred to as his 'gift of irony', communicates the grotesque reversal of fortune whereby, having accessed the domestic inner sanctum, it is the Means Test inspector, a complete stranger, who now sits at the family table, 'where grace used to be said and friends used to laugh over tea', while they [the Cooks] 'stood trembling before him' (*MM*, 263). In the extract below, the narrator records Jane Cook's abhorrence of such indignities by employing biblical syntax and imagery that posits such encroachment as not far short of sexual violation:

> Her hate was towards those who permitted the sacred veil to be torn down from before any family hearth, baring unto nakedness the minds and souls of those sitting around the fire speaking of things which bound them together. Men in content allowed it to be done to their fellow men, not knowing what they did. Jack was sad about it, his hate was against the big fact that such a system could be. Jane hated her fellow-beings, her husband included, and hate now tainted her whole being. (*MM*, 67)

The contagion of Jane's enmity is self-evident. With four repetitions of the word hate, her feelings are in extremis. That unemployment operates to distort the Cooks' domestic and familial equilibrium is evident in the following passage:

> The chaotic period of adjustment, from 'saving' to 'drawing', from a smooth domestic economy to a bewildering strain to make ends meet, had bared the nerves of man and wife, had weakened them morally. Swear words were much nearer the surface in Jane; they came through Jack with ease now, but only in secret as yet [...] they felt better apart, somehow, the knowledge of how, what and where they were did not crowd so closely then—so heavily. Jack was glad of the "signing mornings", of fine days when he could be in the garden or walking about the commons. Jane was relieved, too, to see his back for a while; she could never quite adjust herself to having a man on the hearth continually. (*MM*, 137, 138)

'For better, or for worse, in plenty and in want, in sickness and in health', the Cooks' wedding vows must have begun to ring hollow; not only theirs but those many others, who, under similarly straitened circumstances, must have identified and possibly relished the opportunity to spend some time apart. As Carole Snee remarks:

> Jack's unemployment means that he and his wife are forced by external factors to modify the traditional segregation of roles found in mining

> communities. They both have to recognise that her love for Jack is partially determined by his ability to provide for her and her child... Love does not conquer all, and is itself revealed as part of the social framework, not something existing outside it.[33]

Despite the implacable anxieties and intrusions of the external world, throughout his tribulations, Jack Cook's overriding concern is to find work:

> [B]ut until the opportunity came, if it ever did, and that doubt had begun to be very insistent [...] his mental time must be wholly taken in keeping his little world steady. On the face of it this little world *seemed* easily capable of being managed, everything was so straightforward, so determined—a fixed rate of income, three human beings to be catered for (my emphasis). (*MM*, 6)

In this further ironic interlude, Brierley's narrator lures the reader into believing that, viewed objectively, Jack's immediate responsibilities, his 'little world', *ought* not prove too difficult to maintain. The word 'seemed' flags up an ironic intervention here, for although one might be tempted to agree, Brierley's use of the past participle undercuts the meaning, its intention the opposite to that being said.

Asking why the novel became the appropriate form with which to communicate accounts of working-class experience and what it offers working-class writers that sociological or historical accounts do not, Simon Dentith proposes the answer lies in 'irony'.[34] The novel, he believes, 'provides as one of its characteristic modes, the use of irony, but that, in part because of this inheritance of irony, it is especially hospitable to a different kind of irony that is in fact a characteristic resource of the speech communities from which the novelists emerge'.[35] One may readily find examples of what Dentith describes as the bourgeois novel's 'ironic gaze at the delusions of the protagonist' in the intellectual aspirations of George Eliot's Dorothea Brooke in *Middlemarch*, or the hapless Richard Carstone as he attempts to secure his inheritance from the estate of Jarndyce and Jarndyce in Dickens' *Bleak House*. Each of these characters is illustrative of the 'ironic gaze', undertaken by the 'transcendent' or affirmative narrative viewpoint presented in the nineteenth-century realist text. As Dentith suggests, 'this is one of the principal generic possibilities that the novel provides. [This] it may be said, is what novels do.'[36] In describing what he judged 'the characteristic note of working-class writing in the thirties', its 'particular tone of voice', a 'tone of sardonic worldly wisdom often characterised by ironic understatement or by the choice of telling anecdote', Dentith touches upon Richard Hoggart's remarks in respect of D. H. Lawrence's 'voice' above.[37] Martha Vicinus traces the presence of tone of voice and irony in working-class speech patterns by reference to Music Hall performance, Chartist writing and nineteenth-century Chap books. Explaining that irony was 'a characteristic resource of working-class speech communities', which though is 'at times debilitating', she hastens to affirm that '[i]ronic distance [...] acted as self-protection; life was often desperate enough, but few survived on complaints, and humour proved to be the backbone of a developing class-consciousness'.[38]

Elements of the 'ironic gaze' are again taken up in the following passage where Brierley's narrator records the myriad purchases one is able to make upon receipt of the meagre twenty five shillings and three pence allowed by the Public Assistance Committee, 'Which, after rent, rates and sick club', were considered sufficient to provide:

> [F]ood, clothes, coal, light and the hundred and one things which are included in the connotation of the term 'a home'. And moreover, the two heads of the household were always on hand to keep the home on the top level of domestic efficiency; never was the bewildered wife presented with a problem which would have to wait until her husband returned from an eight-hour exile at the pit. He was always on hand with advice or help. She was relieved too, from more than half of the practical management of the household, so that she could never justly claim like some wives and mothers in Wingrove that she was a 'slave with not a minute to call her own'. (*MM*, 7)

In what seems a parody of the jaunty, third-person, Pathe newsreel 'voice-over', Brierley uses self-deprecation, understatement and not a little acerbic wit to register the awkward presence of 'the bewildered wife's' unemployed spouse as he negotiates the enforced conviviality of the hom-escape, where, once more, the traditional segregation of roles noted by Carole Snee is upturned and ironised. Michael Pickering and Kevin Roberts follow Martha Vicinus here by suggesting how this process might function as a defence mechanism: 'Ironic humour is in fact a distinctive tone of class and proletarian self-consciousness, expressing moods that range from laconic self-resignation to buoyant self-confidence and pride.'[39] In their discussion of the working-class writer Jack Common, they suggest it was 'precisely this humour and irony that allowed him to explore his own life at a distance and for its generality [...] he is just as much interested in the representative nature of his fate as in his own unique and particular circumstances'.[40] Brierley employs these devices to precisely the same effect; a tone of laconic resignation permeates the above passage and undercuts conventional assumptions regarding the respective heads of the household. Like Jack Common, Brierley saw the representational potential of his own experience, for, just as with the stand-up comedian's 'observation-humour', Brierley's verbal irony depended upon readers' mutual recognition of shared circumstance or, in the case of middle-class readers, a finely tuned empathic response. His rootedness in the mining community and close acquaintance with the depredations of unemployment enabled him to construct ironies which, if only temporarily, went some way to alleviating the misery of the many like himself having to 'scrape by' on preposterously inadequate state benefits.

Rather than communicating cynicism or humour, the following passage finds Brierley deploying irony to underline unemployment's darker, more destructive effects. It follows the narrator's explanation of how Labour Exchange officials offered a dispensation to the long-term unemployed whereby they were excused the indignity of 'signing-on' on a daily basis, provided they sign a document once each week stating they have not worked (and hence not received any income) during the intervening period. The remaining days of the week subsequently considered their own, to do with 'as they pleased'. Irony and tone of voice again point up the sheer waste of human potential here. In mapping the descent towards 'disintegration and crisis', the following passage, far from celebrating any sense of liberation or release, reveals how, rather than 'doing as they please', such listless unstructured days only provide the workless collier with further opportunities for anxiety, contemplation and dark introspection as their inability to provide for their families becomes internalised as personal failure:

> The rest of the time they were free, free to work in their homes and gardens, free surreptitiously to earn a few bob or two working for other folks (until some swine reported them and they were either summoned or had a week or two's money stopped), free to be nagged at all day long by a petulant wife, free to feel the pride they had in a home and children becoming attenuated until it disappeared altogether and one of the two qualities, indifference or an enduring poignancy, was bared, free to brood with want around them, frightened by visions of the river, the canal, the reservoir; sometimes seeing an awful significance in the strong arm of a tree, the hook in the

> ceiling, the razor they shave with; having to hurry to the fields to breathe deeply, firmly, there to curse and swear not only at external things but the foolish weakness of themselves. (*MM*, 131)

The iterations of 'free' in this passage are set against the unemployed miners' embarrassment of time; the irony is clearly manifest in the opposite of what is said, as they were never wholly free from anxiety. A markedly less-than-liberating experience, unemployment here is presented more as the condition of 'unfreedom', especially for individuals enmeshed within the capitalist mode of production where, as Marcuse suggests, 'cultural values as well as the physical and psychological powers of men have become commodities [...] The situation of the Labour market is what directly determines the freedom of men and the possibilities of life, and is always dependent on the dynamics of society as a whole'.[41] Once severed from the all-pervasive market, the industrial worker finds that there is simply and abruptly nowhere to go. Here, rather than ironically tracing what Pickering and Robins suggest as the ironic trajectory from 'laconic resignation to buoyant self-confidence', the mood is one of unimpeded descent: a charting of the fall from cheery resignation to grim foreboding.[42] In his discussion of the mining novel, Graham Holderness remarks upon the hazards of the coalface describing how 'Each "little thing", each minute detail of empirical observation, contains a strange otherworld of dark anxiety and existential terror [...] the naturalistic surface is constantly fracturing to disclose these underground fears'.[43] Paradoxically, even when 'out of work' and 'released' from the ardours of this gruelling and dangerous occupation, there is little opportunity to experience 'freedom', be it physical or emotional respite, the demoralising effects of unemployment merely pushing its victims to deeper and darker levels of introspection.

Moving to a wider formal analysis, the remainder of this discussion will consider how the stylistic decisions undertaken by Brierley contribute to his novel's uniqueness. As indicated in the introduction, critics such as John Fordham are keen to stress the dialectical nature of working-class writing and the use of forms 'fundamentally at odds with traditional representational modes' with which they have been commonly yet cursorily associated. Fordham illustrates this by reference to Liverpool writer James Hanley but notes how the departure from traditional realist modes was equally evident in Walter Brierley where:

> [T]he episodic and metaphoric nature of [his] works suggests a less realist and more expressionistic level of reading consistent with a perception that human beings are determined by forces external to their individual will. [And that] the narrative focus on a 'means test man' or a 'sandwichman' precisely represents those conditions of unemployment where the social relations of human beings have been reduced to a static or reified state.[44]

The episodic form of *Means Test Man* is relevant here. As commented upon earlier, the days of the week prior to the Means Test inspector's visit each provide incidents that give rise to psychological reflection on the part of the protagonist. Usually taking the shape of 'realisations', or 'awakenings' of consciousness, unlike the Joycean epiphany however, such instances reveal how the Cooks' relationship to the 'real world' has instead become coloured by the feelings of despair engendered in their circumscribed existence. Beyond loss of remuneration, by severing individuals' links with the working population at large, unemployment also functions as a form of social rejection or banishment. Lukacs' theory of *reification* asserts that, owing to industrial capitalism's increasingly specialised methods of production, workers converge with and become mere extensions of the machines they operate, and come to exist as products, objects—ultimately as mere commodities themselves. Demeaning as this is, the term was conventionally (in Marxist criticism) applied to members of the industrial proletariat 'fortunate' enough to exchange their labour for a wage and to remain in full-time employment. However, during the periods of capitalist crisis where employment is often revealed as a less-than-stable proposition, the 'jobless worker' is subject to humiliations on a wholly different scale. Discussing their predicament in *Means Test Man*, Graham Holderness suggests, '[the Cook's] condition is not simply one of poverty, but one of extreme alienation' and conjectures that 'their experience, if released into the even certainty of the real (bourgeois) world would drive that world to madness'.[45] He considers that the effects of long-term unemployment reveal the Cooks to occupy a social and psychological 'double-bind' between their faith in the 'real world' and their existence in the actual'.[46] By denying his right to work, and support his family, unemployment closes down Jack's belief that he holds any stake in his economic destiny. 'No longer', to paraphrase Dickens' *David Copperfield*, 'the hero of his own life', but now a mere 'commodity', more disconcertingly an 'unmarketable' commodity, Jack Cook's experience exemplifies the final devastating and exquisite consequences of long-term unemployment.

It is ironic that the cruellest element of unemployment lies in the abundance of free time one is given to contemplate the situation. In the passage below, Brierley describes the febrile atmosphere where, with temperaments at breaking point, man and wife walk on eggshells in the confines of their home. Sunday, once the day of leisure, traditionally a family day and hitherto the high point of the working week, has now become a day like any other, simply one more to be endured:

> Sunday … Everything was held up the world could do without those workers who were in regular employment even, so there was no hope for those who were seeking it. Hope was foolishness on this day, optimism mere futility, nothing to do but sit and wait for it to pass; a dangerous day, too, when a moment's weakness might lead to the very core of domestic accord being poisoned or ripped away. (*MM*, 66)

To escape the tedium, Jack and his son embark on a long walk, their route passing by the pithead buildings of the colliery where Jack had been employed for ten years prior to his lay-off. Here, lying squat and huddled together, the engine houses, blacksmiths' and joiners' shops that comprise this industrial landscape are found in their Sunday longueurs, and where, in the manner of Auden's 'Who stands, the crux left by the watershed', they appear to rebuke the complacent observer by communicating some deeper significance.[47] Providing an appropriate backdrop, Brierley's anthropomorphic description has a dispiriting effect upon Jack:

> A hate was warming him, sickening him, its source some vague sense of loss. He had worked there ten years, the place was part of him, he was part of the place. In was an eagerness, [*sic*] a willingness to go back, to live with it again, but there was no room for him there. It rejected him. Such was infinitely worse than love rejection, this was being rejection, the denial of the activity, the pleasure, the whole richness of life, health, security, independence. (*MM*, 87)

Jack's social isolation transcends even the indignities of reification and finds Brierley groping to articulate his protagonist's 'vague sense of loss'. Recalling, Ryle and Soper's discussion above, 'in the social orientation of his labours, the deployment of skills and expenditure of effort' and his responsiveness to 'the forms of objectification provided by work', Jack's occupation had proven a positive experience.[48] Brierley's narrator nonetheless depicts Jack's redundancy in the terms of a broken relationship, with unemployment shown to be more emotionally debilitating than 'love rejection'. Unable to rationalise his predicament as one shared by other members of his community, and more widely his class, Jack has internalised the situation, viewing it as a personal failing: one that is manifest in the wholesale denial and rejection of his very being. Effectively ostracised from society—more properly a society organised around the capitalist relations of production symbolised by the impassive, pithead buildings—the language of Jack's reverie is thus consonant with the reified consciousness described by John Fordham where:

> [T]he experience of reification determines its use of figurative language and the non-realist quality of its forms. Thus the writing itself, while it is often grounded in an ostensible realism, will nonetheless adopt descriptive or allegorical modes in which meaning does not so much depend upon a realist plausibility, but on a symbolic or metaphoric representation of a 'reified' consciousness.[49]

Following Fordham by describing a 'real world explicitly differentiated from the experience of the unemployed', Graham Holderness attributes the Cooks' predicament to the fact '[they] occupy a peripheral dimension of extreme deprivation, watching the world from behind a barrier of separation' and cites the following passage in which Brierley's narrator focalises the wider implications from Jane Cook's perspective:

> [T]hey were penned in a small space in the world like a lot of cattle and were provided with what was thought enough for them. Thousands of harassed men, women and children were penned with them, beings with no independence, no freedom, underfed, underclothed, not trusted. (*MM*, 55)

Jane's use of such terms as 'penned in' and 'pinion' (the clipping of a bird's flight feathers in order to keep it captive) combine with the 'cattle' simile and other metaphorical representations to underline the impoverishment of the unemployed. Such figurations appear later in the novel as Brierley tracks the Cooks' progressive dehumanisation by likening them to bacteria or microbial spores, 'They were like plants and animals, like any sort of life which existed where the wind blew bleakly all the time, stunted, without nature, of no use to the world' (*MM*, 269).

Brierley's use of imagery derives from intense psychological introspection; here, 'the violent emotions welling up from the innermost recesses of the subconscious' that are characteristic of expressionism's hostility to the conventions of the realist novel viewed as the literary manifestation of bourgeois ideology.[50] Brierley's 'escape from traditional realist convention' is thus revealed in linguistic experimentation and his astute psychological delineations of character. The untrammelled anger with which Jack and Jane Cook react to their predicament moves from stolid realism towards the expressionistic depictions of reality he had discovered in Lawrence. As Peter Nicholls suggests, 'Like the Cubists, the Expressionists were interested in arriving at unfamiliar images of the world through calculated images of distortion.'[51] While assenting to John Fordham's caution that such pronouncements 'rel[y] on an understanding of modernism as a gradual and emergent discourse within the realist text', one might play devil's advocate and posit the view that the distorted imagery by which his characters voice their dissatisfactions may have stemmed more from Brierley's wish to emulate Lawrence than to subvert or break from the constraining influence of the realist mode.

As a provisional, 'working' definition of Expressionism, Kristian Sotriffer proposes:

> [Expressionism's] underlying characteristic [...] consists of an over-intensification of experience, a rejection of the classical canon, a distortion and exaggeration bordering on the hysterical, a shattering of traditional forms and the reordering of fragments to make vehicles for changed thinking and sensation, and a new, more critical and empathic approach to the world. [52]

These iconoclastic intensifications and figurative distortions were anathema to Lukacs, who took issue with Naturalism, Expressionism and subsequent modernist modes, believing that 'emotionally and intellectually the modernist schools remain frozen in their own immediacy; [failing] to pierce the surface to discover the underlying essence; the real factors that relate their experiences to the hidden social forces that produce them'.[53] Rather than simply reflecting the despair and futility of bourgeois existence, Lukacs believed the artist must penetrate history's superficial, surface appearance to comprehend instead the totality of the social processes that constituted contemporary capitalist society.

Such expressionistic renderings of experience naturally invoke the figure of D. H. Lawrence, who, as I have intimated, exerted a powerful hold on the imaginations of the Birmingham group writers, especially Brierley, Allen and Hampson. Andy Croft indicates, 'there was no readily available, familiar, native, national, working-class literary tradition to which they could see themselves belonging. All they had was D. H. Lawrence.'[54] This was not without irony for, according to Andrew Harrison, having established a reputation as a 'regional' and, by connotation, working-class author:

> Lawrence's first instinct was *not* to produce social realist works like 'Odour of Chrysanthemums' and *Sons and Lovers.* It was only at the instigation of his early mentors Ford Madox Hueffer and Edward Garnett, who had an eye to literary commerce, that Lawrence began documenting Eastwood life and reproducing the routines, speech patterns and mannerisms of the mining community.[55]

However, the correspondence between Brierley, Hampson and Allen held by Derby local Studies Library, whilst invaluable in detailing their collaboration, also testifies to Lawrence's status as their literary mentor. In a letter dated 11 September 1934, Allen informs Brierley he would forward him a copy of the unexpurgated American edition of *The Rainbow*, adding, 'as you'll see, it is a copy pinched from a circulating library, a most respectable place. They'd got it in the window. I realised that they couldn't possibly know the book was banned, so I thought I'd relieve them of harbouring such unpleasant stuff'.[56] In a further letter, Allen comments that although it was some years since he read it, '*The Rainbow* was probably the best of D.H.L. […] the great scene is probably the chapter towards the end of the book where the girl is chased by the horses. Seems to me the greatest piece of imaginative writing since Dostoievsky [*sic*]'.[57] The following extract from a letter written by Allen reveals the extent to which Brierley had imbibed elements of the Lawrencian metaphysic:

> If I understand you rightly, you are interested primarily in—here I fumble for words—the mystery of the human heart, the deep instinctive feelings, the springs of action. The dark mysteries. The essence of things. I belive [*sic*] I see quite clearly what you mean, but it's difficult to express. It means your affinities are really with Lawrence—as John has already pointed out—and with Wordsworth. You are interested at the point where life begins to show itself. Am I getting near?[58]

Walter Allen believed himself conditioned to admire Lawrence, '[h]is upbringing and social background were close enough to mine to make it almost inevitable that I should identify with him. He was a working-class boy with no advantages except his talent'.[59] That John Hampson was equally enamoured of the Nottinghamshire writer is evident in his correspondence with Brierley. In a letter dated 27 July 1934, a perplexed Hampson informs Brierley that '*Brothers and Lovers* (the American imprint of his *Strip Jack Naked*) arrived from New York this morning: on the wrapper I am described as the heir apparent to D. H. Lawrence. I am looking forward to the American reviews with curiosity'.[60] As the Brierley correspondence with Walter Allen and John Hampson reveals, all three were votaries at the shrine of D. H. Lawrence, Brierley perhaps more so for—in terms of his geographical location in the East Midland coalfield, social status and class mobility—Lawrence clearly functioned in the dual role of local hero and literary mentor. Whilst powerful, the Lawrencian influence has nonetheless overshadowed Brierley's reputation. For, rather than studiously emulating Lawrence, Brierley's accounts of colliery experience were actually based upon lived-experience *as* a collier.[61] Conscious that there was 'something more to life than the pit', Brierley's short stories and novels interrogate the heroic mythology of masculine labour. Fearful of death or personal injury, Brierley was able to describe the harsh, energy-sapping realities of pit work as only one accustomed to its ardours could.

Despite Lukacs' disparaging assessment of modernist modes, there are episodes in *Means Test Man* where Brierley's writing clearly maps onto Kristian Sotriffer's definition of Expressionism and is supportive of John Fordham's view:

> In the interests of accurate documentation of conditions, [proletarian] writing, although relying on established codes of realism, discloses the influences of European modernism, in which narrative movement is towards isolation, disintegration and crisis rather than towards [realism's] affirmative resolution.[62]

While often characterised as social or documentary realists confined, possibly condemned, to writing within the parameters of the dominant representational form, Brierley's, and indeed Birmingham group fictions in general, kicked against the restraining and affirmative traces of traditional realism and, as had been shown, were by no means unresponsive to experimentation and innovation. Again, as Fordham suggests:

> In working-class writing, the bourgeois novel's convention of internal focalisation will be replaced by a figural representation of consciousness [...] This

> is why the category of "realism" is not always an adequate means of analysing the working-class novel: its formal properties often derive from models or traditions outside the literary mainstream.[63]

Rather than following the narrow prescriptivism of socialist realism or simply decanting the content of his experience into the readily available modes of naturalism, traditional bourgeois realism or formal autobiography, Brierley's account of the Cooks' tribulations deploys a range of formal devices in order to further his indictment of contemporary social policy. Though not engaging, progressive and declining, possibly unable to offer any practical political solution to the depredations wrought by long-term unemployment or the intrusive violations of the Means Test, Brierley's novel was, as evident from contemporary reviews and sales, successful in communicating the dispiriting and debilitating experience of unemployment to a wider public and also to fostering a greater awareness of the iniquities endured by the working classes under the Means Test and which ultimately led to its abolition in 1941.[64]

The somewhat reluctant assimilation of Brierley's novel into the contemporary pantheon of working-class writing, owing to a perceived lack of political commitment, can in retrospect be seen to have 'thrown the baby out with the bath water'. Far from being a naïve attempt to emulate realist or naturalist narrative, *Means Test Man* is, on the contrary, a carefully constructed and confidently ambitious work. In its amalgamation of traditional and modernist modes, Brierley's distinctive 'manner of speaking', his 'tone of voice' and the wealth of psychological insight he brings to the novel reveal it as a significant and powerful intervention in the working-class canon.

John Hampson: 'Man About the House'

It was their short stories that had initially brought the Birmingham writers to the attention of Edward O'Brien, who appreciated how their conception of the short form had broken with an earlier tradition he believed was inclined to 'the 'pretty' and 'wistful', its being at best 'a Georgian lyric that remained unaware of its own time and inhibited from social contact beyond that of its own class'.[65] Acknowledging that the poets Auden, Day-Lewis and Spender 'wish[ed] to come out of the ivory tower and to have strong social sympathies', Edward J. O'Brien nevertheless sensed some ill ease and discomfort attached.[66] Such tentative fraternisation with the workers—what Steve Ellis refers to as 'privileged pseudo-proletarianism'—and Frank Kermode's somewhat depressing suggestion that, sincere motivations aside, 'the company of middle-class friends was more congenial', had certainly not dissuaded the writers of the Birmingham group from crossing such social barriers. Indeed, in terms of their proximity to working-class livelihoods and their own class origins, it would be more accurate to say that there existed no barriers to surmount.[67] The reading that follows will examine John Hampson's modernist treatment of the short story form, where, in echoing John Fordham's remarks, rather than tracing the realist parabola from crisis to closure and resolution, the modernist short story conversely resists such closure, by remaining open-ended and unresolved.[68]

Written five years before W. H. Auden's 'September 1, 1939', John Hampson's 'Man About the House' is illustrative of Auden's aphoristic assertion that 'Those to whom evil is done/Do evil in return'. Though rather than merely restating this regrettable truism, Hampson's exploration of a family enduring the stresses of unemployment probes beneath the trauma of immediate circumstance to reveal the external inertias informing its protagonist's behaviour. The fact that the story's principle characters are often addressed as 'the Man', or 'the Woman', and that the boy remains unnamed throughout, gesture towards the 'universality' H. E. Bates perceived in the short form and thus imbuing Hampson's story with a parabolic or fabular quality.[69] The modern short story's intrinsic brevity has led contemporary theorists to consider it a hospitable medium for innovation and experimentation. Adrian Hunter relates how, on finishing Katherine Mansfield's 'The Daughters of the Late Colonel', one day in 1921, Thomas Hardy assumed there would be a sequel. He didn't recognise the ending as an ending, or the story as complete in itself'.[70] Hunter says, 'Hardy's bafflement was by no means unusual, but reflect[ed] the extent to which this new species of story ran against the precepts and expectations readers customarily brought to a piece of narrative fiction.'[71] Hunter touches upon an important element here, for innovations in both the contemporary novel and short story specifically aimed to disrupt the expectations established in the conventions of bourgeois realism.

In its detailed focus upon a single scene or event, in some respects analogous to a Victorian narrative painting, the modern short story allows little, if any, space for the creation or dissolution of enigma found in conventional narrative forms, as Ian Reid suggests:

> [T]he action of a short story [...] need have no completed pattern at all. It may be virtually without start or finish, representing only a state of affairs rather than a sequence of events [...] Chekhov himself once remarked: "I think that when one has finished writing a short story one should delete the beginning and the end". In discarding patterns of enclosure [and disclosure] the short-story writer can perhaps discover a freedom and imaginative truth inherent in this genre.[72]

It is therefore unsurprising that the short form has been considered ideally suited to capturing the fragmentary and fleeting experience of modernity. In its absence of plot, its focus on a single incident and a palpable 'resistance to closure or completion', Hampson's *Man About The House* breaks with the affirmative inertia of 'conventional cultural and signifying systems' and moves nearer the modernist short story as defined by Dominic Head.[73] Contrary to Edgar Allan Poe's *unifying* effects, Head suggests the modern short story's use of *disunifying* effects such as irresolution provide a more comprehensive definition of the contemporary form which, despite a seeming lack of closure, nevertheless '[makes] its point in a closed, manageable narrative period' and is clearly complete.[74] Rather than delivering the comforting assurance of a resolution, John Hampson's story 'repudiat[es] conventional fictional representations of experience' and, though ostensibly realist in terms of its content, is shown to display formal characteristics of a decidedly modernist tendency.[75] In order to locate the political force of the modern short story, Head proposes we apply Althusser's concept of 'relative autonomy' which 'involves seeing the disruptive literary gesture [...] as something which is simultaneously conditioned by, yet critical of its ideological context, a context which can be equated with literary conventions and whatever world-view they encompass'.[76] Simply put, Althusser conceives the artwork as an ideologically privileged form of knowledge independent of *conventionally constructed discourse* and, as such, capable of questioning the received wisdoms *of* this discourse. Head indicates that in his 'Letter In Reply To Andres Despre', Althusser 'outlines the concept of relative autonomy in art'.[77] Asserting that he '[does not] *rank real art among the ideologies*, although art does have a quite particular and specific relationship with ideology', Althusser accords art privileged status which (in the case of literature) enables the reader 'to "[*see*]", "[*perceive*]" and "[*feel*]" the *ideology* from which it is born, in which it bathes and from which it detaches itself as art, and to which it *alludes*'.[78] He illustrates his point by reference to the works of Balzac and Solzhenitsyn, for, as he tells Despre:

> Balzac and Solszenitsyn [*sic*] give us a view of ideology to which their work alludes and with which it is constantly fed, a view which presupposes a *retreat*, and *internal distantiation* from the very ideology from which their novels emerged. They make us 'perceive' (but not know) in some sense *from the inside*, by *an internal distance*, the very ideology from which they are held (original emphasis).[79]

John Fordham approaches this discussion by way of the 'textual class struggle [...] determined by an essentially oppositional stance and immanent social critique' he discovers in the work of James Hanley, and cites Theodor Adorno's notion of the artwork's '*dual essence*' as something which is 'ideological through and through and at the same time, because of its autonomy, that which criticises society in its very being' (my emphasis).[80] In privileging aesthetic autonomy over ideology, Adorno's conception of the negative dialectic immanent in a practically useless art closely resembles Althusser's notion of 'relative autonomy'. Fordham unpicks Adorno's theory further:

> Art for its continuing existence, depends upon the economic and institutional dissemination of its products, and thus preserves the status quo in its collusion with commodity fetishism. Yet, because of its aesthetic identity as 'truth content' it functions as essentially autonomous from, as non-identical with, the empirically real world of commodities and thus in implicit opposition to it.[81]

Applying Althusser's concept of relative autonomy' to Hampson's short story, one may begin to appreciate how, while Head cautions against 'putting too much weight upon so slight a document as the "Letter on Art", the concept of relative autonomy proves valuable as "a signpost to the politicising of the aesthetic as a valuable contextual category"'.[82] Head continues:

> The dual essence of art—its simultaneous contextual dependence and contextual critique—is only viable if the context can be made available through the text. History, that is to say, has to exist as an extra-textual reality which locates and defines literary production. This may amount to no more than an imperfect reconstruction by the critic, based on a personal period-knowledge, but

> it is this element of referentiality which redeems the knowledge of art from the 'subjectless discourse of conceptual science' and gives it a context.[83]

The 'dual essence' of 'contextual dependence and contextual critique' appears in Hampson's narrative where the contemporary economic slump functions as Dominic Head's 'extra-textual reality'. Reuben's frustration and psychological confusion arise from his inability to understand the seeming recalcitrance of a world operating beyond the perimeter of his own ideological imaginary. The contradictory nature of Reuben's and Lena's real world experience therefore has implications for the formal element of the story, and in this respect they share their condition with the Cooks in Brierley's *Means Test Man*, where, as Graham Holderness suggests, 'the fact that the social and psychological condition of the characters is defined as one of extreme alienation radically alters the signifying potentialities of the apparently naturalistic style'.[84]

> The man sat still, glowering over his thoughts. Being out of work was no game for a healthy sort of bloke. For eighteen months, now, he'd hung about, doing a bit in the garden, earning infrequent shillings for cutting other people's grass and hedges. Having nothing to do made a man sick and weary, made him feel useless and done for. It was awful being about, getting in Lena's way, now that he had become conscious of her irritation and watched for it to show in her face when he came into the house during the day hours, when he should have been at work. She annoyed him, too, especially the way in which she spoiled the lad. Out of all reason that was. (*MA*, 3, 4.)

Once more, articulated in the idiom of its protagonist by a third-person narrator, the use of free-indirect discourse communicates the sense of purposelessness and psychological anxiety experienced by the unemployed and clearly draws upon Hampson's own experience and proximity to such familial and marital dysfunction. As Carole Snee remarks of Brierley's *Means Test Man*:

> [The Cooks] are forced by external factors to modify the traditional separation of conjugal roles [...] They both have to realise that [Jane's] love for Jack is partially determined by his ability to provide for her and her child. In charting this process Brierley brings into focus the nature of interpersonal relationships in a capitalist society. [85]

Hampson's protagonists must likewise dispense with idealised or romantic notions; their straitened circumstances expose the cruel reality in Carole Snee's observation that: 'Love does not conquer all, and is itself revealed as part of the social framework, not something existing outside it.'[86]

Peopled by just three characters: a mother (Lena), her husband (Reuben) and their son (unnamed), *Man About The House* centres upon the incident in which Lena confronts her husband in the act of brutally disciplining their son for associating with a group of other boys, considered a negative influence:

> "Oh! You brute!" she screamed.
>
> "Can't I leave you alone with the kid for two or three hours without you having to set about him!"
>
> Reuben looked up sullenly. "It's what he's been asking for these last three months, or over. He ain't had enough yet."
>
> "Don't you dare hit him no more!"
>
> He raised the weapon and brought it down three times in quick succession, then stood the boy on his feet and smiled as the woman rushed forward to gather him to her.
>
> "There, there," she comforted, but the boy pulled himself free and stood, still crying and ashamed, striving to rub the tingling smart away with the palms of his hand. (*MA*, 9)

Once considered the panacea for child misbehaviour, a 'good hiding' was frequently administered alongside the Victorian notion of 'character building', wherein such disciplinary mitigations as 'it never harmed anyone' or 'spare the rod, spoil the child' abounded. We're told that Reuben experienced such beatings at the hands of his own father, information that clearly adds weight to psychological theories of behavioural patterning. Undeniably disproportionate given the trivial nature of the boy's misdemeanour, such premeditated punishment would constitute child abuse today. Nonetheless, without wishing to understate its manifest cruelty, the following analysis posits Reuben as less the aggressor and more a victim of circumstance and proposes 'Man About The House' be read as a moral fable which serves as an indictment of the factors informing the protagonist's behaviour, its didactic function addressed to cause rather than effect.

Beyond Reuben and Lena engaging in further recriminations before retiring, there is little further development in the story; its closing scene finds Reuben entering the bedroom and staring solemnly into a mirror by the light of a solitary candle:

As he stood there, naked, the woman's sleepy voice called: "Blow out that light and come to bed can't you!"

He watched the pale ghost's thin lips twist into a bitter grin, then laughed softly, conscious of his own power and virility. He was still master of his own house; he'd show her something, yet.

Pinching the hot flame from the wick he yawned.

Getting into bed he lay on his back in the warmth, staring into the glowing blackness, remembering different days.

A warm searching hand came, caressing him gently. Pretty nigh eleven years ago, Lena and himself had cycled over to Frolesworth. She had drunk a glass of stout that night. The bicycles had gone, months back, for what they would fetch.

"Reuben," the woman whispered.

He lay still. Should he make it up again? Let her soothe, comfort, and snare him into sleep?

"Reuben," she whispered again, tightening her hand on him.

"None of that, now," he said roughly. He rolled over and lay, back towards her, staring into darkness. (*MA*, 19)

As was remarked in the discussion of Walter Brierley's *Means Test Man*, and as we shall discover in Walter Allen's *Innocence Is Drowned*, the psychological trauma attendant on long-term unemployment is frequently marked by a parallel deterioration in a character's physiognomy. Prior to turning in, Reuben had momentarily ruminated on his appearance: 'The face looked hard and thin, deep lines marred both mouth and brow'. The ardours of unemployment are registered as disfigurements not wholly dissimilar to the process of deindustrialisation itself, which Phil O'Brien describes as 'a violent and criminal act, morally wrong and unfair to the people who are its victims; they are literally "crushed" under the weight of such change'.[87] On Reuben and Lena eventually finding sleep, Hampson's story 'ends' without affirmation, resolution or any indication of how their situation might change for the better. As with Brierley's Cooks, the metaphor of 'incarceration' seems appropriate; the forward momentum in their lives having stalled, rather than following a linear 'progression', they are constrained to repetition and circularity which, until the external circumstances dictating their predicament are significantly transformed, will ensure their lives will remain locked in a downward spiral of inhibition and frustration.

Catherine Belsey suggests, 'It is these incompatibilities and contradictions within what is taken for granted which exert a pressure on individuals to seek new, non-contradictory subject positions.'[88] Belsey illustrates this by reference to the position of women who are simultaneously produced and inhibited by contradictory discourses: 'Very broadly they participate in the liberal humanist discourse of freedom, self-determination and rationality and at the same time in a specifically feminine discourse of submission, relative inadequacy and irrational intuition.'[89] According to Belsey:

> The attempt to locate a single and coherent subject position within these contradictory discourses, and in consequence to find a non-contradictory pattern of behaviour, can create intolerable pressures. One way of responding to this situation is to retreat from the contradictions and from the discourse itself, to become 'sick'—more women than men are treated for mental illness.[90]

Belsey considers, 'women are not an isolated case however. The class structure also produces contradictory subject-positions which precipitate changes in social relations not only between whole classes but between concrete individuals within those classes.'[91] Belsey's illustration of 'incompatible and contradictory discourses' holds good for Hampson's short story. By applying an Althusserian 'symptomatic' reading, it is possible to reveal the contradictory nature of the contemporary social formation (ideology)—whilst extolling the high moral virtue of the work ethic and the value of family life, the liberal humanist discourse of self-determination and independence, it is ironically this very discourse that prevents Reuben, Lena and their son from achieving its ideals. Simply stated, Reuben's experience of unemployment determines his position as 'non-identical' with the societal norm that determines women 'look after the house' while men 'go out to work'. Owing to his inability to fulfil his historically defined role as 'family breadwinner', Reuben is prey to psychological confusions which, as with the women described by Belsey, are manifest in mental ill-health which, in Hampson's short story, is registered in the protagonist's *dis*-ease as revealed in the violent attempt to regain his perceived loss of status.

A 'symptomatic' reading of 'Man About The House' would locate it therefore as a modernist text whose political indictment emerges in the tension generated between formal convention and formal disruption. In this respect, Hampson's method conforms closely to the process Fordham identifies in Hanley's writing where 'The nature of social reality emerges in the dialectical relation between the form of the work of art—for example the bourgeois novel and what in essence negates it, what is non-identical with it [in which the] representation of the extremes of a particular class experience is an expression of the non-identical: a negation of the affirmative ideology of bourgeois society, expressing what is essentially outside itself'.[92]

Hampson understood that poverty and the sense of failure engendered by it exacted an excessively high toll on family relationships. Recourse to autobiographical forms as a means to achieve catharsis is a recurring factor in Hampson's narratives, and this aspect of his work is examined more fully by reference to Max Saunders' discussion of 'Autobiografiction' in the following chapter. However, given his involvement with the Hogarth Press and Bloomsbury, it is not beyond the bounds of possibility that Virginia Woolf would empathise closely with this aspect of Hampson's writing. Louise DeSalvo explains how, in *To The Lighthouse*, Woolf had herself attempted to erase the impact of her father's violence by writing about it, and similarly to quell her mother's voice—the one telling her the only proper role for women was to serve men—which had previously obsessed her. Woolf believed that in writing: 'I did for myself what psychoanalysts do for their patients. I expressed some very long and deeply felt emotion. And, in expressing it I explained it and then laid it to rest.'[93] In this respect it is possible to consider William Plomer's characterisation of Hampson's *Saturday Night at The Greyhound* as a 'case-history' in a more positive light.[94] Rather than having a confessional or exculpatory function, Hampson's stories may be better read as indictments of the external pressures imposed upon families by the such external factors as the Means Test or Unemployment, in which case, to paraphrase Louise DeSalvo, they would be better construed as forms of public testimony whereby personal suffering (Hampson's experience of the spiritual and physical debasement brought about by economic impoverishment) is transformed into art.[95]

Arguing that the category of realism was not always adequate to the task of analysing the working-class novel, John Fordham suggests, 'the bourgeois novel's convention of internal focalisation will be displaced by figural representations of consciousness, the reified worker transformed into automaton or machine part'.[96] This process was underlined in the discussion of *Means Test Man*, where it was shown how 'figural representations' were achieved by distortions closer at times to expressionist rather than realist practice. However, whilst formally innovative in this respect, Brierley's narrative technique remained otherwise conventional, the events impinging upon the Cooks' life recounted largely from the standpoint of a single omniscient, third-person narrator. Reading Walter Allen's

Innocence Is Drowned directly after Brierley's novel, one is immediately struck by the differences in narrative technique. In what remains very much a novel of working-class life informed by perspectives gleaned as an 'insider', Allen's working-class status as grammar school scholarship boy, university graduate in English literature, habitué of the Birmingham film society, literary critic and novelist, clearly exposed him to a wider repertoire of literary influence than that of his Birmingham group companions Halward and Brierley. A comparison of the Birmingham group authors' educational experiences underscores the importance of not viewing working-class writers monolithically. Ross McKibbin and Valentine Cunningham have each cautioned against such stereotyping, likewise Tony Davies, who is critical of conceptions which ignore '[T]he highly varied social, ethnic and occupational composition of the working class, the active and continuously productive nature of experience and [...] appropriate forms of representation in constantly changing circumstances'.[97] It is to Walter Allen's 'representation' of the 'constantly changing circumstances' of provincial working-class life during the darkening months of the 1930s that I now turn.

Walter Allen: *Innocence Is Drowned*

As with Walter Brierley's *Means Test Man*, and his own *Blind Man's Ditch*, Allen's first published novel *Innocence Is Drowned* is episodic in structure and focuses largely upon the dynamics of a working-class family focalised from the perspective of each of its members during a three-day period. Its title derives from Yeats' *The Second Coming*, which, as Allen informs us, 'in a gracious and charming letter', the Irish poet gave his permission to quote. Published late in 1938 against the backdrop of a national psyche barely recovered from the economic downturn of the 1920s and now teetering towards a further European conflict, the closing months of the decade witnessed a period of heightened political awareness and anxiety amongst the population at large. E. M. Forster referred to the post-Munich period in his article titled 'The 1939 state', in which, as Steve Ellis indicates, the lower case 's' captures the prevailing mood of both political and psychological consternation.[98] As the novel's title suggests, older certitudes could no longer be relied upon; a sense of foreboding hung in the air. Allen records, 'The age was seen as either an age of apocalypse as in Yeats' poem or in the grip of an 'obscure malaise' as in Auden's, 'What shall we say of England, this country of ours where no-one is well?'[99]

Diluvian imagery is pervasive, Allen's title suggested the 'drowning' of innocence, whereas, Orwell's George Bowling is presented as a floundering swimmer who, as with Allen's protagonist, laments the change taking place in the world around him asking: 'Does anyone who isn't dead from the neck up doubt that there's a bad time coming? We don't even know what it will be, and yet we know it is coming. Perhaps a war, perhaps a slump—no knowing except that it'll be something bad.'[100] Although Lukacs would claim that 'richness and profundity of created characters relies upon the richness and profundity of the total social process', contemporary events, though far from 'rich or profound', had nonetheless provided fertile ground for Walter Allen's imagination.[101] To use a culinary term, his novel *reduced* the nation's social and political anxieties to the more manageable dynamic of a provincial family unit striving beneath the shadow of catastrophe. Again, this process aligns with Raymond Williams' formulation in that it provides 'a sense of the quality of life at a particular place and time: a sense of the ways in which particular activities combined into a way of thinking and living' and thus captures 'the area of interaction between the official consciousness of an epoch and the whole process of actually living its consequences'.[102] John Hampson describes Allen's literary modus operandi as follows:

> Allen's books deal with the provincial scene; they indicate the turmoil existing beneath the dull surface of an industrial town. His three novels *Innocence Is Drowned*, *Living Space* and *Blind Man's Ditch* are concerned with existence in the thirties, his pictures are grim yet lively, for he can see what lies behind the trim undistinguished façade which a provincial town presents to the stranger. Allen takes a small section of the community and shows what happens to them over a short space of time. Among his types are always the bohemian intellectual and the spiv, or would be crook.[103]

As he told Andy Croft, Allen considered the pre-war decade 'a great period, a great time for the novel of specific place', and although remaining politically committed throughout his career, as was remarked above, he had been equally 'swayed by aesthetic considerations'.[104] Allen's literary aesthetic at this time consisted of three principal strands: firstly, the genius loci built on his familiarity with and nearness to the Birmingham working classes and his desire to represent them in fiction; secondly, the formal potential he discovered in the 'collective' novel, in which the outlook of a single protagonist or omniscient narrator is substituted for a multiplicity of character viewpoints enabling a more democratic, plurality of perspective; and thirdly, narrative experimentation, an attempt to emulate in literature the montage techniques, editing, juxtaposition and cross-cutting employed in documentary cinema. Doubtless, such noble aims would have met with the approval of Margaret Storm Jameson. In fact, Storm Jameson had set out a theory of documentary writing which stressed the importance of visual presentation, suggesting:

> A well-placed novelist might bring out a double-sided record: one day or one week in the life of a family of five living in one of the wealthier residential districts of the West End (if he or she can find one which has so far forgotten itself as to breed) set down opposite the life during the same length of time of a similar, Paddington, Hoxton Lambeth family. [...] As the photographer does, so must the writer keep himself out of the picture while working ceaselessly to present the *fact* from a striking (poignant, ironic, penetrating, significant) angle.[105]

Storm Jameson's comments effectively paraphrase Walter Allen's approach, as he described it to Andy Croft, and, given that Allen self-avowedly sought to appropriate and deploy cinematic effects in his novel, it seems practical to approach *Innocence Is Drowned* by exploring it from a filmic perspective. It is also important to remember that Allen's novel was produced within the Jamesian aesthetic of vision, a critical orthodoxy that emphasised a preference for *showing*, rather than *telling*, and which, when combined with the burgeoning influence of the documentary film and mass-observation movements, exerted a powerful influence on the contemporary novel. Catherine Belsey suggests that in '[e]schewing the subjectivity of Romantic and Victorian periods that had culminated in Eliot and Yeats', the prose fiction of later years adopted a different perspective whereby 'intrusion by the author comes to seem an impropriety; impersonal narration, "showing" (the truth), rather than "telling" it, is a requirement of prose fiction by the end of the nineteenth-century'.[106] It was believed that *showing* enabled greater objectivity, detachment and dramatic verity as registered in the abandonment of the 'omniscient', and simultaneously 'intrusive' narrative voice, as witnessed, and often disparaged, in the work of nineteenth-century realist writers. David Lodge notes how 'the Jamesian aesthetic of vision; the preference for "showing" rather than "telling" remained dominant in criticism of the novel during the

1920s, thirties and 1940s'.[107] Given Leslie Halward's observation that the Birmingham writers 'met periodically for the purpose of explaining each to the other where he was wrong', one might speculate the showing/tellings debate formed the topic of some heated discussion. Indeed, the discussion as to whether, 'showing' did offer itself as the literary panacea to treat such writerly qualms, continued throughout the pre-war decade and well beyond. However, in *Narrative Discourse* (1972), Gerard Genette would caution those adopting a too-credulous enthusiasm:

> [F]rom our own strictly analytic point of view it must be added [...] that the very idea of *showing*, like that of imitation or narrative representation (and even more so because of its naively visual character), is completely illusory: in contrast to dramatic representation, no narrative can "show" or "imitate" the story it tells. All it can do is tell it in a matter which is detailed, precise, "alive," and in that way, give more or less the *'illusion of mimesis'*.[108]

Based upon his artisan father: 'a silversmith's engraver, designer and die-sinker who had spent a year at grammar school—long enough to give him the rudiments of Latin grammar and an insatiable thirst for learning'—we initially encounter Walter Allen's ageing, tubercular and unemployed protagonist Dick Gardiner as he struggles to retain his status as the family patriarch.[109] The novel is loosely threaded by a blackmail plot in which Dick Gardiner's rebellious second son Eric, arrogant and impervious to his father's designs, embarks upon a criminal act. The dramatis personae include: elder son Ralph, who is studying at Birmingham's Mason College (later Birmingham University) and is currently in a relationship with the socially sophisticated and superior Monica Craven, a graduate of Newnham College, Cambridge; Sydney, the youngest son is currently at grammar school and represents his father's last opportunity to exert paternal influence; and finally, attempting to hold familial body and soul together, Rose, Dick's hard-working 'doubly oppressed' wife, who takes in ironing to supplement the family income.

This chapter's focus on unemployment involves wrenching Allen's sick and ageing patriarch, from the confines of the family unit, in order to examine the deleterious effects and psychological perturbations which lead to not only the 'unmanning' of this once-craft-proud artisan but also his political reconstitution as, jolted from his erstwhile innocence and naiveté, he comes to appreciate the wider implications of worklessness in a seemingly unsympathetic world. Set in the second-city slowly lifting itself from the slough of economic depression, Allen's novel portrays a provincial, working-class household, worlds apart from Brierley's alienated collier and family out on the Derbyshire coalfields. Differences in the social, geographical, occupational and educational settings would have major implications for the kind of novel he produced.

Birmingham's expansion and economic recovery during the middle period of the 1930s led to the city's increasing demand for skilled engineering workers. The professions of toolmaking, pattern-making and die-sinking comprised a craft-proud aristocracy conscious of its own power and importance.[110] This was not always collectively or socially conducive however, as Ross McKibbin indicates: 'The status-consciousness that accompanied craft-pride undermined working-class *esprit de corps* as much as it did that of any other class.'[111] Having contracted TB owing to long hours as a toolmaker during the Great War, Allen's sick and unemployed artisan is the embodiment of the type described by Robert Tressell:

> The skilled artisan does not as a rule take part in such a procession except as a very last resource…And all the time he strives to keep up an appearance of being well to do, and would be highly indignant if anyone suggested that he was really in a position of abject, miserable poverty […] he tries to bluff his betters that he has some mysterious private means of which they know nothing, and conceals his poverty as if it were a crime.[112]

The 'episodes' upon which the following will focus trace Dick Gardiner's progress from individualistic, craft-proud patriarch and lead to his critique, outrage and, ultimately, what might be descried as the raising of his political consciousness with regard to the failings of an economic system and ideology he perceives as creating and seemingly sanctioning such wastage of human potential.

It is around the family dining table that we first encounter the Gardiner family. Eldest son Ralph is out visiting his girlfriend, while his younger siblings Eric and Sydney sit consuming bread and cheese. Mrs. Gardiner serves up cocoa, while her husband Dick enthusiastically surveys a quantity of wood and quietly muses over his plans to construct a bookcase:

> Now the wood had come he would be able to get to work again. The very sight of it gave new strength and suppleness to his fine fingers. Soon they would be holding a plane again […] When Joe had first promised him the

wood he had planned to sell the bookcase [...] but now, damned if he'd sell it. (*ID*, 11)

Relating to an earlier conversation between Dick Gardiner and a companion, the narrator's account of Dick's musings communicate obliquely not only the physical and mental atrophy visited upon the workless craftsman but also the rejuvenative nature of creative activity: of being in control and doing something purposive. Capturing both the artisan's craft-pride and independence, it reflects Dick Gardiner's refusal to consider himself a mere commodity or of assessing the produce of his labours purely in terms of exchange value alone. 'People thought that because you were out of work you had to do everything for money', thought Dick, 'No; Ralph should have [them]' (*ID*, 12). Rather than merely realising their nominal exchange value, the bookshelves represent something more than a commodity.[113]

Though not supplying the portentous metaphor of Leonard Bast's encounter with them in Forster's *Howards End*, Dick Gardiner's bookshelves nonetheless carry a symbolic function. Initially envisaged to house his son Ralph's university textbooks, they also function metonymically for Dick Gardiner's own, unrealised academic aspirations. Ralph is currently studying at Birmingham University, where he is expected to take a first. However, whilst courting and simultaneously intimidated by his girlfriend—Newnham College educated, Monica Craven, recently 'on the rebound' from her troubled relationship with Derek, 'the most brilliant man in Cambridge'—Ralph is Derek's antithesis owing to a lack of self-esteem and his strong sense of class inferiority. However, despite Monica's assumption that Ralph will become a schoolmaster, Ralph however has different ideas:

Schoolmaster indeed! He winced at the snob phrase. [...] He did not want to be a schoolmaster.[114] He would be an elementary schoolteacher, in the class from which he had sprung. The educational system had transplanted him from elementary school to university by way of the municipal secondary school. If he got a good degree the same process would land him a job in another secondary school. That must be resisted. Now, he wanted only to teach the children of the very poor, those whom the educational system left untouched and unprovided for, who wanted direction and encouragement more than the others. (*ID*, 28)

Ralph sees education very much in terms of the German concept of *Bildung*: the altruistic process of acquiring knowledge and disseminating it to one's community, a notion he shares with his fictional counterpart Arthur Gardner in Walter Brierley's *Sandwichman*. However, Ralph's noble sentiments are not echoed by his brother Eric, who, rather than realising Dick Gardiner's vicarious wish that his sons become doctors or schoolmasters, has instead left school at the earliest opportunity to take position as a jeweller's apprentice. Unmoved by his father's importunity, Eric epitomises teenage rebellion, the relationship between Gardiner senior and his second son articulating the generational dissonance identified by Raymond Williams whereby:

> One generation may train its successor, with reasonable success, in the social character or the general cultural pattern, but the new generation will have its own structure of feeling, which will not appear to have 'come from' anywhere. [...] The new generation responds in its own unique ways to the world it is inheriting [...] yet feeling its whole life in certain ways differently, and shaping its creative response in a new structure of feeling.[115]

Outwardly aggressive and opinionated, Eric is a psychologically complex character: '[N]ot tough and hardboiled but merely potentially so', he, along with Eugene Lorimer in *Blind Man's Ditch*, represents the amateur criminal type John Hampson considers the stock characters in Allen's fiction, each standing as figurations of the wider evil permeating existence in the closing months of the 1930s.

As we discover, Dick Gardiner's 'pride' precedes his 'fall'. Temporarily buoyed by his recovered self-esteem, Dick's reverie continues as he recalls his recent misfortunes in the passage below where the continual rebuffs he describes both test and begin to respond to the kinds of question asked by the social researchers Beales and Lambert, who asked: 'When a man loses his job, how long does he continue looking hopefully for a new one?' Dick's experience is representative of that shared by thousands in the real world, and here Allen's narrator communicates the tribulations and indignities confronting those seeking work:

> During his illness the thought of the tramp looking for work day after day had been agony to him; almost he had not wanted to get well again, going over the continual rebuffs he had met with and, worse still the discouraged talk of the men hanging around the factory gates. 'They don't want us old 'uns any longer.' They all said that. (*ID*, 16)

As we saw in his correspondence with Walter Brierley, John Hampson stressed the need to 'make capital of each and every difference between the state of the man in employment and the man workless'. Allen shared in this exchange and, along with Brierley, was doubtless a beneficiary of Hampson's advice. In the following extract, Allen contrasts the rejuvenating effects of creative activity with Dick's negative experience of unemployment, and, as the opening scene develops, his narrator provides further access to Dick's sanguine imaginings, where, his equilibrium partially restored, more positive thoughts emerge:

> Suddenly, gazing at the smoothly planed planks, the future seemed easy and obvious to Mr. Gardiner. It was absurd to have despaired so long. New strength was in him; he felt ill no longer; his fingers ached to be at their labour. If he felt as well tomorrow he knew he would get a job. [...] He sat up and leaned forward, elbows on the arm of his chair. His eyes shone brightly. It was urgent that they [his family] should share his joy and satisfaction. (*ID*, 17)

As further potentialities reveal themselves, we move from Dick's internalised imaginings to his voiced, though emptily optimistic, declaration:

> 'I reckon we'll soon be in calm weather,' he said. The words poured out excitedly. 'As soon as I get my strength back we'll be in calm weather. I'll get a job then.' His hands gesticulated. 'We'll move out of this lousy dump, into a decent neighbourhood. He jerked his thumb viciously at the wall. "We'll say goodbye to old Creeping Jesus next door, we'll...'
>
> '*You won't get another job* (my italics).
>
> Mr. Gardiner stopped. Eric was sitting there, grinning sarcastically, his smile a smile of malicious triumph. 'Who d'you think's going to give you a job?'
>
> Mr. Gardiner's mouth was dry. "That's not the way to speak to your dad," cried Mrs. Gardiner. "For two pins I'd give you a hiding old as you are!" Mr. Gardiner clutched at the arms of his chair, his legs weak again, as though decomposing into fluid. The boy smiled his twisted grin, hugging the secret within him. He was in good humour with himself and the world. "Aw nuts!" he said. For a moment there was silence. Mr. Gardiner stared in front of him. Weariness flooded his whole being. *Saying a thing like that in front of young Sydney.* He tried to speak, but no words came. He felt suddenly old, and the tears formed behind his eyes. His heart fluttered. *Saying a thing like that!* Mrs. Gardiner spoke quietly: "Sydney, go to bed, I'll see to

> your books." Silently, shamefacedly, the boy edged from his chair. "Good night all," he said, feeling his voice go high and strangled. Nobody answered. (*ID*, 18)

At the outset of this passage, Dick Gardiner's hopes for better times were internalised. His thoughts rendered chaotically and fragmentally as they present themselves in his mind. However, between these snatches of dialogue, Allen's narrator employs a restricted diegetic mode in order to recount the 'manner' in which Dick Gardiner's words are spoken: 'the words poured out excitedly', 'his hands gesticulated', but declining to comment or make judgement upon them. While presented as mimesis, as Genette indicated, the notion of 'showing' here remains 'illusory': the sequence of events being registered *verbally*, whereas in a drama or film these paralinguistic details would be either enacted or communicated by means of close-up, or 'zooming in', to reveal the speaker's actions as a bystander might observe them.

Typographically set-off from the remainder of the passage, the line '*You won't get another job*' abruptly silences Dick Gardiner's enthusiastic reverie, the absence of the *he/she said* (epic-preterite) contrives to make the interjection appear unattributed, as though coming from nowhere. As the sting of the remark fades, external focalisation reveals Eric as its originator; again, by adopting the restricted diegetic mode, his guilt is revealed purely by reference to his facial expression 'sitting there grinning sarcastically, his smile a smile of malicious triumph'. The line offers readers an insight into Eric's personality, his cynical, threatening tone and brusque reference to his father in the second person being indicative of his disrespect and congruent with Allen's subsequent development of his character. Eric's rebuttal of his father's dreams is doubly insensitive: initially crushing in being uttered just at the moment when Dick Gardiner was beginning to think more positively, and additionally due to its utterance in the dining room: the family hearth, the otherwise inviolate womb of the working-class household once considered a sanctuary from such harsh external realities.

Eric's words certainly have an unsettling effect. The narrative focus returns immediately to his father, whose reactions are relayed purely by 'showing' his physical response: 'Mr. Gardiner clutched at the arm of his chair, his legs weak again as if decomposing into fluid' (*ID*, 18). Though clearly shocked at Eric's outburst, Mrs Gardiner has calmed a little and encourages Sydney, the youngest son, to go to bed. Again, Allen's narrator registers that she 'spoke quietly', which, by describing the *manner* in which her words were uttered, is appropriate to situating her as the long-suffering and dutiful matriarch charged with pouring oil upon the troubled waters of family conflict. The most curious line in the passage is the italicised: *Saying a thing like that in front of young Sydney*. The gerundive is representative of Dick Gardiner's internalised, unvoiced feelings and emphasises the enormity of Eric's remark, unable to speak and sticking all the more firmly in Dick's craw owing to his 'public' humiliation. Eric's words not only undermine Dick Gardiner's role as family patriarch but more so because they contain the kernel of an inescapable truth, and they serve to underline the crueller reality that he may never work again. As if to underscore the febrile tension of this dinner-table 'domestic', Allen focalises young Sydney's 'shamefaced discomfort' and the 'strangled pitch' of his voice as he says his goodnights and the dinner table 'scene' closes.

As the novel progresses, Dick Gardiner comes to perceive how things are for his generation and class. Taking its title from Yeats' 'The Second Coming', Allen must have been aware of the Irish poet's pronouncement regarding change and impermanence: that 'Things fall apart; the centre cannot hold'.[116] Too old, sick and powerless to effect any change, his protagonist Dick Gardiner's 'ceremony of innocence is [certainly] drowned', his once-haughty artisan demeanour eroded as he reconciles himself to the implications of long-term unemployment. This discomfiting realisation is cemented when he moves from the sanctuary of the domestic homescape to the public sphere of the Central Library reading room. Sheltered from the elements and providing warmth and companionship, it is here, confronted with the degradations suffered by his ageing and defeated contemporaries, that the foundations of Dick's hubris are shaken, and he finally throws his lot in with his fellow men. Glancing disinterestedly at a copy of *The Tatler*, his usual reading matter having been appropriated by one of the unemployed and dozing denizens of the reading room, Dick Gardiner peruses photographs of upper-class 'society' lounging on the Riviera:

> [P]ictures of ladies and gentlemen in evening dress posed in restaurants with bottles in buckets at their feet ; a full-page picture of a girl holding a Scots terrier—"Miss…, lovely daughter of Captain and Lady…, one of the season's most popular debutantes"; pictures of ladies and gentlemen in bathing costumes lying under the Riviera sun. Resentment smouldered in Mr. Gardiner. He turned hastily to the advertisements and saw a picture of a proud lady in a fur coat and a prouder lady head thrown back and breasts jutting triangularly forth, wearing somebody's corsets. He glanced about:

> putting a paper like that in a public library seemed to him a bloody insult. The man next to him snored gently. Mr. Gardiner looked at him. His head was placed in his folded arms that lay in a loop on the table. His old bowler hat tipped forward showed a mat of thick white hair. He had a piece of red rag around his neck. A sweetish sickly smell came up from his body. Cautiously Mr. Gardiner peeped under the table. The man had no socks and was wearing a pair of broken brogues; under a toe-cap a dirt-encrusted toe protruded coyly. (*ID*, 161,162)

Presented in chopped fragments, the clipped, telegraphic style of Dick's reading mimics his perfunctory scanning of the society magazine and registers his indifference to its frivolous material. Allen uses free indirect speech to render his thoughts: '[P]utting a paper like that in a public library seemed to him a bloody insult', and he deploys typographical ellipses as though suggesting, not without irony, why read any further? 'Resentment smouldered in Mr Gardiner', the images of bathing costumes, fur coats and lingerie that fill the pages of the magazine represent a world wholly inaccessible to Dick Gardiner and his class. Whilst such images doubtless reverberated in Dick Gardiner's psyche, against these images Allen juxtaposes Dick's wife—ground down by a lifetime's hard work and forced by ill-circumstance to take in ironing—against Mrs Gamble, the fortunate wife of a local accountant who drinks orange juice for breakfast and stays in bed until midday and whose gowns and silk lingerie form the basis of Rose's workload.

Unlike the cross-class montage provided in the photo-essays of *Picture Post*, *The Tatler* was directed towards a middle- and upper-class readership in which celebrities, investment bankers and aristocrats sat side by side. Recoiling angrily at the magazine's fawning adulation of these overindulged socialites, Dick considers the magazine's very existence an affront to the dignity of the beaten and defeated humanity he finds in the reading room. As Lara Feigel observes:

> The contrasting of rich and poor through montage came to dominate both Russian and German cinema in the late 1920s and was used explicitly in Fritz Lang's *Metropolis* (1927) where [...] the beleaguered, dehumanised mass of dark-clothed workers is juxtaposed with the upper classes, dressed in white and frolicking in the sun.[117]

In the remaining lines of the 'Library' scene, Allen continues to emulate cinematic effects and changes of narrative viewpoint to register Dick Gardiner's anger as he contrasts the images of these rich socialites with the indignities suffered by members of the unemployed working class. Again the sequence beginning 'The man next to him snored gently' and culminating in [...] 'a dirt encrusted toe protruding coyly' provides a graphic image and owes much to Allen's Sunday evenings spent at the Birmingham Film Society, where he absorbed the lessons of Eisensteinian shock montage. Emulating the techniques of documentary cinema, Allen's Dick Gardiner functions as the novel's camera eye and centre of consciousness. By montaging the lives of the privileged classes against those of the destitute habitués of the library reading room, Allen engages his readers as active participants in the construction of the novel's political meaning and, in so doing, reveals his solidarity with the downtrodden. The montage technique employed in his literary 'screening' of the disparities between elite and subordinate classes is thus revealed as a deeply political act. As with Brierley, the absence of prescriptive or overtly political rhetoric in Allen's novel is not to condemn it as apolitical. Indeed, despite the tendency towards political or sectarian prescriptivism current in the contemporary and later criticism of working-class writing, Allen's approach aligns more closely to the Marxist concept of 'objective partisanship'. In his correspondence with Minna Kautsky, Frederick Engels explained:

> He was by no means averse to fiction with a political 'tendency' but that it was wrong for an author to be *openly* partisan. The political tendency must emerge unobtrusively from the dramatised situations; only in this indirect way could revolutionary fiction work effectively on the bourgeois consciousness of its readers.[118]

A more expansive account of a literary work's sociopolitical function (or message) is to be found in the writings of Theodor Adorno. Informed by the notion of negative dialectics, which proposes the significance of autonomous art lies in its 'functionlessness', Adorno doubts the efficacy of a literary work to communicate an overt social message—especially the kind of engagé writing promoted by Sartre in *What is Literature?*—believing instead that the inclusion of 'propositional content' resulted in the artwork's aesthetic being subsumed beneath 'a superior universal concept': its message, with the consequence that the literary text came to resemble less an artwork than a philosophical treatise'.[119] Adorno held that the 'rudiments of external meaning are the irreducibly non-artistic elements in art. Its formal principle lies not in them but in the dialectic of both moments—which accomplishes the transformation of meanings within it'.[120] Rather than freighting his narrative with authorial commentary, therefore, Allen's 'cinematic realism' presents the conflicts and opposing realities of the contemporary social divide 'non-propositionally'; his novel's critique emerging, as Engels proposed, 'unobtrusively from the dramatised situations', and, as Adorno suggests, in 'the dialectic of both moments' within the work itself, allowing the ideas presented to speak for themselves.[121] The fact that Allen's consciously 'visual' mode of representation was successful in communicating the dialectic enabled his readers to position themselves within the frame of his story, as though witnessing events first-hand; in this way, he was able to generate an affective response, as attested by such early reviewers as Wilfred Gibson, who considered Allen gave 'an utterly convincing picture of a working-class family', and Edwin Muir, who perceived 'the writing is so transparent, the observation so unexaggerated, that *we seem to be seeing everything with our own eyes.* And what we see in these few figures is the life of a whole class' (my emphasis).[122]

Though formally innovative, the naturalist genre with which working-class literature has often been associated had met with criticism from Western Marxists such as Lukacs on the grounds that 'by restricting itself *exclusively* to the faithful reproduction of immediate reality [it] robbed literature of its power to give a living and dynamic picture of the essential driving forces of history'.[123] While Lukacs' conception of the totality is relevant to those epochs in which the *momentous* events of history unfurled themselves, it overlooks the fact that certain epochs were perhaps *less momentous* than others. As we have seen, the early years of what came to be known as the 'low dishonest decade' were not always conducive to producing 'the richness and profundity of the total social process' that Lukacs desired, the working class's confrontation with immediate circumstance in the shape of unemployment certainly presenting as an imaginative barrier. Andres Gorz uses the metaphor of an army to highlight the difficulty of understanding the totality of the social process from a position of exclusion within it:

> Seen from the summit, an army resembles an intelligent animal with a single head, commanding thousands of arms and legs. But the animal does not exist for itself. The unit commanders and individual soldiers are ignorant of both the overall strategic plan and the entire movement of the army. All that they know are the orders and local, partial movements whose overall meaning escapes them.[124]

Touching on the ideological impulse informing what he terms the 'Myth of Collective Appropriation', Gorz' asserts, '[I]t is impossible to see the overall process in its entirety and to get the overall goal that is built into the workings of this gigantic machinery internalised by each individual and reflected in everyone's work. And this impossibility has, of course, been deliberately created in order to guarantee capitalist domination.'[125]

In the opening lines of Dickens' *David Copperfield*, the young David speculates, '[w]hether I shall turn out to be the hero of my own life, or whether that station will be held by anybody else [...]'.[126] Dickens was particularly fortunate; alongside contemporaries such as Tolstoy and Balzac, he was able to become the hero of his own life. These pages reveal how the exercise of individual agency was rarely an option for the authors and protagonists of the narratives discussed here, nor likewise the working classes whose lived-experience they set out to represent.

Referencing Robert D. Putnam's and Shaylyn Garrett's *The Upswing* (2020), Martin Kettle explains how 'the 1950s [represented] the swelling summit in the middle of the "I-We-I" bell curve of American life between the economic free-for-all of the 1890s, the era of greater co-operation mid-20th century, and the turbo-charged renewal of individualism, inequality and partisanship of the 2020s'.[127] As the trope has it, what happens in America sooner or later surfaces here, and surely the 'we' summit of Britain's sociopolitical, bell curve might be said to have arrived following the tranche of social reforms that issued in the 'post-war consensus'. As with America, the mid-twentieth-century social agitation evident in Britain had included the voices of minorities, who, driven less from self-seeking or individualistic motives, or believing they possessed sole-agency rights to alienation, merely expressed a desire for inclusion and the wish to avoid falling further. In a recent TV interview, ex-president Barack Obama outlined the historical, zig-zag progression of American social and human rights movements from abolitionism to the suffragettes, from union movement to feminism through LGBQT activism and Black Lives Matter, before concluding: '*we the people*, by which we mean not just a handful—not just property-owning white males—*all have a seat at the table*' (my emphasis).[128] Although Obama's 'inclusivity imperative' outlines the nature of the *political* task, it also predicates an examination of the overlapping categories of disadvantage experienced by working people labouring beneath the broad parameters of the class, race and gender trilogy. As Ben Clarke and Nick Hubble indicate, this specifically necessitates '[c]hanging the ways in which the working classes are represented and understood [...] [and requires] not only recognising the agency of working class people, their ability to speak about their own interests, but the diversity of experiences and identities potentially encompassed by the category "working class" itself'.[129] That the Birmingham group writers showed themselves as responsive to the diversity of experience and categories of disadvantage to which working people were exposed *beyond*, though often running in parallel *with*, issues of class, race and gender, is therefore encouraging of this book's adoption of an intersectional approach in the chapter which follows.

Notes

1. To the respectable working-class family, the Means Test was an unprecedented intrusion into their privacy, as well as the symbol of a mean-spirited and vindictive state. 'The Means Test was tantamount to a new Poor Law in working-class demonology, and remains an abiding image of the period'. Ian Haywood, *Working-Class Fiction: From Chartism to Trainspotting* (Plymouth: Northcote House Publishers Ltd, 1997), p. 37.
2. Walter Allen, *Tradition and Dream*, p. 142.
3. Joseph Freeman and others, Introduction, *Proletarian Literature in the United States: An Anthology* (London: Lawrence and Wishart Ltd, 1935), p. 6.
4. Ibid.
5. The power of the visual image is not to be understated. In a recent article commenting upon the seeming public complacency in the face of rising upsurge in deaths attributed to the Covid pandemic, behavioural psychologist Robert West remarked: 'One thing we know about humans is our emotions are stirred by images, they're not stirred by numbers.' Hannah Devlin Guardian article: 'Why Britons are tolerating sky-high Covid rates—and why this may not last. *The Guardian*, Friday 15 October 2021.
6. Beales, H. L. and R. S. Lambert, eds, *Memoirs of the Unemployed* (London: Victor Gollancz, 1973), p. 7.
7. Juliet Gardiner, *The Thirties: An Intimate History*, p. 62.
8. Ibid. Beveridge's involvement and the various committees on which he sat during the years 1940–41 issued in what later became known as the 'Beveridge Report'. This document essentially gave rise to the social reforms and legislation underpinning the Welfare State.
9. Beales and Lambert, *Memoirs*, p. 7.
10. Ibid, pp. 7, 25.

11. Terry Eagleton, *Marxism and Literary Criticism* (London: Methuen & Co. Ltd, 1987), p. 18. Eagleton's, discussion at this point was geared to addressing the ideological element of Marxist criticism more than the working-class fiction's social function per se.
12. Beales and Lambert, *Memoirs*, p. 9.
13. M. Jahoda, P. F. Lazarfeld, and H. Zeisel, *Die Arbeitslosen von Marienthal* (Leipzig, 1933), and English edn., *Marienthal: The Sociography of an Unemployed Community* (London, 1972). Cited in Ross McKibbin, *The ideologies of Class*, p. 229.
14. Ibid, p. 253. McKibbin suggests, '*Marienthal* [was] a rather hit-or-miss description of a single-industry village of exceptionally high long-term unemployment from which only limited conclusions can be drawn.' Unfortunately, some of the findings of this research were subsequently discredited—largely owing to the local specifics of the control sample—being, as Ross McKibbin suggests, little more than 'truistic'.
15. Beales and Lambert, *Memoirs*, p. 91. Andy Croft refers to the occasionally archaic element in Brierley's language.
16. Walter Brierley, 'Frustration and Bitterness: A Colliery Banksman' in Beales and Lambert, *Memoirs*, p. 93.
17. *Turning Point*. A talk given by Brierley to the BBC, on 20 January 1965, detailing his life up to the publication of *Means Test Man* and his resumption of employment on his appointment as a Welfare Officer for Derby Education Authority. Brierley Papers DL282. Derby Local Studies Library. In the *Listener* article, beyond divulging his occupation as 'A Colliery Banksman', Brierley remained otherwise anonymous. Mrs Perowne had presumably written to *the Listener's* editors requesting the invitation be forwarded to the writer of the article.
18. Ibid, p 112.
19. Walter Brierley, 'Frustration and Bitterness', in Beales and Lambert, *Memoirs*, p. 96.
20. Christopher Hilliard believed Halward's epiphanic claim, 'The sudden urge to express [himself] laid hold as unexpectedly as a fever', was not 'wholly unreliable'. Although Hilliard was careful to add that the impulse to write 'is not to affirm the existence of some timeless creative urge wired into "human nature." There may be such an urge, but the notion of it is also part of the body of popular ideas about creativity and art that were current in early and mid-twentieth century Britain'. Christopher Hilliard, *To Exercise Our Talents*, pp. 113, 127.
21. John Hampson, Letter to Brierley. 21 April 1934. DLS 282.
22. Ibid.
23. Ibid.

24. Derby Local Studies Library holds copies of some one hundred letters from Walter Allen and John Hampson offering Brierley advice and encouragement. Their correspondence with the Derbyshire writer reveals a deep friendship based upon mutual professional respect rather than beneficence or altruism.
25. Christopher Hilliard, *To Exercise Our Talents*, p. 113.
26. Chris Baldick, *The Modern Movement*, p. 184.
27. John Fordham, *James Hanley Modernism*, p. 4.
28. Richard Hoggart, *Speaking To Each Other* (London: Penguin Books, 1973), p. 185 et seq.
29. Ibid.
30. Ramon Lopez Ortega, 'The Language of the Working-Class Novel of the 1930s'. In H. Gustav Klaus *The Socialist Novel in Britain*, 122-144. p. 124.
31. Walter Allen, *Tradition and Dream*, p. 215.
32. Ken Worpole was discussing the Liverpool writer James Hanley but his comments, as will be seen, are equally applicable to Brierley's procedure. Ken Worpole, Dockers and Detectives, p. 90.
33. Carole Snee. 'Walter Brierley: A Test Case'. In *Red Letters*, p. 12.
34. Simon Dentith, 'Tone of Voice in Industrial Writing of the 1930s'. Eds, Gustav Klaus and Stephen Knight, *British Industrial Fictions*, 99-111. p. 99.
35. Ibid, p. 100.
36. Ibid, p. 104.
37. Ibid, p. 100.
38. Martha Vicinus, *The Industrial Muse: A Study in Nineteenth Century British Working-Class Literature* (London: Croome Helm, 1974), p .38.
39. Pickering. Michael and Kevin Robins, Eds, 'A Revolutionary Materialist with a Leg Free': The Autobiographical Novels of Jack Common'. In Jeremy Hawthorn, *The British Working-Class Novel in the Twentieth Century* (London: Edward Arnold, 1984), 77-92. p. 79.
40. Ibid.
41. Herbert Marcuse, *Studies in Critical Philosophy* (London: NLB, 1972), p. 129.
42. Michael Pickering and Kevin Robins cited in Simon Dentith Chapter 'Tone of Voice in Industrial Writing in the 1930s'. In Klaus and Knight, *British Industrial Fictions*, p. 105.
43. Graham Holderness, 'Miners and the Novel'. In Jeremy Hawthorn, Ed, *The British Working-Class Novel*, p. 27.
44. John Fordham, *James Hanley: Modernism and the Working-Class*, p. 4.
45. Ibid, p. 26.
46. Ibid.

47. Though claiming 'Tramlines and slagheaps and pieces of machinery' as his 'ideal' scenery. 'Letter to Lord Byron' (1936), in an earlier poem 'Who stands, the crux left of the watershed' (1927), Auden appears to have been less ambivalent regarding industrial landscapes. Rather than attaching sentimental or romantic value, the observer should reflect on the daily struggle and ever-present danger of injury or death for those who had worked in such hazardous occupations.
48. Ryle. Martin and Kate Soper, *To Relish the Sublime,* p. 186.
49. John Fordham, *James Hanley,* p. 4.
50. Peter Nicholls, *Modernisms: A Literary Guide* (London: Macmillan Press Limited, 1995), p. 142
51. Ibid.
52. Kristian Sotriffer, in Jack F. Stewart. 'Expressionism in the Rainbow', *Novel: A Journal on Fiction,* 13 (1980), 296-315. p. 297.
53. Fredric Jameson, Ed, *Aesthetics and Politics,* pp. 36, 37.
54. Andy Croft, *Red Letters,* p. 81.
55. Andrew Harrison, 'The Regional Modernism of D. H. Lawrence and James Joyce', in Neal Alexander and James Moran, *Regional Modernisms* (Edinburgh: Edinburgh University Press, 2013), p. 46.
56. Walter Allen Letter to Brierley 11 September 1934. Brierley Papers. DL282. Derby Local Studies Library.
57. Walter Allen Letter to Brierley 17 September 1934. Brierley Papers. DL282. Derby Local Studies Library.
58. Walter Allen Letter to Brierley 11 November 1934. Brierley Papers. DL282. Derby Local Studies Library.
59. Walter Allen, *As I walked Down,* p. 18.
60. John Hampson Letter to Brierley 27 July 1934. Brierley Papers. DL282. Derby Local Studies Library.
61. Although praising *Means Test Man* for its 'recreation of his own empirical observations of life on the dole', Carole Snee's charge that in *Sandwichman* Brierley merely used Lawrence as a lens with which to see the world and 'as a substitute for his own understanding', is, as I aim to show, unjustified. 'Working-Class Literature or Proletarian Writing', in Clark Jon, Margot Heinemann and others, *Culture and Crisis,* pp. 180, 181.
62. John Fordham, Chapter 'Working Class Fiction across the Century', in Robert Caserio, *The Cambridge Companion to the Twentieth-Century English Novel* (Cambridge: Cambridge University Press, 2009), 131-145. p. 136.
63. Ibid, p. 132.
64. According to Andy Croft, Oliver Baldwin, the Labour MP and son of three times Conservative prime minister Stanley Baldwin, demanded, 'Every MP should read it!' [*Means Test Man*]. Though whether novels of

this sort were influential on policymakers remains a moot point. The election of the Attlee government and the welfare changes brought about in the post-war consensus following the Second World War do suggest something of a delayed reaction following changes in the national attitude and a raised social conscience.

65. Edward J. O' Brien, Introduction. p. viii. Leslie Halward, *To Tea on Sunday* (London: Methuen & Co. Ltd, 1936).
66. Ibid.
67. Steve Ellis, *British Writers and the Approach of World War II,* p. 174. ; Frank Kermode, *History and Value.* p. 34.
68. John Fordham, Chapter: 'Working Class Fiction across the century' in Robert Caserio, *Cambridge Companion To The Twentieth Century English Novel,* p. 136.
69. H. E. Bates, *The Modern Short-Story,* pp. 24, 25.
70. Adrian Hunter, *The Cambridge Introduction to the Short Story in English* (Cambridge: Cambridge University Press, 2007), p. 44.
71. Ibid.
72. Ian Reid, *The Short Story* (London and New York: Methuen, 1977), pp. 62, 63.
73. Dominic Head, *The Modernist Short Story: A Study in Theory and Practice* (Cambridge: Cambridge University Press, 1992), pp. 1-36.
74. Ibid, p. 194.
75. Ibid.
76. Ibid, p. 26.
77. Ibid, p. 27.
78. Ibid.
79. Louis Althusser. 'A letter on Art in reply to André Daspre', in *Lenin And Philosophy And Other Essays,* Louis Althusser (New York: Monthly Review Press, 1971), p. 223.
80. John Fordham, *James Hanley: Modernism and the Working Class,* p. 77.
81. Ibid.
82. Dominic Head, *The Modernist Short Story,* p. 28.
83. Ibid.
84. Graham Holderness, 'Miners and the Novel' in Jeremy Hawthorn, *The British Working-Class Novel,* pp. 26, 27.
85. Carole Snee, 'Walter Brierley: A Test Case', *Red Letters,* p. 12.
86. Ibid.
87. Phil O'Brien. 'The De-Industrial Novel: Twenty First Century British Fiction', in Clarke, Ben and Nick Hubble' *Working-Class Writing,* 229-.246. p. 233.
88. Catherine Belsey, *Critical Practice,* p. 65.
89. Ibid.

90. Ibid.
91. Ibid, p. 66.
92. John Fordham, *James Hanley*, p. 79.
93. Virginia Woolf, 'A Sketch of the Past.' In *Moments of Being* (New York: Harcourt Brace Johanovich, 1985), cited in Louise DeSalvo, *Writing as a Way of Healing: How Telling Our Stories Transforms Our Lives* (Great Britain: Womens Press, 1999), p. 40.
94. William Plomer, in Christopher Hawtree introduction to John Hampson, *Saturday Night at the Greyhound* (London: Hogarth Press, 1986), p. 4.
95. Louise De Salvo, *Writing as a Way of Healing*, p. 41.
96. John Fordham, 'Working-class fiction across the Century.' Robert Caserio, *Cambridge Companion to the Twentieth-Century English Novel*, p. 132.
97. Tony Davies, 'Unfinished Business: Realism and Working-Class Writing' in Jeremy Hawthorn, ed, *The British Working-Class Novel in the Twentieth Century*, 125-136. p. 126.
98. Steve Ellis, *British Writers*, p. 1.
99. Walter Allen, *As I Walked Down*, p. 44.
100. George Orwell, *Coming Up for Air* (London: Penguin Books, 1980), p. 168.
101. Gyorgy Lukacs, Article in the New Hungarian Quarterly, vol xiii, No. 47. (Autumn 1972). Cited in Terry Eagleton, *Marxism and Literary Criticism*, p. 30.
102. Phil O'Brien, Chapter, 'The De-Industrial Novel: Twenty-First century British Fiction', in Clarke. Ben, and Nick Hubble, Eds, *Working-Class Writing*, 229-246. p. 229; Raymond Williams, *The Long Revolution*, pp. 62-68.
103. John Hampson, 'In the Underground II'. John Lehmann, Ed, *The Penguin New Writing*. 28.
(London: Penguin Books, 1947), p. 138.
104. Walter Allen, 'Thirties Fiction A View From the Seventies', *Twentieth Century Literature'* 20. (1974), 245-251. p. 246.
105. Postgate, Raymond and Margaret Storm Jameson, Eds, 'Writing in Revolt: Theory and Examples' *Fact*, No 4, p. 15.
106. Catherine Belsey, *Critical Practice*, p. 68.
107. David Lodge, *After Bakhtin: Essays on Fiction and Criticism* (London: Routledge, 1990), pp. 47, 48.
108. Gerard Genette, *Narrative Discourse* (Ithaca New York: Cornell University Press, 1980), p. 164.
109. Walter Allen, *As I Walked Down*, pp. 2, 3.

110. Craft-pride, real and legitimate if exaggerated, was deeply divisive, and more than one local labour party foundered on disputes between skilled and unskilled union members. Ross McKibbin, *The Ideologies of Class,* p. 37.
111. Ibid.
112. Robert Tressell, *The Ragged Trousered Philanthropists* (London: Paladin, 1991), p. 288.
113. Arnold Hauser describes the bourgeois ethic of good workmanship which sees the criterion of aesthetic value in flawless technique and careful execution. *The Social History of Art: Naturalism, Impressionism, The Film Age. Volume IV,* (London: Routledge, 1989), p. 105.
114. 'Schoolmaster': The term was conventionally used to describe male teaching staff at 'public schools', and survives in today's independent sector.
115. Raymond Williams, *The Long Revolution*, p. 49.
116. William Butler Yeats, Stanza One line three, 'The Second Coming', From 'Michael Robartes and The Dancer', (1921). In W. B. Yeats, *The Poems,* Introduction and Edited by Daniel Albright, (London: J. M. Dent and Sons Ltd, 1992).
117. Lara Feigel, *Literature, Cinema and Politics,* pp. 21, 22.
118. Terry Eagleton, *Marxism and Literary Criticism,* p. 46.
119. Theodor Adorno, in Jameson, Ed, *Aesthetics and Politics,* p. 178.
120. Ibid.
121. Ibid.
122. This notion of readerly positioning is discussed by Lawrence F. Hanley in 'Cultural Work and Class Politics: Re-Reading and Remaking proletarian Literature in the United States.' *Modern Fiction Studies,* 38, 3, Fall 1992. Explaining Kenneth Burke's term 'representative anecdote', Hanley suggests the term describes the process whereby middle-class or otherwise uncommitted characters are initiated into a knowledge of class conflict and hence into solidarity with the oppressed, subordinated working classes. Hanley refers to this as the theme of 'crossing' its chief effect being to transport listeners/readers across the class boundaries that divide proletariat and bourgeoisie. pp. 715—732. p. 723. Extracts from publicity reviews shown in Allen's second published novel *Blind Man's Ditch* taken from Wilfred Gibson *Manchester Guardian* and Edwin Muir *Listener,* (undated).
123. George Lukacs, *The Historical Novel* (London: Merlin Press, 1962), p. 206.
124. Andre Gorz, *Farewell to the Working Class: An Essay on Post-Industrial Socialism* (London: Pluto Press, 1980), p. 30
125. Ibid, p. 31.

126. Charles Dickens, *The Personal History of David Copperfield* (London: Hazell, Watson & Viney, Ltd, 1935), p. 9.
127. Martin Kettle, 'The toxic polarisation of our politics can be reversed, but it will take humility', *The Guardian*, Thursday 26 November2020.
128. 'David Olusuga talks to Barack Obama', BBC One, Wednesday 18 November 2020.
129. Clarke, Ben and Nick Hubble, *Working-Class Writing*, p. 4.

CHAPTER 4

Writing Their Selves: Authorial Subjectivity and Representation in Birmingham Group Narrative

> Some of the most important work currently being done in literary theory and literary history centers [*sic*] on the discursive strategies by which marginalized subjects articulate selfhood and challenge dominant cultures. The study of proletarian fiction, which is replete with images and voices of the dispossessed seeking possession, makes an important contribution to this inquiry.[...] the political discourse in proletarian fiction centrally addresses the intersections of class with gender and race and thus bears directly on many key issues in contemporary cultural studies.[1]

It is to explore the 'voices of the dispossessed seeking possession' to whom Barbara Foley alludes in the above passage that this chapter will now focus. Foley's assertion predicates a deeper analysis of authorial subjectivity in the narratives of the Birmingham group writers, who, as this chapter's title has aimed to capture beneath the veil of pseudonymity, 'literally' have written themselves into their narratives. Moving from the thematic consideration of work and unemployment central to critical discussions of working-class literature in the 1930s and, to escape the 150-year shadow cast by the sociopolitical preoccupations of what Paul Mason defines 'a predominantly white, male, manual labour force', this chapter will employ an intersectional methodology in order to examine aspects of working-class culture hitherto neglected or overlooked.[2] Although the class-based analyses of working-class literature would continue throughout the 1930s, Karl Radek's repudiation of Proletkult methods and his wish to adopt

R. Harriott, *The Birmingham Group*,
https://doi.org/10.1007/978-3-031-14383-0_4

policies aimed to promote wider class allegiance in the fight against fascism led to a softening of Comintern's Third-Period 'class-against-class' policies and found erstwhile sectarian and patriarchal discussions placed temporarily in abeyance. These changes were mirrored in a critical climate which, by attracting fellow-travelling middle-class writers, served to imbue social-realism with a fuller appreciation of the aesthetic that, in line with the critical ambitions of this book, might begin to open up the literary element in working-class writing and enable a more holistic discussion of contemporary working-class experience.

The position taken in this chapter nevertheless dissents from the view that intersectionality is a 'retreat from class' and stresses the importance of retaining a class-based analysis as the 'explanatory framework' within which to consider the manifold categories of disadvantage under which working people's lives were subsumed.[3] Whilst aiming to explore cultural categories neglected due to the traditional emphasis on class struggle alone, the following discussion follows Victor Wallis in urging that, 'in terms of "real world" praxis, *class* has a strategic or binding function that does not pertain to any of the other lines of oppression: it brings together, potentially into a coherent force, *all* the constituencies that are held down by the single most concentrated power in contemporary society, that of capital itself (original emphasis)'.[4]

More recent discussions of working-class literature have encouraged a critical engagement attuned to aspects of working-class experience reaching beyond the narrowly patriarchal, and, although she does not use the term 'intersectionality' directly, Nicola Wilson reiterates Peter Williams' assertion that 'work and workplace have dominated our conceptions of the ways social relations and institutions are constituted and reproduced. All else, it seems, has been regarded as secondary and as a reflection of the primary relations established through work'.[5] Wilson also references the work of historian Joanna Bourke, who, drawing from working-class autobiographies, argued that the principal loci of class awareness and identity were 'not the factory floor nor trade union' but 'emerged from the routine activities of everyday life'.[6]

An important aspect of Wilson's survey of the home in working-class fiction hinges on the distinction she makes between representations of 'observed' and 'inhabited' space and their implications regarding the formal elements in working-class literature. She illustrates this distinction by reference to the writing of Robert Tressell and D. H. Lawrence.

Explaining why 'Tressell's detailed description of observed space, "his often clear instruction to 'readoff the home for character'" (a rhetoric of domesticity), has generally fallen foul of critical favour', she contrasts *The Ragged Trousered Philanthropists* with the work of D. H. Lawrence, in which 'the home is not "read" in this way, but constitutes instead an existential, "living, inhabited space"', created through the actions and habitation of its characters.[7] Arguing that the experience of class is frequently 'understood [...] in only the narrowest of terms, [implying] misleadingly that working-class writing must be political or politicised', Wilson maintains that '[f]or many on the Left, analyses of society that spoke of the struggle in terms of anything but class (defined in terms of the politics of the male workplace), were regarded as divisive and disloyal to the cause'.[8] Yet, while there is currently a move towards adopting more appropriate perspectives from which to evaluate working-class narrative, the 'traditional', politically biased agenda has proven tenacious and, as registered in H. Gustav Klaus' remarks, has persisted until quite recently.

Nick Hubble's *The Proletarian Answer to the Modernist Question* (2017) is similarly encouraging of an intersectional approach, positing 1930s proletarian writing not merely as *peripheral*, but *central* to 'reconciling the individual with the collective', a task which, following Alick West, he identifies as having exercised both modernist writer and Marxist critic alike during the early decades of the twentieth century (my emphasis).[9] Like Wilson, Hubble laments the preponderance of narrowly political readings, and he therefore views women's political and intellectual history as a key factor in his exploration of working-class narrative. Observing how 'the revaluation of proletarian literature since the collapse of Eastern European Communism in 1989 [...] relieved some of the ideological constraints that had inhibit[ed] unbiased criticism', he fully endorses the intersectional approach asserting that issues of gender, sexuality and familial relations not only provide a more appropriate 'way in' to the analysis of working-class texts but that the perspectives these offer should be adopted more widely:

> In the quarter of a century [since] Hynes *The Auden Generation,* the proletarian literature of the thirties had not only become a major area of study but also had been demonstrated to exceed the workplace-set masculine concerns that had become associated with working-class writing in the post-war period by pre-figuring very contemporary feminist concerns.[10]

In the readings which follow, intersectionality functions as the critical apparatus with which to prise open notions of working-class identity for too long occluded by perspectives founded solely upon patriarchal concerns and class-based assumptions. Linking the Birmingham group writers to the struggles of socially marginalised and disenfranchised characters they describe in their narratives will both illuminate and foster a greater awareness *of* and imaginative solidarity *with* the lived-experience of the second city's working people. Writing as 'insiders', the Birmingham group's proximity to the working people not only strengthened the veracity of their accounts of working-class life but, in so doing, would hopefully provide succour to those enduring its travails. For as Stephen Reynolds indicated:

> [T]hose in the Slough of Despond themselves gain courage and endurance from the knowledge that someone else has been there too, has found it just as endurable and has come through. How helpful is that writer as a guide through the Slough, how calming and comforting his sympathy.[11]

These lines constitute a significant aspect of Reynolds' 'pitch' for the hybrid autobiographical form he developed in the early years of the twentieth century and more recently taken up in Max Saunders *Self-Impression: Life Writing, Autobiografiction, and the Forms of Modern Literature* (2010). Saunders explains the term as coined and defined in Reynolds' *Speaker* article of 1906 in which Reynolds claimed autobiografiction as the formal repository for 'anything that reacts strongly on the mind' as 'spiritual experience': any emotion, beautiful thing, work of art, sorrow, religion or love, which intensifies a man's existence; 'anything in short that directly touches his soul'.[12] It is important to make a distinction between the terms *autobiography* and *autobiographical*, as Reynolds' hybrid genre possibly problematises matters. Saunders indicates Reynolds distinguished 'autobiographical fiction' from his portmanteau term by suggesting the latter lies at the intersection where autobiography, fiction and discursive writing meet, and he therefore advocated its use as an appropriate medium through which 'the complex individual might express himself'.[13]

Reynolds believed the qualities of intimacy and directness inherent in autobiografiction: its potential for recounting and recasting the spiritual experience of the introspective individual *as that of another* whilst simultaneously providing an appropriate means by which to express and *conceal one's identity* as central factors in its utility, Saunders indicates that this assertion probably derived from the fact that 'as a homosexual, writing only a decade after the Wilde trial', '[Reynolds] would have been particularly sensible of the need to be guarded about his intimate life'.[14] Saunders also draws attention to the genre's cathartic potential, noting how 'Reynold's closes his essay [by urging] how autobiografiction's chief significance lies in the psychological consolation it offers'.[15] Nick Hubble adopts Saunders' perspective suggesting that 'autobiografiction' offers itself as a 'new critical paradigm' with which to read proletarian/modernist works because 'it exceeds autobiographical fiction by allowing writers to transform themselves performatively and represent a different understanding of selfhood'.[16] Hubble illustrates how 'autobiografiction' might function in this way in his reading of Naomi Motchison's *We Have Been Warned*, in which he suggests:

> Autobiografiction can include material that writers may prefer not to own in their own person; but rather than suggesting that their fiction gives them away, either consciously or unconsciously, they are claiming that the fictional permits a *fuller* autobiography. This is partly a matter of its being able to include the shameful as well as the honourable, and thus assemble a more complete, more human picture.[17]

This is apparent in the analysis of the Birmingham group narratives below where, rather than following the more traditional confessional or autobiographical modes available, the hybrid form they adopted was enabling of a 'fictionalised' performative transformation which, for want of a more hospitable generic term, might be better considered as 'autobiografiction'.

Fortunately, as registered throughout this book, as traditional critiques of working-class narrative have decreased, works formerly considered politically quiescent are beginning to receive the kinds of attention enabled by more appropriate critical perspectives. However, this renewed focus upon works dealing in the everyday experience of the working class is not to suggest that it had been wholly absent in earlier accounts. For a long while, Richard Hoggart's dewy-eyed recollection of his pre-war Yorkshire childhood in *The Uses of Literacy* (1957) facilitated a collective, somewhat sentimentalised, remembrance of working-class *temps perdu*, as did George Orwell's nostalgic yearning for the blissful content of the worker's fireside which, though possibly granting a 'better chance of happiness' than that afforded the 'educated man', was nonetheless predicated on a family 'breadwinner' who, in Orwell's formulation, was inevitably male, 'in steady work and drawing good wages'.[18]

Despite their misplaced reverie, the opinions of Orwell and Hoggart seem relatively benign when set beside those of the Auden set, who collectively seem to affirm Cyril Connolly's pronouncement that 'there is no more sombre enemy of good art than the pram in the hall'.[19] Fortunately, Valentine Cunningham saw fit to censure the 'bourgeois old boys' for their seeming reluctance to discuss gender, women or children, his observations inadvertently encouraging of and adding further stimulus to the intersectional approach adopted here.[20] Cunningham cites Virginia Woolf's address to the Conference of the Workers' Educational Association in 1940, where, referring to those [women] like herself who had not been through 'the male preserves of private and public schooling', she insisted, '[reading women] are not going to leave writing to be done for us by a small class of well-to-do young men—who have only a pinch, a thimbleful of experience to give us'.[21] The target of her animus was of course the Auden set, and her address (not without a degree of irony) was later published as 'The Leaning Tower', in John Lehmann's *Folios of New Writing* II.[22] As Cunningham rightly saw, Woolf's metaphors of the thimbleful [suggested the 'Old Boys'] were unconscionably complicit in preserving the 'gendered binary' referred to above; he continues:

> If women came off badly in much '30s writing so, inevitably, did the presentation of the family.
>
> Family life flourishes, one notices, among the works of proletarian authors and in the so-called proletarian fictions. Not so among the texts of the bourgeois Old Boys. Which is why among the few heterosexual male authors in that class of writer there is a certain assertiveness about their marriedness.[23]

Woolf's contention that the male alumni of private and public schools showed such conspicuous unfamiliarity with women and the family, despite [having flourished] in the work of proletarian authors, lends further support to the focus of this chapter. If only to allow a little more air into the discussion of working-class prose literature, Woolf's sidelining of the Leaning Tower writers proves a welcome intervention.

As it is hoped this book's reading of the second city has begun to show, while never less than political, the ideological commitment of Birmingham group writers is registered more *subtly*, yet paradoxically more *powerfully*, in a politics of form. John Fordham suggests that the Liverpool writer James Hanley's refusal to utilise the characteristic monological structure of the conventional realist novel and his preference for modernist methods of treating social phenomena resonates with Theodor Adorno's proposal that 'art indicts by refraining from express indictment'.[24] In *Aesthetic Theory*, Adorno suggests, 'Real denunciation is probably only a capacity of form which is overlooked by a social aesthetic that believes in themes. What is socially decisive in artworks is the content [*inhalt*] that becomes eloquent through the works formal structures'.[25] The readings below follow Adorno's observation by revealing the Birmingham group writers as heavily invested in strategies of formal innovation. Defined as the politicisation of narratological and formal analysis, Greta Olsen and Sarah Copland emphasise how 'a politics of form' seeks to 'unite the formalist analysis of texts with readings that aim to uncover how structures of social power are expressed in and by, as well as challenged by aesthetic form'. [26] Given the symbiosis between formal method and thematic content (thematic here defined as reflecting class-based issues and aspects of society), it often proves difficult to isolate 'narrative' from 'discourse', and it will be seen that some reference to the aestheticisation of politics has already been intimated in Chap. 2. However, the analysis undertaken in this chapter approaches matters from the 'politicisation of the aesthetic' and will avoid repetition owing to its focus on passages selected from several different narratives.

The novels analysed in this chapter are Walter Brierley's *Sandwichman* (1937) and John Hampson's *Saturday Night at the Greyhound* (1931). Applying Barbara Foley's generic criteria, *Sandwichman* falls awkwardly between the categories of 'Proletarian Autobiography' and 'Proletarian Bildungsroman.[27] In conventional usage, 'bildungsroman' identifies the 'classic' form of the bourgeois novel which traces the fortunes of a single protagonist as he/she overcomes the hurdles encountered on the path to 'maturation'. Brierley's *Sandwichman* differs markedly in this respect; its protagonist—a thinly veiled, pseudonymous representation of its author—seeks 'improvement' via the 'academic education' he feels denied due to his lowly class status. Recording the obstacles placed before his working-class *litterateur* as he wrestles the conflicting demands of work and study, Brierley's novel might, in this respect, be better described an 'anti-bildungsroman'. Again, if one were to employ Foley's generic criteria, John Hampson's *Saturday Night at the Greyhound* would be labelled a

'Proletarian Social Novel' owing to its exploration of the events, intrigues and relationships that befall staff, visitors and habitués of the eponymous Derbyshire public house from a range of character perspectives. As with Brierley's novel, Hampson's narrative is suffused with detail deriving from its author's personal experience, and though Barbara Foley's specific generic criteria function provisionally, there seems a case for arguing that, generically speaking, 'autobiografiction' therefore proves a more comprehensive and accommodating critical lens through which to discuss both novels.

In addition to its analysis of the two novels, this chapter will examine contrasting treatments of the short story. Here, Leslie Halward's 'A Broken Engagement' responds readily to an intersectional reading in its sensitive exploration of the woman's position within the prevailing social ethos, especially with regard to marriage, care and ageing. Stylistically at some departure from Halward, Peter Chamberlain's exercises and short stories exploit the genres of 'found' sketch, comedy and satire, which, by employing snippets of overheard conversation and stream-of-consciousness technique, aimed to depict both working- and middle-class existence. Running their short stories together enables a comparison of the short form as produced by writers from differing sides of the contemporary class divide and proves strangely revealing, for here, in terms of 'authenticity': the prerequisite that a working-class writer be *from* the working-classes, Leslie Halward though identifying chauvinistically with 'his own people' is found, somewhat ironically, to be less 'class-conscious' than 'fellow-travelling' Birmingham group companion Peter Chamberlain.

A Reluctant Collier? Walter Brierley: 'Body'

As the foregoing discussion has revealed, Walter Brierley's narratives repeatedly reference the hardships of the collier's life. Rather than heroic, he likens pit work to '[the] bestial creature that devours men and women, by feeding on their labour and destroying their lives' which Graham Holderness discerned in Zola's *Germinal*.[28] Charting its protagonist's heartfelt intuition that 'there was something better in life than the pit', and by evidencing its author's resistance to prevailing notions of masculinity, the Brierley short story that commences this chapter will set the tone for the ensuing discussion of the Derbyshire writer's second novel: *Sandwichman*.[29]

The adoption of an autobiografictional mode is clear from the outset of 'Body' as Brierley channels his own negative and fearful experience of pit work into the characterisation of young Harry Rogers who——ripped untimely from the most rudimentary, elementary education——has been thrust into colliery life.[30] The eldest of seven siblings and of a sensitive disposition, Harry is conflicted between a sense of familial duty, the requirement he contribute to the family coffers in order to supplement his father's meagre wage, and, constructed on a hazy intuition that life may have something better to offer, a fervent desire to escape an occupation he loathes. Unable to maintain the stoic resignation of the 'Big Jims', -Joes or -Jocks, those romanticised titans who comprise what Valentine Cunningham identifies as the 'Bigness cult' in working-class fiction, Harry lacks both the physical stamina necessary to perform his labours and the mental stamina to withstand the baiting of co-workers who continually bully and intimidate him.[31] Brierley portrays Harry as imprisoned in an occupation to which he feels totally unsuited. Whereas other working-class novels treat a young worker's often troublesome 'initiation' as a 'rite of passage', something reluctantly endured but ultimately surmounted, Harry remains inconsolable.

During the interwar period, as was remarked in the reading of Halward's 'Belcher's Hod' above, male-dominated workplaces were (often still are) beset by what R. W. Connell terms 'hegemonic masculinity', a persona requiring that men be 'active', 'aggressive', 'daring and tough' or, failing this, should suppress any evidence to the contrary.[32] Defined as a patriarchal outlook 'that legitimises men's dominant position in society and justifies the subordination of the common male population and women, and other marginalised ways of being a man', as shown in John Hampson's 'Man About The House', hegemonic masculinity provides a further illustration of the way in which male-oriented convention was able to exert a destructive influence upon both individual and family life.[33] Shunned by his tougher contemporaries, Harry finds a more enlightened workplace ally in the shape of Shirley the colliery chargeman, who (as had Brierley himself) is studying Latin, English and Logic and hopes to access university. Shirley's academic ambitions kindle a similar interest in Harry, who, owing to family circumstances, was unable to pursue a scholarship and had been set to work the day after leaving school.

Following an incident in which Harry mistakenly releases a loaded coal tram potentially causing injury, he is severely reprimanded.[34] In what would have resulted in his sacking had Shirley not intervened, his despondency only deepens. His predicament akin to that of those reluctant and terrified Great War infantrymen, Harry contemplates self-mutilation by placing his hand between the heaving coal trams or putting his foot on the track so as to gain some respite in the form of certificated medical absence. He determines against this however, speculating that sheer exhaustion might induce a 'legitimate' physical collapse or faint and thus no longer necessitate what he sees as a potentially dishonest and distressingly painful course of action.

On his arrival home, Harry enters the wash house and overhears his parents talking outside:

> "is our Harry workin' ta-morrer?"
> "No."
> "That's a bad job, it's not as if 'e got any dole."
> He splashed about the shallow bowl of water, then swilled double-hansful [*sic*] into his face. But for all that, the sob which was born suddenly within him rushed out and sounded above the splashing. (*B*, 517)

Harry's identity crisis, his sensitivity to his parents' hardship and his inchoate gropings for a means of escape are anti-systemic. His physical inability and reluctance to function merely as a cog or unit in the means of production, a mere 'Body', combine in a sense of individual agency and present as a form of micro-resistance. Though uncertain of who he is, he's sure of who he isn't, and in this respect 'Body' functions as a counter-narrative to works in which patriarchal notions of workplace behaviour and masculine solidarity are valorised. Though (at this juncture) presumably unacquainted with the Marxist terminology of alienation, exploitation or commodification, Harry's inner conflict assumes a more universal significance, his irrepressible, primal sob the cry of the exploited worker echoing down the generations.

Brierley's Harry Rogers would have found a sympathetic counterpart in Harold Heslop's Joe Tarrant the protagonist of *Gate of a Strange Field*, a character whose 'sensitivity' and 'imagination' likewise mark him out from his co-workers. As Pamela Fox explains, '[Joe's] eagerness at the age of fourteen to enter the colliery is first inspired, then dampened, by his free-ranging mind. The anticipated "adventure" of work soon fades into the reality of "slavery", the "shackles of industry" imprisoning him.' [35] While Brierley's protagonist dreamed of pursuing the kind of education provided by the WEA (doubtless reflecting Brierley's own chosen academic route),

Heslop's Joe Tarrant opts for the 'Labor [*sic*] press' and later 'the "vortex" of institutionalised worker education', he found in the Plebs League, although as Fox indicates:

> Heslop's novel is much more openly conflicted about the authenticity of working-class epistemology taught from above. Its distrust of the Marxist education movement, the principal source of influence on (and often the source of) worker-intellectuals like [Frank] Owen and [Larry] Meath, calls into question the forms of [collective] agency privileged in [the novels of Tressell and Greenwood].[36]

As with Jonathan Rose's autodidacts, the overtures of Marxist theory gained little purchase in the imaginations of Brierley and Heslop or their fictional protagonists.[37] Nevertheless, the male-oriented, masculine ethos of colliery life would remain the departure point for characters such as Harry Stokes and Joe Tarrant, not to mention their creators, as they embarked upon their respective journeys of educational self-cultivation.

The various paths to self-discovery noted in the middle-class intellectuals' desire to 'go over' and, conversely, in the working-class' individual's desire, simply to desire 'something better', are illustrative of the political dilemma confronting both 1930s working-class writers and their middle-class counterparts as together they wrestled the competing claims of individual and collective agency. As registered in Alick West's aphoristic 'When I do not know any longer who are the "we" to whom "I" belong I do not know any longer who "I" am either'.[38] These distinctions were constitutive of one's political allegiance during the 1930s, although, succinct as West's aphorism is, a more conciliatory formulation may have lain in Ralph Fox's opinion:

> [E]ach man has, as it were a dual history, since he is at the same time a type, a man with a social history, and an individual, a man with a personal history. The two of course, even though they may be in glaring conflict, are also one, a unity, in so far as the latter is eventually conditioned by the former, though this does not and should not imply that in art the social type must dominate the individual personality.[39]

The 'I/We' dilemma had continued to assume significance in the pre-war period where, as Valentine Cunningham suggests, 'self-abandonment' became for many 'the only salvation for the shattered modernist self [...] and represented the veriest orthodoxy of the Communist Party and *Left*

Review', though possibly sneering at the Auden set, of whom he asserted, 'all were agreed on which side redemption lay in the contemporary war on pronouns'.[40] The socially sublimating impulse Cunningham describes runs against the grain of the methodology taken in the remainder of this chapter where, in drawing upon notions of individual identity and consciousness, it will suggest that, rather than undermining collective agency, narrative representations of the individual "I" fuse with the collective "We" to provide a fuller, intersubjective, understanding of working-class experience.[41]

For many during the interwar period, ill-education, lack of education or, as we encountered it in 'Body', the pre-1944 Education Act form of schooling meted out to working-class children had remained—whilst a vast improvement on the nineteenth century, utilitarian pedagogy outlined in Dickens' *Hard Times*—in essence rudimentary, often leaving its recipients ill-equipped to cope with much beyond the most basic intellectual requirements. In terms of the intersectional analysis undertaken here, this served to disadvantage working-class children not only economically but also spiritually and culturally. Helen Lynd's observation, 'Shame, while touched off by a specific, often outwardly trivial, occurrence initially felt as revealing one's inadequacies, may also confront one with unrecognised desires of one's own and the inadequacy of society in giving expression to these desires', is particularly appropriate here.[42] Knowledge, more specifically the *pursuit* of knowledge via higher or further education is none other than a manifestation of desire: the oblique expression of a working-class individual's sense of lack or disadvantage and one which occurs as something of a leitmotif in working-class writing. Whether couched in terms of 'self-improvement' or, as connoted (usually negatively) in the term *embourgeoisification*, it is often treated ambiguously and considered a source of tension in working-class culture, where, as Richard Hoggart indicates:

> [T]here is often a mistrust of 'book-learning'. Are you any better off (i.e. happier) as a clerk or a teacher? What good does it do you? Parents who refuse, as a few still do, to allow their children to take up scholarships are not always thinking of the fact that they would have to be fed and clothed for much longer; at the back of this is the vaguely formulated but strong doubt of the value of education. That doubt acquires some of its force from the group-sense itself: for the group seeks to conserve, and may impede an inclination in any of its members to make a change, to leave the group, or be different.[43]

The outbreak of social conscience that impelled members of the privileged and well-educated elite to embark upon their cultural diaspora had not been all one-way-traffic, the phenomena of cross-class mobility was echoed by members of the working class who sought the cultural capital they believed might be attained following academic study. As shown in the discussion of Walter Allen's novels, Birmingham narratives frequently chart the progress of characters seeking to acquire a level of cultural capital by means of educational advancement. In *Sandwichman*, Walter Brierley traces the academic aspirations and misfortunes of his protagonist Arthur Gardner, literary counterpart to Hardy's tragic autodidact Jude Fawley and the hapless Leonard Bast, the object of Forster's satire in *Howards End*, who each shares a 'relish for the sublime' and are determined to challenge the fixity of prevailing middle-class perspectives which characterise them as unworldly and idealistic.[44] As Pamela Fox indicates, the desire for cultural-capital often morphs into an indictment *of* and resistance *to* the societal inequalities working-class people believe are pitted against them. E. M. Forster's Leonard Bast is cautionary in this respect, '[a]ttacked by one of the upper-class characters, he symbolically grabs a bookcase for support'; unfortunately it falls, crushing him, and causes a fatal heart attack. 'Such are the dangers of higher education', John Carey suggests, especially 'when it is pursued by the wrong people'.[45] However, Rachel Howarth seeks to rescue Forster from Carey's cynicism by indicating that having begun teaching at the Working Men's College in 1902, Forster continued to do so for twenty years, thus demonstrating his profound interest in the cultural development of working-class people. Dissenting from Carey's viewpoint and seemingly in conversation with Pamela Fox, Howarth argues that Leonard's demise functions as a comment on a society that leaves the working class 'underfed in every way. It reflects social constraints, rather than indicting the innate abilities of a poverty-stricken working-class man'.[46]

The foregoing discussion of 'Body' is illustrative of the fact that not all male protagonists of working-class narrative would, or might wish to, conform to prevalent notions of masculinity, whether by emulating the forward-gazing, lantern-jawed, visionaries of socialist realism, the 'hard body' imagery of the American New Deal mural, or the kinds of masculine hegemony described above. However, the fact that as recently as 2016 the *New Statesman* would publish an article entitled 'How to be a man: The quiet crisis of masculinity' is testimony to the persistence of this gendered-binary and attitudes deriving from it.[47] Brierley's short story is not only illustrative of Helen Merrell Lynd's shame dynamic but also prefigurative of Alick West's 'I'/'We' dichotomy in registering the plight of subjects unwilling to submerge their individuality or wholly abandon themselves to the demands of collective convention. As Hubble observes:

> Plenty of proletarian literature [...] turns on a combination of shame and autobiografiction; for example, Brierley and Heslop (who both draw upon the example of Lawrence's autobiografiction), Gibbon (who draws on Lawrence and Joyce), Carnie Holdsworth and [Ellen] Wilkinson all self-consciously, sometimes playfully—even to the point of self-parody—portray their selves as imaginary fictions dependent on an intersubjective relationship with other imaginary portraits drawn from their experience'.[48]

Walter Brierley: *Sandwichman*

Following his completion of *Means Test Man* and an exchange of congratulatory correspondence from Walter Allen and John Hampson, Brierley received a further letter from Hampson encouraging him to '[s]tart another book as soon as [possible], your own history, in the form of a fiction should be excellent'.[49] Walter Allen agreed, adding:

> I think John's suggestion is good. You should do an autobiographical novel now, keeping it as objective as possible. The usual itch to write other people's books! But I think I'd be tempted to restrict the book first of all to boyhood and youth in the pits. You could carry on then in another. That's probably bad advice, I don't know. All I know is that you can do a faithful book showing the rhythm of the workers lives without any marring propaganda or hysteria. Like Wilfred Owen's war poetry, where he says in his preface "The poetry is the Pity"—and the pity is unstated.[50]

As he made clear, Allen abjured facile, politicised polemic, believing, with Marx and Engels, that ideas should spring naturally from the characters themselves rather than merely functioning as a mouthpiece for their author's views. The autobiographical novel that Hampson and Allen encouraged Brierley to write would follow shortly, though not entirely as they had envisaged. Far from a conventional autobiography, Brierley's novel offered instead an unremittingly bleak and subjective account of the difficulties encountered by a member of the working-class foolish enough to embark upon the path of educational self-cultivation.

As Ian Haywood points out, while retaining a focus on the 'emasculated male worker', *Sandwichman* develops 'the critique of patriarchal attitudes' its author had begun in *Means Test Man*. However, whereas the injustices heaped upon the family in the earlier novel derived from external factors, the tragedy depicted in *Sandwichman* is the product of its protagonist's/author's own ambition.[51] Generically speaking, *Sandwichman* departs from the anglicised notion of the *Bildungsroman*, conventionally defined as an account of its protagonist's progress to maturity and insight, which is hardly compatible with the irrevocable descent and tragic outcome which awaits Brierley's protagonist. Modelled on his own experience of pit life and his subsequent failure to gain a scholarship for full-time study at Nottingham University, Brierley must have begun to ruminate upon how his particular experience of educational self-realisation and its negative implications for interpersonal relationships might be shaped into a novel. Instead of producing the formal autobiography that his Birmingham companions had suggested, Brierley would decant both the defeats and the successes of his personal experience into a hybrid form closely resembling Stephen Reynold's conception of an *autobiografiction* whose fictional element, as Nick Hubble indicates (see page145), would paradoxically enable a fuller autobiographical account of his experiences.[52]

In addition to his employment at the colliery, Arthur Gardner is studying part-time at Trentingham University College (a barely disguised Nottingham University) and is currently courting girlfriend Nancy Maugham. Arthur is twenty-three years old, an only child whose father had been killed at the outset of the Great War. Following her husband's death, his mother, Mrs Gardner remarried. Her second husband, Albert Shirley, along with his sons Albert and Sidney (we are not told the fate of the former Mrs Shirley) become Arthur's stepfather and stepbrothers, respectively. Albert Shirley is presented as having fallen upon hard times: 'Until his early twenties he had held a good position in a large co-operative society, but, owing to some misdemeanour had been compelled to seek a livelihood at an occupation where an exemplary moral character was no essential' (*SM*, 6). Ian Haywood suggests that what ensues as the stepfather's 'vindictive behaviour' and his attempts to frustrate Arthur's plans stem from an envy borne of his own 'downward mobility'.[53] Arthur's mother typifies the respectable working-class woman that adverse circumstances have reduced to genteel poverty, and, in this respect she may be likened to D. H. Lawrence's Gertrude Morel, or Rose, Dick Gardiner's long-suffering wife in Walter Allen's *Innocence Is Drowned*.

Brierley's narrator informs us that 'All three [boys] were intelligent, their mother's endowment, yet the two Shirleys lacked drive each and the capacity to reach forward, aware of the moment only, though filling each richly but without point' (*SM*, 6). Arthur's mother had nonetheless sought to inculcate a level of artistic sensibility amongst the boys, and though it is perhaps inevitable she dote on her biological son, her stepsons are not without a degree of accomplishment. Albert listens to radio symphony concerts and is knowledgeable in the classics, whilst Sidney is described as a competent reader of the 'plainer-mannered authors of France' (*SM*, 6).

From the novel's outset, Arthur's single-minded devotion to his studies is shown to precipitate family conflict; this creates difficulties in his relationship with girlfriend Nancy and tensions at his place of work. Having arrived home early one evening prior to his stepfather and stepbrothers, Arthur seats himself for the evening meal and quietly apprises his mother of his academic progress. As with Lawrence's Gertrude Morel, she offers encouragement but is concerned Arthur's reserves of energy will be quickly depleted, spread so thinly as they are between work, girlfriend and study, especially with examinations imminent. Arthur responds with bluff confidence: 'Don't you worry, mum', [...] 'In October Is'll say good-by to the black hole and be a black-gowned undergrad' (*SM*, 4). Unconvinced by her son's self-assurance, she retorts, 'Don't you harp on that. You never know what might happen'. Though clearly proud of her son's fortitude, this tender mother-son colloquy is abruptly terminated by the sound of 'slurring nailed boots on the yard' (*SM*, 4). This grating sound closes down any further discussion by signalling the return of her husband and stepsons from the pit, whereupon the mood quickly changes. As Arthur retires to the front room to commence his evening's studies:

> She watched him go, her eyes were warm, the spirit in her face reached out as if to fuse with his in some kind of victorious peace. But she cleaned her face of all expression when her husband and other two sons clattered into the kitchen and clinked their tin drums on to the back of the sink, then threw their coats, caps and scarves on to Arthur's by the fireplace. That expression never shone from her eyes except on the occasions when she was alone with her eldest son. It was not that she loved him more than the others. (*SM*, 5)

This extract provides a useful 'way in' to Brierley's narrative, and although the use of irony and some of the broader aspects of Brierley's style were analysed in the discussion of *Means Test Man*, it is worth commenting on the formal devices he employs in this novel, which, despite their economy of means, communicate a wealth of information in respect of characterisation and the wider aspects of familial behaviour with which Brierley engages. As delineated above, Arthur's retreat to the front room immediately underscores his separation from the existential flux of family life. Watching him go Arthur's mother feels it necessary to suppress her pride and contain any expression of shared joy in her eldest son lest it be construed as favouritism by his stepbrothers. John Lucas suggests that his mother's encouragement and dreams for Arthur's success register the implicit 'rejection of [the] life that [her husband] has had to accept as all that's on offer' and necessitate she adopt an attitude of circumspection and diplomacy.[54]

As illustrated in the above passage, the grind of hobnailed boots has become something of a trope in the mining novel, their sound often measuring the comings and goings of the proletarian day. Here in announcing the Shirleys' homecoming, the alliterated 'k' sounds momentarily expunge the last remnants of quiet confidentiality shared between Arthur and his mother, the clattering intrusion of external reality is also registered by a change in her facial expression. Functioning figuratively, the scraping sound of the boots not only signifies the coarseness and ugliness of the occupation from which Arthur desires to escape, but also seems to mock him in the attempt. Likewise the coats, caps and scarves, which, thrown on top of Arthur's belongings, enact a metaphorical smothering: a collective resistance towards those having the temerity to defy both cultural and patriarchal convention. Richard Hoggart remarks how individuals seeking to 'take up some educational activity—so as to "work for their class" or "improve themselves"—tend to be ambiguously regarded' by the working-class community and though Arthur's stepbrothers are not without their own cultural enthusiasms, these are pursued in the more socially acceptable form of hobbies or interests, rather than potentially 'class-alienating' activities.[55] Arthur's stepfather articulates Hoggart's assertion and demonstrates the suspicion directed at 'self-improvers' when he opines that Arthur '[t]hinks because "e knows a bit o" blasted "istory an" 'alf a dozen French words that "e"s too good for t'pit' (*SM*, 101). Arthur's plans to better himself undeniably generate conflict within the domestic sphere. According to Philip Gorski, John Hampson and Walter Allen had advised Brierley against making Arthur illegitimate. He doesn't explain why, though one imagines the stepfather/stepson relationship might offer more dramatic potential for familial conflict in what was already a volatile domestic environment. In *The Uses of Literacy*, Richard Hoggart points to the importance of the matriarchal role, more specifically that of family arbitrator, and is unequivocal in his conviction that 'once established as the mother of the family, the working-class wife comes into her own' [...]. 'She is then the pivot of the home, as it is practically the whole of her world. She, more than the father, holds it together.'[56] This was certainly the portion allotted to Gertrude Morel in Lawrence's *Sons and Lovers*, and, having read examples of the quick close relationships, the cut and thrust of working-class life described by his spiritual mentor, these were undoubtedly patterns of working-class experience Brierley similarly wished to present.

What is already a tense situation quickly comes to a head. Despite his mother's caution, Arthur has spread himself too thinly between work, his girlfriend and his studies; fatigue leads to an argument at his place of work, which results in an accident and damage that sets the colliery's schedule back two days, and, as a consequence of which, he is dismissed.[57] There are implications in terms of domestic and emotional economies: what his mother foresees as her husband's angry response to this development are devastating. Again, Brierley communicates the mother's anguish by reference to her physical response alone, 'Her mouth was loose, her eyes dull, the hope she had carried because of him faded, her whole physical being drooped' (*SM*, 99). Following her husband's return from work, an unholy row ensues. Affronted by his stepfather's hectoring tone, Arthur demands to know 'who the hell he thinks [he is]?', to which his antagonist storms:

> 'An' who the hell are you?' The man rose from his chair but Arthur did not flinch.
>
> 'You'll find your clothes and books chucked out on to t'yard if you don't 'ave less of your damned buck.' His arm came up but lowered again as he saw the young man's mouth line.' 'Bloody young mon-funk.' [...] '[Arthur] turned away in disgust, saw his mother leaning heavily on the table, her face grey even to her lips, a glazed empty look was in her eyes which blinked as if the lids were hardly capable of function'. (*SM*, 101)

Following a walk to cool down, Arthur returns home. 'His mother was seated on the sofa, her hands resting on her lap. She looked like a sick animal' (*SM*, 101). Once again, the mother's feelings are communicated by her physical appearance alone: her acquiescent, defeated posture more closely resembling a state of repose. Having confided to Arthur that these familial tensions are pulling her apart, she appears emotionally drained and pleads with Arthur to avoid further confrontation, advising, 'say nothing back to him' [...]. 'He's the master here, and he'll show it' [...]. 'He's been on since you went out. He'll be on, now, for a week or more, especially if he gets in the pub every night' (*SM*, 102), Again, an intersectional reading proves helpful here as it brings into focus gendered relationships overlooked or treated as peripheral to more overtly political discussions of working-class literature. Whilst not advocating Brierley as a proto-feminist, the above extracts reveal him as a conscious and sympathetic observer of the women's position in contemporary society. Doubly disenfranchised by patriarchal and class oppression founded on notions of the living-wage and male breadwinner models, such ideological constructions fostered a gender ideology in which 'femininity served as the counterpoint to an aggressive masculinity' and which, as revealed here, whether actual, threatened or proximal, ultimately became for many working-class women a 'hierarchical relationship enforced through violence'.[58]

The depiction of Arthur's relationship with Nancy once more reveals Brierley's empathy for the woman's experience, just as they had proved for Richard Hoggart's 'scholarship boy'. Arthur's studies demand that he is 'more and more alone'.[59] His single-minded devotion creates distance not only between family and workmates but also between himself and Nancy. Ian Haywood suggests that her predilection for dances, pictures and nice clothes represents the battle line Arthur draws between the philistinism of mass culture (what Haywood refers to as Orwell's palliatives) and the barely attainable salvation of higher culture—which, as noted in the discussion of Walter Allen's *Blind Man's Ditch*, was also one of the 'battle lines' Eugene Lorimer had drawn in his quest for cultural capital.[60] Again, intersectionality provides a useful framework for this discussion because here, rather than dismissing Nancy as merely shallow and superficial, it might be fairer to view her as a victim of the 'capitalist institutionalising of social relations', the 'absorption of the dominant ideology' that Carole Snee identifies in her discussion of Jane Cook in *Means Test Man*.[61] Nancy's 'learned behaviour', the female counterpart to the 'male breadwinner model' which, as Nicola Wilson indicates, 'was a key part of Trade Union policy from the mid-nineteenth century to the inter-war period, and has been seen by historians as a gendered and spatial ideology which underpinned the historical development of the British working-classes'.[62] More sinned against than sinning, Nancy's desire for the material fulfilment promoted in such idealised notions as the companionate marriage and the fantasy projections of popular cinema should not be dismissed out of hand. Pamela Fox uses the term 'benevolent spectators' to describe the tendency to condescension shown towards working-class women not only by male literary critics but also by feminist scholars critical of female material desire. Noting 'the desire for some degree of *gender*-marked difference' in the writing of working-class women (original emphasis), Fox maintains that as readers of this literature, 'we are still troubled by that "narrow plot," threatened by its implications' [...]. 'The "desire" which it names enacts a refusal of the boundaries circumscribing working-class existence and cultural production.'[63] In short, desire may function to resist societal values, or rather the values of respectability projected downwards by bourgeois society. Traditional attitudes run deep and Nancy's behaviour is not entirely blameworthy for there is clearly an element of parental collusion here too, as Arthur reflects:

> She could think of nothing but the pictures on Saturday evenings at one time. Now he couldn't get her near, except about once a month. They must go and lie in the fields, or prop themselves up against stiles and fences. And last Saturday she had asked him to tea, and her father and mother had gone out at six o'clock. It would have to stop. (*SM*, 49)

The parallels with a similar episode in Hardy's *Jude the Obscure* are clear. Arabella employed a similar strategy, telling her mother, 'He's shy: and I can't get 'un to come when you are here. I shall let him slip through my fingers if I don't mind, much as I care for 'n!'.[64] Both novels trace the fortunes of their protagonists' educational aspirations while simultaneously registering the distractions of their loved ones.[65]

Compared with the critique of political quietism and passivity levelled at *Means Test Man*, the critical reception of *Sandwichman* was relatively subdued. Changes in Comintern policy—from the third period 'class-against-class' period to the exigencies of the 'popular front'—created a critical environment less hostile to works previously perceived as lacking a political agenda and one in which intellectuals and writers hitherto considered reactionary were now welcomed by the CPGB in order to assist in humanity's fight against fascism. This seeming volte face would prove problematic for certain authors. Andy Croft records how Harold

Heslop's *Gate of a Strange Field* had fallen foul of such 'third period' prescriptivism. It seems Heslop's Lawrencian treatment of colliery life had met with the censure of the ILPs *New Leader* reviewer and similarly his later *Last Cage Down* for its '"over-sexed" treatment'. As Croft maintains, 'as long as the Left endorsed a mixture of sectarianism, puritanism, anti-intellectualism, and anti-Utopianism, it could not respond to the one intellectual and literary influence (Lawrence) that the miner novelists looked to'.[66] Croft records that having made a 'penitent and committed attempt [...] to answer his critics' in *Last Cage Down* (1935), a cruel irony awaited Heslop, for by the time his novel was published, the third period had passed. His writing, now under the aegis of modified popular front directives, was considered 'too wholesale in its criticisms of trade union officials' and 'a little too sectarian for these days'.[67] Brierley was luckier however; written against the changing backcloth of Comintern policy, the reception of his second novel was more positive. Reviewing *Sandwichman* in the *Daily Worker*, B. L. Coombes described it as 'a worthy successor to *Means Test Man*' and, as Croft indicates, 'praised it for precisely those qualities the paper had found lacking in that novel two years earlier', remarking that 'Mr. Brierley has not attempted to overdramatize his story. He has told it naturally and quietly'.[68] Despite such critical adjustments, there still remained pockets of resistance in certain quarters. Philip Gorski believes the novel's 'subject matter and "apolitical" approach made it unpopular with respectively: the guardians of the Great Tradition on one hand and a mechanical Marxism on the other'.[69] The latter is evident in the remarks of Carole Snee, and although she had praised *Means Test Man* effusively for its depiction of how social inertias distorted domestic relationships and gender-related issues, she judged that in *Sandwichman* Brierley had neglected 'the Litmus paper of his own experience'.[70] This seems hardly fair, as an individual who spent some four years pursuing his dream of a higher education, Brierley tapped deeply into his emotions to recount with honesty what must have been a painful experience. That Snee gives Brierley's account short shrift is not entirely surprising for she sees education, particularly the kind of WEA course undertaken by Brierley, as a betrayal of class values because it precipitates movement away from one's class roots: '[Brierley's] education never becomes a way of understanding himself, his world, or his class, rather it becomes a process of alienation.'[71] The text of *Sandwichman* does not endorse this view however, for as Brierley's narrator tells us:

> He was no snob; he seemed to realise even as he thought, and was content to know, that, however far he reached from the practical atmosphere of his class, he would still be one of them, no better than the miner conscious of life. He didn't want to be either. Examples of climbing under managers and deputies shot to his mind and shuddered him. (*SM*, 49)

Again, Brierley's narration of Arthur Gardner's thoughts echo those of Walter Allen's Ralph Gardiner, who, rather than harbouring ambitions to become a public schoolmaster, saw his role as an educator of the poor and is once more revealing of the unity of purpose threading the Birmingham writers and their narratives. It might also be noted that the German concept of *Bildung*, taken as 'formation' in its more usual British connotation as being synonymous with the realist representational mode, was initially pursued as a form of individual educational *self*-cultivation, for rather than being conceived as an appropriation of cultural capital for its own sake, it was considered a process whereby the knowledge gained was viewed as intellectual capital to be disseminated for the benefit and development of one's community and society at large.[72] In this respect, Arthur's desire to teach, to restore something to his class rather than being self-orientated or economically instrumental, is more honourable than Snee allows. By dismissing Arthur's educational aspiration as 'self-interest', Snee illustrates the Marxist position in the 'I'/'We' debate by demonstrating the difficulty of reconciling individual self-realisation with group consciousness. Given her preference for 'proletarian writing that exhibits a greater awareness of class as its primary determinant' rather than the artistic pretensions of a working-class *literature*', Snee's political allegiance is clear, and, though not in conformity with the views expressed here, is nonetheless consistent.[73]

Although D. H. Lawrence exerted a powerful influence over working-class writers, and specifically those of the Birmingham group, it is mistaken to claim, as does Carole Snee, that Walter Brierley merely worked in his shadow. MacDonald Daly reminds us that their respective life experience was markedly different.[74] Just as in *Sons and Lovers* Paul Morel had sought to avoid becoming a 'prisoner of industrialism', so too Lawrence himself who baulked at the prospect of being incarcerated within the 'relations of production'.[75] By contrast, Walter Brierley was thoroughly enmeshed *within* the relations of production, more so during the periods of unemployment when he became, somewhat paradoxically, the 'vulnerable victim of exclusion *from* them (my emphasis)'. In his varied roles as miner, member of the unemployed and parent, Brierley's life within the mining community provided him with negative experiences and insights simply unavailable and unimaginable to Lawrence.[76]

Whilst this discussion makes reference to Richard Hoggart's account of the working-class scholarship boy, Ian Haywood reminds us that Brierley's novel detailing working-class educational aspiration had preceded Hoggart's account by some twenty years.[77] Philip Gorski presses further explaining that 'whereas Hoggart *describes* the attempted transition, Brierley *dramatises* it in novel form thus achieving greater power and complexity' (original emphasis).[78] It appeared that in his determination to discover there was 'something more to life than the pit' and in describing the barriers placed before those bent upon securing their 'non-alienated destiny', Brierley was attempting to work through his own personal demons and 'to discover', in Jonathan Rose's words, 'how his individual life fitted into the larger society'.[79]

Notions of subjectivity and representation are foregrounded as Brierley engineers the following 'set-piece' in which Arthur explains his (and possibly Brierley's own) position in the 'I'/'We' debate. During a dispute in which his friend David Neil has been angered by a fellow student's defamatory remarks concerning Trade Union leaders, Arthur attempts to placate his friend by articulating his own perplexity: 'I know why you're angry Dave but I couldn't be angry at a remark like that—I couldn't really. I can't grasp the idea of class somehow. I never know a man as a miner or a coal-owner; they're just individuals to me, pushing forward through life' (*SM*, 61). Arthur continues: 'I'm glad I'm not like either of you with your emphasised feels [*sic*] of indifference on one hand, and contact on the other. What he won't recognise is that there are others beside himself; you that there are others beyond your particular clique' (*SM*, 62). As Brierley shows elsewhere in the novel, Arthur is perplexed at the difficulty of reconciling his individuality and urge to self-realisation with that of group or collective interests; as Ian Haywood suggests, 'Arthur's understanding of the links between education and emancipation are still forming', again one may speculate that Brierley may have been coming to terms with this linkage himself.[80] As Philip Gorski claims, rather than attempting to reconcile the 'worlds of work and culture [that had] long been too polarised', Brierley's achievement lay in revealing the workings of this polarity and its effects through the action of his novel'.[81] In its pseudonymous, 'autobiografictional' conflation of Walter Brierley and Arthur Gardner, *Sandwichman*, though offering little by way of solution, provides a sympathetic representation of the difficulties encountered in the troubling attempt to reconcile individual consciousness with communal solidarity.

Chapter 3 of this book made reference to the work of practitioners and critics of the short story who had become impatient with the invidious comparisons made between their chosen form and the novel and who believed the short story was better conceived as a literary genre in its own right. Its suitability as a medium for depicting a single event or episode lent itself readily to the Birmingham writers' scenes of working-class life. The following section analyses contrasting treatments of the short form as produced by Leslie Halward and Peter Chamberlain, respectively. Given the foregoing discussion of *Sandwichman*, one would have been hard pressed to characterise Walter Brierley as a member of the bourgeois elite, yet this is exactly the position taken by Birmingham's Leslie Halward, who expresses the view that 'The worst thing that could happen to a young working-class man [*sic*] with a desire to write about his people [...] is that he be sent to a College or a University. Once such a young man gets 'education' into his system, becomes a student and has a taste of culture, all is lost'.[82] Halward's ressentiment was evident in his contribution to a *London Mercury* symposium titled, 'The Coming of Proletarian Literature'.[83] Despite Halward's renowned vitriol towards class 'outsiders', his ire was not reserved for these alone. Rejecting the dubious advantage to be gained from academic studies, Halward also considered Walter Brierley's and Frederick C. Boden's attendance on the Nottingham University extension course akin to treachery. However, as with Brierley's and Hampson's narratives, Halward's own no-nonsense depictions of working-class experience recovered the voices of those lost in contemporary sectarian readings. As we saw in 'Belcher's Hod', Halward was psychologically percipient probing diligently beneath the tough exterior of his characters to discover their inner fears and vulnerability. This was no less the case in his sensitive portrayal of his female protagonists. Owing to the requirement that women 'man' the factories of Birmingham and other provincial cities during the Great War, Victorian axioms such as 'a woman's place is in the home' became increasingly untenable. Nevertheless, a significant number of working-class women remained in, or returned to, varieties of unpaid labour in the shape of child-rearing, caring, cleaning, cooking, domestic conflict arbitration and the myriad responsibilities with which they dutifully, but often reluctantly, engaged in the family home. As we have seen, the overlapping social categorisations highlighted in an intersectional reading reveal that many women were indeed doubly, often triply, oppressed, economic circumstances dictating their lives proceeded unremarked, unrewarded and not uncommonly subject to violence. The following discussion of Halward's short story 'The Broken Engagement' finds its author's class loyalties extending to solidarity with his contemporary female counterparts and engaging in the 'critique of patriarchal attitudes' that Ian Haywood discerned in the writing of Walter Brierley.[84] As Paul Lester observes, 'Halward's feel for working-class culture include[d] a sympathetic understanding of the burden's imposed by women's traditional domestic role.'[85]

Leslie Halward: 'A Broken Engagement'

While ostensibly examining the breakdown of a working-class relationship, Leslie Halward's 'A Broken Engagement' delves further by providing a moving account of the self-sacrifice undertaken by its female protagonist in order to care for her sick and ageing mother. Here Halward makes effective use of the short form by revealing a seemingly inconsequential quotidian event as an instance of the heroic ordinariness of everyday life and giving voice to those often neglected in contemporary accounts. At the story's outset, Halward introduces us to his protagonists, Vincent Broome and Annie Grove:

> He had a pale, podgy face, a squat nose with gaping nostrils and a loose mouth, the lips thick, the lower one slightly protruding. His broad, flat skull was bald at the front, and at the back his oily black hair stuck out behind his ears and over his jacket collar like tufts of blackened grass. His mild, expressionless brown eyes gazed inquiringly through the powerful lenses of his steel-rimmed spectacles.
>
> She was a year older than he. Her name was Annie Grove. She was so thin that she looked ill-nourished. Her body was as straight, as flat, and hard-looking as a board. There was a deep hollow between two cord-like sinews at the base of her meagre neck. Her nose was long, thin, and pointed, as if it had been nipped sharply between thumb and finger, and the end of it, against the dead white of her face, showed red. Her mouth was so small, the lips so tightly compressed, that it might have been sewn up with invisible thread. She had grey eyes, large and round as fish's eyes, and a great mass of mousy hair that was piled up on top of her head like a helmet. (*BE*, 77)

This rather unforgiving portrayal certainly illustrates the 'caustic point of view' Cyril Connolly discerned in Halward's writing, his unprepossessing characters presented almost as Dickensian grotesques, both ageing, he oily and unkempt, she emaciated and ill-nourished.[86] Having been engaged for several years, their love has soured; to this extent their ordinariness and sullen acceptance mark them less as Dickensian, and more the classic Chekhovian subjects. Though at times bordering on the cruel, Halward's descriptive 'disinterestedness' derives from knowledge gained under Chekov's tutelage: 'If you want to touch your reader's heart you must be cold.'[87] That he was unflinching in his adherence to Chekhov's advice was apparent to Walter Allen, who considered:

> Halward made himself the most objective of writers, and the most economical; his prose is admirably direct and terse; no opinions are expressed. [...] He was dealing with characters who were deprived and largely dispossessed, and they do not necessarily arouse his sympathy; they interest him.[88]

In terms of the observed/inhabited space distinction mentioned earlier, Halward was not averse to providing descriptive detail as in the following extract where the dank chill of the front room and its furnishings provide an appropriate backcloth to the couple's mood and physical appearance:

> They sat on the old-fashioned horsehair sofa in the front room of the house where she lived with her mother. The room was small and overcrowded with ancient furniture. Heavy plush curtains, like blankets, covered the window, and another hung over the door to keep out the draught. The room was lit by one of two gas-jets fixed on either side of the chimney breast, there was a gas fire at their feet, but this was turned so low that the little warmth it gave out did not reach them. In spite of its stuffy appearance the room was chill and smelt damp. (*BE*, 78)

Expressing a preference for 'showing' rather than 'telling', the following passage finds Halward once more heeding his mentor Chekhov's advice:

> Vincent and Annie had sat in silence for a long time, the man leaning forward with his forearms on his thighs, his head bowed, his fat, moist hands at one moment clasped together and at another awkwardly dangling between his knees; the woman upright, her hands lying loosely in her lap, her head

> high, as she gazed at the photograph of a lady in a dress with leg of mutton sleeves that stood in the middle of the mantle shelf. (*BE*, 78)

Presented in the form of a tableau, the couple's self-conscious body language and the reference to the photograph combine with the earlier description to create an airless, stale atmosphere appropriate to their deteriorating affections. Though no word is spoken, such visual descriptions heighten the reader's sense of apprehension. 'At last the woman spoke':

> "I've been thinking over things, Vincent," she said, still looking at the photograph, as if speaking to it instead of to the man at her side. "I think we should both be better off if we were free." ... "I don't want you to take this too hardly or to think too badly of me," she went on, hurriedly, as if afraid of forgetting some part of what she wanted to say. "I've not made my mind up on an impulse, as a young girl might. I'm not a young girl, Vincent. I'm old enough to know what I really feel, to be certain of myself when I decide anything. I've thought about this for a long time Vincent. I'm sure it would be better if we were to part. I'm sure we should both be a great deal happier." (*BE*, 79)

It seems Annie doth protest too much. Though expressing her thoughts as a kind of release: as the couple's mutually advantageous liberation from the conventions of contemporary courtship, the repeated 'I's in the above passage are undermined by her glance towards the photograph (her mother) and, likewise the haste of her utterances lest she forget some part of what was clearly a well-rehearsed speech. Together these persuade the reader that her decision to break the engagement is occasioned more by extrinsic circumstance than personal desire. As we learn at the end of the story, Annie had been conflicted between pursuing her relationship with Vincent and (pre–Welfare State) convention that determined the duty of care generally fell to the 'family', namely a woman.

Having 'walked out together' for some seven years, an extended period owing to economic circumstances, and with the romantic first flushes of courtship long since vanished, Annie and Vincent's engagement, whilst dutifully and honourably following the conventions of contemporary betrothal, has become jaded and mechanical, a grim persistence at best.[89] Yet, for his part Vincent seems initially rather shocked at Annie's suggestion. A residual desire to continue their engagement persists: 'There's my course', he reminds her, his voice curiously high pitched in tone. 'I'm studying hard. In a year I may be a salesman. If you could wait another year—' (*BE*, 79). Some further exchanges follow before Annie rises from the sofa, 'Here's your ring, Vincent', she said. And pulled it off her finger and gave it to him. Vincent's response bringing to mind H. G. Wells' 'simple soul' Arthur Kipps:

> Not until that moment had he realized the full significance of what had occurred. Now it filled his mind like a flood of blinding light in a darkened room. He was free! He was no longer tied to this woman. She could no longer hinder him, no longer hold him back. His mind leapt to the future. He would leave Dobsons and go to another town. He would work hard at his course. In a year or two he would be a salesman. Then, without this millstone round his neck, he would climb—move upwards, always upwards, until finally he reached the top. Alone he would rise to the very pinnacle of success. (*BE*, 80, 81)

It takes Vincent some moments to register the fuller implications of his release, but Halward's use of free-indirect narrative combined with the third-person pronoun 'she' and the demonstrative 'this woman' clearly register the emotional space which has opened up between the couple. The verbs 'tied', 'hinder', 'hold back' each indicative of Vincent's erstwhile constraint as he is released from the obligations of this desultory relationship. Free to pursue his destiny, Vincent's imaginary contrasts movingly with Annie's reality. After he leaves, she returns to the living room to find her mother sitting in a straight-backed chair near the table. 'In the gas light she looked incredibly old. Her face was yellow and deeply wrinkled, like cracked parchment.'

> Presently the old woman looked up. Her eyes were two tiny black points.
> 'Have you told him?' she asked.
> 'Yes', replied the daughter
> 'What did he say?'
> 'Nothing.'
> There was a further long silence.
> Then, the old woman said, 'I'll have my milk now, Annie'. (*BE*, 82)

Having settled her mother to sleep, Annie retires herself. '[She] did not try to sleep. She did not even close her eyes. She lay awake thinking of what life had in store for her' (*BE*, 83).

> She knew now that she would never see Vincent again. She knew that she would never marry. She told herself that she would find happiness in another, and perhaps a better, way. She thought of her mother's words. 'I don't know what I should do without you,' and felt a deep glow of pride. Her mother needed her. 'As long as she lives,' she thought, 'I'll never leave her. I shall be doing my duty. And I shall be content.' But even as she thought this she turned her face to the pillow and began to sob as if her heart would break. (*BE*, 83)

In this poignant closing scene, Halward reveals the full implications of Annie's situation. Prior to Beveridge's eradication of the five 'Giant Evils', working-class people had generally been unable to access private nursing facilities; it fell upon wives and daughters to care for sick or elderly relatives. Forfeiting her own desires and interests, Annie determines on self-abnegation. In drawing together the interconnections between categories of disadvantage such as gender, health and age, 'A Broken Engagement' responds to a variety of intersectional factors obscured by the prevailing emphasis on class alone.

Generally speaking, the constituency of Leslie Halward's 'selving' had been informed by attitudes forged in the masculine ethos of the workplace and in consequence looked back to the 'common style of proletarian life' that Eric Hobsbawm believed was, by the 1950s, in full retreat. This situation is alluded to in Halward's radio drama *Afternoon at Excelsior Lodge* (1960), which, in terms of authorial subjectivity, those 'barely revealed and concealed aspects of an author's life he may not have wished to own', might, following Stephen Reynold's definition of 'autobiografiction', be better described as an 'autobiodrama'.[90] Written as a 'two-hander', its dramatis personae feature a neglected author of short stories, Mark Finsbury, and would-be writer, Vernon Ross, loosely modelled upon and representing Leslie Halward and Geoffrey Trease, respectively.[91] In terms of the 'I/We' dilemma mentioned above, the play's somewhat threadbare mask of pseudonymity enabled Halward to reflect upon his own life experience: on how war service and the experience of moving to the Worcestershire village of Guarlford had inadvertently severed him from 'his people' both geographically and spiritually, for, detached from the urban habitus that constituted the fount of his authorial identity, Halward, as the following lines reveal, had effectively made himself redundant:

Ross:	Did you think you were forgotten?
Finsbury:	It's a hell of a long time since I had reason to think otherwise.
Ross:	Did the war make much difference to you?
Finsbury:	It finished me.
Ross:	You mean, as a writer?
Finsbury:	As a writer.
Ross:	I should have thought
Finsbury:	Before the war I was writing about the *poor* working-class, the unemployed, at first hand. I was one of 'em. Since the war there haven't been any. The people I used to write about no longer exist. I can't *feel* anything for factory workers who knock up fifteen or twenty (or thirty) quid in a five day week, have a fortnight's holiday with pay, and go off in their own cars.
Ross:	You don't think they're worth writing about?
Finsbury:	I didn't say that. They might be. I just don't know 'em, that's all. There Aren't any of my working-class left. There will be in a few years, the way things are going. Then I might be able to start again. I wonder if the missus has put that kettle on. (*EL*, 4)

Peter Chamberlain: An Eavesdropper's Secrets: 'Mr. Marris' Reputation' and 'What the Hell?'

In terms of subject matter and style, Halward's treatment of the short form contrasts dramatically with that of Peter Chamberlain, whose stories, rather than constructed from lived-experience of working-class life, are lighter in tone and, in this respect, may be likened to the comic invention of the American short story writer O. Henry. Walter Allen is disparaging of O. Henry, considering his work formulaic and partially responsible for the short story's descent into 'the swamps of journalism and magazine fiction' during the early years of the twentieth century.[92] However, H. E. Bates nurtured a secret admiration, considering him 'a trickster—the supreme example in the history of the short story of the showman 'wrapping it up so that the fools don't know it'.[93] O. Henry's 'wrapping it up' often consisted in the twist-in-the-tale ending, and it is Chamberlain's use of this device in 'Mr Marris's Reputation' and elsewhere that prompts the appropriation of Graham Greene's term 'Entertainments' here to distinguish his working-class 'slices of life' from the more avant-garde and experimental pieces.[94] As Andy Croft indicates, in terms of both subject matter and style, '[Chamberlain's] stories defy characterisation [...] Their only common character is rather the enormous *variety* of subject, setting, style, voice and vocabulary, evoking different levels of class and culture (original emphasis)'.[95] Though Croft cites a sizeable extract from 'What the Hell?' he provides little, if any, critical commentary. Beyond the initial praise of I. A. Richards and the personal reminiscences of Walter Allen and Leslie Halward, there remained little, if any, further discussion of his work for almost thirty years. This would appear in 2011 and was provided by Bashir Abu-Manneh who, in researching the short stories published in the *New Statesman* between 1913 and 1939, discussed Chamberlain's work in relation to that of V. S. Pritchett.[96] Echoing the position taken here, Abu-Manneh finds:

> [The realist] interest in everyday life and experience [...] shows how domestic, communal and workplace concerns informed the fictional practices of working-class and lower-middle-class writers during this period, focusing upon works in which class and realism take centre stage in a critical landscape 'dominated by modernism and empire'.[97]

While remarking positively on Chamberlain's formal innovation, Abu-Manneh registers a preference for working-class writing that displays the social commitment and the ordinariness of working-class life he found in the work of V.S. Pritchett, as a consequence of which his views on modernism in general, and Chamberlain's writing in particular, are downgraded. On the one hand, this is helpful for Abu-Manneh's argument provides a useful framework for the following discussion; on the other, it is unfortunate because Chamberlain's writing is discussed less on its own merits than as a critical foil to that of Pritchett. In Abu-Manneh's opinion, Pritchett's perspective as a member of the lower middle class enabled him to draw more 'highly-individuated social portraits' unlike those written in the 'detached documentary' style of Chamberlain, where he finds 'no sense in the encounter that the reader really knows the characters described, or has been shown what makes them distinctive individuals'.[98]

The following analysis of Chamberlain's short stories, whilst in accord with Abu-Manneh's praise of V. S. Pritchett—a writer whose class status is in many ways closer to Leslie Halward than Peter Chamberlain—takes issue with the charge of inauthenticity registered in his description of Chamberlain's style as 'detached and documentary'.[99] To arraign Chamberlain on the grounds that his middle-class background proved—as with the criticisms levelled at, though clearly refuted in the work of Henry Green—a barrier to his knowledge of working-class experience amounts to a summary dismissal, at once disqualifying not only Chamberlain but anyone from 'outside' the working classes writing about them. Fortunately, this view has become less widespread. As the foregoing discussion has remarked, changes in Comintern policy directives were transformed from the proletkult hard line to the softening of approach exigent upon the adoption of popular front policies. Barbara Foley indicates how, following the 1934 Soviet Writers Congress, the emphasis in the art/propaganda debate was upon writing in which 'There was no necessity for the authors of socialist realist texts to come from the ranks of the proletariat'.[100] Peter Chamberlain's observational skills and ear for working-class dialogue enabled him to engage fully with Comintern's new directive in the construction of authentic, convincing slices of working-class life, which combined comedy, individuation and compassion without lapsing into caricature, condescension or sentimentality.

Abu-Manneh's negative response to Chamberlain's working-class *tranche de vie* is also revealed in the pejorative connotations he attaches to the adjective 'Documentary'. He explains this by reference to 'Documentary exactitudes', the term coined by Valentine Cunningham, who had employed it to describe the properties 'called upon to aid the outside, bourgeois observer of working-class life, as the best substitute available for the inside information he was short on'.[101] Considered as theatrical 'props', or 'Staffage', the pre-painted 'stick-on' characters employed by eighteenth-century landscape painters, the notion of 'documentary exactitudes' resonates with the 'materialism' Virginia Woolf discerned in Arnold Bennett's prose, whose 'craftsmanship' she asserted ironically, allowed 'not so much as a draught between the frames of the windows, or a crack in the boards'.[102] As has been shown, Birmingham's Leslie Halward enthusiastically policed the boundaries of working-class prose and disliked intensely 'the casual contact and occasional eavesdropping' engaged in by middle-class individuals in order to divine the nature of working-class experience.[103] 'Eavesdropping' is a double-edged sword however, and whilst communicating Halward's displeasure at such literary 'slumming', it functioned more positively in respect of Chamberlain for whom it had furnished a wealth of sincerely and authentically recorded working-class subject material. Bringing this unlikely pair into conversation with one another affords an opportunity to contrast Halward's experientially informed narratives with Chamberlain's more imaginatively conceived *tranche de vie*. The fact that Chamberlain employed 'Documentary exactitudes' or 'reality effects' should not invalidate the truth-to-life or authenticity of his stories per se, for to insist, as Woolf accused Bennett, that the employment of *realia* was an evasion or substitute for a fuller psychological delineation of character is untenable, as W. H. Auden suggests:

> The only genuine meaning of the word 'documentary' is true-to-life. Any *gesture*, any *expression*, any *dialogue* or *sound effect*, any *scenery* that strikes the audience [reader] as true-to-life is documentary whether obtained in the studio (i.e. crafted/staged) or on location (in the world). [...] The effect of film is to create a powerful emotional attitude towards the emotional material presented. [...] on the screen you never see *a* man digging in a field, but always Mr. McGregor digging in a ten acre meadow. It goes far beyond the novel in this. (My emphasis)[104]

That Auden saw the documentary film camera's indefatigable appetite as surpassing the scope of the novel is not to negate the imaginative writer's achievement. As with a cinema audience, the reader's emotional attitude to the words on the page is formed by 'relating' the plausibility of fictional representation to their own experience, and Chamberlain's use of 'documentary exactitudes' was aimed at precisely this effect. The following synopsis of Chamberlain's 'Mr. Marris' Reputation' is provided in order that the reader may judge for himself.[105]

Best described as a 'comic slice-of-life', or as a 'working-class comedy of manners', Chamberlain's story is set within the blackened, smoke encrusted walls of the Railway Hotel.

> Between it and the embankment a steep path, made from the cinders of forgotten engines, led up to the derelict station, forming a much prized Lovers Lane, so that a glass of port and an old-and-mild would often be the prelude to giggles and scuffling in its friendly darkness. (*WH*, 103)

Recounting the events that took place in this bleak industrial landscape where Eros came calling and Mr. Marris acquired his 'reputation', it is here we encounter in medias res the swarthy Alf Marris 'smelling of tarry rope, and wearing a permanent cloth cap' along with his two companions Bert Stamps and Bert Jemson in the _moke room (the 's' having long since disappeared) of their regular Saturday haunt. Alf Marris is drawn by the allure of the attractive and striking Saturday barmaid Miss Fowler, whereupon, encouraged and emboldened by her smile, he ventures to engage her in conversation.

> 'Fine evening?' he tried doubtfully.
>
> Yes, isn't it replied Miss Fowler, as nice as you please, dazzling him with a perfectly ravishing smile, and nodding her head so that the ear-rings hopped about skittishly.
>
> Deeming this intimacy sufficient for the moment, he uttered a melancholy 'Ho' and carefully carried the beer back to the table. (*WH*, 106)

Surprised, possibly taken aback, to find his conversational gambit so warmly reciprocated, Alf Marris is temporarily lost for words his eyes continue to trace Miss Fowler's movements behind the bar. Surprised at Alf's uncustomary largesse, his drinking companions look on dumbstruck as the 'usually so-kept-to-herself' Miss Fowler 'thawed, and told him, as though it were the most natural thing in the world, that she would take a glass of port, thank you, and her respects, she was sure' (*WH*, 107). Miss Fowler's vivacious demeanour is represented anthropomorphically by the description of 'beer bubbl[ing] from the tap overflowing slightly and dribbling into the jug set to catch it below', with Chamberlain's narrator communicating Alf's thoughts via the use of free indirect discourse to describe 'the strong neck and the green earrings that came bursting from the wild wood of her hair, black as his own coals'. Chamberlain thus underscores his protagonists' mutual attractedness and propels the story towards the 'assignation' in which Alf Marris acquires his 'reputation'. Drinking-up time follows apace, during which Alf's companions voice alternately their expressions of disbelief and encouragement at the seeming success of Alf's romantic stratagem, whereupon, surprised by his own extraordinary daring, Alf basks assuredly in his self-modesty and is content merely to utter an acknowledging 'Ar' during the lacunae in their excited and gabbled commentary.

> Setting down their empty mugs, and calling goodnight, they were departing when it happened. Miss Fowler, industriously polishing a glass, leant across the counter and called, apparently to the whole group, 'See you outside'. (*WH*, 108)

Clearly thrown into a panic, '[f]or a moment all three stood with wide-open mouths, rooted to the ground, then higgledy-piggledy scrambled through the door, Mr. Marris noticeably unsteadily' (*WH*, 109). Ill at ease in this new found situation, Alf's companions wave their respective goodnights before hurriedly departing and leaving him to contemplate the situation alone. Outside, while leaning against a lamppost, with one half of his mind telling him she was a 'clinking piece of stuff', the other annoyed at his friends' desertion, a couple emerge from Lovers Lane and stare in Alf's direction, whereupon, hearing the bolt of the pub door withdrawn, Alf's nerve fails. Almost running, he blunders off in the opposite direction; it was an extra half-mile's journey home. However, by taking this route, he would be certain not to encounter his companions and avoid the need to disabuse them regarding the outcome of his misbegotten lovers' tryst. Dramatic irony works its subtle effects: Chamberlain's readers, privy to what 'actually happened' and where, added 'comic' value derives from the knowledge that this ageing Lothario's long detour home was simply an artefact of some lingering and residual masculine pride.

While disparaging of Chamberlain's working-class tales, Abu-Manneh offers a more encouraging, though qualified, response to the experimental pieces. That Peter Chamberlain was a tireless observer of his own social milieu, is evident in the following extract from 'Suburban Exercise' that appeared in the *New Statesman* on the 23 February 1935[106]:

> They have spoiled the master's shirts at the laundry again; they will have to make us an allowance that is all.
>
> These tennis balls will be clean enough for the Holloways.
>
> At last we have heard of a satisfactory parlour-maid; she has first-class references from one of the Gillotts who live in Hastings Road—quite a big house—but she asks too much money. Girls just will not go into service these days.
>
> In the shrubbery are lying the torn-up pieces of somebody's golf card.
>
> Her son is at school at Eastbourne, and getting on very well she says.
>
> Our roses have done very well this year; we have had a magnificent show, although we only have a man in twice a week to keep the place tidy.
>
> They are taking it in part exchange for a new Austin. It has done us very well and never let us down, but Gerald feels that he wants something different I suppose. (*WH*, 61–63)

Although these snippets are presented as anonymous pieces of everyday speech, they are not wholly transparent. Wrested from their original context and re-presented in the manner of a surrealist collage, these textual fragments behave in a similar manner to the objects and figures (the phantasmagoria) assembled in Walter Benjamin's Arcades Project, whereby, as J. M. Coetzee's definitional analysis proposes, 'they act spontaneously to give off political energy'. In so doing, the fragments constitute the dialectical image, dialectical movement frozen for a moment, open for inspection, dialectics at a standstill: 'Only dialectical images are genuine images.'[107] Delivered employing the elaborated linguistic code and subject material freighted with middle-class signifiers, Chamberlain's slivers of dialogue are unquestionably parodic, their cumulative effect issuing in a satirical treatment that looks forward to John Betjeman's *Summoned by Bells*. As a member of the middle classes himself, Chamberlain was both alert to their idiom and well placed to 'eavesdrop' and parody their forms of utterance. In 'Belgravian Exercise', he moves from the suburban milieu to tackle a more elevated and cosmopolitan demographic.[108] Here, numbered and extended extracts create a sequential montage that parallels the visual imagery of *Picture Post*, or more closely Walter Ruttman's silent film *Berlin: Symphony of a Metropolis*, in which the recording of arbitrary incidents from everyday life provides a non-narrative, stream-of-consciousness commentary taking in human interactions, random objects, shop window displays, signs and notices, and the many other phenomena to be observed on a typical day in one of the capital's most affluent areas:

> 7. The driver of the taxi, which the two ladies hailed just before reaching the square, affected to be unaware of the dark looks given him by his colleagues, who were already waiting on the rank.
>
> 9. Further along the Square some dozen women and about half as many girls are standing on the pavement. What are they waiting for? They are expecting the children of the Duke and Duchess of Kent to leave for their walk, and do not appear to notice the cold wind which is blowing from the North.
>
> 21. From the Palladium the voice of Miss Gracie Fields, popular light comedienne, is repeated first by one wireless then another, so that, as I walk over the rough stones, her song is loud and continuous. She is singing to the tenants of the only 'conversion' in the mews, she is singing to the King and Queen, she is singing to the whole of the British Isles. Because of the command performance, many people have stayed at home tonight.[109]

What Abu-Manneh terms Chamberlain's 'Snapshot Documentary' is clearly redolent of the ethnographic turn discussed in the introduction. In Chamberlain's *objet trouve*, the 'Documentary' impulse is turned in upon itself. The 'configuration', Stuart Hall identified as 'The Social Eye of *Picture Post*', and which developed the social consciousness of wartime Britain', is now turned upon the observer and his own caste.[110] The process of observation and social eavesdropping is clearly evident in Chamberlain's working- and middle-class renderings which, deriving from real life, provide the kinds of insight provided by Mass-Observation's participant observers. Whether drawn from reality or imaginative artifice, Chamberlain's 'exercises' are constructed from close observation—indeed, from what might be described as the sine qua non of the imaginative writer: the ability to listen—and present as micro-sketches of the middle-class world he knew intimately and which offer insights into lives and identities far beyond the working-class milieu that had constituted the Birmingham group's more usual fayre.

Though at times comic and employing a 'twist-in-the-tail' conclusion, Chamberlain's stylistic approach in the experimental pieces owes less to O. Henry than John O'Hara. Recording that it was Chamberlain who introduced him to O'Hara's writing by lending him *Appointment in Samarra* and *The Doctor's Son*, Walter Allen describes John O'Hara as amongst the American 'novelists who came of age during the thirties when the condition of society as a major theme was all but inescapable'.[111] Testifying to the power of his imaginative prose, Allen explains: 'The great strength of John O'Hara, [...] had always lain in precise, exhaustively detailed description of provincial society', concluding that although it is fiction, '[O'Hara's] *Appointment in Samarra* is probably the best and most illuminating account we have of the class system of a white American town'.[112] Whether O'Hara's American narratives raised Chamberlain's political consciousness is a moot point, that his 'way of seeing' influenced the English writer is unquestionable. In a *New Yorker* article titled 'The Eavesdropper's Secret: On John O'Hara', Charles McGrath reads against the grain of Leslie Halward's abrupt dismissal, by not only legitimising eavesdropping, but in elevating it to something of an art form. Describing O'Hara as 'one of the great listeners of American fiction', he explains:

> [*The New Yorker*] became a place where [O'Hara] could develop his talent almost experimentally—without the pressures that went with novel writing. His earliest efforts, like most of what the magazine was publishing then, were virtually plotless little sketches—often snatches of overheard dialogue: a lonely man in a diner, for example, reminiscing about an old girlfriend. ('So Nan and I just chatted about nothing at all. I didn't make a pass at her and finally she suddenly stopped talking and I knew she was tired so I went home. Funny how you get over a girl like that').[113]

Chamberlain followed O'Hara's *New Yorker* strategy by using the pages of Britain's *New Statesman* to hone his craft, and, just as O'Hara made satirical play of American small town Babbittry, so Chamberlain laid bare the trivial pre-occupations of his English, middle-class peers often, as McGrath remarked of O'Hara, 'in a manner as fond as it is pointed'.[114]

In 'What the Hell?' Chamberlain renews his focus on working-class characters, more specifically that apotheosis of 1930s and wartime petty criminality: the 'spiv', the type John Hampson described as 'a comparatively recent comer to fiction', and one who, despite nefarious black marketeering, aroused a degree of sympathy amongst those eager to purchase those goods to which he (female spivs are curiously unrecorded) appeared to have unlimited access.[115] Formally speaking, Chamberlain's *very* short story takes the form of an interior monologue or soliloquy in which the speaker addresses a silent interlocutor possibly a friend or perhaps the reader.[116] It is difficult to speculate on Chamberlain's aims or purpose here, although his 'insider knowledge' may well be read as an encoded critique of bourgeois values. In its imagining of another's experience and operating in the moment where autobiography, fiction and the essay intersect, 'What the Hell?' is not, generically speaking, beyond the parameters of autobiografiction.[117] Chamberlain's spiv character exposes the vacuity of rabid consumerism revealing that 'the narrow plot of acquisitiveness' is not restricted to female desire alone. Unlike Brierley's scholarly outsiders, Chamberlain's creation has more in common with Leslie Halward's reputation-seeking Jim Belcher, for, as with Halward, Chamberlain is equally percipient in discerning the vulnerability lying beneath his protagonist's veneer of machismo.

'What the Hell?' drew the attention of I. A. Richards, who, having read it in the *New Statesman*, 'sent Chamberlain a postcard saying the story was the most original thing he had read for several years'.[118] Chamberlain's portrait of this 'Yewgottabetough' school graduate was certainly innovative, simultaneously a study in the use of 'Documentary exactitudes', a paean to rampant consumerism and, in its anticipative treatment of the spiv type, looking forward to Graham Greene's Pinky in *Brighton Rock* (1938), before moving beyond to the Milk Bars, Kitchen Sinks and Angry Young Men of post-war Britain.[119] The spiv character was by no means exclusive to the London scene as we saw in the behaviour of the would-be blackmailer Eric Gardiner and Eugene Lorimer's con man mentor James Bartholomew, who lurked furtively within the pages of Walter Allen's fictions. Andy Croft remarks that Hampson attributed the ascendancy of the spiv to the vogue for 'grim autobiographies' of the criminal underworld that were popular and influential during the 1930s and constituted a form of writing he thought appropriate for an audience 'living in a threatened society' and which he recommended for giving 'the authentic flavour of the present times', 'unsentimental, realistic and contemporary'.[120] On face value, 'What the Hell?' is a catalogue of material possessions: listing luxury goods, jewellery and accessories, and clothes, shoes, luggage and furniture, and referencing interior design, the speaker's good taste and social aspirations before culminating, somewhat disconcertingly, with people. Abu-Manneh suggests we read it as a satire on the 'bourgeois documentary' form prevalent in 1930s literature and epitomised in such journals as *Fact*, where the 'bourgeois documentary approach' is deployed 'against its dominant form and twist[ed] back upon itself' in such a way that 'a discourse used to read across the class divide' is turned to describing its own social origins'.[121] The view taken here aligns with Abu-Manneh, though whereas the 'bourgeois documentary approach' had merely recorded working-class objects or experience in order to create descriptive authenticity, 'What the Hell?' instead considers such items more dismissively as though an indictment of middle-class values. Described by a working-class subject who appears sceptical of their value, rather than accoutrements, they appear as encumbrances, which, though satisfying his immediate wants, fail to satisfy his needs and thus reveal themselves as the unfulfilling objects of material desire whose power, once possessed, mysteriously evaporates.

'What The Hell?' begins with Chamberlain's speaker assuring his readers 'I got most everything I *want*. Look at it all ways I have. Well then [my italics]...' (*WH*, 1). The speaker's brusque idiom sets the tone:

> My gold cigarette-case is real class; it cost a mint of money in Regent Street. And I got a silver one; a big 'un with fine markings. Mostly I carry fags in the packet though. I can smoke expensive muck if I choose, but I like the twenty a bob best. (*WH*, 1)

Despite the flippant tone, the speaker undercuts the 'refinement' these luxury items purportedly confer by indicating a preference for carrying 'fags in the packet', which expresses a level of groundedness rather than ostentation. In a similar manner, he describes the impracticality of a gold wristwatch, 'which don't keep good time but looks swell, with a funny sort of face you can't read very well, but it's smart, with a metal thing for a strap, gold, that Jim told me was nancy (obsolete slang term: effeminate male/homosexual), only that's just his jealousy I guess' (*WH*, 1).[122] The speaker's initial claims are frequently undercut in this manner. We move from descriptions of jewellery to clothes, shoes and travel goods to the interior of his flat. Here we're told: 'You can see everything's posh at a glance. Furnished complete by a bloke who knew his job. He ought, he charged enough, Christ knows' (*WH*, 2, 3). Again, in a commodity-oriented world, value is determined in purely monetary terms simply by reference to an item's cost, rather than the quality of its workmanship. The speaker's comments reveal his unfamiliarity with the nature of 'luxury' items where an item's price is measured in terms of the skills expended in its decorative embellishment rather than their practical necessity or function alone.

Chamberlain employs 'ungrammatical first-person narration' to construct his 'crisp, honest, down-to-earth and heroically ordinary' working-class speaker.[123] In the absence of further identifying detail, by using an appropriately restricted linguistic code, punctuated by tersely expressed opinions and the curious tone of self-deprecation, Chamberlain's character seemingly self-creates. Taking its speaker's shallow materialism at face value, one may read Chamberlain's story as a simple satire on consumerism. However, there is room for an alternative reading, for having amassed his cache of luxury items (cultural capital) presumably in order to be well-thought of by others, behind the speaker's braggadocio lurks a desperately insecure individual whose possessions fail to reciprocate the sense of value he invests in them. These material objects found wanting, he seeks the reassurance of others to bolster his self-esteem:

> And I got taste too; the girls in shops always tell me that. Pictures and rugs and ornaments and knick-knacks all in the very best of style. But nothing simply because it's expensive… 'When I give a party people come. No matter who they are, and some of them are real swells, they come. And they're always very civil to me. (*WH*, 3)

The naivety registered in his dealings with the 'real swells' from outside his own social milieu and whose approval he so desperately wants is conspicuous, but turns several shades darker when extended to his relationships with women who are described purely in terms of exchange value, as goods to be purchased rather than relationships to be formed:

> You should have seen the bit I took abroad last year. As smart a piece as any I saw in Nice. She cost a heap of money, but she was good value. I've had the real goods throw themselves at me in this very room. The better class they are the more loving they seem to be. You'd be surprised at the things some of them do. And finely built girls too, Of course it's the money most of them want—I'm not such a fool as not to know that—but after all.... (*WH*, 3)

As Nicola Caramina suggests, '[t]he demands of a consumer society replace love with Eros and sensuality. In a society based upon consumerism and the commodification of individuals, even love becomes instrumental as it is bought and sold in a market of social exchange where individuals become objectified with disposable brands'.[124] Chamberlain's 'possession proud' protagonist thus offers himself as a further male exemplar of the 'narrow plot of acquisitiveness and desire' Virginia Woolf had discerned in the writing of working-class women. As Pamela Fox maintains, the acquisitive impulse merely registers the working-class individual's simple requirement for something better in life and, in this respect, may be viewed as a form of resistance which, 'posed against more explicitly oppositional narrative formulas, [...] impels the writing of a secondary plot that tells another, equally pressing, class story'.[125] However, in 'What The Hell?', rather than adopting the condescending perspective of the 'benevolent spectator', Chamberlain withheld narratorial judgement in permitting his working-class protagonist to speak for himself.

The interest of Chamberlain's characterisation lies in the fact that, despite his character's bluff exterior and seemingly credulous desire for material possessions, there remains an underlying degree of self-knowledge, the recognition that whether 'girls' or 'swells', 'it's the money most of them want—I'm not such a fool as to not know that'. Just as the initial allure of his material possessions is found wanting, so too the adulation of the free-loading, fair-weather friends he hopes to 'purchase' but whose attentions will doubtless evaporate when the money runs out. Fortunately, he values older, long-standing friendships more. As he grudgingly remarks in the closing lines, 'And I'm generous with it. Nothing's too good for a friend of mine. Yes, I've got pretty well everything I want. Well then? What the sweet Hell?' (*WH*, 4). Closing with a near repetition of the opening line, Chamberlain's story registers both the circularity and the insatiability of consumer desire.

John Hampson: *Saturday Night at the Greyhound*

Chapter 2 examined John Hampson's short story 'Man About The House' by considering some of the prevailing cultural issues raised by its content, particularly the male breadwinner model and contemporary notions of masculinity. As this book has remarked, issues of gender were frequently seen as peripheral to traditional critiques of working-class writing yet, as Christopher Hilliard indicates, 'representing domestic situations implicitly emphasise[s] there is more to working-class life than work'.[126] As is hopefully becoming clear, notions of identity are currently undergoing reassessment and scrutiny. The following analysis of John Hampson's *Saturday Night at the Greyhound* takes its cue from Stanislava Dikova's review of Nick Hubble's *The Proletarian Answer to the Modernist Question*, which, while largely affirmative of Nick Hubble's project, suggests that 'placing greater emphasis on queer writers and authors from cross-cultural backgrounds might provide a fuller picture of intersectionality'.[127] Hampson's novel affords a unique opportunity to examine issues of working-class culture from this perspective and also enables its readers to consider intersubjective relationships at both *intra*- and *inter*-class level. As has been shown, many of the autobiographical and sociocultural issues that permeate Hampson's shorter fiction were already visible in his novels, surfacing in a series of *bildungsromane* in which the protagonist's world-view was frequently that of the homosexual and whose persona was frequently constructed from the author's own lived experience. Hampson's representations therefore assist in the recovery of what, certainly during the interwar years, was not so much a 'submerged' as a 'legislatively suppressed' authorial voice. Once more, *Saturday Night at the Greyhound* attests to the fact that the narratives of the Birmingham group not only respond to but also were often pre-figurative of more recent critical approaches to the discussion of the working-class literature of this and subsequent periods.

The realist novel's impulse to document and describe was discussed earlier with reference to Nicola Wilson's distinction between 'observed' and 'inhabited' space. John Hampson's novels make frequent reference to 'observed' space, and, in *O Providence* (1932), this becomes a formal device whereby the novel's four sections (Five Ways, The House in Laurel Road, Rowantree End and Park View) are constructed around the vicissitudes of the Stonetun family's experience at each location. Charting their fortunes from the self-evidently opulent, tree-lined avenues and large staff required to service 'Five Ways' to 'the six-foot square of ragged grass bordered by dry-brown earth' which constituted 'Laurel Road's' front garden, the youngest child Justin Stonetun (the Hampson persona) describes how, temporarily thrown upon their uppers, the Stonetuns experience life within the humble confines of the artisanal home's restricted dimensions: 'The house itself was small and narrow, possessing a thin hall, a narrow stairway and nine small rooms. Allys Stonetun loathed it. [...] the house was furnished barely, essential things, beds and chairs, a table. A few more pieces too, her own personal possessions, relics of other days' (*OP*, 106). The proximity and lack of privacy is emphasised from a child's perspective as Justin describes his father, 'face smeary with lather', calling the children to wake, and in the sharing of bedrooms where an elder brother impatiently helps dress a younger sibling, with the mother downstairs in the kitchen where 'she worked like a galley slave sewing and scrimping'. Outside '[a] tram-car came rattling along [...] as crowds of dark-clad people hurried along the pavements, men on bicycles pushed along the roadway. So many things to see' (*OP*, 106). The shaping influence of the familial and domestic—the 'close quick relationships', 'the continuous flow and recoil of sympathy', 'the essential process of living' that Raymond Williams found in D. H. Lawrence's writing, not to mention the Nottingham writer's profound influence on Hampson, are clearly evident in the scenes described here.[128]

In *Strip Jack Naked* (1934), the central character Ted Borlay (a further incarnation of the Hampson persona) undertakes to marry Laura, the wife of his recently deceased elder brother Alf, upon whom Ted has become fixated and enslaved. Laura and Ted's marriage begins somewhat vicariously; initially a substitute for Ted's cathectic projections, the marriage to Laura will allow him to foster his brother's child. From Laura's perspective, this course of action owes more to moral and economic necessity, that is, the need to provide for the child, though in time the couple are reconciled to their new found situation and move from beneath the shadow cast by Alf's death to enjoy a companionate marriage with a second child and hence a family of their own. Again the Lawrencian influence is plain, no less in the American edition of *Strip Jack Naked*—retitled '*Brothers and Lovers*' to avoid a clash with Douglas Goldring's novel of the same name—than in its content where, as Mercer Hampson Simpson, explains:

> In *Sons and Lovers* Paul Morel's mother-fixation prevents his marrying until after her death as, it seems, was the case with Lawrence himself. Hampson's American title is perhaps more apposite than his British one since, though Tom was mentally—psychically, in his imagination, not physically—his brother's lover, both brothers are, in turn Laura's lovers; and again as with Lawrence, not until the death of the dominating loved one in the family is the surviving lover free to choose another partner outside his family.[129]

Although Hampson's literary output was the most prolific of the Birmingham group writers, the following discussion is necessarily curtailed due to limitations of space, not to mention the limited availability of Hampson's novels. The foregoing observations were greatly assisted by Mercer F. Hampson Simpson's M. A. dissertation 'The Novels of John Hampson' (1975), which, beyond Walter Allen's critical evaluations, contemporary reviews and 'introductions' to reprints of *Saturday Night at the Greyhound*, provides, to my knowledge, the only extended discussion of Hampson's writing.[130] The plot-based summaries of *O Providence* and *Strip Jack Naked* examine the 'psychological aetiology' that Mercer F. Hampson Simpson believed was a persistent factor in Hampson's work. Though biographically accurate and informative, his 'account of Hampson's life and work' inevitably suffers by being a product of its time. Written in 1975, a mere eight years after the decriminalisation of homosexual acts registered in the Sexual Offences Act of 1967 and other changes in clinical criteria that had only recently ceased to consider homosexuality a mental illness, Mercer F. Hampson Simpson's assessment is therefore skewed by the prevailing discourse that regarded homosexuality as requiring concealment rather than disclosure, a motivation which, certainly from the more enlightened perspective of today, appears as none other than prudish solicitude.[131] Such attitudes are articulated in Mercer Hampson Simpson's comment that *Strip Jack Naked* represented an attempt to project a more normative account of himself; he suggests, '[John Hampson] *must* have felt that the time had come to attempt an artistic escape from the *limitations of his personality*'—a view which, in the absence of an autobiography or explicit biographical detail, is unverifiable and more possibly a function of Mercer F. Hampson Simpson's presumption.[132] However, given contemporary attitudes, it is undoubtedly possible that Hampson may have wished to conceal his homosexuality, though whether he believed he might escape the 'limitations of his personality' by having his characters adopt the 'active' (as opposed to passive) role of the heterosexual male privileged in contemporary normative accounts of sexuality is another question. Mercer F. Hampson Simpson nevertheless rehearses prevailing psychoanalytical concepts to press his view that Hampson *wanted* to assume a more active masculine role, and he consequently reads Ted Borlay's marriage to Laura as 'a move from homosexual to heterosexual, from passive role to active role', and suggests that Hampson sought to create *positive* centres in his novels as opposed to 'flatly homosexual ones' (my emphasis).[133] This clearly has implications, for although Mercer F. Hampson Simpson's discussion is sensitive to their author's homosexuality, it is apparent that he considered it a constraining, at times, negative influence upon the works themselves. Written ten years prior to Mercer Hampson Simpson's account however, a somewhat more enlightened and percipient Walter Allen saw that:

> In almost all Hampson's novels there appears the figure of the young man, often a youngest son—Tom in *Saturday Night at the Greyhound*, Johnny in *Family Curse*—who is, or sees himself to be in permanent estrangement from society because he is a homosexual. He is wiser, more clear-sighted, more disinterested, than the other characters; he sees through them and foresees the consequences of their behaviour, even though he may be powerless to prevent them; though he participates in the action, he is also its chorus.[134]

Perceptive in itself, Allen's encomium certainly encourages a positive reading of the novels, one that is particularly alive to the sensitivity with which Hampson imbued his characterisations and one certainly more attuned to the critical requirements of our own times.

As outlined in the discussion of Walter Brierley's incursion into the world of publishing, John Hampson proved a passionate advocate of working-class writers. That Hampson's altruistic leaning had been earlier reciprocated by Leonard and Virginia Woolf at the Hogarth Press confirms Helen Southworth's assessment that literary life did indeed exist beyond the capital, and, as her eponymous conference paper 'Outside The Magic (And Tyrannical) Triangle of London, Oxford and Cambridge' makes clear, a further factor in the Woolfs' support of Hampson might have been that other publishing houses were actively seeking working-class fiction at this time.[135]

Although the Hogarth Press would publish *Saturday Night at the Greyhound* in 1931, Hampson's first submission to the Woolfs had been

Go Seek a Stranger. Resembling E. M. Forster's *Maurice* in being an account of 'a happier year', Southworth describes the novel as an 'explicitly homosexual work, […]' '[one] universally judged his best, by among others Virginia Woolf' and 'offers a sympathetic portrait of the dilemma of the homosexual man in the 1920s and 1930s'. Doubtless sympathetic regarding Hampson's sexual orientation and clearly registering their impatience with regard to current censorship legislation, Southworth records, 'The Woolfs' experience with Joyce's *Ulysses*, for which they were unable to find a printer willing to risk prosecution on obscenity charges, and their involvement with Radclyffe Hall's *The Well of Loneliness* trial 'appeared to have made them wary and 'likely discouraged them from publishing' Hampson's novel or similarly controversial works'.[136] Unfortunately, Leonard Woolf 'found himself compelled to reject [it]', telling Hampson, '[the work] has interested us greatly and has such merits that we should have liked to publish', but that 'unfortunately we do not think that this would be possible under present circumstances'.[137]

Although rejected by Jonathan Cape in 1929, Helen Southworth says: '[*Saturday Night at the Greyhound*] worked well with the Woolfs' mandate at the press which was to launch new authors and to publish work that would not find a home in a mainstream publishing house'.[138] Having submitted *Saturday Night at the Greyhound* and *O Providence* at the same time, the reader's report, while considering *O Providence* the more remarkable of the two novels, had urged the Woolfs to publish *Saturday Night* at the Greyhound first, suggesting it might 'attract more attention' and commenting, somewhat cryptically, 'the writer seems to me extraordinarily unaffected by any conventional attitude to life. He describes what he sees with his own eyes and makes his experience actual to the reader. He never plays tricks to bring his story into line with the conventional novel. the result is the most unusual impression of complete truthfulness.'[139] Whether in his coded allusion to 'conventional attitudes, or the more irascible tone he later adopted – possibly a reflection of the 'Bloomsbury attitude' towards fashionable 'metropolitan' tastes – when assuring the Woolfs that: 'neither book has the pretentious writing or obvious psychological complications which would appeal to middle-brows'.[140] He signed off by suggesting: 'In any case the author should be encouraged to continue writing. He seems to me the most interesting new novelist I have come across for several years.'

As will be seen, *Saturday Night at the Greyhound* offers a faithful depiction of working-class lives which, according to the Hogarth Press historian

J. H. Willis, offered the Woolfs 'an uncharted literary landscape', 'written', as Helen Southworth points out, in a style wholly appropriate to its subject matter.[141] Discussing the latter in relation to Liverpool author James Hanley's formal innovations, Ben Clarke references John Cowper Powys' description of the Liverpool writer's 'bald, bleak, stripped, winnowed and harrowed style' as one befitting the 'most modern school of aesthetics', that is to say, the 'hard-boiled' American style: the 'yougottabetough' school as coined by Cyril Connolly; it was clearly an aesthetic approach that sat well with Hampson, who, as remarked upon by Walter Allen, had little patience with the niceties of 'fine writing'.[142]

Again, in terms of an appropriate critical framework against which to evaluate Hampson's work, the intersectional approach proves helpful by supporting the analysis of a gendered dynamic operating within these class-based narratives whilst simultaneously addressing the question of authorial subjectivity. Nevertheless, while fully supportive of Hampson's project, Walter Allen's perceptive comments are balanced by those of William Plomer, who, having read *O Providence*, wrote to Hampson, remarking, 'the whole thing seems to me interesting as a case history rather than as a work of literature'.[143] Plomer's observation reiterates the issue of visibility: the dilemma of concealment and disclosure regarding issues of sexual orientation in the pre-war decade and which necessarily prompts a fuller examination of the autobiographical and cathartic elements in Hampson's writing. Indeed, by describing *O Providence* as *autobiographical* rather than autobiography per se, Mercer F. Hampson Simpson points up the subtle distinction between adjective and noun that once more resonates in the term 'autobiografiction'. Probably unaware of Stephen Reynolds generic coinage, Hampson's novels, as with those of his Birmingham group compeers, are readily assimilated into the bounds of this capacious form. The spiritual experience engendered by love, its complications, sorrows and the intensified emotions that Reynolds describes were doubtless familiar to the sensitive and complex Hampson. By creating fictional characters able to articulate and express his concerns and pre-occupations, in 'recasting the spiritual experience of the introspective individual as that of another', Hampson stumbled upon a means of literary expression and a mode of psychological consolation: a salve for both himself and his readers that resembled closely Stephen Reynold's autobiografiction.

In some respects, *Saturday Night at the Greyhound* might be considered more suitable for inclusion in the discussion of 'work' undertaken in Chap. 1, for as Christopher Hilliard suggests:

> Depicting the working-class at play was another aspect of the concern to represent writers' "own people" on their own terms.' Pubs have an understandable prominence in this literature, not just because of their place in working-class leisure, but also because the pub is a site where work and leisure meet.[144]

Nevertheless, Hilliard indicates: 'Despite its setting, the novel is no ode to the people's alehouse.'[145] Originally conceived as a play, the three parts of Hampson's novel are set in the eponymous public house and take place during the eight hours which constitute the publican's working 'day'. Divided thus—'Nightfall at the Greyhound', 'The House Opens' and 'The House Closes'—it follows the Aristotelian unities in providing not only the narrow spatial compass of tragedy but also the temporal divisions comprising exposition, complication and resolution. Hampson's novel traces the fortunes of its central characters Freddy Flack, his wife Ivy and her brother Tom Oakley as they attempt, though ultimately fail, to run a public house in the East Midland coalfield.[146]

Having worked for their parents in the well-run and successful Crown & Cushion public house in Birmingham, both Ivy and Tom were able to live well, buy nice clothes and enjoy a social life and social status commensurate with that of the petty-bourgeoisie.[147] Having gone their separate ways, Ivy through marriage and Tom to find work in London, brother and sister are reunited following the untimely deaths—within an hour of one another—of their parents. Each sibling receives an inheritance of £250; the cautious Tom banks his portion, while Ivy views hers as capital with which to embark upon a business venture with her husband Freddy. Six months later, Tom receives a letter from his sister informing him that she and Freddy intend to run a public house and imploring him to join them.[148] The charming Freddy Flack is irresponsible, spendthrift and promiscuous. However, Ivy, well schooled in the licensed trade by respectable and professional Birmingham victuallers, is cautious, conscientious and professional. Alternately, besotted, charmed and not a little suspicious of her wayward husband, it is hoped that by investing her inheritance in the public house, she may placate his restlessness. 'The sum [being] too small to get any but the meanest of out-of-the-way houses in Birmingham', their enterprise commences in Grovelace (Ashover), a small mining village in the East Midland coalfield, their aim being to make enough money before returning to Birmingham and the prospect of managing a larger more lucrative concern (*SN*, 41).

Functioning as the Hampson persona described by Walter Allen above, Ivy's brother Tom dotes on his sister and is disparaging of her marriage to the irresponsible Freddy Flack. William Plomer characterised Fred and Ivy's marriage as 'a mating of attractive irresponsibility with wishful thinking'.[149] Once ensconced in the Greyhound and its bleak environs, the Flack ménage is augmented by two further pairs of characters: initially, two locals: the embittered Mrs Tapin, a charwoman, and her daughter, the attractive, ambitious Clara, as barmaid. Added to Hampson's cast are two overnight visitors: the anodyne Roy Grovedon, son of the late village Squire, and his sophisticated, rather pretentious, London girlfriend, Ruth Dorme. With 'casting' complete, Hampson's principals are set to perform their roles amidst a chorus of generally unsympathetic villagers.[150]

Having established 'a complete community encompassing the whole social spectrum', Hampson has only to light the blue touch paper and retire as his highly combustible characters began to ignite in a narrative fiction where aphorisms such as 'character is action' and 'a man's character is his fate' leave little room for conjecture as to how the story would end.[151] Unable to escape the clutches of providence, Fred proceeds to squander the pub's takings by ingratiating himself to the locals in the mistaken belief that he can manipulate and cajole them into liking him. Christopher Hawtree remarks how 'Hampson was able to show with hideous plausibility how the night's remorseless sequence of events had their diverse origins in circumstances and conditions that go back not only months, but years', and as Mercer F. Hampson Simpson suggests, there was an 'Ibsenite certainty' in all of this, although the workings of the malign fate that stalked Thomas Hardy's fictions may likewise have hovered offstage.[152] Yet, unlike the gentle folk who comprised Hardy's rustic chorus in Wessex, the Derbyshire miners are tough. Engaged daily in tearing their living from the raw earth, they are schooled in hardship and shown to be ruthless and wily; indeed, it is they who manipulate the incomers. With the exception of Tom Oakley, the other characters show little self-knowledge or capacity to reflect on their behaviour. Whether Hampson, as he suspected, overdetermined his characters' fates is unclear, though in writing to his publisher that 'the characters lack resistance to providence', he had appeared to nurture some regret.[153] The air of tragic inevitability is pervasive and ultimately ensures that Fred, Ivy and Tom will lose their livelihood and any future possibility of realising their dreams.

In its overlapping of class, gender and setting, *Saturday Night at the Greyhound* almost anticipates an intersectional reading. Drawing from his childhood experience to portray the male characters of Freddy Flack and Tom Oakley and having traced not only their differing life trajectories but also how notions of authorial subjectivity become worked into fictional representations, it is through these characterisations that the autobiografictional notion of 'concealment' comes into play. Hampson contrasts the thoughtful Tom Oakley—who, as a gay man in the 1930s, not unsurprisingly wishes to remain prudent in his discretion—with the philandering, foolhardy and ingratiating Freddy, who hopes to gain the locals' respect and approval. We're told how 'in giving him life Freddy's mother died' and that, neglected by a 'hard and distant father', he was indulged by a spinster aunt who worshipped him, 'no matter what trouble he got into, she found an excuse for him' [...]. A strong desire for popularity and a distinct aptness for games won Freddy a certain amount of success amongst his school fellows' (*SN*, 62). On his father's death at the tender age of fifteen, 'Miss Flack found in him her ideal man; broad-shouldered and slim, his proud bearing and arrogant manner were, she felt, supremely masculine. To wait on him hand and foot seemed only his due; she did it willingly, and he let her' (*SN*, 63).

Having placed the 'broad-shouldered and slim' ideal of manhood that is Freddie Flack atop the marble plinth of essentialist and misogynistic presumption, in making Tom Oakley, to use an old-fashioned term, the 'hero' of his novel, and, by reading against the grain of pre-war sexual politics, Hampson subverts not only Miss Flack's but also contemporary culture's celebration of masculine sexuality. While clearly oblivious regarding present-day notions of identity and gender-constructedness, Hampson saw 'nurture' as a significant factor in identity formation, and in this respect his narrative is prefigurative of the work of Judith Butler and Eve Sedgwick. Doubtless ideologically interpellated within the contemporary purview that legitimized a belief in female inferiority, Mercer F. Hampson Simpson attributed John Hampson's 'passivity' and 'bias' (sexual orientation) to 'childhood ill-health [which] isolated him from the rough-and-tumble of normal boyish pursuits and friendships and made him dependent firstly upon elder women and ultimately upon himself'.[154] The character of Tom Oakley therefore represents the antithesis to prevailing conceptions of masculinity. Having suffered paternal abuse as a child and raised by nursemaids and female carers, rather than developing into the 'arrogant' and 'supremely masculine' type represented by Freddy, John Hampson had become more sensible of the woman's position and chose instead to represent himself pseudonymously as the thoughtful and sensitive Tom.

As intimated earlier, though this book's periodisation is limiting in that it is unable to provide an intersectional analysis of ethnic or racial categories, Hampson's story does articulate the predicament of the 'incomer' in what is an unfamiliar, and in this case relatively hostile, environment. The contrast between Tom and Ivy's comfortable existence in Birmingham and the experience they undergo in their new location is marked. While homesickness accounts for feelings of separation from the domestic known and familiar, immersion in a seemingly hostile environment has more far-reaching consequences in terms of cultural displacement. Psychoanalyst Karim G. Dajani explains how '[removing] a person from a location organised by a particular set of cultural practices and placing them in another location organised by a substantially different set of cultural practices—can shock and alter the ego'.[155] Dajani employs Bourdieu's concept of habitus: 'the set of durable transposable dispositions inculcated from a collective in which an individual is embedded' as the means by which to analyse the impact of 'cultural dislocation' on bi-cultural patients.[156] While the 'shock' and hostility experienced by the immigrant normally derives from more dramatic and contrasting extra-cultural practice such as language or dress codes, the principle in which newcomers appear as a threat and experience hostility from a host community is in essence the same. Ivy Flack found the Derbyshire folk rebarbative, and although 'they had some virtues' [...], their vices seemed many. 'They were slow to like strangers, though quick enough to hate. She knew how to treat them in their own coin with contempt and haughtiness' (*SN*, 47). As the following passage reveals, Ivy feels her cultural dislocation sorely:

> She did not care for serving in the tap-room. There the men seemed to keep their natural rough hardness, in the smoke-room and bar they behaved with an affected restraint as though they were at a funeral. But in the tap-room their rough vigour alarmed her, they were utterly different from the saucy Birmingham boys, with whom she was fully able to cope. (*SN*, 86)

Ivy's brother's response too is illustrative here for, despite his lower-middle-class status, the locals find virtue in Tom; they respect both his work ethic and, paradoxically, his aloofness, and to a certain extent their feelings are reciprocated, as Hampson's narrator explains:

> [Tom] in turn gained respect for them. They were difficult to understand, these people; their hard exterior hostility was something he had never met before. The gaunt countryside was reflected in their grim faces. Suffering and poverty made them hard and callous in their speech, though drink betrayed them, as sentimental. Always on Saturday evening they sang old songs, preferring the mawkish type. Even the children possessed no pity; the harshness of life eliminated it from them. At first Tom thought them animals, their fierceness, frightened him. They laughed harshly at stories of cruelty that turned him sick. In spite of it all, he admired them; their persistent struggle to gain the means of their existence was great in its way. (*SN*, 70)

In this way, Hampson captures the contradictory nature of Tom's encounter—simultaneously one of alarm and admiration—with the inhabitants of a 'location organized by a substantially different set of cultural practices'.[157] The 'shock' Tom registers doubtless owes much to Hampson's own petty-bourgeois origins and upbringing. In correspondence with Mercer F. Hampson Simpson, Leslie Halward remarked, 'I always felt that although he had a great compassion for the working class he was too genteel to write convincingly about them.'[158] Halward's observation illustrates the liminal nature of the Birmingham writers whose social status, as has been suggested, ranged instead across a continuum of positions *within* the 'broad church' of narratives defined as working-class literature. As remarked, Leslie Halward's conception of 'authenticity' had been constructed largely from contemporary male-oriented critiques of workplace and labour relations. His conception of the working class was of a distinct caste rather than sociopolitical construct. Yet his assessment of Hampson was not wholly inaccurate, for although the above passage finds Hampson's 'narrator' describing 'Tom's' feelings, it might equally be seen as the genteel Hampson in dialogue with himself as he attempts to determine his own identity and social status.

John Hampson was under no illusion regarding his dual attitude in respect of class. Despite his high regard for these Derbyshire sons (daughters and offspring) of toil, his narrator concluded the above passage by asserting, 'There was not one of them with whom he would have changed places; sooner he would have died' (*SN*, 70). One might be excused here for believing that Tom was evoking the kind of revulsion expressed by individual members of the genteel middle-class/literary intelligentsia towards the masses; however, Hampson's narrator qualifies this:

> The singing was a herd movement, a mass urge to something they felt better than their daily existence. As a mass Tom disliked them, but many of them as individuals he liked very much. […] Tom sighed, who was he to judge them? He could not have endured life as they led it. There was no merit in despising genuine hardship. The poverty of the country folk seemed even more distressing than that of the townspeople. It seemed the rule rather than the exception. (*SN*, 112)

It is worth reminding ourselves that the Soviet Writers Congress of 1934 initiated a dismantling of hitherto prescriptive notions regarding authenticity and class origin disseminated by Proletkult in favour of a social realism attuned to the perspectives of both working- and middle-class writers 'prepared to write Balzac-style nineteenth-century realism in support of the class struggle'.[159] Nick Hubble cites from William Empson's *Some Versions of Pastoral* in which Empson suggested pastoral presented as an alternative to a proletarian literature per se, by bridging 'the social divide between the metropolitan intelligentsia, and the workers, farmers and peasants', arguing that its 'double-attitude', that of the 'complex man to the simple one ("I am in one way better, in another not so good")' offered a more appropriate means by which to realise the social changes advocated at the Soviet Writers Congress.[160] As Hubble explains, it was by such means that the term 'proletarian literature' underwent reconfiguration from *sectarian* to more *heterogeneous* purposes and was thus able to offer intersubjective encounters from a variety of positions with 'the key intersubjective connections often as much between genders as classes' (my emphasis).[161]

Having fallen upon circumstances similar to those experienced by his parents, Hampson's narrative not only provides an authentic and detailed exploration of his socially displaced city dwellers but also presents an *intra*-class perspective revealing the harshness of working-class lived-experience beyond the urban centre where, rather than engaging in rural idealisation, Hampson's coalfield publicans wholly subvert any romanticised notion of the bucolic or provincial. As Mercer F. Hampson Simpson remarks: '[I]n its realistic depiction of the social conditions obtaining in the area, [the] novel relates to the themes of social amelioration, so popular amongst his contemporaries of the 1930's.'[162]

Notwithstanding his unflinching portrayal of the locals, Hampson doesn't forego the opportunity to indulge his distaste at the pretentions of the Metropolitan intellectual elite as represented in the figures of Roy Grovedon and Ruth Dorme. Although Mercer F. Hampson Simpson considered this a weakness in the novel, he conceded it was probably Hampson's intention 'to give social depth by providing a cross-section of Grovelace society as well as added comment from intellectual, sophisticated London'; he nonetheless considered their appearance rather contrived.[163] This reading counters Mercer F. Hampson Simpson's position, for in its presentation of a social cross-section, John Hampson's aim was in close accord with Margaret Storm Jameson's concept of 'Soundings' whereby, as Elizabeth Maslin explains, '[Jameson] offered readers a chance to measure the depths of a contemporary crisis through close inspection of a sample community containing all the critical elements'.[164] As this book has remarked, the documentary film movement became the 'Jakobsonian dominant' during the interwar period, its techniques, in particular the montage effect, being enthusiastically appropriated and incorporated into novelistic technique.[165] John Hampson having adopted these devices early on, as Lara Feigel indicates:

> *Saturday Night at the Greyhound* employs cross-class montage to juxtapose the young squire, and his friend Ruth, with the working-class local people who run and patronise the Greyhound Pub. Hampson montages their perspectives on each other, so that Ruth is mocked for idealising the working class: "these people she felt really lived" (*SN*, 95) and, at the same time, the working-class Mrs. Tapin is mocked for immediately coming to the wrong conclusion about Ruth and assuming that she is a prostitute: "If Master Roy wanted fancy women he had better seek elsewhere". (*SN*, 122)[166]

Unlike their male counterparts in the novel, the female characters are more resolute, the venal and embittered Mrs Tapin excessively so. Possibly staged as a warning to Freddy Flack against taking liberties with her daughter Clara, she viciously kills the Flack's pet Greyhound. Mercer F. Hampson Simpson suggests the Tapins function as allegorical figures: Mrs Tapin and her daughter Clara representing 'destructive and active' characters, respectively.[167] In the following character résumé, Hampson's narrator condenses descriptive detail to summarise the subplot whilst revealing the calculated reasoning behind their motivations: 'Mrs. Tapin liked [her daughter's] guile. It was worthy of her own skill. She had always been clever with men herself. Though it took her five years to get the old Squire after her. But she had done it and got a husband into the bargain. Times had changed the men were not so easy as they used to be' (*SN*, 62).

The working-class Tapins are subsequently montaged against the visitors. On Ruth Dorme's arrival at the Greyhound, Hampson's narrator loses no time cutting to the quick their Metropolitan perceptions. Having advised Ruth that she would most likely be served 'bread, cheese and pickled onions', Roy Grovedon returns from the kitchen to inform her that 'Tomato soup, tinned, will be ready for us in five minutes' (*SN*, 92). The adjective 'tinned' clearly registers Roy's misgivings and reflects wider class attitudes concerning the nutritional value of working-class foodstuffs. As John Carey ruefully remarks, '[w]e saw that E. M. Forster's Leonard Bast eats tinned food, a practice that is meant to tell us something significant about Leonard, and not to his advantage'.[168] Ruth is intrigued nevertheless:

> A meal at the Greyhound might be amusing. It would be something to talk about. Anything, so long as it had novelty, that was the thing nowadays. People would enjoy hearing of her meal among the miners. If it proved too ghastly she could embroider it a little. Ruth Dorme, an unmarried woman of thirty, found life rather boring in spite of her money. She was fairly clever and considered to be an intellectual by her friends. Knowing that, she let it rule her life. She dare not say or do anything she considered traitorous to the intellect with which she allowed herself to be endowed. Few people liked her. (*SN*, 89–90)

Imagining herself as a cultural anthropologist returning to the city with tales of the uncivilised provinces, Hampson's narrator quietly dismantles Ruth's metropolitan pretensions. In the following passage, Hampson deploys the 'rhetoric of domesticity' to consider the Greyhound's guest room, where having decided to eat and stay overnight, we proceed to the first of Ruth's 'readings':

> While waiting for the next course, she photographed the room on her memory. It was quaint, possessing a certain stiff formality, not unlike a stage-setting. Over the fireplace hung an enlarged photo of a pleasant-faced old man, probably the landlady's father. Two huge and hideous blue vases flanked it. Ruth considered them gravely "No wonder," she said, "the

> working-classes do not care to use their best rooms." After a quick look round Roy agreed. The room was obviously a museum of family happenings, the collected result of many marriages and deaths. (*SN*, 93)

As Hampson's narrator intimates, there is something calculated and premeditated in Ruth's persona, her remarks to Roy in the above extract contrast dramatically with her outward opinion as expressed to Ivy below:

> The spare room was beautiful, Ruth decided immediately. The furniture was of dark oak in severe lines, the bedstead was big and looked most comfortable. On the walls was a milk-grey paper; three narrow frames of black wood containing silhouettes were their only ornaments. The curtains and bedspread were of pale grey cretonne patterned with a formal design of cornflowers. Narrow bedside carpets of a matching blue shade were on the dark wooden floor. By the bedside stood a tiny arm-chair upholstered in dark grey plush. Ruth turned to Ivy. "What an exquisite room," she said. (*SN*, 99)

Here Hampson effectively turns the notion of 'observed' space on its head, the above passage ostensibly revealing more about Ruth than the interior she describes. Having catalogued the greys that comprise the muted colour scheme of what seems a particularly drab and depressing room, Ruth's choice of the adjective 'exquisite' appears either disingenuous or at best condescending. This said, it is not implausible to believe that the restricted palette of this utilitarian décor may have been momentarily tangential with the ephemeral nature of metropolitan taste.[169]

In rendering a wide range of characters, Hampson's novel provides a detailed exploration of intersubjective relationships by means of both intra- and inter-class montage. Rather than being considered negatively, the perspectives Hampson offered as a gay man, should be acknowledged as a positive force. Although he may have sought to repress his homosexuality, his narratives reveal him as alive and sensitive to discriminatory systems of class and gender that unfortunately are still relevant today. As Andy Croft observes:

> [I]n the thirties [Hampson] briefly pioneered a form of intense autobiographical fiction, combining a 'hard-boiled' prose style with experiments in narrative technique. He found in provincial middle-class family life the materials of Greek tragedy, and confronted his own sexual history in fiction at a time when honesty in such matters was difficult,

championing the emotionally disinherited and the weak in a decade dominated by the institutionalised bullying he so hated.[170]

In assisting the recovery of submerged voices eclipsed by sectarian readings, and, for wresting an alternative 'way of seeing' from the myopia of what had been a predominantly 'male gaze', the intersectional approach has proven invaluable. Ever alert to the complexities of class, setting, gender and familial relationships, it provides a more nuanced and sympathetic critical apparatus with which to address the subject material of Birmingham group narratives. In a period and occupation where hegemonic masculinity was the order of the day, and where the heroic miner, lionised by figures such as Orwell, had come to symbolise working-class solidarity, the Oliver Twist-like temerity of Brierley's Arthur Gardner in asking for something 'more' would surely have been greeted as weak-kneed individualism. *Sandwichman* told a different tale however, for its protagonist's confrontation with sectarian convention had been informed by the tragic consequences of Brierley's own lived experience. Though ultimately doomed to his public humiliation in the 'stocks' of an advertiser's sandwich board, Arthur's desire for something better than a 'life down the pit' exacted a terrible price. Using a generic template resembling Stephen Reynold's 'autobiografiction' which, as Max Saunders proposes, 'facilitate[d] readers' empathy, not just because it [cut] the material free from the name and person of the author, but because the aesthetic work that fiction performs on autobiography encouraged greater imaginative engagement with the material', Brierley was able to communicate the negative experience of his educational deprivation to a wider public. Whether William Beveridge read Brierley's *Sandwichman* is unknown, although 'Ignorance'—his shorthand for greater public access to educational opportunity—constituted one of the 'Five Giants' addressed in his series of post-war reforms.

Leslie Halward's objective stance and the pitiless precision with which he presented the tragic nature of Annie's self-sacrifice attains its universal significance by attesting to the distinct sadness behind all such selfless acts. 'A Broken Engagement' aligns with Frank O'Connor's conception of the short story as a means of giving voice to the members of 'submerged population groups' with Annie's self-sacrifice standing in for that of the myriad unheard, non-heroic individuals who provide such an intense awareness of human fortitude.[171] In 'Mr. Marris' Reputation', Peter Chamberlain showed it was possible to write about working-class life without having been born into it and that the possession of writerly skills based upon close observation could successfully furnish authentic accounts of working-class experience. In 'What The Hell?' Peter Chamberlain's spiv character remarks with droll self-mockery upon the value of his possessions. As his portfolio enlarges to include women and friendships as objects of consumption, the story offers a jarring critique not only of the objects themselves but also of the values both cultural and material that Chamberlain's own caste foisted upon the working classes. John Hampson's *Saturday Night at the Greyhound*, explored intersectional categories of class, place and gender. As had Brierley, Hampson developed what was effectively an 'autobiografictional' genre with which to examine the psychological experience of cultural displacement by deploying the techniques of documentary montage to analyse notions of class. Hampson's *Saturday Night at the Greyhound* is in many ways prescient of more recent developments in both the novel form and the critical analysis of it. As with his novels and short stories, his narratives customarily offer the psychological consolation of one having experienced the hardships his protagonists endure. As Stephen Reynolds had claimed, autobiografiction 'cut the material free from the name and person of the author'. In Hampson's case, it provided a formal mode by which to encode and conceal his homosexuality in a decade where prevailing attitudes, derived in part from notions of a hegemonic masculinity and the kinds of misogynistic assumptions which had informed the sectarian, male-oriented critique of working-class literature, would have proven detrimental.

As was indicated in the introduction, Ben Clarke and Nick Hubble stress that '[a]ny return to working-class writing must be informed by feminist, post-colonial and queer studies, exploring the intersections of class with *gender, ethnic and sexual identities* rather than reverting to earlier critical methods from which these categories were largely absent (my emphasis)'.[172] The methodologies adopted in this chapter were adopted to follow their adjurations and have proven central in examining how authorial subjectivity frequently surfaced in Birmingham group narratives. As Pamela Fox suggests, shame theorist '[Helen] Lynd had only to consult the working-class fictional texts of the subsequent period to glimpse her theory worked out in narrative form'.[173] By placing authors and characters in dialogue with one another in this way, the narratives of the Birmingham group writers can be seen as both anticipative and responsive in respect of Lynd's theories.

Owing to their mis-identification as local exemplars of the wider, more militant variety of proletarian realist literature 'frequently untroubled by any substantive engagement with the actual texts or reflection on the term itself', the Birmingham group writers have suffered unwarranted oversight and neglect.[174] The recovery of their work is hardly begun; yet, taken as documents recording the 'complexities of working-class experience, which political, historical and sociological accounts often erase', their narratives both function as a record of working-class culture in the 1930s and provide a valuable resource for working-class culture now, where, as Nick Hubble suggests:

> Such a culture—because it includes everyday resistance, subjectivity and intersubjectivity, material desires and a challenge to traditional gender relations, and links them to an understanding of capitalist social relations—provides resources from which to build social relations for the radically changed conditions now emerging in the twenty-first century.[175]

Notes

1. Barbara Foley, *Radical Representations*, Preface, p. ix.
2. Paul Mason, *Postcapitalism* (London: Penguin Books, 2016), p. 177.
3. Barbara Foley, 'Intersectionality: A Marxist Critique', *New Labor Forum*, 28.3. (2018) 10-13, p. 11. <doi: 10.1177/1095796019867944> [accessed 25-07-2020]
4. Victor Wallis, 'Intersectionality's Binding Agent: The Political Primacy of Class', *New Political Science*, 37. 4. (2015), 604-619. p. 610. <doi: 10.1080/07393148.2015.1089032> [accessed 21-10-2020]
5. Peter Williams, 'Constituting Class and Gender: A Social History of the Home, 1700—1901', in Nigel Thrift and Peter Williams eds, *Class and Space: The Making of Urban Society,* (London, 1987), pp. 154-204, p. 154. In Nicola Wilson, *Home in British Working-Class Fiction,* p. 15.
6. Joanna Bourke, *Working-Class Cultures in Britain 1890—1960: Gender, Class and Ethnicity* (London and New York: Routledge, 1994), p. 4. In Wilson, *Home in British Working-Class Fiction,* p. 2.
7. Nicola Wilson, Ibid, p.39.
8. Ibid, p. 69.
9. Alick West's aphorism 'When I do not know any longer who are the "we" to whom I belong. I do not know any longer who "I" am either', Alick West, *Crisis and Criticism & Literary Essays* (London: Lawrence and

Wishart, 1975), p. 19. Cited in Nick Hubble, *The Proletarian Answer*. Introduction, p. 1.
10. Ibid, p. 33.
11. Stephen Reynolds 'Autobiografiction' in Max Saunders, *Self-Impression: Life-Writing, Autobiografiction, & the Forms of Modern Literature* (Oxford: Oxford University Press, 2013), p. 174.
12. Stephen Reynolds. 'Autobiografiction', *Speaker*, New Series, 15, 366, (October 1906). In Max Saunders, *Self- Impression,* pp. 166-179. p. 169.
13. Ibid.
14. Ibid, pp. 172, 173.
15. Ibid, p. 175.
16. Nick Hubble, *The Proletarian Answer*, p. 18.
17. Max Saunders, *Self-Impression*, p. 205, cited in Hubble, *The Proletarian Answer*, p. 18.
18. George Orwell, *The Road to Wigan Pier* (London: Penguin Books, 1984), p. 104.
19. Cyril Connolly, *Enemies of Promise* (London: Penguin Books, 1979) p. 127.
20. Cunningham, *British Writers*, p. 152.
21. Virginia Woolf cited in Cunningham, *British Writers,* pp. 151, 152.
22. *Folios of New Writing,* Spring 1941, 'The Leaning Tower: Replies' comprised three articles: The Falling Tower, Below the Tower, The Tower that Once, written by Edward Upward, B. L. Coombes and Louis MacNeice respectively, with 'A Postscript' by John Lehmann defending the 'Leaning Tower' writers against Woolf's animadversions. pp. 42-46.
23. Cunningham *British Writers*, p. 152
24. John Fordham, *James Hanley: Modernism,* p. 130.
25. Theodor Adorno, *Aesthetic Theory* (London: Bloomsbury, 2017), p. 313.
26. Sarah Copland and Greta Olson, 'Towards a Politics of Form', *European Journal of English Studies,* 20 (2016). 207-221, p. 207.
27. Barbara Foley, *Radical Representations*, pp. 284-398.
28. Graham Holderness, 'Miners and the Novel', in Jeremy Hawthorn Ed, *The British Working Class Novel,* p. 22.
29. Philip Gorski, Introduction, p. viii. Walter Brierley, *Sandwichman* (London: Merlin Press, 1990).
30. Walter Brierley, 'Body', in John Hackney, *No Want of Meat Sir!: Being a Collection of Stories Edited by John Hackney* (London: Grayson & Grayson, 1936), p. 517.
31. Cunningham, *British Writers*, pp. 310, 311. Cf. Leslie Halward's Jim Belcher in the discussion of 'Belcher's Hod', qv, Chapter 1, p. 35. et seq.
32. Flood, Michael, 'Toxic Masculinity: A Primer and Commentary, <XY Online. Net 2018> [accessed 07-07-2018]

33. Ibid.
34. An incident Brierley reworked as the cause of Arthur Gardner's dismissal in *Sandwichman*.
35. Harold Heslop's *The Gate of a Strange Field* (1929) in Pamela Fox, *Class Fictions*, p. 83.
36. Worker intellectuals as emblems of class agency: Frank Owen from Robert Tressell's *The Ragged Trousered Philanthropists*, and Larry Meath from Walter Greenwood's *Love on the Dole*, Pamela Fox, *Class Fictions*, p. 79.
37. Jonathan Rose, *The Intellectual Life*, p. 298.
38. Alick West, *Crisis and Criticism* (London: Lawrence and Wishart, 1975), p. 19.
39. Ralph Fox, *The Novel and the People* (London: Lawrence and Wishart, 1937), p. 34.
40. Valentine Cunningham, *British Writers*, p. 219.
41. Barbara Foley sees the reader's identification with the protagonists of proletarian fiction as a means of positioning the reader to undergo an education of their own, thereby experiencing an ideological effect very different from that accompanying the classic bildungsroman. Proletarian fictions 'posit the synecdochic relation of their protagonists to their social groups. But they speak for a collective, not an individual self'. *Radical Representations*, p. 284.
42. Pamela Fox, *Class Fictions*, p. 16.
43. Richard Hoggart, *Uses of Literacy*, p. 64.
44. The expression 'to relish the sublime' is from Matthew Arnold. *Culture and Anarchy*. Arnold cites these words from an obscure satire by John Arbuthnot a contemporary of Swift and Pope. p. 3. Ryle, Martin and Kate Soper *To Relish the Sublime*, p. 3.
45. John Carey, *The Intellectuals and the Masses: Pride and Prejudice Among the Literary Intelligensia, 1880-1939* (London: Faber and Faber, 1992), p. 19.
46. Rachel Haworth, 'Abyss: Class and Culture in Howards End', *Cambridge Author's Project* (2009) <https://www.english.cam.ac.uk> [accessed 06-09-2019]
47. Owen Jones, 'How To Be A Man: The Quiet Crisis of Masculinity', New Statesman, 7 June 2016. <http://www.newstatesman.com/politics/uk/2016/06how-be-man> [accessed 16-09-2019].
48. Nick Hubble, *The Proletarian Answer*, p. 47.
49. Letter John Hampson to Walter Brierley. 12 September 1934. Walter Brierley Papers. DL282. Derby Local Studies Library and family services.
50. Letter Walter Allen to Walter Brierley. 17 September 1934. Walter Brierley Papers. DL282. Derby Local Studies Library and family services.
51. Ian Haywood, *Working-Class Fiction*, pp. 65, 68.

52. Nick Hubble, *The Proletarian Answer*, p. 18.
53. Ian Haywood, *Working-Class Fiction*, p. 68.
54. John Lucas, 'Walter Brierley & Leslie Williamson'. Home Up. p. 3. <https://www.pennilesspress.co.uk> [Accessed 22-1-2018].
55. Richard Hoggart, *The Uses of Literacy*, p. 63.
56. Richard Hoggart, *The Uses of Literacy*, p. 27.
57. This real life incident is similar to that described in Brierley's short story 'Body'.
58. Stephen Brooke, 'Gender and Working-Class Identity in Britain During the 1950s', *Journal of Social History*, 773-95. p. 776.
59. Richard Hoggart, *The Uses of Literacy*, p. 244.
60. Ian Haywood, *Working-Class Fiction*, p. 32.
61. Carole Snee, 'Working Class Literature or Proletarian Writing' in Jon Clark and others, *Culture and Crisis*, p. 179.
62. Nicola Wilson, *Home in British Working-Class Fiction*, p. 50.
63. Pamela Fox, *Class Fictions*, pp. 25, 26.
64. Thomas Hardy, *Jude the Obscure* (London: Penguin Books, 1985), p. 98.
65. Walter Brierley references Hardy's novel, Arthur describing it as 'not a very pleasant one' on returning home to find his mother reading it. *Sandwichman*, p. 213.
66. Andy Croft, *Red Letter Days*, p. 84.
67. Ibid.
68. Ibid, p. 85.
69. Philip Gorski, Introduction, Walter Brierley, *Sandwichman*, p. xv.
70. Carol Snee. 'Working-Class Literature or Proletarian Writing?' in Clark and Others. *Culture and Crisis*, p. 180.
71. Carol Snee. Ibid.; The WEA courses attended by both D.H. Lawrence and Walter Brierley had been devised on the principle of political neutrality and founded on the Arnoldian conception of literary culture. In this respect, the WEA 'was—and has remained—an organisation *for* rather than *of* the working class'. Janet Batsleer and others, *Rewriting English: Cultural Politics of Gender and Class* (London; Methuen & Co, 1985), p. 50.
72. Noam Chomsky, *On Anarchism* (London: Penguin Books, 2013), p. 133. It was the Prussian philosopher and educationist Wilhelm von Humboldt's wish that education, considered as truth and virtue, must be disseminated to such an extent that it extended to others and to the benefit of society at large.
73. Carole Snee, 'Working-Class Literature or Proletarian Writing?' in Jon Clark, *Culture and Crisis*, p. 166.
74. Macdonald Daly, 'D.H. Lawrence and Walter Brierley', *Journal of D. H. Lawrence Studies*, 4 (1986), p.28.

75. D. H. Lawrence, *Sons and Lovers* (London: Penguin Books, 2006), p. 89; Macdonald Daly, 'D. H. Lawrence and Walter Brierley', *Journal of D. H. Lawrence Studies,* 4 (1986).
76. Macdonald Daly, Ibid.
77. Haywood, *Working-Class Fiction,* p. 68.
78. Philip Gorski, introduction to Walter Brierley, *Sandwichman,* p. viii.
79. Jonathan Rose, *The Intellectual Life of the British Working-Classes,* p. 277.
80. Ian Haywood, *Working-Class Fiction,* p. 69.
81. Philip Gorski, introduction to Walter Brierley, *Sandwichman*, p. xvi.
82. 'Talk to Fircroft Working Men's College Birmingham', Halward Papers. MS1293/106/30. The Library of Birmingham.
83. The Coming of Proletarian Literature: A Symposium, *London Mercury,* May 1936.
84. Ian Haywood, *Working-Class Fiction,* p. 65.
85. Paul Lester, *The Road to Excelsior Lodge* (Birmingham: Protean Publications, 1988), p. 12.
86. Cyril Connolly, in Andy Croft, *Red Letter Days*, pp. 168, 169.
87. Leslie Halward, *Let Me Tell You*, p. 227.
88. Walter Allen, *The Short Story in English* (Oxford: Clarendon Press, 1981), p. 275.
89. Ibid, pp. 142, 143.
90. Following the war and the failure to find a market for his short stories, Halward turned to playwriting for radio (the BBC Home Service) in which he achieved some local notoriety to the extent that in the late 1950s *The Sunday Mercury* could remark that Halward 'had come to be known as 'the voice of the Midlands'. *Sunday Mercury,* 26 May 1957. Paul Lester, *The Road to Excelsior Lodge,* p. 18.
91. Geoffrey Trease (11.8.1909—27.1.1998), a Midlands writer who lived near Leslie Halward in Colwall, Worcestershire.
92. Walter Allen, *The Short Story In English,* p. 60.
93. H. E. Bates, *The Modern Short Story*, p. 59.
94. Graham Green employed the term 'entertainments' to distinguish between his thrillers and his 'Literary' works.
95. Andy Croft, 'The Birmingham Group: Literary Life Between Two Wars', *London Magazine, 23* (1983), p. 20.
96. Bashir Abu Manneh, *Fiction of the New Statesman*
97. Ibid, 'Introduction: Realism and Class' p. xi.
98. Ibid, p. 196.
99. Ibid.
100. Barbara Foley cited in Ronald Paul '"A Culture of the People": Politics and Working-Class Literature in Left Review, 1934-1938', *Left History,* 8. 1. (2002), 61-76. p. 72.
101. Valentine Cunningham, *British Writers*, p. 303.

102. Virginia Woolf, 'Modern Fiction' in Lawrence Rainey, Modernism an Anthology (Oxford: Blackwell Publishing, 2005), p. 897.
103. Leslie Halward, 'Writing about the Working-Class'. A talk given at Fircroft Workingmen's College Birmingham, 8 October 1939, Halward Papers. The Library of Birmingham, MS1293/106/30.
104. Auden, W. H. and Edward Mendelson, ed, *The English Auden*, p. 355.
105. Peter Chamberlain, W*hat The Sweet Hell*? (New York: Henry Holt and Company, 1935), p. 103.
106. The story first appeared in the *New Statesman* (23 February 1935), p. 245-6. Later collected in the anthology *What the Sweet Hell?* (USA: Henry Holt and Company, 1935).
107. J. M. Coetzee, 'The Man Who went Shopping for The Truth', Review of Walter Benjamin, *The Arcades Project,* translated from the German and French by Howard Eiland and Kevin Mclaughlin.
108. *New Statesman*, 12 November 1938. p. 777.
109. Ibid.
110. Nick Hubble, 'The Intermodern Assumption of the Future' in Kristen Bluemel, *Intermodernism,* p. 172.; The reference to the 'Jakobsonian dominant' in Keith Williams 'Post/Modern Documentary: Orwell, Agee and the New Reportage' in Keith Williams and Stephen Matthews, *Rewriting the Thirties,* p. 164.
111. Walter Allen, *Tradition and Dream*, p. 182.
112. Ibid, p. 183.
113. Charles McGrath, 'The Eavesdropper's Secret: On John O'Hara', In *The New Yorker,* 22 September 2016.
114. Ibid.
115. John Hampson, 'Movements in the Underground, II', John Lehmann Ed, The Penguin New Writing, No 28, (London: Penguin Books, 1946), p. 133.
116. J. A. Cuddon, *The Penguin Dictionary of Literary Terms and Literary Theory* (London: Penguin Books, 1998), pp. 418, 517.
117. Max Saunders, *Self-Impression,* p. 171.
118. Walter Allen, *As I Walked Down,* p. 68.
119. The 'Yewgottabe Tough' school, coinage is attributed to Cyril Connolly's 'New Statesman' article, 1 February 1936. Connolly was referring to the British emulation of American novels, for example *The Postman Always Rings Twice* and the enthusiasm for similar 'low-life' novels of underworld Britain: James Curtis' *The Gilt Kid* (1936), Robert Westerby's *Wide Boys Never Work,* (1937) and Graham Greene's *Brighton Rock* (1938), to name but a few.
120. Andy Croft, *Red Letter Days,* pp. 170, 171.
121. Ibid, p. 194.

122. American expression. Nancy Boy was a gay burlesque character from the 1930s.
123. Bashir Abu-Manneh, *Fiction of the New Statesman*, p. 193.
124. Nicola Caramina, 'Self-Concept in Consumer Behaviour: A Psychoanalytical Investigation Working Paper Series'. (2018) <https://www.academia.edi/36927375/Self-Concept-in-Consumer-Behaviour>. p. 67.
125. Pamela Fox, *Class Fictions*, p. 26.
126. Christopher Hilliard, *To Exercise Our Talents*, p. 121.
127. Stanislava Dikova, 'Book Review: The Proletarian Answer to the Modernist Question by Nick Hubble', (2018) <Https://Lse.ac.uk/lsereviewofbooks.> [accessed 22.4.2019]. Unpaginated.
128. Raymond Williams, *Culture and Society*, p. 205.
129. Mercer Hampson Simpson, 'The Novels of John Hampson', (Master of Arts, 1975). M.A. Dissertation. University of South Wales Library Services. p. 54.
130. Ibid. This is not to overlook Helen Southworth's *Leonard & Virginia Woolf, The Hogarth Press and the Networks of Modernism* (see below pp. 178, 179), which has provided valuable insights into Hampson and his relationship with Literary London.
131. Following considerable research, the American Psychological Association removed homosexuality from the *DSM* (*Diagnostic and Statistical manual of Sexual Disorders*), thus removing the stigma of mental illness that had long been associated with it. However, it was not until as recently as 1987 that homosexuality would completely fall from the *DSM*.
132. Mercer Hampson Simpson, 'The Novels of John Hampson', p. 51.
133. Ibid.
134. Walter Allen, *Tradition and Dream*, pp. 226, 227.
135. Helen Southworth, Conference paper 'Outside the Magic (And Tyrannical) Triangle of London, Oxford and Cambridge': John Hampson the Woolfs, and The Hogarth Press. In *Woolfian Boundaries: Selected papers from the Sixteenth Annual International Conference on Virginia Woolf*, Edited by Anna Burrells, Steve Ellis, Deborah Parsons and Kathryn Simpson, (Clemson South Carolina: Clemson University Press, 2007), pp. 43—50. P. 46.
136. Helen Southworth, 'Outside the Magic', p. 48.
137. Helen Southworth, Editor, *Leonard and Virginia Woolf, the Hogarth Press and the Networks of Modernism*, (Edinburgh: Edinburgh University Press, 2010), p. 218.
138. Helen Southworth's conference paper 'Outside the Magic' p. 46.
139. Reader's Report, MS2750/153/3, 'Modernist Archives Publishing Project'.

140. Ibid.
141. Helen Southworth, 'Outside the Magic', p. 45.
142. Ben Clarke, 'Working-class Writing and Experimentation', in Clarke and Hubble, *Working-Class Writing: Theory and Practice*, p. 29. William Plomer, while sharing Hampson's distaste for the 'fine writing & pretentiousness which abounds in these days', wondered whether Hampson's spare, angular style was 'quite literary enough'. Helen Southworth. 'Outside the Magic, p. 47.
143. William Plomer cited in Christopher Hawtree, Introduction, p. iv. John Hampson, *Saturday Night at the Greyhound* (London: The Hogarth Press, 1986).
144. Christopher Hilliard, *To Exercise Our Talents*, p. 121.
145. Ibid, p. 22.
146. 'The Greyhound' in Grovelace was based upon 'The Kettle Inn' in Ashover, Derbyshire, where Hampson had worked 'in part protection' of his beloved sister Mona.
147. The Crown & Cushion, Perry Barr, Birmingham was, until its recent demolition, a well-known Birmingham public house.
148. This element of the story derives from Hampson's own experience as a barman and 'part-protect[or]'in helping his beloved sister Mona, represented pseudonymously as (Ivy Flack in *Saturday Night*) and (Mercy in *O Providence)* run a public house in the North Derbyshire mining village of Ashover. Christopher Hawtree, Introduction, p. ii. John Hampson, *Saturday Night at the Greyhound*. As Hawtree points out, the same pub (The Nettle Inn) also figured unnamed in the first of three volumes of Graham Greene's autobiography, *A Sort of Life*. (1971).
149. William Plomer, introduction to the 1950 reprint of *Saturday Night at the Greyhound*, cited in Mercer Hampson Simpson. 'The Novels of John Hampson.' M. A. Dissertation, University of Wales, p. 48.
150. Ibid, p. 39.
151. The first, attributed to Aristotle, is often employed by theatre critics to show how a character's actions, 'what they do', rather than 'what they say' determine their personality/fate. The second is attributed to Heraclitus. *The Oxford Dictionary of Quotations* (Oxford: Oxford University Press, 1996), 12, p. 333.
152. Christopher Hawtree, Introduction, John Hampson *Saturday Night at the Greyhound*, p. 4.
153. Ibid. Writing to Cape his publishers denigrating [*Saturday Night at the Greyhound*] Hampson asserted that he was 'not interested in it'. 'The characters lack resistance to providence. For that reason I feel half-hearted about them.' Letter 20 December 1929, cf. also letter to Leonard Woolf [Hogarth Press] 8 June 1930. Footnote 1, p. 18. p. 40. Mercer Hampson Simpson, M.A. Dissertation, 'The Novels of John Hampson'.

154. Mercer F. Hampson Simpson following his reference to a passage from Havelock Ellis *Studies in the Psychology of Sex* (1901), 1915, based upon Havelock Ellis' reading of Freud's 'Some Neurotic mechanisms in Jealousy, Paranoia and Homosexuality', (1922), The Complete Psychological Works (1957), 1973, xviii. Though questionable today, such theories were still current when Mercer F. Hampson Simpson had referenced them. Mercer F. Hampson Simpson. 'The Novels of John Hampson', p. 12.
155. Karim G. Dajani, 'Cultural Dislocation and Ego Functions: Some Considerations in the Analysis of Bi-Cultural Patients', *International Journal of Applied Psychoanalytic Studies,* 15 (2018). p.186.
156. Ibid.
157. Karim G. Dajani, 'Cultural Dislocation', p. 186.
158. Leslie Halward, Letter to MHS 23 July 1974. In Mercer Hampson Simpson. 'The Novels of John Hampson.' Footnote I, p. 22.
159. Nick Hubble, *The Proletarian Answer*, p. 4
160. Ibid, p. 14.
161. Nick Hubble, *The Proletarian Answer*, p. 7.
162. Mercer Hampson Simpson, 'The Novels of John Hampson', p. 46.
163. Ibid, p. 48.
164. Elizabeth Maslen, 'A Cassandra With Clout: Storm Jameson Little Englander And Good European', in Kristen Bluemel, *Intermodernism*, 21-37. p. 27.
165. Williams, Keith and Stephen Matthews, *Rewriting the Thirties*, pp. 164, 165.
166. Lara Feigal, 'Buggery and Montage: Birmingham and Bloomsbury in the 1930s', in Anna Burrells and others *Woolfian Boundaries* (South Carolina: Clemson University, 2007), p. 55.
167. Mercer Hampson Simpson. 'The Novels of John Hampson', p. 39.
168. John Carey, *The Intellectuals and the Masses*, p. 21. Carey provides several other examples.
169. Interestingly, Ruth Dorme's character chimes with K. D. M. Snell's view that the term 'regional' 'is open to various understandings, but usually involves belittlement of any form of cultural life other than that supplied by the metropolis. It assumes metropolitan arbitration of taste, the superiority of metropolitan people and expression over those of locality—as though metropolis and locality were mutually exclusive terms'. The Regional Novel in Britain.
170. Andy Croft, *Oxford Dictionary of National Biography*. Entry for Simpson, John, Frederick Norman Hampson [Known as John Hampson] (1901—1955), p. 2.

171. Frank O'Connor, 'The Lonely Voice: A Study of the Short-Story' in *Short-Story Theories*, ed, Charles May (Ohio: Ohio University Press, 1963), p. 86.
172. Clarke, Ben and Nick Hubble, *Working-Class Writing*, p. 5.
173. Pamela Fox, *Class Fictions*, p. 203.
174. Ben Clarke, Review of 'Nick Hubble, The Proletarian Answer to the Modernist Question', University of North Carolina, Greensboro, (2017), https://academic.oup,com/res/article-abstract/69/291/811/4980910> [accessed 15-11-2019]
175. Nick Hubble, *The Proletarian Answer*, p. 40.

CHAPTER 5

Conclusion

At the risk of making the 'inflated claims' cautioned against at the outset of this book, I have nevertheless been struck by how the literary productions of the Birmingham group writers collectively and consistently provided practical resolutions to many of the prevailing theoretical concerns, critical debates and expectations addressing the production of working-class literature produced during the pre-war decade. Aware that the concluding chapter of a scholarly monograph should ordinarily provide a brief summation of its foregoing material, I hereby offer notice that—as this preamble may have begun to signal—rather than quietly bringing matters to a close, the first of two concluding sections, 'Coda: Dispersal', will press beyond the 1930s, when their star was in the ascendant, to consider the fate of the Birmingham group writers and their city as the country slowly began to emerge from the war years into the grey dawn of the 1950s and the early glimmerings of a Welfare State. Expressed as an ongoing narrative, this section will trace the remaining years of the Birmingham writers' literary careers, thus bringing to a close the biographical account provided in the introduction.

The Birmingham writers' literary critical engagement with the second city during the pre-war decade, especially in terms of its anticipation and response to criteria attendant upon the more recent theoretical discussion of 1930s literature, presents as an important and exemplary contribution to what is a continuing and flourishing critical conversation in academia and one that may also be seen to inform the revitalised tradition of

R. Harriott, *The Birmingham Group*,
https://doi.org/10.1007/978-3-031-14383-0_5

working-class writing currently underway. Casting forward, the second of two concluding sections will therefore address the work of the Birmingham group writers and their narratives as a legacy and consider the implications of this as both influence and heritage: a resource of hope for later generations of working-class writers and cultural commentators unaware of what an early champion of their work Edward O'Brien termed their 'natural community of achievement'.

Coda: Dispersal

> During the past few years the attentive reader who scanned the English literary scene might have noticed that a new group of writers was emerging in the Midlands, chiefly in and near Birmingham. These writers, who lay no claim to a common purpose, and whose work developed spontaneously without any close common association, have nevertheless a good deal in common, and it was my pleasure as one of the editors of "New Stories" to discover in them this natural community of achievement when they first submitted stories to that magazine. John Hampson and Walter Brierley have already made a definite position for themselves with their novels, and Peter Chamberlain has won deserved recognition for his collection of short stories. Walter Allen is one of the group and not the least distinguished, but from the beginning it has seemed to me that Leslie Halward…[1]

Leslie Halward cited O'Brien's lines in his autobiography *Let Me Tell You* (1938). Originally forming the opening paragraph in the latter's introduction to Halward's first collected volume of short stories *To Tea on Sunday* (1936), it was possibly modesty that prevented Halward from continuing to cite this passage, for O'Brien made further reference praising him as the 'most gifted potentially' and his 'achievement […] so far the most substantial' of the Birmingham group writers. However, in characteristic manner, Halward followed the ellipsis ending the above extract by confiding: 'NOW LET ME TELL YOU ABOUT THE "Birmingham Group," [*sic*] which, alas, exists no longer'

> The almost weekly meetings no longer take place in the upper room of a public house off Corporation Street. Allen and Chamberlain have both gone to live in London; I am here in Malvern; only Hampson remains near the city. (Brierley should never have been included, for he lives in Derbyshire and has entered the public-house only once or twice when on a visit).[2]

Despite the dismissive reference to Brierley in Halward's bluff 'eulogy' above, his words ought not distract from the evident tone of regret. While figures such as W. H. Auden philosophised from afar as the decade's 'clever hopes expire[d]', the advent of war held more immediate consequences for those in Britain where preparations increasingly began to impinge upon everyday life. Though career opportunities prompted Walter Allen's and Peter Chamberlain's (always the Londoner at heart) move to the capital, effectively signalling the end of the Birmingham group, the prospect of imminent hostilities undoubtedly cemented its demise; the remaining members either registering for active service or dispersing to home and family. Walter Allen described the months between the Munich agreement and the outbreak of war as 'a period of waiting, as though life and significance were in suspense'.[3] Following his move to London on the strength of publisher Michael Joseph's £25 advance for *Innocence Is Drowned*, Allen found lodgings in the capital and, by securing reviewing work and reading film scripts for MGM, provided himself with a modicum of financial security that enabled the final severing of his links with Birmingham and tentatively established him as a jobbing writer in the capital.[4]

Of the Birmingham group writers, it was Allen alone who, as one of the last 'Men of Letters'-style literary critics, managed to extend his writing career beyond 1945. A literary education, combined with skills learned from journalism, reviewing and lecturing, equipped him with a portfolio ripe for adaption and fine-tuning beyond the war years. Although *All In A Lifetime* (1959), a 'biografictional' account of his father, constituted his most successful (in terms of sales) novel, his (formal) autobiography, *As I Walked Down New Grub Street* (1981), and two important works of popular criticism provide a useful overview of the nation's literary firmament from the closing years of the Victorian period up to the outbreak of the Second World War, and remain a valuable resource for those seeking insights into the period itself and offer insightful detail on its literary offering both in Britain and in America.[5] Yet, though having successfully negotiated the hazards of 'New Grub Street', Allen is barely considered today, if remembered at all, is as a critic and reviewer, or his position as literary editor of the *New Statesman*, rather than as a novelist. In what was ever a precarious profession, the fortunes of his Birmingham group contemporaries would be even less assured.

Married in 1936, Halward and his wife Gwen moved from Birmingham to a cottage they named *O Providence* (after Hampson's novel) in the village of Guarlford near Malvern, Worcestershire. As Halward confidently recorded in the closing lines of his autobiography, 'Yes, we have got what we have so long waited for – each other and our cottage in the country. And let me tell you, we are very happy.'[6] Unfortunately, on his return to civilian life following war service in the RAF, Halward, as his fictional persona Finsbury recounts in the radio play 'Afternoon at Excelsior Lodge', was unable to pick up his literary ambitions from where he left off, having effectively severed himself from the city and his roots in the urban lived experience he had once described so knowledgeably. As Walter Allen suggested, '[t]he working-class stories that he continued to write seemed like carbon copies of his Thirties stories.' He was, I think, the victim of his own lack of education and adaptability, and of the lack of imagination of bodies like the BBC that failed to exploit his talents.'[7]

On 1 January 1935, Walter Brierley received a letter of acceptance from Methuen agreeing to publish *Means Test Man*, and on the very same day stepped from the privations of unemployment to take up work as a timekeeper at an engineering works in Derby. Possibly as a result of his studies whilst a collier, he would later secure work as a Child Welfare Officer in Derby, a position in which he was to remain until his retirement in 1965.[8] The success of *Means Test Man* would not be repeated. Beyond the novels *Sandwichman* (1937), *Dalby Green* (1939) and *Danny* (1940), and the occasional short story, Brierley was unable to get any further significant work published.[9]

Suffering narcolepsy and, according to Walter Allen, having successfully hidden it from the Army medical corps during his initial examination and throughout the war, Peter Chamberlain fulfilled his military ambition to become a motorcycling instructor by attaining the rank of sergeant. Unfortunately, more detailed biographical information remains elusive, though it seems that, following hostilities, Chamberlain returned to civilian life where, although no longer producing prose narratives (no evidence to the contrary has come to light), he remained in post as editor of *Motor Cyclist* magazine until the early 1950s.

Having tried to enlist in the RAF, but being rejected on health grounds, John Hampson's health continued to deteriorate. A further novel, *A Bag of Stones*, was published in 1952, but cumulative critical neglect found his reputation in decline. Following a further illness and failed attempt to discharge himself from care, Hampson died in Solihull General Hospital on 26 December 1955.

Short-lived as it had been, in addressing hitherto neglected aspects of working-class culture and simultaneously exploring the potential of their own lived-experience as source material for their narratives, the Birmingham group writers lived up to Edward O'Brien's praise of their early promise. Neither propagandistic nor quietist, the liminal space occupied by their narratives is not be construed as political 'fence-sitting'; on the contrary, their narratives illustrate collectively the quality of what the American literary theorist and critic Kenneth Burke terms 'Addressedness', a rhetorical position which identified and defined an author's ideological allegiance *to* or alignment *with* a specific audience and/or sociopolitical perspective without necessarily being overtly propagandistic or hortatory. Although asserting that 'addressedness' was politically neutral and applicable to either working-class or bourgeois writing, Burke considered proletarian literature was addressed to the people *for* the people.[10] It is therefore to reiterate how, despite the experiential diversity of its authors, the writing of the Birmingham group nonetheless remains ideologically radical and presents collectively as the valid cultural intervention on which the remainder of this conclusion will focus. As critics Barbara Foley and Michael Denning argue in their respective recoveries of American worker writers from this period, the political impetus of working-class narratives is just as likely to be located in the individual writer's subjective experience and formal innovation than in an overtly political or propagandist content.

The Birmingham Group: Reading the Second City in the 1930s has urged the view that, rather than sacrificing literary expression to propagandist rhetoric or adopting traditional realist or naturalistic modes owing to a limited awareness of any alternative representational strategy, the members of the Birmingham group were fully alive to prevailing literary and cultural developments, in particular those deriving from what came to be termed the 'ethnographic turn' and responded accordingly by readily employing aspects of the 'documentary dominant' in their narrative representations. Walter Allen adapted Eisensteinian shock-montage effects and Griersonian 'exposure' strategies learned from his visits to the Birmingham Film Society and applied these to literary narratives that quietly interrogated the injustices of the prevailing social order. *Innocence Is Drowned* deployed cinematic montage techniques in order to present an ideology critique which, to use Marxist terminology, 'laid bare' the gulf between common perceptions and ideological realities. In this way, rather than deploying 'tendential' (authorial/propagandist) rhetoric, Allen contrived that his political message would emerge naturally from the events or situations he described. This was achieved formally via the juxtaposition of contrasting images and the combination of alternating focalisations or vantage points so as to provide a dialectical montage image directed to stirring the reader's political consciousness. As discussed, a degree of curatorial consternation regarding the de-politicising, fantasy-inducing effects of the media and mass entertainment was very much abroad during the 1930s with commercial (Hollywood) cinema being considered a particularly negative influence, merely 'an ideological force to dope the workers.'[11] In *Blind Man's Ditch*, Allen, following Henry Green's example of employing a cinematic grammar, turned the techniques of commercial cinema productions in upon themselves in order to shake individuals from their complacency by presenting what Lara Feigel describes as a 'montage of quickly changing scenes, from differing points of view, to juxtapose the life and thoughts of the upper- and working-class characters and show the perspective of each upon the other'.[12] The late Robert Scholes remarked: '[Montage] was the key device for modernism in the verbal as well as the visual arts.' Bestowed with 'special meanings' by Sergei Eisenstein, he believed the word retained 'permanent currency in discussions not only of film but of modernism in all the arts, if not modernity itself'.[13] That Walter Allen adopted and adapted its repertoire of effects is not to privilege modernism as the formal desideratum of working-class fiction *tout court*, but merely to indicate how Birmingham group writers freely appropriated prevailing representational modes thereby repudiating the charge of 'expressive conservatism' so often levelled at working-class literature. In his adoption of formal devices discovered in cinema and the late modernist/neo-realist novels of Henry Green, Allen reconfigured the traditional realist mode and applied it to a body of narrative writing that looks forward to the work of such post-war surveyors of Birmingham and the deindustrialised Midlands as David Lodge and Jonathan Coe.[14]

Walter Brierley likewise pushed beyond traditional representative convention. *Means Test Man* employed irresolution: a cyclical, rather than linear, plot design resistant to closure; psychological analysis more in tune with modernist interiority, or, as some might claim, solipsistic affectation (though the psychological pre-occupations of Brierley's protagonists could hardly be considered an affectation); and, owing to its often parodic and frequently ironic use of language and imagery, a satire whose distorting perspectives achieved a grotesquery more redolent of expressionism than traditional realist or naturalistic modes.[15] Again, whilst not aiming for the levels of socialist polemic sought by a Berthold Brecht or Walter Benjamin, more recently H. Gustav Klaus, in harnessing these devices, Brierley too could be seen to have *umfunktionert* the traditional realist mode. In *Sandwichman*, he transformed the traditional bildungsroman, in two ways: firstly, by inverting the arc of traditional realist novel's trajectory, the record of an individual's growth from ignorance to maturation, and, secondly, by detailing the obstacles heaped against the working-class individual pursuing self-cultivation, he interrogated the idea of the liberal education itself. Rather than achieving or affirming his protagonist's desires, Brierley shows the tragic consequences of the attempt whilst simultaneously addressing contemporary themes of masculinity, the family breadwinner convention, the position of women in contemporary society and, not least, his own authorial identity. As with John Hampson, it is doubtful whether Brierley would have been familiar with the term, but through a combination of innovation and experimentation, he had inadvertently discovered a hybrid form strangely reminiscent of Stephen Reynold's autobiografiction.

Peter Chamberlain's writing problematised the discussion. Like Henry Green, he was an outsider who wrote *about* and often from the perspective *of* the working class, rather than a working-class insider. While editor of *Motor Cycle* magazine, and, owing to his acquaintance with Hampson's brother Jimmy, a famous racing motorcyclist, Chamberlain arrived in Birmingham, met John Hampson and subsequently joined the Birmingham coterie. A practising and published writer beyond his editorial position at *Motor Cycle,* Chamberlain followed the footsteps of those who came over to the working classes in the wake of Comintern's shift to popular front policies where, as Barbara Foley reminds us, 'the task of writers was now to be seen as mimetic rather than hortatory [...] writers should not engage in agitational polemics that would disrupt realism's illusion of seamless transparency: the objective portrayal of existing realities was adequate testimony to socialist partisanship'.[16] Chamberlain's working-class *tranche de vie* certainly offered objective portrayals of proletarian existence, while the 'portraits' that constituted his 'suburban exercises' provided a cache of *objet-trouve*: surreal 'out of context', micro-images of the middle-class world he knew so intimately. By adapting the 'image-driven' style of the photoessay, injecting elements of comedy and providing parodic insider-perspectives of his own social milieu, Peter Chamberlain's narratives are illustrative of Edward Seaver's claim that 'the compelling factor in a writer's work' derives not from 'the class origin of the writer [...] but his present class alignment, not the period in history, or the characters that he writes about, but his ideological approach to his story and characters'.[17]

Although Leslie Halward may have appreciated, possibly encouraged, the description of his work as proletarian naturalism, it was he of the five Birmingham group writers who remained the closest to Raymond Williams' definition of the working-class writer as 'the *writer* who comes from a working-class family and community'.[18] Consideration of his writing as anything but an objective attempt to capture the quotidian reality of proletarian existence would have been anathema to Halward. Modelling his style and early stories on those of his mentor Chekhov, Halward early assumed his vocation for, facing down bourgeois snobbery, he believed proletarian experience was worth writing about and to this extent acted as amanuensis and spokesman for his class. Simply, in being written his naturalistic narratives present as a cultural intervention and challenge to the established literary canon, yet his 'English' naturalism was more than this. As Walter Allen observed, though 'just as likely to vote Tory as Labour', Halward nonetheless remained a champion of working-class cultural mores and wrote of them with perspicacity and psychological insight. Whether the doubly oppressed woman as housekeeper, wife or carer, the awkward apprentice, the ageing tradesman, the spiv, the drunkard or the courting or newly married couples who people his narratives, he brought the voiceless citizens of his native city to popular attention, his well-tuned ear having prompted E. M. Forster to proclaim him the one working-class writer that made 'the working-class come alive for him'.[19]

Copies of *Saturday Night at the Greyhound* are still easily found, yet, in terms of critical neglect, John Hampson has suffered a fate similar to that of his Birmingham group contemporaries. Nevertheless, to use an overworked expression, his work retains *relevance* today. Coming from a middle-class family fallen on hard times, ill health militated against his receiving any formal education. On leaving, more possibly estranged from, home at an early age, and, in order to escape the domestic turbulence attendant on families living near the breadline, he worked variously as kitchen-hand, barman, waiter and unskilled ancillary occupations in what would now be termed the 'hospitality sector'. Reduced circumstances therefore equipped him with practical experience in lowly occupations which, perceived from the standpoint of a natural sensitivity and emotional intelligence, enabled him to create characters and representations of intersubjective experience at both inter- and intra-class levels. Never overtly political, his authorial perspective nonetheless bespeaks an innate *moral* sensibility. Aware such a distinction may today be contested, this reading enlists the support of the American writer and literary critic Alfred

Kazin. No lover of politically progressive or propagandist literature himself, Kazin had nevertheless excoriated a post-war critic who scorned the 1930s as 'an imbecile decade' and who, as Kazin relates, '[continued to] explain – with the usual assurance of people who have more than enough to eat – that the issues in literature are "not political but moral"'.[20] Having rounded on his interlocutor, Kazin asserted that '[a]nyone who thinks *political* and *moral* are unrelated is certainly living in a world very different from the thirties – or the 1990s' [this writer would add the 2020s].[21]

Of the five Birmingham group members, Hampson's world-view is in many ways the most prescient of twenty-first-century concerns. This is evident in its disengagement with traditional sectarian imperatives and the movement towards a position more in tune with contemporary identity politics. Hampson's narratives reveal how intersections of class, place, sexuality and gender function by making their implications and consequences explicit. In this respect, his work is not only prefigurative of elements in the phallocentrist discussion taken up later by Jacques Derrida, Kate Millett, Judith Butler and Eve Sedgwick but also conversations centring on a 'post-scarcity emotional economy': the kind of society envisaged by Paul Mason and Nick Hubble in which 'there is no inherent conflict between individual self-realisation and group welfare if the type of society is one which is capable of giving self-expression to, and support for, a diverse range of identities and relationships'.[22] Employing a restricted linguistic palette owing more to Dashiel Hammett than Ernest Hemingway, Hampson, as had Walter Allen, adopted modernist techniques such as irresolution, filmic devices such as montage and the social/collective potential of an autobiografictional genre in order to frame the panoply of differing social groupings, regional conventions and social status he discovered in what had been a purportedly 'monolithic' working class.

Though briefly arrested between 1939 and 1945, Britain's transformation from manufacturing to service-based economy had begun prior to the war years, and though Birmingham undoubtedly played an important role in the collective War effort, the high levels of employment necessitated by arms manufacture only provided a brief hiatus in the city's slow but inexorable industrial decline. If it had been assumed that, following the war, things would simply 'return to normal' and that the literary status quo would merely 'pick up from where it had left off', such hopes were unfortunately misbegotten. Walter Allen commented upon the disappearance of the magazines that had published Leslie Halward's stories and the simple fact that after the war his kind of writing was no longer fashionable.

Halward raised similar concerns himself: in his drama 'Afternoon at Excelsior Lodge' (1960), the protagonist, an impoverished, no-longer read and somewhat cynical working-class writer, reflects on the 'bygone world [of the thirties] which the workers, in their new affluence, preferred to forget'. The play's central character Finsbury (Halward) laments that there is no longer a working class he can recognise, although he speculates gloomily, perhaps prophetically, that '[t]here will be in a few years the way things are going. Then I might be able to start again'.[23] Lara Feigel remarks how 'the postwar climate ushered in a new political climate in which political commitment was no longer simple and not necessarily even desirable'[24]:

> The Literary tradition of self-consciously cinematic, politically engaged literature that began in the early 1930s and flourished at the end of the decade was brought to an abrupt halt by the end of the war. [...] Writers such as Sommerfield, Greenwood or Allen never again regained the popularity they had enjoyed in the 1930s, and left-wing tendencies were no longer prerequisites for acceptance in the literary world.[25]

Feigel records 'the writers who had so violently committed themselves both to left-wing politics and to cinema tended to withdraw from both'. Henry Green and Walter Allen each abandoned the use of montage effects, and, as Feigel points, out by the end of the decade 'cinematic technique [though] endemic in the novel [...] was rarely used overtly with a political purpose'.[26] Whether the Birmingham group's demise was attributable solely to changes in individual belief, as with the refutations of Auden or Lehmann, or changes in literary 'fashion' alone is arguable, however, the 'new political climate' that Feigel references above was certainly registered in the post-war consensus. Effectively constituting a reversal of what Fredric Jameson terms 'expressive causality', the sociopolitical changes registered here would reflect negatively on working-class literary production.[27] Ian Haywood speculates that 'if ever a day can be chosen as a turning point in British working-class history, 26th July 1945 must be a prime candidate'.[28] The tranche of reformsinclude 'full employment based upon Keynsian economics; nationalisation of the staple industries; the creation of a welfare state, a National Health Service; universal free education; and state patronage of the arts each enacted on this day effectively saw Beveridge's "Five Giants" banished in one fell swoop'.[29] Cementing Lara Feigel's claim that political commitment was 'no longer simple and not necessarily desirable', the reforms constituting what came to be termed 'the post-war consensus' served—at least for a time—to render the cultural interventions of working-class writers redundant.

For a brief period in the troubled decade leading up to the outbreak of war, the Birmingham group faithfully chronicled the travails of their fellow citizens. Despite Auden's claim that 'poetry makes nothing happen', the Birmingham group writers certainly made a noble effort in the attempt.[30] Benjamin Kohlmann remarks that although some critics have described the establishment of the Welfare State in Britain as the consolidation of the capitalist status quo, [others see it instead] as the deferred outcome of the collectivist aspirations of the preceding decade, and the co-optation of the radicalised lower middle class into a collectivist post-war politics.[31] Whether the narratives of the Birmingham group and others may have moved politicians to make the necessary post-war reforms would be difficult to ascertain, although, as Elinor Taylor suggests, 'the British Novel came to be not just thematically inflected but also formally shaped by popular front politics, and the ways in which *it performed an active role in the production of that politics*' (my emphasis).[32] In the closing lines of his introduction and, in what seems a fitting close to this section, Edward O'Brien remarked how Halward—and by implication his Birmingham group confreres—had successfully broken the inhibition that hindered others from making social contact beyond their class boundaries. Indeed, O'Brien was adamant such barriers did not exist for the Birmingham group writers: 'When they write about life, they accept life and life accepts them. Each accepts the other on his own terms and is content with what he finds.' In short, they have learned that 'Life is never in bad taste. Once that discovery has been made by a writer his art will not be in bad taste. Life is earthy and salty also and it wears old clothes. And life accepts everybody and everything for what they are'.[33]

The Legacy

In respect of literary reclamation projects more generally, this book has aimed to both illustrate and iterate the proposition that the impetus to recover and recuperate a literary work from an earlier period, more specifically here the moment of sociopolitical upheaval that was the 1930s, is motivated in the first instance by a combination of both *intuition* and *expectation*: a belief that such writing, though temporally displaced, may, when measured against the criteria of contemporary cultural and political values, retain some continuing social worth and relevance. This naturally raises the question of legacy, and in focusing initially upon the productive side of the author/reader relationship, the following discussion will seek to develop this idea by reference to notions of both inspiration (authors will have been readers themselves) and 'heritage' in the sense that earlier outpourings of working-class literary production may, though tied closely to their specific historical context, offer themselves as a repository providing accounts of contemporary lived-experience and possibility for future generations of both writers and readers of working-class fiction. In order to determine why this is culturally important, one could do little better than turn to Birmingham's Walter Allen, who, asking why we read novels at all, proposes they function as 'a sort of resistance movement against rigid and impersonal concepts of man and his duties', adding, 'the novel continually ministers to the enlargement of human sympathy; and sympathy implies identification with and understanding of another, putting oneself in someone else's place as we say'.[34] This certainly offers a rationale with which to develop the fuller implications of the 'identification and understanding of another' that Allen proposes, especially as these become manifest in notions of a text's and a reader's political alignments and commitment.

Before looking more closely at these related issues, it is important to consider why working-class or proletarian writing has historically proceeded in a series of fits and starts. Generally speaking, this is owing to the fact that working-class writing occupies a symmetrical position in relation to the socio-economic context from which it arises. As P. J. Keating has pointed out: '[I]t is only during moments of social crisis that any significant number of English novelists have attempted to write fiction centred upon working-class life. The crisis [however] provides a ready-made framework, a way into working-class life.'[35] Although Marx had not outlined a specific theory of economic crises, to take the view that capitalism is subject to cyclical changes of fortune is hardly controversial; indeed, the irregularities of capitalist production serve only to reveal the true nature of its constructedness and precarity. As Terry Eagleton wrote in 2011:

> We are now living in the wake of one of the most devastating crises of capitalism on historical record [...] You can tell that the capitalist system is in trouble when people start talking about capitalism. It indicates that the system has ceased to be as natural as the air we breathe, and can be seen instead as the historically rather recent phenomenon it is.[36]

Such periodic irruptions—economic downturn, depression, meltdown, market forces, stagflation, slow-growth; fluctuation or any of the other sundry euphemisms informing the coded terminology designed to mitigate the failings and stallings that traditionally accompany laissez-faire or (what are reassuringly termed) 'free-market' economics—have consistently provided a backcloth to outpourings of working-class writing. The modern tradition tracing industrialisation and its discontents reaches back to Chartism and runs forwards to the 'Industrial' so-called Condition-of-England novels of the 1840s and 1850s: the 1880s furore at the urban slum; the mass unemployment of the 1930s and was in turn followed by the outbreak of the Second World War and the concomitant determination to begin anew which inscribed the post-war consensus separating ten decades of impoverishment from the new found affluence of the 1950s and 1960s. Though permeated by a series of micro and aftershocks during the intervening period, such moments of crisis unfailingly provided the context for a working-class literature that continues to the present day, and where it is currently 'enjoying'—I use the word ironically—something of a resurgence owing to the processes of deindustrialisation where the acronym TINA and a lethargic 'better-the-devil-you-know' political class still fail to envisage, or even consider, any alternative mode of economic practice.[37] Throughout this period, fictional narratives tracking these periods of crisis have themselves experienced parallel discontinuities, as demands, more specifically lack of demand for objects of cultural production, inversely echo the instabilities in the economic base. The process is circular: by the time material conditions momentarily stabilise, reading fashions change, the traditional outlets, magazines and periodicals that once lent space to accounts of working-class life having succumbed to decreasing sales or closure, thus reducing the efficacy and continuity of a narrative tradition bent upon diagnosing and understanding capitalism's deleterious effects. Perversely, it is during just such moments of crisis that the work of previous practitioners should remain extant and available as a resource. As H. Gustav Klaus suggests, 'a further reason for having the more important working-class novels in print' is the following:

> The history of the socialist novel reveals that again and again, as late as the 1950s, how aspiring worker writers set out not only against all odds but also unaware of the struggles and results of their literary ancestors. Cut off from their very own tradition, every group or generation invariably felt anew that it was starting from scratch, without the benefit of much inherited literary

> experience, without the knowledge of previous achievements and experiments; in fact, quite conversely, all too often overloaded with the 'ballast' of the dominant tradition.[38]

As a long-time champion of working-class and socialist literature, H. Gustav Klaus knew of what he spoke, and Terry Eagleton echoes his sentiments when he observes that:

> There are less 'extreme' phases of bourgeois society in which art [...] becomes trivial and emasculated, because the sterile ideologies it springs from yield it no nourishment. [...] in such an era, the need for explicitly revolutionary art again becomes pressing. It is a question to be seriously considered whether we are not ourselves living in such a time.[39]

As 'austerity bites' once again becomes the mantra, Eagleton's requirement for an 'explicitly revolutionary art' cannot be understated and adds critical weight to Gustav Klaus' argument that recourse to the heritage of one's literary forebears is ever more urgent.

Questions of continuing influence in terms of *direct* intervention through personal contact were discussed earlier regarding John Hampson's and Walter Allen's mentoring of Walter Brierley, similarly as detailed in Hampson's own dealings with the Hogarth Press, which revealed how the comments of a publisher's reader would often influence the successful outcome to publish. However, questions of legacy must also be considered in terms of *indirect* intervention, whereby a body of work might offer itself as a heritage of hope for subsequent generations of working-class writers. As remarked in the opening chapter, the Birmingham writers' literary careers in the 1930s had been 'fenced-in and fenced off' by momentous events: commencing with the Great Depression and closing with the outbreak of the Second World War. The duration of the latter witnessed a sea change in literary tastes but also marked the appearance of a younger generation of writers eager to 'make it new' by setting down accounts of lived working-class experience beyond the horizon of wartime hostilities and a fledgling Welfare State. That tastes change is of course a truism, and while later generations of writers would still have recourse to the wider formal aspects of realist or modernist representational modes, the possibility of the Birmingham group narratives' more context-critical stylistic departures exerting any significant, continuing influence is less than likely. Citing 'Walter Allen's statement about the "montage novel" as "firmly embedded in the past"', Lara Feigel indicates: 'The self-conscious cinematic technique he describes is a mode of writing he "used to do", and not a mode of writing [...] characteristic of the modern novel.'[40] Dated as the Birmingham group's formal innovation may have seemed, surely their subject material would withstand such vicissitudes.

In what was a further reflection of changing post-war attitudes—though arguably tainted by a degree of utopian optimism— one-time champion of the worker-writer John Lehmann added his voice to the post-war clamour of renunciation that now considered the working-class novel very much a child of its [pre-war] time, claiming: 'The conception of working-class literature is itself out of date in the age and country of the welfare state, [...] We are very much nearer a classless society in 1955 than we were in 1935.'[41] Whether Lehmann's prognostication bore fruit would remain to be seen. Fortunately, as Christopher Hilliard observes, there were others, 'later approximations of Edward Garnett [and] John Middleton Murry' [that still] 'kept an eye out for working-class talent', one such being Birmingham's Walter Allen, who remained, *contra* Lehmann, 'a fervent advocate of the working-class novel', and, as reader for the publisher Roland Gant of Michael Joseph, recommended the publication of Keith Waterhouse's first novel *There Is a Happy Land* (1957).[42] Hilliard claims that such 'fervent advocates' could nevertheless prove restrictive by advising authors to 'stick to what they knew'.[43] Articulating the prevailing concern as to whether working-class authors should attempt to write outside of their immediate class experience (ideas above their station), Stuart Laing relates that Walter Allen counselled [Sillitoe], as the 'most exciting chronicler in fiction of contemporary working-class life', to 'get back to [his] factory-hands and Borstal boys'.[44] Interestingly, the effects of the affluent society within which the post-war literary offering first began to appear were remarked upon by the American critic Irving Howe, who registered his own preference for Walter Allen's *All in A Lifetime* (1959), over Alan Sillitoe's *Saturday Night and Sunday Morning*. In a review titled 'The Worker as a Young Tough', Howe compared Sillitoe's novel unfavourably, saying:

> [Allen's novel] provided a sweet tempered retrospect of the life of Billy Ashted, an English worker who at the turn of the century had educated himself to socialist convictions, a measure of intellectuality and, most impressive of all, an enviable degree of civilised humaneness. Surely the socialist movement, for all its failures, has reason to feel that in nurturing such figures it made a genuine contribution to humanity.[45]

Howe, considered 'for all Arthur's energy' the life of Sillitoe's protagonist, 'is sadly limited in scope and value. It is a life bound by ritualistic practice and unexamined assumption, for in the absence of genuine consciousness, his freedom comes to little more than a repetition of familiar acts with increasing violence'.[46] Howe believed it was precisely the civilising extent of Allen's Billy Ashted that Sillitoe's Arthur Seaton lacked. His comments articulate how succeeding generations of writers represent changes in the social fabric. Describing how things were for the submerged and disenfranchised inhabitants of the second city, the narratives of the Birmingham group represent a unique portion of a much wider body of working class from the 1930s in which working-class writers had given voice to the hitherto unheard, having, as John Lehmann noted, 'addressed themselves to the widest possible circles of ordinary people engaged in the daily struggle for existence'.[47]

Despite such discontinuities and changes of emphases, working-class literature continued to be produced in the immediate post-war years and beyond. The first significant outpourings were evident in the work of Alan Sillitoe, John Osborne, Stan Bairstow, John Braine, John Wain and Kingsley Amis, the so-called 'Angry Young Men' whose work informed and was traceable in the British 'New Wave' cinema of the 1960s and continued in Television's take-up of working-class experience in such programmes as *Z Cars* and *Coronation Street*. Whilst clearly an erratic tradition, it was nevertheless one in which the work of the Birmingham writers must be seen to share, for, just as Nick Hubble's description of John Sommerfield's *Trouble in Porter Street* sets out, their narratives had likewise offered:

> [A] form of social-realist urban pastoral, or street life, that arguably became the dominant mode of cultural representation of the British welfare state as manifested in countless post-war dramas, situation comedies and soap operas, such as [Bill] Naughton's radio play *June Evening* (1958) televised nine months before the first broadcast of the series it arguably influenced, *Coronation Street* (1960-).[48]

Hubble suggests the film *Made in Dagenham* (2010), which describes events at the Ford factory in Dagenham Essex that led to the passing of the equal Equal Pay Act, effectively 'mark[ed] the end point of the long 1930s' and 'the utopian aspirations of 1930s proletarian literature'.[49] However, examples of cinematic 'resistance' would resurface four years later when *'Pride'* (2014), though dealing with earlier events, brought matters up to date by tackling neoliberal ideology head on in its romanticised portrayal of the support offered to miners in the Welsh coalfield by lesbian and gay activists during the 1984 strike.[50] Similarly in two notable and more recent documentary drama productions written by Paul Laverty and filmed under the direction of the indefatigable Ken Loach, 'I Daniel Blake' (2016) and 'Sorry We Missed You' (2019), the first addressing the deliberately obfuscated processes aimed to deter welfare benefit claimants from receiving assistance in the form of the benefit payment now termed Universal Credit, and the second describing the experiences, largely negative, of life as a self-employed delivery driver under the precarious and exploitative ethos of working-practices instituted in the name of an uncaring neoliberalism.

Such 'traditional 'content-providers' of working-class writing as, heavy industry with its concomitant aberrations in the division of labour, strikes, unemployment and the Means Test, would themselves become redundant in the immediate post-war period as the transformations instituted in nationalisation, the health service, education, welfare, council housing and other elements of a more progressive consensus came to prevail. However, despite its positive reception, the ideology of 'affluence for all' that initially fuelled the post-war outpouring of working-class literature was set from fair to change for, as Hubble rather chillingly remarks, 'within four years of the passing of the Equal Pay Act in 1975, Neoliberalism [would] replace social democracy as the dominant ideology in Britain'.[51]

That neoliberalism finally slammed the door on three decades of public ownership and the significant reforms instituted by the 1945–1951 Labour Government in turn deriving from 1930s political agitation is a well-documented and, as this book has suggested, indisputable lament. Marking a sharp reversal in the fortunes of working people where, compounded by a pandemic, further retrenchments in welfare provision and a cost-of-living crisis stemming from an increase in global energy prices is rapidly leading to a *status quo ante* position, in which neoliberalism constitutes an assault on the lives of the working-class citizens potentially as dramatic as that endured by their predecessors in the pre-war decade. That working-class literature exists to record and hopefully countervail such iniquities is essential, for as Nicholas Coles insists:

> In Marxist terms class, like sexism and racism, is a name for the institutionalized practice of dominance and subordination on which the social order is

> founded; and writing by working-class people, even when it is neither explicitly 'radical' or 'socialist,' shares with much women's and ethnic writing an implicitly oppositional or alternative relation to that order. It can nurture a spirit of dissent and irreverence towards the dominant culture, and puncture its omnipresence; it may gesture towards, and in some cases directly enact, a new order, a vision of a better world, or at least of a way forward out of the blockages and distortions of present oppression.[52]

Written in 1997, Ian Haywood expresses the wish that his book, 'may give some encouragement to working-class authors who still feel they are denied a literature of their own'.[53] Allowing for the dubious 'benefit' of hindsight in a remark more ominous than perhaps intended, he echoes Coles' sentiments in concluding: 'So long as capitalism requires the existence of a working-class, there will be a working-class literature.' Having cited Jeremy Seabrook's observation that 'the most authentic working-class communities were now to be found in the Third World or in the ranks of 'techno peasant[ry]', Haywood was surely aware that Britain was currently entering the last throes of its industrial phase where, if a local illustration may be adduced, Birmingham's BL (British Leyland, formerly the Austin factory and once the largest motor manufacturing plant in the world) saw closure following its 'fire-sale' to a Chinese conglomerate. Representing the nadir of Birmingham's manufacturing industry, the 2005 closure of 'The Longbridge', as it was known locally, and its subsequent redevelopment as a 'retail park', a euphemism for the vacuous 'Shopping Mall' consumerism designed as a sop, was of a piece with the kinds of deindustrial reconfiguration beginning to reshape the country as a whole in its move to a poorly paid and precarious service-based economy.

Despite the razing of the country's industrial base, the tradition of British working-class writing fortunately continues unabated into the first two decades of the twenty-first century where, as recent commentators have shown, it responds flexibly and more than adequately to these changes in, more possibly, erasures of the country's industrial landscape. Citing Raymond Williams' account of 'the "distinctive physical character" of a specific working-class industrial area', Phil O'Brien asks, 'what happens when [this] working society, which is 'formative and decisive', undergoes fundamental and irrevocable change? What it is like to live through the dismantling of that habitual order and that home?'[54] He proceeds to offer readings of twenty-first-century 'de-industrial' fictions, two of which, Anthony Cartwright's *The Afterglow* (2004) and Catherine O'Flynn's

What was Lost (2007), describe neoliberalism's deleterious effects, which, in echoing the situation outlined above at Longbridge Birmingham (see also pp. 9, 210), trace the demise of the Round Oak Steelworks in Dudley, in which the respective protagonists of each novel ruminate upon issues of class and identity. O'Brien—and surely not without irony—indicates that the closure of the Dudley steelworks and its refashioning as a retail park on one of Margaret Thatcher's 'Enterprise Zones', was '*meant* to tackle unemployment in de-industrial areas during the 1980s' (my emphasis).[55] He suggests that, in recourse to immediate surroundings and circumstance, 'Cartwright and O'Flynn offer "regional" voices engaging in the wider dynamics of neoliberalism as it is felt and understood on and in a local and very specific setting'.[56] In this way, working-class literature continues the tradition of dissent and irreverence towards the dominant (neoliberal) culture noted by Nicholas Coles above. In a footnote, O'Brien foregrounded the notion of heritage by indicating that Cartwright's and O'Flynn's novels belong to a tradition of working-class writing from the West Midlands: 'notably the Birmingham group which included Walter Brierley, John Hampson and Leslie Halward', and, in emphasising the importance of regional publishers in the promotion of working-class writing, had made reference to the Tindal Street Press in Balsall Heath, Birmingham which aimed to foster working-class writing and had proven instrumental in the success of Cartwright and O'Flynn's debut novels.[57] Unfortunately, the demise of this small-scale but nonetheless effective Birmingham publisher was sealed some short while later when, its funding having dried up, the Tindal Street Press ceased to operate independently and subsequently became an imprint of rival London company Profile Books in 2012.

Publication would remain the final hurdle to be jumped by working-class authors aiming to see their work not only in print but also—as the reference (see p. 206) to its somewhat asymmetrical relationship with moments of crisis suggests—essential to the continuation of a radical tradition. As has been seen, over time various initiatives were put in place to encourage working-class writing. However, Hilliard distinguishes between the worker-writer campaigns of the 1930s and what he terms 'the efflorescence of working-class writers in the 1970s'.[58] For whereas the former placed less emphasis on changing the system of publication than in discovering worker-writers, 1970s 'worker-writing' had been linked closely with 'community publishing', where, as Hilliard points out, '[g]roups affiliated with the Federation of Worker Writers and Community Publishers

[FWWCP] tended to regard [the] writing itself as an activity that should be open to everyone in a social democracy'.[59] The kind of publishing offered by the FWWCP derived from a 'perceived incomprehension and condescension from neighbours or people in the media who assumed that writers had to be "special people"'.[60] As set out in Dave Morley's and Ken Worpole's *The Republic of Letters* (1982), its aims were critical of cultural gatekeepers, namely the Arts Council, who fetishised the *writer* rather than the *writing* itself.[61] This Yeatsian 'tell the dancer from the dance' conundrum was resolved by initiatives seeking to strike a balance between the two, one such being Kit De Waal's 'Common People' project, which culminated in an anthology of writing dedicated to: 'everyone who has yearned to see their life on the page, who has hoped one day to read about working-class lives told by the working-class people who lived them.'[62]

In the course of researching this book, my close reading and study of the Birmingham group narratives has enabled a move from the perplexity expressed at the outset to discover that, contrary to pre–popular front critiques of working-class literature which considered the lack of an overtly sectarian or propagandist message a weakness; the restraint, the conspicuous absence of political rhetoric, exercised by the Birmingham writers, functions paradoxically as the more powerful political device. As this project has registered, the theorisation of working-class literature during the 1930s and since is both detailed and complex and one that frequently emerges in the shape of radically conflicting arguments. Yet, whilst somewhat perverse, it is the seemingly contradictory and irreconcilable nature of the form/content debate in conjunction with its associated, art/politics, literature/propaganda, aesthetics/commitment binaries that serve to vitalise the critical discussion keeping it live. As Terry Eagleton suggests: 'as with other philosophical disputes, tension and irresolution serve to ensure its continuance, [...] the question of how "progressive" art needs to be to be valid is an *historical* question, not one to be settled for all time.'[63]

Nevertheless, as it is hoped this book has shown, the practical application of these contending theories, especially during the 1930s would remain very much in the hands of the writers themselves. Indeed, having demonstrated the contradictory nature of certain theoretical positions, one might play devil's advocate by inverting the whole process and asking how the *theory* stood up against the *practice*, not only of the Birmingham group writers but also of other working-class writers from this period whose work, notwithstanding their unfamiliarity with both prevailing and more recent theoretical discussions, seems to have encapsulated so many of its criteria. In a review of Phil O'Brien's *The Working Class and Twenty-First Century British Fiction: Deindustrialisation, Demonisation, Resistance*, Joseph Williams touches this very point, suggesting that the word 'resistance' in the book's subtitle refers to the act of writing itself, and that the novels discussed by O'Brien (see p. 200) both 'name and resist the forces of demonisation and therefore provide sites of resistance to the damaging logics and inequalities of capital'.[64] More pertinent however, certainly with regard to the notion of literary *practice* outweighing *theory*, are the 'wider implications' of this argument, for, 'rather than conceiving of the novel as a simple representational form', O'Brien suggests that, 'fictional writing can make significant interventions into critical and theoretical discourse, owing to the flexibility of the novel form itself rather than as conceptual prose, or the 'novel of ideas' *per se*, in this way it offers itself not merely as 'simple reflection' [but as a] 'powerful intervention[n] into both class discourse and the drastic changes to class formation in Britain brought about by the ideologies of neoliberalism'.[65] The idea that imaginative fictions are *able* to, or, put more forcefully, *should*, intervene in class discourse aligns closely with Walter Benjamin's adjuration, as cited in Eagleton, that 'rather than uncritically accepting the existing forces of artistic production, artists should revolutionise those forces and in so doing create new social relations between artist and audience'.[66] As Benjamin remarks:

> What matters in the [sphere of literary production] is the exemplary character of production, which is able, first to induce other producers to produce, and second, to put an improved apparatus at their disposal. And this apparatus is better, the more consumers it is able to turn into producers—that is readers or spectators into collaborators.[67]

Having argued the case for a politics of form as against notions of applied tendency or propagandist rhetoric, the 'literary work as political intervention' proposition is certainly one with which this book would align, with the caveat that the promise of any collaborative impetus arising from such interventions is also dependent upon a politically aligned and sympathetic readership. Citing Chantal Mouffe, Greta Olsen and Sarah Copland indicate that: 'artistic practices play a role in the constitution and maintenance of the symbolic order, or in its challenging and this is why they necessarily have a political dimension [...]' to understand the fuller implications of this process involves, 'the necessity of reading not only aesthetic forms but also modes of interpretation in politically acute ways'.[68]

Rather than 'uncritically accepting the tools handed down to them', the Birmingham writers of the 1930s were able to extend the relationship between writer and audience, not only during this period of heightened political crises but also as a legacy and resource in the continuing struggle.[69] That working-class writing has traditionally functioned as the cultural arena in which this discourse of dissent is played out is important; the recovery and recuperation of neglected, overlooked or forgotten narratives matters considerably because the processes of identification and alignment they engender lead to a greater consciousness and questioning of class division. Readers' exposure to and understanding of a radical tradition in which earlier trials and struggles had been surmounted is therefore vital, for in this way working-class literature presents as a rhetorical resource in the ongoing struggle against the assaults of a resurgent capitalism constructed so arbitrarily and precariously upon neoliberal assumptions. The intersectional reading of working-class texts likewise contributes to this process by placing greater emphasis upon the need to generate 'scholarship, art and activism' built on 'solidarity in difference' rather than the hitherto limiting image of the 'blue collar' as sole class signifier.[70] In bringing the moral, political and literary into orbit with one another, working-class literature is therefore in and of itself vitally important, and as Ben Clarke and Nick Hubble maintain, it is 'essential [...] because it insists upon the specificity of working-class experience, which political, historical and sociological accounts often erase'.[71] In this respect, the Birmingham group novels and short stories foster not only an awareness and greater critical attention to issues of class and the working class in particular which not only seek to 'extend both the methods and objects of literary study' but also serve to situate imaginative literature as the sun around which the related humanities discourses of cultural studies, history and philosophy revolve.[72]

Whether one may take solace from previous moments of capitalism's self-doubt as a means to explain and understand contemporary sociopolitical crises is perhaps dependent upon whether one follows Karl Marx's formulation that 'History repeats itself, first as tragedy, second as farce' or alternatively George Santayana's view that, 'Those who do not remember the past are condemned to repeat it'. Whether celebratory or salutary, political parties of both Left and Right have regularly trawled the 1930s for spiritual succour, the habit of 'comparison' being deeply ingrained. Jonathan Freedland recently described the nineteen-thirties as 'rhetorical shorthand' a 'two word warning from history'.[73] Indeed, such repeated invocations of the 1930s have become something of a journalistic trope, standing either as measure of human fortitude during a time of political uncertainty or, more ominously, the malign spur to political initiatives of a more extreme variety. However, while the Wall Street crash, and its economic aftermath still remain powerfully evocative, this singular focus on the economic and political aspects of the decade has tended to obscure other areas of contemporary experience which might benefit equally from the 'warnings of history,' especially those relating to the intersectional, 'holy trinity' of class, race and gender issues so frequently neglected and overlooked owing to the prevailing focus on male-oriented concerns. Introducing *A History of 1930s British Literature*, Benjamin Kohlmann and Matthew Taunton assert:

> If nothing else, we hope that by bringing together the most innovative recent scholarship on the decade, this book will permanently dislodge the perception of the 1930s as an aberration. But we also hope that this volume demonstrates the centrality and continuing vitality of 1930s literary culture well beyond the political instrumentalisation and presentist reductions that have so often hampered a fuller understanding of the decade.[74]

The formal diversity of the Birmingham group narratives described how things were for the unheard citizens of Britain's second city in the chaotic years between the Wall Street Crash and the build-up to the Second World War. For too long overlooked or dismissed as 'guilty by association' with working-class literary productions that merely adopted traditional realist modes or paid blind obeisance to ideological strictures regarding what *ought* to constitute a working-class literature or, in Raymond William's words, by merely 'applying tendency,' the Birmingham writers supply abundant testimony to that brief period in the 1930s when, as Andy Croft observes:

> The Left seems to have genuinely understood how culture works, how impossible it is to legislate for the imagination, how different books can come to life in such different people's heads, how the unlikeliest of texts can make the heart beat faster in the unlikeliest of readers, how most of us win our ideas about ourselves, others, our society, about the possibilities of being human in our time from the culture we inhabit.[75]

It seems fitting to close this study by citing the words of Andy Croft, whose pioneering work provided some of this project's earliest insights into working-class writing from the 1930s and the Birmingham writers in particular. It is hoped that in sharing his sentiments with the work of more recent scholars, *The Birmingham Group: Reading the Second City in the 1930s* will similarly 'dislodge perceptions of the 1930s as an aberration' and that the recovery of the Birmingham group narratives may spur further research into their work.[76] Owing to the breadth of their literary output, this study could have been undertaken from a range of differing perspectives employing illustrative examples from the many narratives untouched in this cursory selection. There is consequently much potential for further exploration. Whether one approaches their works individually or in terms of genre, whether the focus be on the novel, short story, radio-drama or criticism, taken collectively this corpus of imaginative prose writing patiently awaits the rediscovery of both scholars and future generation of working-class authors temporally severed from or simply unaware of Birmingham's short-lived but once vibrant tradition of working-class writing.

Notes

1. Edward O'Brien. Introduction p. vii. Leslie Halward, *To Tea on Sunday,* cited in Halward, *Let Me Tell You*. p. 244.
2. Leslie Halward, *Let Me Tell You,* pp. 244, 245.
3. Walter Allen, *As I Walked*, p. 114.
4. Ibid, p. 96.
5. Walter Allen, *The English Novel: A Short Critical History* (1954) and *Tradition and Dream: The English and American Novel from the Twenties to Our Time* (1964). These two works possibly represent the swansong of traditional English literary criticism prior to the upsurge of feminist, colonial, and cultural–materialist critiques which came to dominate critical discussion from the late 1960s onwards. *Tradition and Dream* represents a pioneering early attempt by an English critic to provide an overview of contemporary American literature.
6. Leslie Halward, *Let Me Tell You*, p. 288.
7. Walter Allen, *As I Walked*, p. 70.
8. Andy Croft Introduction, Walter Brierley, *Means Test Man*, p. xii.
9. Ibid.
10. Kenneth Burke, *Rhetoric of Motives* (Berkeley and Los Angeles: California University Press, 1969).

11. Lara Feigel, *Literature, Cinema and Politics*, p. 118.
12. Ibid, p. 136.
13. Robert Scholes, *Paradox of Modernism* (New Haven and London: Yale University Press, 2006), pp. 96, 97.
14. Cf. David Lodge's *Nice Work* (1988) for its montaged exploration of conflicting political ideologies, and also Jonathan Coe's *Middle-England* (2018), pp. 255-263, for its use of similar devices to examine the processes of deindustrialisation (The closure of the Longbridge car plant in Birmingham).
15. Jack Windle explains Bakhtin asserted that 'the essential principle of grotesque realism is degradation, that is, the lowering of all that is high, spiritual, ideal, abstract; it is to transfer to the material level, to the sphere of earth and body'. In Clarke, Ben and Nick Hubble, *Working-Class Writing*, 41-60. p. 51.
16. Barbara Foley, *Radical Representations*, pp. 162, 163.
17. Edward Seaver, American Literary Theorist and critic in Barabara Foley, p. 119.
18. Raymond Williams. 'Working-Class, Proletarian, Socialist: Problems in Some Welsh Novels', in H. Gustav Klaus, *The Socialist Novel in Britain*, p. 114.
19. Andy Croft, *Red Letter Days*, p. 169.
20. Alfred Kazin, introduction, p. vii, Henry Roth, *Call It Sleep* (London: Penguin Books, 2006).
21. Ibid.
22. Nick Hubble, *The Proletarian Answer*, p. 20.
23. Paul Lester, *The Road to Excelsior Lodge*, p. 21.
24. Lara Feigel, *Literature, Cinema and Politics*, p. 235.
25. Ibid, p. 233.
26. Ibid, p. 235.
27. Fredric Jameson, *The Political Unconscious: Narrative as a socially symbolic act*, (London and New York: Routledge, 2009), p. 10.
28. Ian Haywood, *Working-Class Fiction*, p. 88.
29. The Beveridge Report identified Want, Disease, Squalor, Ignorance and Idleness as the 'Five Giants' constituting the social deprivation needing to be addressed by the post-war consensus registered in the Labour Party's 1945 General Election victory.
30. See note 64, page 139, regarding publication and praise of Brierley's *Means Test Man*.
31. Benjamin Kohlmann, 'Fashioning the 1930s' in James Smith Ed, *The Cambridge Companion To British Literature Of The 1930s*, (Cambridge: Cambridge University Press, 2019), pp. 224–238. p. 233, 4.
32. Elinor Taylor, *The Popular Front Novel In Britain 1934–1940*, p. 17.

33. Edward J. O'Brien, introduction, p. x. Leslie Halward, *To Tea on Sunday.*
34. Walter Allen, *Reading a Novel,* (London: Phoenix House Ltd, 1949), p. 22.
35. P. J Keating, *The working classes in Victorian fiction*, (London: Routledge and Kegan Paul, 1971). p. 124.
36. Terry Eagleton, *Why Marx Was Right*, (Newhaven & London: Yale University Press, 2011). Introduction, pp. x, xi.
37. De- Industrialisation. Phil O'Brien importantly stresses the distinction between post- and de- prefixes here, suggesting that 'Post' has adverbial connotations in the sense of 'after', 'following' or 'subsequent to' a particular event, whereas 'De-' implies an act, something done and continuing, thus raising the notion of deliberation an ideological act undertaken in the act/process of class shaping.
38. H.Gustav Klaus, *The Socialist Novel in Britain,* pp. 5, 6.
39. Terry Eagleton, *Marxism and Literary Criticism*, p. 58.
40. Lara Feigel, *Literature, Cinema and Politics 1930 – 1945*. p. 235.
41. John Lehmann, *New Writing in Europe*, (Harmondsworth: Allen Lane, Penguin, 1940). Foreword p. 13.
42. Christopher Hilliard, *To Exercise Our Talents*, p. 253.
43. Ibid. p. 254.
44. Stuart Laing, *Representations of Working-Class Life 1957 – 1964* (London: Macmillan, 1986). p.80.
45. Irving Howe, 'The Worker as Young Tough', Review of Alan Sillitoe, *Saturday Night and Sunday Morning. Nation* 24th August 1959. pp. 27 – 28.
46. Ibid.
47. John Lehmann, *New Writing in Europe*. p. 13.
48. Nick Hubble, 'Proletarian Writing in the 1930s', in Kohlmann, Benjamin and Matthew Taunton Eds, *A History of 1930s British Literature* (Cambridge: Cambridge University Press, 2019), pp. 44–57. p. 55.
49. Ibid.
50. There is a view that the account provided by 'Pride', although based upon actual events, tends to obscure the fact that a long-standing and formidable tradition of resistance had been a consistent feature of life in the Welsh mining valleys.
51. Ibid.
52. Nicholas Coles, 'Democratizing Literature: Issues in Teaching Working-Class Literature'. *College English*, 48, 7, (Nov 86), pp. 664–680. P. 672.
53. Ian Haywood, *Working-class Fiction: from Chartism to Trainspotting,* p. 160.
54. Phil O'Brien, 'The Deindustrial Novel: Twenty-First Century British Fiction and the Working-Class', in Clarke and Hubble Eds: *Working-Class Writing: Theory and Practice,* pp. 229–246. p. 230.
55. Ibid, pp. 239, 240.

56. Ibid, p. 239.
57. Ibid, p. 245.
58. Christopher Hilliard, *To Exercise Our Talents*, p. 142.
59. Ibid, pp. 142 -143.
60. Ibid, p. 282.
61. Morley, Dave and Ken Worpole Eds, *The Republic of Letters: Working-Class Writing and Local Publishing*, (London: Comedia Publishing Group, 1982), pp. 138–139. Though folding in 2007, the FWWCP would continue in spirit as further initiatives sought to encourage working-class writers into print. Notable amongst these is Kit De Waal's Common People Project. Running for a twelve-month period from 2018 to 2019, it sought, as had the FWWCP, to bring together regional writing development agencies in order to 'create a strategic model of intervention to address the under-representation of working-class writers'. Supporting the professional development programme via National Lottery Funding, the Arts Council fared better this time around; however, the project also aimed to break the 'class ceiling' that had hitherto dissuaded and discouraged unpublished and would-be worker-writers from achieving successful outcomes. Details of the scheme are to be found in Katy Shaw's research report: *Common People: Breaking the Class Ceiling In UK Publishing*, produced in conjunction with New Writing North; Writing West Midlands and Northumbria University. Although further collections of working-class writing and essays are planned, the literary fruits of this project are available in (editor Kit De Waal's excellent) *Common People: An Anthology of Working-Class Writers* (London: Unbound, 2019).
62. Kit De Waal, *Common People: An Anthology of Working-Class Writers*, (London: Unbound 2019), p. xii.
63. Terry Eagleton, *Marxism and Literary Criticism*, p. 57.
64. 'Key Words: A Journal of Cultural Materialism', 19, 2021. (Leicester: Raymond Williams Society, 2021). Joseph Williams, Review of Phil O'Brien: *The Working Class and Twenty First Century British Fiction: Deindustrialisation, Demonisation, Resistance,* (Abingdon: Routledge, 2020). pp. 98–100.
65. Ibid.
66. Terry Eagleton, *Marxism and Literature*, pp. 61-62.
67. Walter Benjamin, The Author as Producer', *Selected Writings, Volume 2*. p. 777.
68. Chantal Mouffe, Agnostics: Thinking the World Politically (London: Verso, 2013), p. 91. Cited in Copland, Sarah and Greta Olsen, 'A Politics of Form', *European Journal of English Studies*, 20. (2016), pp. 207–221, p 207.

69. Chantal Mouffe, Agnostics: Thinking the World Politically (London: Verso, 2013), p. 91. Cited in Copland, Sarah and Greta Olsen, 'A Politics of Form', *European Journal of English Studies*, 20. (2016), pp. 207–221, p 207.
70. Sara Appel, 'A Turn of the Sphere: The Place of Class in Intersectional Analysis', *A History of American Working-Class Literature,* Ed, Coles, Nicholas, and Paul Lauter, pp. 406–423, p. 408.
71. Ben Clarke and Nick Hubble, Introduction, *Working-Class Writing,* p. 5.
72. Ibid.
73. Jonathan Freedland, 'The 1930s were humanity's darkest, bloodiest hour. Are you paying attention?' *The Guardian*, Saturday 11 March, 2017.
74. Kohlmann, Benjamin and Matthew Taunton Eds, *A History of 1930s British Literature* (Cambridge: Cambridge University Press, 2019), p. 12.
75. Andy Croft, *Red Letter Days*, p. 9.
76. Regarding the recovery of the Birmingham group novels and short stories, cf p. 49 n1.

Works Cited

Primary Sources

Allen, Walter, *All in a Lifetime* (1959), introduction Alan Sillitoe. (London: Hogarth Press, 1986).

Allen, Walter, *As I Walked Down New Grub Street* (London: Heinemann, 1981a).

Allen, Walter, *Blind Man's Ditch* (London: Michael Joseph Ltd, 1939).

Allen, Walter, *Innocence Is Drowned* (London: Michael Joseph Ltd, 1938).

Brierley, Walter, *Means-Test Man (*1935), Introduction Andy Croft, (Nottingham: Spokesman, 2011).

Brierley, Walter, *Sandwichman* (1937), Introduction Philip Gorski, (London: Merlin Press, 1990).

Brierley, Walter, 'Body' in *No Want of Meat Sir! Being a Collection of Short-Stories,* Ed, John Hackney (London: Grayson and Grayson, 1936).

Brierley, Walter, 'Transition', in *'Under Thirty' An Anthology*, Ed, Michael Harrison, (London: Rich and Cowan, 1939).

Chamberlain, Peter, *What the Sweet Hell?* (New York: Henry Holt and Company, 1935).

Green, Henry, *Living* (1929), *Loving, Living and Party Going,* Introduction Sebastian Faulks, (London: Viking, 2005a).

Green, Henry, *Surviving: The Uncollected Writings of Henry Green* (New York: Penguin Books, 1992a).

Halward, Leslie, *Gus and Ida* (London: Michael Joseph Ltd, 1939).

Halward, Leslie, *Let Me Tell You* (London: Michael Joseph Ltd, 1938a).

Halward, Leslie, *The Money's Alright and Other Stories* (London: Michael Joseph, 1938b).

R. Harriott, *The Birmingham Group*,
https://doi.org/10.1007/978-3-031-14383-0

Halward, Leslie, *To Tea on Sunday* (London: Methuen & Co. Ltd., 1936).

Hampson, John, *Man About the House* (London: Grayson & Grayson, 1935).

Hampson, John, *Saturday Night at the Greyhound* (1931), Introduction Christopher Hawtree, (London: The Hogarth Press, 1986).

Secondary Sources

Abu-Manneh, Bashir, *Fiction of the New Statesman 1913 - 1939,* (Delaware: University of Delaware Press, 2011.

Adorno, Theodor, *Aesthetic Theory* (London: Bloomsbury, 1970).

Alexander, Neal, and James Moran, *Regional Modernisms* (Edinburgh: Edinburgh University Press, 2013).

Allen, Walter, *The English Novel: A Short Critical Introduction* (London: J. M. Dent & Sons Ltd 1954).

Allen, Walter, 'An Artist of the Thirties', in John Lehmann, Ed, Folios of New Writing (London: Hogarth Press, 1931).

Allen, Walter, 'Point Counter Point Revisited, *Studies in the Novel,* 9.4 (1977), 373-377. http://www.jstor.org/stable/29531885 [accessed 17-03-2018]

Allen, Walter, *The Short Story in English* (Oxford: Clarendon Press, 1981b).

Allen, Walter, 'An Interview in New York with Walter Allen', *Studies in the Novel,* 3. 4. (1971), 405-429. <http://www.jstor.org/stable/29531486> [accessed 17-03-2018]

Allen, Walter, 'Thirties Fiction: A View from the Seventies', *Twentieth Century Literature,* 20, (1974). 245-251. <http://www.jstor.org/stable/440642> [accessed 15-06-2016]

Allen, Walter, *Tradition and Dream : The English and American Novel from the Twenties to Our Time*

Althusser, Louis, 'A Letter on Art in Reply to Andres Daspre' in *Lenin And Philosophy And Other Essays* (London: Monthly Review Press, 1971). 221-227.

Anthony, P.D., *The Ideology of Work* (London: Tavistock Publications Limited, 1977).

Armengol, Joseph M., 'Gendering the Great Depression: Rethinking the Male Body in 1930s American Culture and Literature', *Journal of Gender Studies,* 23 (2013), 59-68.

Arnold, Matthew, *Matthew Arnold Selected Prose.* (Middlesex: Penguin Books Ltd, 1970).

Auden, W.H., and Edward Mendelson, Ed, *The English Auden: Poems, Essays and Dramatic Writings 1927 - 1939* (London: Faber, 1989).

Austen, Jane, *Emma* (London: Penguin Books, 1996).

Bachelard, Gaston, and John R. Stilgoe introduction, *The Poetics of Space,* Trans. Maria Jolas (Boston: Beacon Press, 1994).

Baldick, Chris, *The Modern Movement,* Vol 10, The Oxford English Literary History, ed, Jonathan Bate. (Oxford: OUP, 2004).

Bates, H.E., *The Modern Short Story: From 1809 to 1953.* (London: Robert Hale, 1988).

Batsleer, Janet, Tony Davies, Rebecca O'Rourke, and Chris Weedon, *Rewriting English: Cultural Politics of Gender and Class,* ed, Terence Hawkes, *New Accents* (London Methuen & Co, 1985).

Baxendale, John, *Priestley's England: J. B. Priestley and English Culture* (Manchester: Manchester University Press, 2007).

Beales, H. L., and R. S. Lambert, *Memoirs of the Unemployed* (London: Victor Gollancz, 1973).

Beja, Alice, 'Proletarian Literature, An Unidentified Literary Object', *L'Atelier,* 7.1 (2015), 68-78.

Belsey, Catherine, *Critical Practice.* ed. Terence Hawks, *New Accents* (London: Routledge, 1980).

Benjamin, Walter, 'The Storyteller Reflections on the Works of Nikolai Leskov', (Cornell). 1-14. <https://arl.human.cornell.edu> [accessed 26-02-2020]

Bergonzi, Bernard, *Reading The Thirties: Texts and Contexts* (London: The Macmillan Press Ltd, 1978).

Bergonzi, Bernard, 'Walter Earnest Allen', *Oxford Dictionary of National Biography* (Oxford: Oxford University Press, 2004).

Birkett, Jennifer, *Margaret Storm Jameson: A Life* (Oxford: Oxford University Press, 2009).

Birkett, Jennifer and Chiara Briganti, eds, *Margaret Storm Jameson Writing in Dialogue*, (Cambridge Scholars Publishing, 2007).

Bluemel, Kristen, *Intermodernism: Literary Culture in Mid-Twentieth-Century Britain* (Edinburgh: Edinburgh University Press, 2009).

Blythe, Ronald, *The Age of Illusion: Glimpses of Britain between the Wars 1919-1940* (Oxford: Oxford University Press, 1963).

Bradbury, Malcolm, *The Modern British Novel* (London: Secker & Warburg, 1993).

Briggs, Asa, *Victorian Cities* (London: Penguin Books Limited, 1990).

Bronner, Stephen Eric, *Critical Theory: A Very Short Introduction* (Oxford: Oxford University Press, 2011).

Brooke, Stephen, 'Gender and Working-Class Identity in Britain During the 1950s', *Journal of Social History,* 34. (2001), 773-795.

Caesar, Adrian, *Dividing Lines: Poetry, Class and Ideology in the 1930s* (Manchester: Manchester University Press, 1991).

Caramina, Nicola, 'Self-Concept in Consumer Behaviour: A Psychoanalytical Investigation Working Paper Series.' (2018), <https://www.academia.edi/36927375/Self-Concept-in-consumer-behaviour> [accessed 23-06-2018]

Carey, John, *The Intellectuals and the Masses: Pride and Prejudice among the Literary Intelligentsia, 1880 - 1939* (London: Faber and Faber, 1992).

Cartwright, Anthony, *The Afterglow* (Birmingham: The Tindal Street Press Limited, 2004).

Caserio, Robert L., Ed, *The Cambridge Companion to the Twentieth-Century English Novel* (Cambridge: Cambridge University Press, 2009).

Chomsky, Noam, *On Anarchism*, (London: Penguin Books, 1913).

Clark, Jon, Margot Heinemann, David Margolies, and Carole Snee, *Culture and Crisis in Britain in the 30's* (London: Lawrence and Wishart Ltd, 1979).

Clarke, Ben, review of 'Nick Hubble. The Proletarian Answer to the Modernist Question', in *University of North Carolina at Greensboro.* (2017). <https://academic.oup,com/res/abstract/69/291/811/4980910> [accessed 24-06-2018]

Clarke, Ben, and Nick Hubble, Eds, *Working-Class Writing: Theory and Practice* (Switzerland: Palgrave Macmillan, 2018).

Coetzee, J. M. 'The Man Who Went Shopping for the Truth', *New York Review of Books* article reprinted in *The Guardian,* 20th January 2001. Review of Walter Benjamin, *The Arcades Project,* new translation Howard Eiland and Kevin McLaughlin published by Belknap Press/ Harvard University Press.

Coles, Nicholas, 'Democratizing Literature: Issues in Teaching Working-Class Literature', *College English*, 48, 7, (Nov, 1986), pp, 664 – 680. https://www.jstor.org/stable/377367 [Accessed 18-01-2022]

Coles, Nicholas, and Paul Lauter, Eds, *A History of American Working-Class Literature*, (Cambridge: Cambridge University Press, 2017).

Connell, R. W., *Masculinities* (Berkeley: University of California Press, 2005).

Connell, R. W., and James W. Messerschmidt, 'Hegemonic Masculinity', *Gender & Society*, 19 (2016), 829-59.

Connolly, Cyril. *Enemies of Promise* (London: Penguin Books, 1979).

Cook, Chris, 'The Work Ethic in the 1930s', *History Today*, 33. 7. (1983). <https://www.historytoday.com> [accessed 14-07-2018]

Copland, Sarah, and Greta Olsen, 'A Politics of Form', *European Journal of English Studies*, 20. (2016), 207-221.

Croft, Andy, 'The Birmingham Group: Literary Life between Two Wars', *London Magazine,* 23 (1983).

Croft, Andy, *Red Letter Days* (London: Lawrence & Wishart, 1990).

Cuddon, J. A., *The Penguin Dictionary of Literary Terms and Literary Theory* (London: Penguin Books, 1998).

Curtis, James, *The Gilt Kid* (London: Penguin Books, 1947).

Cunningham, Valentine, *British Writers of the Thirties* (Oxford: Clarendon Press, 1988).

Dajani, Karim, 'The Ego's Habitus: An Examination of the Role Culture Plays in Structuring the Ego', *International Journal of Applied Psychoanalytical Studies*, 14 (2001), 273-81.

Dajani, Karim G., 'Cultural Dislocation and Ego Functions: Some Considerations in the Analysis of Bi-Cultural Patients', *International Journal of Applied Psychoanalytic Studies,* 15 (2018), 16-28.

Daly, Macdonald, 'D.H. Lawrence and Walter Brierley', *Journal of D. H. Lawrence Studies,* 4 (1986), 22-9.

Davies, Tony, 'Unfinished Business: Realism and Working-Class Writing', in Jeremy Hawthorn, Ed, *The British Working-Class Novel in the Twentieth Century* (London: Edwin Arnold, 1984), 125-136.

DeSalvo, Louise, *Writing as a Way of Healing: How telling Our Stories Transforms Our Lives* (London: The Women's Press, 1999).

De Waal, Kit, *Common People: An anthology of working-class writers* (London: Unbound, 2019).

Dickens, Charles, *The Personal History of David Copperfield* (London: Hazel, Watson & Viney Ltd, 1935).

Dikova, Stanislava, Review (26-10-2019) of: Nick Hubble, *The Proletarian Answer to the Modernist Question* (2017), 1-4. <https://LSEblogs.lse.ac.uk> [accessed 04-07-2019]

Eagleton, Terry, *Criticism and Ideology: A Study in Marxist Literary Theory* (London: Verso, 1976).

Eagleton, Terry, *The English Novel: An Introduction* (Oxford: Blackwell Publishing, 2005).

Eagleton, Terry, *Marxism and Literary Criticism.* (London: Methuen & Co. Ltd, 1987).

Eagleton, Terry, *Why Marx Was Right* (Yale: Yale University Press, 2011).

Ellis, Steve, *British Writers and the Approach of World War II* (Cambridge: Cambridge University Press, 2015).

Empson, William, *Some Versions of Pastoral* (London: Hogarth Press, 1986).

Farrell, James T., *A Note on Literary Criticism* (London: Constable & Co Ltd, 1936).

Feigel, Lara, *Literature, Cinema and Politics 1930 - 1945* (Edinburgh: Edinburgh University Press, 2010).

Feigel, Lara, 'Buggery and Montage: Birmingham and Bloomsbury in the 1930s', in Burrells, Anna, Steve Ellis, Deborah Parsons, and Kathryn Simpson, *Woolfian Boundaries* (South Carolina: Clemson, 2007) 51-57.

Flood, Michael, *Toxic masculinity: A Primer and commentary* <XY Online. Net 2018.> [accessed 07-07-2018]

Foley, Barbara, *Radical Representations: Politics and Form In U.S. Political Fiction, 1929-1941* (Durham and London: Duke University Press, 1993).

Foley, Barbara, 'Intersectionality: A Marxist Critique', *New Labor Forum,* 28.3. (2018), 10-13.

Fordham, John, 'James Hanley and the Project of Modernity', *Critical Survey,* 10.3. Literature of the Thirties (1998), 56- 61 <http://www.jstor.org/stable/41556796> [accessed 05-07-2019]

Fordham, John, *James Hanley Modernism and the Working Class* (Cardiff: University of Wales, 2002).

Fox, Pamela, *Class Fictions: Shame and Resistance in the British Working-Class Novel. 1890 - 1945.* (Durham, North Carolina: Duke University Press, 1994).

Fox, Ralph, *The Novel and the People* (London: Lawrence and Wishart, 1937).

Freeman, Joseph, 'Introduction' *Proletarian Literature in the United States* (London: Lawrence and Wishart, Ltd, 1935).

Gardiner, Juliet, *The Thirties: An Intimate History* (London: Harper Press 2011).

Gasiorek, Andrzej, *Post-War British Fiction: Realism and After* (London: Edward Arnold, 1995).

Genette, Gerard, *Narrative Discourse* (Ithaca New York: Cornell University Press, 1980).

Gerke, Daniel, 'Raymond Williams and Andrez Gorz: Class, Communism, Humanism', in *The Raymond Williams Society* (RWS Blog, 2019). <https://raymondwilliams.co.uk> [accessed 14-03-2019]

Gloversmith, Frank, *Class Culture and Social Change: A New View of the Thirties* (Sussex: The Harvester Press, 1980).

Gorz, Andre, *Farewell to the Working Class: An Essay on Post-Industrial Socialism*, Trans, Michael Sonenscher (London: Pluto Press, 1980).

Goulding, Simon, *'From Where I Stand', Orientation and Location in the Textual Landscape: An Analysis of the Novels of Patrick Hamilton and George Orwell* ' (Unpublished PhD Thesis. University of Birmingham, 2006).

Green, Henry, *Surviving: The Uncollected Writings of Henry Green* (New York: Penguin Books, 1992b).

Green, Henry, *Loving, Living and Party Going* (London: Viking, 2005b).

Greenwood, Walter, *Love on the Dole*. Penguin edn (London: Jonathan Cape, 1933).

Grierson, John, *Cinema Quarterly*, 1. 1. (Autumn, 1983).

Gustav Klaus, H., *The Literature of Labour* (Brighton: The Harvester Press, 1985).

Gustav Klaus, H., *The Socialist Novel in Britain* (Brighton: Harvester Press, 1982).

Gustav Klaus, H., *Tramps Workmates and Revolutionaries: Working-Class Stories of the 1920's* (London: Journeyman Press, 1993).

Gustav Klaus, H., and Stephen Knight, Eds, *British Industrial Fictions* (Cardiff: University of Wales Press, 2000).

Hackney, John, *No Want of Meat Sir! Being a Collection of Stories Edited by John Hackney* (London: Grayson & Grayson, 1936).

Hampson Simpson, Mercer, 'The Novels of John Hampson' (Master of Arts Dissertation, University of Wales, 1975). University of Reading Special Collection Services.

Hardy, Thomas, *Jude The Obscure* (London: Penguin, 1985).

Haworth, Rachel, 'Abyss: Class and Culture in Howard's End', in *Cambridge Authors Project* (2009). <https://www.english.cam.ac.uk> [accessed 06-09-2019]

Hawthorn, Jeremy, Ed, *The British Working-Class Novel in the Twentieth Century*, Stratford-Upon-Avon Studies (London: Edward Arnold, 1984).

Haywood, Ian, *Working-Class Fiction: From Chartism to Trainspotting* (Plymouth: Northcote House Publishers Ltd, 1997).

Head, Dominic, *The Modernist Short Story: A Study in Theory and Practice* (Cambridge: Cambridge University Press, 1992).

Hentea, Marius, 'Fictions of Class and Community in Henry Green's "Living"', *Studies in the Novel*, 42.3 (Fall 2010) 321-339. < https://www.jstor.org/stable/41203476> [accessed 05-09-2018]

Highmore, Ben, Essay 'Everyday life and the birth of Mass Observation', <https://www.masssobservation.amdigital.co.uk.> [accessed 17-03-2017]

Hill Collins, Patricia, and Sirma Bilge, *Intersectionality, Key Concepts* (Cambridge: Polity, 2016).

Hilliard, Christopher, 'Modernism and the Common Writer', in *Historical Journal*, 48. 3. (Sep 2005) 769-787 <http://www.jstor.org/stable/4091722> [accessed 05-08-2016]

Hilliard, Christopher, 'Producers by Hand and by Brain: Working-Class Writers and Left-Wing Publishers in 1930s Britain', *The Journal of Modern History University of Chicago*, 78.1. (2006a). 37- 65. <https://www.jstor.org/stable/10.1086/499794> [accessed 19-07-2016]

Hilliard, Christopher, *To Exercise Our Talents: The Democratization of Writing in Britain* (Cambridge Massachusetts: Harvard University Press, 2006b).

Hilton, Jack. Caliban Boswelling, University of Nottingham University Library, MS JH/1/1/24.

Hobsbawm, Eric, 'The Forward March of Labour Halted', *Marxism Today*, September (1978), 279-86.

Hoggart, Richard, *Speaking to Each Other*, Vol Two (London: Penguin Books, 1973).

Hoggart, Richard, *The Uses of Literacy* (Middlesex: Penguin Books Limited, 1960).

Hubble, Nick, *Mass Observation and Everyday Life* (Hampshire: Palgrave Macmillan, 2006).

Hubble, Nick, *The Proletarian Answer to the Modernist Question* (Edinburgh: Edinburgh University Press, 2019).

Hunter, Adrian, *The Cambridge Introduction to the Short Story in English*. (Cambridge: Cambridge University Press, 2007).

Hunter, G. Frederick, 'Commitment and Autonomy in Art: Antimonies of Frankfurt Esthetic Theory', *Berkeley Journal of Sociology*, Vol 30, (1985). pp. 41 – 64. p. 42.

Hynes, Samuel, *The Auden Generation: Literature and Politics in England in the 1930's* (London: The Bodley Head, 1976).

James, David, 'Zadie Smith's Style of Thinking', *Post 45*, 5. (22.09.2020). <https://post45.org.?p=12358&preview=true> [accessed 30-10-2020]

Jameson, Fredric, Ed, *Aesthetics and Politics* (London: Verso, 1990).

Jameson, Fredric, *The Political Unconscious: Narrative as a Socially Symbolic Act*, (London and New York, 2009).

Jefferies, Stuart *Grand Hotel Abyss* (London: Verso, 2016).

Jeffery, Tom, 'Mass Observation Archive Occasional Paper 10', (Sussex: University of Sussex, 1999).

Johnson, Roy, 'The Proletarian Novel', *Literature and History*, 2. (1975), 84-95.

Jones, Owen, 'How to Be a Man: The Quiet Crisis of Masculinity' in *New Statesman* (London: 2016). <https://newstatesman.com/politics/uk/2016/06/how be man> [accessed 16-09-2019]

Jones, Peter, ed, *Imagist Poetry* (Harmondsworth: Penguin Books, 1972).

Kermode, Frank, *History and Value* (Oxford: Clarendon Press, 1988).

Kohlmann, Benjamin, and Matthew Taunton, *A History of 1930s British Literature* (Cambridge: Cambridge University Press, 2019).

Koloktroni, Vassiliki, Jane Goldman, and Olga Taxidou, *Modernism: An Anthology of Sources and Documents.* 2013 edn (Edinburgh: Edinburgh University Press, 1998).

Lawrence, D. H., *Sons and Lovers* (London: Penguin Classics, 2006).

Ledbetter, Kenneth, 'Henry Roth's Call It Sleep: The Revival of a Proletarian Novel', *Twentieth Century Literature*, 12. 3. (1966), 123-130.

Lehmann, John, *The Penguin New Writing*, Vol. II (London: Penguin Books, 1939).

Lehmann, John, Editor, *Folios of New Writing*, Vol III, (London, Hogarth Press, 1941).

Lester, Paul, *The Road to Excelsior Lodge: The Writings of Leslie Halward* (Birmingham: Protean Publications, 1988).

Lodge, David, 'Birmingham Dire Blame Jane Austen', *Daily Telegraph*, 4th April 2008.

Lodge, David, *As I Was Walking Down Bristol Street* Central, Independent Television Production, 1983.

Lodge, David, *Working With Structuralism: Essays and Reviews on Nineteenth and Twentieth century Literature* (London: Routledge and Kegan Paul, 1981).

Lucas, John, *The 1930s: A Challenge to Orthodoxy* (London: Harvester Press Ltd, 1978).

Lucas, John, 'Walter Brierley and Leslie Williamson', Essay, Home Up site <https;//www.penniless press.co.uk> [accessed 22-01-2018]

Lukacs, Georg, *The Historical Novel*, (London: Merlin Press, 1982).

MacKay, Marina, and Lyndsey Stonebridge, Eds, *British Fiction after Modernism: The Novel at Mid-Century* (London: Palgrave, 2007).

MacNeice, Louis, *The Strings Are False: An Unfinished Autobiography* (London: Faber And Faber, 1965).

MacNeice, Louis, *The Collected Poems of Louis MacNeice* (London: Faber and Faber, 1979).

MacNeice, Louis, *I Crossed the Minch* (London: Longman, Green, 1938).

Marcus, Laura, and Peter Nicholls, *The Cambridge History of Twentieth Century Literature* (Cambridge: Cambridge University Press, 2004).

Maslen, Elizabeth, 'The Case for Storm Jameson', in *British Fiction after Modernism: The Novel at Mid-Century*, ed. by Marina MacKay and Lyndsey Stonebridge (Hampshire: Palgrave Macmillan, 2007), 33-41.

Mason, Paul, *Postcapitalism* (London: Penguin Books, 2016).

Matejka, Ladislav and Krystina Pomorska, Eds, *Readings in Russian Poetics: Formalist and Structuralist Views* (Michigan: Ann Arbor, 1978).

Matz, Jesse, Review, 'Intermodernism: Literary Culture in Mid-Twentieth-Century Britain' *Modernism/modernity*, 18.3. (September 2011), 665-667.

McGrath, Charles, 'The Eavesdropper's Secret: On John O'Hara', *The New Yorker* September 22nd 2016.

McKibbin, Ross, *The Ideologies of Class: Social Relations in Britain 1880-1950* (Oxford: Oxford University Press, 1990).

McManus, Matthew, Editor, *What is Post-Modern Conservatism?: Essays on our Hugely Tremendous Times* (Winchester: Zero Books, 2020).

Miller, Tyrus, 'Documentary / Modernism: Convergence and Complementarity in the 1930s', in *Modernism / modernity*, 9. 2. (2002), 226-241.

Nicholls, Peter, *Modernisms* (London: Macmillan Press Ltd, 1995).

Nuttall, William, 'The Proletarian Reader', *The London Mercury* (1936), 502-507. <https://warwick.ac.uk> [accessed 12-12-2018]

Nuttall, William, and Leslie Halward, 'The Coming of the Proletarian Literature. A Symposium', *The London Mercury* (1936). <https://warwick.ac.uk> [accessed 12-12-2018] 10-15.

O'Connor, Frank, 'The Lonely Voice: A Study of the Short-Story', in Charles May, Ed, *Short-Story Theories* (Athens, Ohio: Ohio University Press, 1963), 83-93.

O'Flynn, Catherine, *What Was Lost* (Birmingham: Tindal Street Press Limited, 2007).

O'Rourke, Rebecca, 'Were There No Women?: British Working-Class Writing in the Interwar Period', *Literature and History*, 1. 4. (1988), 48-63.

Orwell, George, *Inside the Whale and Other Essays* (Harmondsworth: Penguin Books, 1980).

Paul, Ronald, '"A Culture of the People": Politics and Working-Class Literature in Left Review, 1934 38', *Left History*, 8. 1. (2002), 61-76.

Perkin, Harold, '"The Condescension of Posterity." The Recent Historiography of the English Working Class', *Social Science History*, 3. (1978), 87-101.

Radek, Karl, 'Contemporary World Literature and the Tasks of Proletarian Art' Speech to the Soviet Writers Conference (August 1934), Marxists Internet Archive, <https://www.marxists.org> [accessed 21-10-2020]

Rainey, Lawrence, *Modernism an Anthology* (Oxford: Blackwell Publishing, 2005).

Reid, Ian *The Short Story* (London and New York: Methuen, 1977).
Remy, Michel, Tessa Sidey, Silvano Levy, and Pheobe Tulip, *Surrealism in Birmingham 1935 - 1954* (Banbury: Birmingham Museum and Art Gallery, 2000).
Reynolds, Stephen, 'Autobiografiction', *Speaker,* New Series, 15 (1906), 28-30.
Rose, Jonathan, *The Intellectual Life of the British Working Classes* (New Haven/ London: Yale University Press, 2001).
Roth, Henry, *Call It Sleep,* Ed, Alfred Kazin, (Penguin Classics, 2006).
Ryle, Martin, and Kate Soper, *To Relish the Sublime: Culture and Self-Realisation in Postmodern Times* (London: Verso, 2002).
Sartre, John-Paul, *What Is Literature?* (New York: Philosophical Library, 1950).
Saunders, Max, *Self-Impression: Life-Writing, Autobiografiction, & the Forms of Modern Literature* (Oxford: Oxford University Press, 2010).
Scholes, Robert, *Paradoxy of Modernism* (New Haven, London: Yale University Press, 2006).
Selden, Raman, *A Reader's Guide to Contemporary Literary Theory (5th Edition),* Eds. Raman Selden, Peter Widdowson and Peter Booker. (Harlow: Pearson Education Limited, 2005).
Smith, David *Socialist Propaganda in the Twentieth-Century British Novel* (London: The Macmillan Press Ltd, 1978).
Smith, James, *The Cambridge Companion to British Literature of the 1930s* (Cambridge: Cambridge University Press, 2019).
Snee, Carole, 'Walter Brierley: A Test Case', *Red Letters Communist Party Literature Journal,* 3. (Autumn 1976), 11-13.
Snell, K. D. M., Ed, *The Regional Novel in Britain and Ireland 1800 - 1990* (Cambridge: Cambridge University Press, 1998).
Sotriffer, Kristian, cited in Jack Stewart 'Expressionism in the Rainbow', *Novel: A Forum On Fiction,* 13. 3. (1980). 296-315. <https://www.jstor.org/stable/1344862> [accessed 28-11-2017]
Southworth, Helen, *Leonard & Virginia Woolf: The Hogarth Press and the Networks of Modernism,* (Edinburgh: Edinburgh University Press, 2010).
Southworth, Helen, 'Outside the Magic (and Tyrannical) Triangle of London-Oxford-Cambridge': John Hampson, The Woolfs, and the Hogarth Press,' Woolfian Boundaries, *Selected Papers from the Sixteenth Annual International Conference on Virginia Woolf* Edited; Ellis, Steve, Deborah Parsons, Anna Burrells, Kathryn Simpson, (South Carolina, Clemson University Press, 2006), 43 – 50.
Stallworthy, Jon, *Louis Macneice* (London: Faber & Faber, 1995).
Standing, Guy, *The Precariat: The New Dangerous Class* (London: Bloomsbury Academic, 2011).
Storm Jameson, Margaret, 'Writing in Revolt: Theory and Examples' in Postgate, Raymond and Margaret Storm Jameson, Eds, *Fact No 4.* 1. 4. (1937), 9-18.

Taylor, D. J., *The Prose Factory: Literary Life in England Since 1918* (London: Vintage, 2016).

Taylor, Elinor, *The Popular Front Novel in Britain 1934 - 1940*, (Chicago: Haymarket Books, 2018).

Thompson, E. P., *The Making of the English Working Class* (London: Pelican, 1963).

Todd, Selina, *The People: The Rise and Fall of the Working Class* (London: John Murray, 2015).

Treglown, Jeremy, *Romancing: The Life and Work of Henry Green* (London: Faber and Faber, 2000).

Tressell, Robert, *The Ragged Trousered Philanthropists* (1914). Introduction Alan Sillitoe, (London: Paladin 1991).

Uglow, Jennie, *The Lunar Men: The Friends Who Made The Future* (London: Faber and Faber, 2002)

Upton, Chris, *A History of Birmingham* (Stroud: Phillimore, 2012).

Vicinus, Martha, *The Industrial Muse: A Study in Nineteenth Century British Working-Class Literature* (London: Croom Helm, 1974).

Wallace, Victor, 'Intersectionality's Binding Agent': The Political Primacy of Class, *New Political Science,* 37. 4. (2015), 604-619. <doi 10.1080/07393148.2015.1089032> [accessed 21-10-2020]

Waugh, Patricia, *Literary Theory and Criticism* (Oxford: Oxford University Press, 2006).

West, Alick, *Crisis and Criticism & Literary Essays* (London: Lawrence and Wishart, 1975).

Williams-Ellis, Amabel, 'Nine Workers Describe a Shift at Work', *Left Review,* 1. 6. (1935), 201-216.

Williams, Keith, and Steven Matthews, eds, *Rewriting the Thirties: Modernism and After,* Series: Studies in Twentieth Century Literature, Ed, Stan Smith (Harlow, Essex: Longman Limited, 1997).

Williams, Raymond, *Culture and Society 1780-1950* (Harmondsworth: Penguin Books, 1982).

Williams, Raymond, 'A Lecture on Realism', *Afterall: A Journal of Art, Context and Enquiry.* 5. (2002), 106-115.

Williams, Raymond, *The Long Revolution* (London: The Hogarth Press, 1992).

Williams, Raymond, *Writing in Society* (London: Verso Editions, 1985).

Williams, Raymond, and Geoff Dyer, *Politics and Letters: Interviews with New Left Review* (London: Verso, 2015).

Wilson, Nicola, *Home in British Working-Class Fiction* (Farnham, Surrey: Ashgate, 2015).

Windle, Jack, 'Love on the Dole: What Life Means for Those at the Bottom', *Literature and History,* third series 20. 2. (2011), 35-47.

Wipf-Miller, Carol A., 'Fictions of "Going Over": Henry Green and the New Realism', *Twentieth Century Literature,* 44. 2. (1998), 135-54.

Woolf, Virginia, 'The Cinema', *The Nation and Athenaeum*, xxxix, 13. (3rd July 1926).

Worpole, Ken, *Dockers and Detectives: Popular Reading Popular Writing* (London: Verso, 1983).

Worpole, Ken, Dave Morley, editors, *The Republic of Letters: Working-Class Writing and Local Publishing* (London: Comedia Publishing Group, 1982).

Yeats, W. B. *The Poems,* (London: J. M. Dent and Sons, 1992).

Zuidervaart, Lambert, 'The Social Significance of Autonomous Art', *The Journal of Aesthetics and Art Criticism,* 48. (1990), 61-77.

Index[1]

[1] Note: Page numbers followed by 'n' refer to notes.

R. Harriott, *The Birmingham Group*,
https://doi.org/10.1007/978-3-031-14383-0

Printed by Printforce, United Kingdom